Motorcycle Mechanics

George Lear

Northern Virginia Community College

Lynn S. Mosher

California Polytechnic State University

Prentice-Hall, Inc., Englewood Cliffs, New Jersey

Library of Congress Cataloging in Publication Data

LEAR, GEORGE.
    Motorcycle mechanics.

    Includes index.
    1. Motorcycles—Maintenance and repair. 2. Motor-
cycles. 3. Motorcycling. I. Mosher, Lynn, joint
author. II. Title.
TL440.L4   629.28'7'75   76-22532
ISBN   0-13-604090-x

Printed in the United States of America

10   9   8   7   6   5   4   3

PRENTICE-HALL INTERNATIONAL, INC., London
PRENTICE-HALL OF AUSTRALIA PTY. LIMITED, Sydney
PRENTICE-HALL OF CANADA, LTD., Toronto
PRENTICE-HALL OF INDIA PRIVATE LIMITED, New Delhi
PRENTICE-HALL OF JAPAN, INC., Tokyo
PRENTICE-HALL OF SOUTHEAST ASIA PTE. LTD., Singapore

Contents

Preface

Motorcycles are an established part of the transportation system in the world. As the number of motorcycles purchased in the United States has approached one million each year, the need to provide maintenance for all those machines has increased in importance.

Many technical schools have started programs to train motorcycle mechanics. A motorcycle mechanics program was developed at Northern Virginia Community College in 1973. One major problem then was the lack of an adequate written theory and practical mechanical step-by-step instruction text for a student to follow in learning motorcycle mechanics. This book evolved from our attempt to solve that problem.

Motorcycle Mechanics has been written to provide the student mechanic or motorcycle owner with basic theory, practical inspection, and repair techniques to accomplish a thorough, safe, and successful maintenance and repair process.

As this text was drafted, revised, rewritten, and expanded, a good number of people and organizations helped us with the project. We wish to thank Linda Potts for her clerical efforts, Dave Sessums for his technical advice, and the companies for their assistance in this project: particularly, American Honda Motor Co., Inc.; Triumph Norton Inc.; Pacific Basic Trading Co. for Hodaka Motorcycles; U. S. Suzuki Motors Corp.; Kawasaki Motors Corp.; AMF Harley-Davidson Motor Co.; Yamaha International Corp.; AC Spark Plug Division of General Motors; Intertec Publishing Corp.; Clymer Publications; Fairfax Honda, Fairfax, VA; San Luis Cyclery, San Luis Obispo, CA; and the Sports Center, San Luis Obispo, CA.

GEORGE LEAR

LYNN S. MOSHER

unit 1

The Motorcycle

Ever since wheels started rolling, people have designed vehicles with one, two, three, four, and more wheels to get themselves and their cargo from one place to another. Very early transportation designs—say, in Roman times—were two-wheeled carts and chariots and four-wheeled carriages and wagons.

Much later someone put one of the two wheels in front of the other, and a crank and pedals on the front wheel, to invent the bicycle. Small, light, and requiring no horses or other people to pull them around, the bikes gained popularity rapidly. Of course when combustion engines were invented, someone had to try to hang one on a bike to make a motorcycle. This didn't happen immediately because even the smallest of the early engines were very heavy.

EARLY MOTORCYCLES

Some of the first powered two-wheelers were steam engine bikes (Fig. 1-1). Production started in 1885 with Gottlieb Daimler's motor bicycle (Fig. 1-2). After 1900, U. S. manufacturers included the names of "Indian" and "Thor" (Fig.

1-3). Harley and Davidson built their first bike in 1903 (Fig. 1-4).

Very soon multicylinder machines appeared, including twins and the four-cylinder Henderson (Fig. 1-5). World War I used thousands of motorcycles, many with sidecars (Fig. 1-6). During this period many Americans were introduced to motorcycling. Most bikes of that era were what are now called "hard-tails." They had no rear suspension system and often no front suspension system. The seats had large springs to improve rider comfort (Fig. 1-7). Front suspensions of that time were undampened coil springs or leaf springs.

There were not many design changes through the 30s and 40s. In the 50s major changes included the development of front telescopic forks and rear swing arms, both with hydraulic damping—that is, shock absorbers. The 50s also saw the combination motor and gear box become common. These unit engine and transmission bikes were lighter weight and cleaner in design. The early 60s saw Japanese production of both two-and four-strokers, with a resultant increase in the popularity of motorcycling. Sales and registrations of motorcycles went from less than a mil-

1

Fig. 1-1 Steam motorcycle (Clymer Publications)

Fig. 1-2 Daimler's first motor bicycle (Clymer Publications)

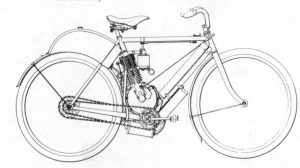

Fig. 1-3 1902 Thor motor bicycle (Clymer Publications)

Fig. 1-4 Harley-Davidson motorcycle, circa 1903 (Clymer Publications)

Fig. 1-5 Early multi-cylinder Henderson (Clymer Publications)

Fig. 1–6 WW I motorcycle with sidecar (Clymer Publications)

Fig. 1–7 The 1930 Excelsior "hardtail" (Clymer Publications)

lion in 1960 to close to five million in 1970. Because fuel costs are increasing, acceptance by Americans of the motorcycle as a regular transportation vehicle will see many more bikes on the road in the next five to ten years.

Two other areas of riding will also help increase the number of bike sales. Mini and trail bike riding are rapidly growing sports. More people are finding trail riding an enjoyable outdoor activity in which groups and families can participate. Introduction of big multicylinder cruisers is increasing the numbers who are trying long-distance trips by motorcycle. Motorcycle camping is also gaining in popularity.

CURRENT MOTORCYCLES

Mini-Bike

Any bike with wheels 12″ or less in diameter fits into this classification. The wheels are usually pressed steel or cast alloy. Engines range from bolt-on lawn mower two- and four-strokers with direct chain drive and an automatic clutch, to more sophisticated engines with multispeed transmissions and lever-operated clutches (Fig. 1–8, 1–9).

These bikes usually weigh less than 125 pounds, and their engines range from 2 1/2 to 10 horsepower. Typical wheel bases range from 32″ to 48″. Kids get started in the powered bike busi-

Fig. 1–9 Sophisticated Suzuki mini-bike (U.S. Suzuki Motor Corporation)

ness with these bikes and begin to learn about things mechanical. However, not very many end up with any kind of legal license tags. Venturesome adults might even find a mini-bike useful for errands.

Trail Motorcycles

The designs of bikes in the trail class have common features even though there will always be arguments as to what makes a trail bike. Once you get out there and ride, certain features become important. Trail bikes need a raised exhaust, out of the way of rocks and logs (Fig. 1–10). Lower gear ratios are needed. Smaller counter-shaft sprockets, larger rear wheel sprockets, additional transmission speeds or dual range transmissions are part of the design (Fig. 1–11).

Fig. 1–8 A low-cost mini-bike

Fig. 1–10 Honda trail bike (American Honda Motor Company)

Fig. 1–11   Honda trail 90 (American Honda Motor Company)

Fig. 1–13   High front-wheel fender clearance

Trail bikes generally exhibit some kind of engine protection, often a double down-tube skid-plate affair (Fig. 1–12). Engines are as compact as possible so as not to stick out on either side and take a beating.

Fender clearance is as much as 5 or 6 inches to allow for long suspension travel and prevent mud packing between the tire and fender (Fig. 1–13). Foot pegs stick out in such a way that they need special consideration for trail riding. Pegs that are spring-loaded and folding can move with the rock then snap back to be useful again (Fig. 1–14).

Tires make a bike go, and knobbies are needed to bite into the dirt and gravel that the trail rider usually finds (Fig. 1–15).

A really important consideration in a trail machine is weight. It gets very hard to pull much over 200 pounds out of a mud hole or over a log. The Penton Trials 125 has an aluminum frame for quick handling at slow speed.

Fig. 1–14   Folding foot peg

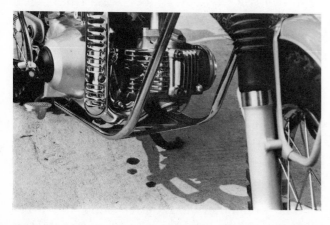

Fig. 1–12   Honda Trail 90 skid plate with double down tube mounting.

Fig. 1–15   Knobbie tire tread for trail riding

Fig. 1–16 The three-wheeled Honda ATC 90 ATV (American Honda Motor Company)

Fig. 1–17 A combination street-trail model (American Honda Motor Company)

Fig. 1–18 The Suzuki 250 cc street bike

Fig. 1–19 A middle-weight street bike

Enduro

Enduro bikes are supposed to do just that, endure. Look for larger wheels, five- and six-speed transmissions, a business-only frame and chassis without any luggage racks or buddy pegs, wider handlebars that are cross-braced, and long suspension travel.

Cycle-Based All Terrain Vehicles (A.T.V.)

These jumbo-wheeled two-wheelers or cycle-based three-wheelers are designed to go where other cycles can't. The two-wheelers are made for serious climbing and rough terrain while the three-wheelers are for the less experienced rider or a whole family try-it-out type of machine (Fig. 1–16).

Combination Street and Trail

Many will say, and it does seem true, that a bike can't be designed to be tops at trail riding and still be a good long-distance street machine. There are some pretty reasonable compromises available for those who want both, but have enough money for only one. These bikes will generally have universal tread tires, high exhaust systems, folding foot pegs, braced handlebars, and lower gearing than street models (Fig. 1–17).

Street Bikes

The commuter and tourer will find street bikes with all the legal lights and turn signals, low fenders, extra instrumentation, buddy seats and pegs, hand rails and more and more cylinders per bike. Sizes range from under 100 cc to over 1200 cc. Extra equipment such as wind screens and fairings, saddle bags, and the occasional side car are also part of the street scene. The around-town commuter would include the 90- to 250-cc group, some with electric starting (Fig. 1–18).

Combination commuter-tourer street bikes range from 250 to 500 cc, of which the Honda 350–360 is most common (Fig. 1–19). The touring to super bike includes the BMW and the liquid cooled four cylinder opposed Honda 1000. (Figs. 1–20, 1–21).

Fig. 1–20　A large solid tourer

BASIC MOTORCYCLE SYSTEMS

As a bike owner or mechanic, you should become familiar with the basic motorcycle systems which include:

The frame
Wheels and brakes
Suspension
Engine
Drive train
Fuel system
Ignition system
Electrical system

Fig. 1–21　A large modern 4-cylinder tourer

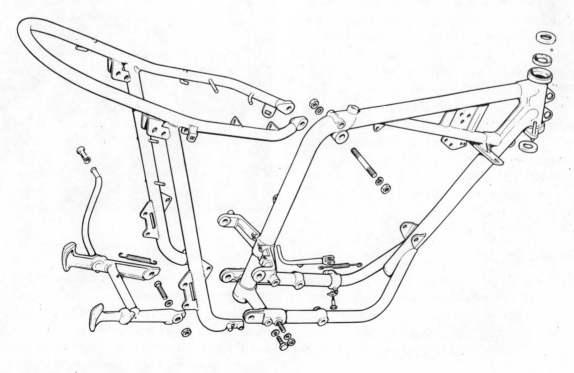

Fig. 1–22　Tube frame on a Triumph (Triumph Norton Incorporated)

Fig. 1–23 A typical stamped box frame (American Honda Motor Company)

Learning about bikes is easiest when you study one system at a time. So here is a brief view of what is in each system. (Later chapters provide details.)

Frame

Motorcycle frames are usually steel tubing or stampings welded into a rigid unit. Some bikes have aluminum or other light alloy frames for special-purpose riding. The most common system is the tubular frame swing-arm type (Fig. 1–22). The stamped box frame is limited to light, small-engine bikes in one or two makes (Fig. 1–23). When you study some of the older bikes you will find that up to the early 50s bikes had rigid rear "hard-tail" suspension. The frame also includes the mounting brackets for attaching other components such as stands and seats. The longer seats are dual purpose: to allow the rider to shift position and for buddy riding.

Wheels and Brakes

Most motorcycle wheels are spoked for lighter weight, fairly low cost, and reasonable rigidity. Cast alloy wheels are now being used on some bikes, but they are expensive. Stamped or pressed steel wheels are found on some mini bikes (Fig. 1–24).

(a)

(b)

(c)

Fig. 1–24 Typical spoke, cast, and stamped wheels

Motorcycle brake systems are either the internal expanding drum type or the newer and better disc brakes (Fig. 1–25). The brakes are applied with a lever and cable system, mechanical rod linkage, or hydraulic systems that use fluid under pressure to operate the brake.

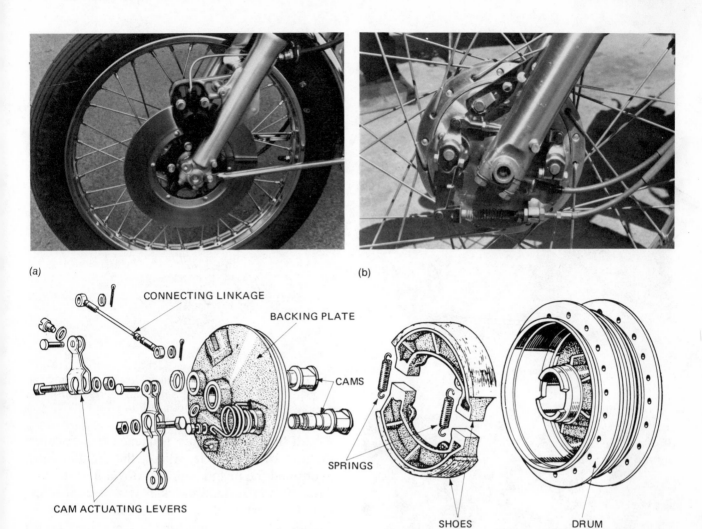

(a)   (b)

CONNECTING LINKAGE

BACKING PLATE

CAMS

SPRINGS

CAM ACTUATING LEVERS

SHOES   DRUM

Fig. 1–25 Disc brake (a) and drum brake (b) with exploded view below, showing drum shoes, backing plate, and connections

Suspension

The most common front suspension system is the telescopic forks that use a combination of sliding tubes, internal springs, and hydraulic dampening to provide a smooth ride (Fig. 1–26). Some riders still favor the Earles type of front suspension as a more forgiving off-road suspension (Fig. 1–27).

The rear suspension consists of swing arms that attach the frame to the rear wheels. Coil-spring shock absorber combinations are attached near the axle on the swing arm and are fixed to a solid frame point above (Fig. 1–28).

Engine

Talk to any motorcycle enthusiast and the first topic is likely to be about some new motorcycle engine or why two-strokes are better than

Fig. 1–26 Telescopic front forks

four-strokes, or vice versa. No doubt about it, the engine on a bike is the biggest concern.

What is the difference in engines? Well, let's start with how a four-stroke engine works—four-stroke first because most cars and light trucks use

Fig. 1–27   Earles-type front forks

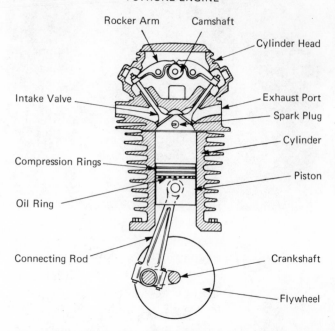

Fig. 1–29   Four-stroke piston engine parts, showing cylinder, head, piston, rings, rod, valves, spark plug, crankshaft, and flywheel

Fig. 1–28   Swing arm with combination coil-spring shocks

the same type. The basic parts are shown in Fig. 1–29. The cylinder and head make a container in which the fuel is burned. The piston gives the burning air-fuel mixture something to push or move, converting the fuel energy to motion. The piston rings help to seal the burning air-fuel mixture in the cylinder. The valves cover the openings through which air and fuel are let in and the exhaust (burned gas) is let out. The spark plug ignites (starts the burning) the air-fuel mixture. The connecting rod and crankshaft together convert the up-and-down motion of the piston to rotary motion which is then used to turn the rear wheel of the motorcycle.

All this happens in a sequence that is called the four-stroke cycle. First, the intake valve opens and the piston is drawn down into the cylinder by the turning crankshaft and connecting rod. This first stroke draws air and fuel into the cylinder. Actually, atmospheric pressure forces air and fuel into the vacuum created when the piston is pulled down in the cylinder. Figure 1–30 shows the sequence of the four strokes.

The intake valve closes at the end of the intake stroke. The second stroke in the cycle is the piston moving toward the top of the cylinder, compressing (squeezing) the air-fuel mixture. The volume left when the piston reaches the top of its travel is only about one-eighth or one-ninth of the amount when the piston was at the bottom on the intake stroke. This highly compressed air-fuel mixture is then ignited by the spark plug.

The third stroke occurs when the piston is pushed down by the power of rapidly burning fuel-air mixture. When the gases (fuel and air) burn, very high pressures are developed, which thrust the piston down with considerable force. This energy is transferred from the moving piston by the connecting rod to the crankshaft. Some is stored by the flywheel in the form of rotary motion to turn the engine through the other three strokes, the rest is used to move the motorcycle.

10

On the fourth stroke, the piston is moved back toward the top of the cylinder with the exhaust valve open. Burnt air-fuel gases (now called exhaust gas) are forced out of the cylinder to complete the four-stroke cycle. This series of strokes repeats over and over, each power stroke adding to the motion of the bike.

Advantages of this engine type are more efficient fuel use and durability. Disadvantages, as compared to the two-stroke engines, are more parts to operate and heavier weight per horsepower output.

Two-stroke engines operate by using a cylinder and piston somewhat like the four-stroke operation except that there is more overlap in the functions. Let's look at what happens. Intake air-fuel mixture enters the cylinder from the crankcase, through a port (a hole in the cylinder wall) at the bottom of the downward piston stroke. The first of the two strokes sees the piston traveling up, compressing the air-fuel mixture (Fig. 1–31). This compression stroke is much like the one in the four-stroke cycle. At the same time, the crankcase port from the carburetor is uncovered

by the bottom of the piston. This allows the air-fuel mixture to enter the crankcase. When the piston travels down, the mixture is compressed and passes readily into the cylinder by way of the transfer passage.

Ignition of the air-fuel mixture by the spark plug occurs just before the piston reaches top dead center (TDC) of the cylinder. At ignition, the piston is thrust down and transmits the power of the expanding gases through the connecting rod to the crankshaft—just like the four-stroke. As the two-stroke piston nears the bottom of the cylinder, the exhaust port is uncovered and the burnt gases rush out of the cylinder. A little farther down the cylinder wall the piston uncovers the intake port. The next air-fuel mixture, coming into the engine via the crankcase and under low compression by the piston coming down, can now rush up into the cylinder, filling it and forcing out more of the burnt gas through the exhaust port.

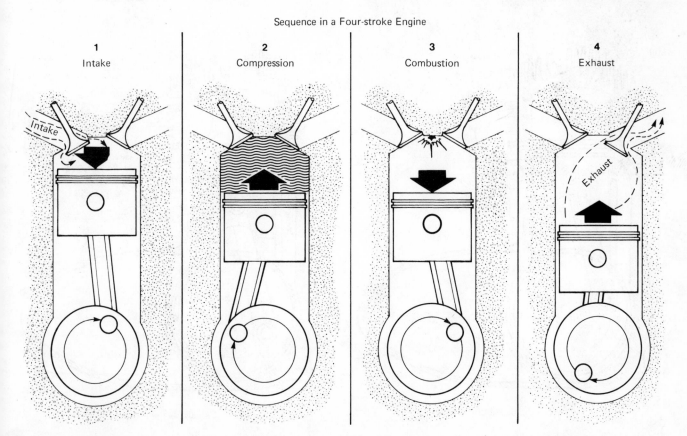

Sequence in a Four-stroke Engine

| 1 | 2 | 3 | 4 |
| Intake | Compression | Combustion | Exhaust |

Fig. 1–30 The four-stroke cycle, showing intake, compression, power (combustion) and exhaust (Kawasaki Motors Corporation)

Two-stroke Engine Cycle
(Sequence of 4)

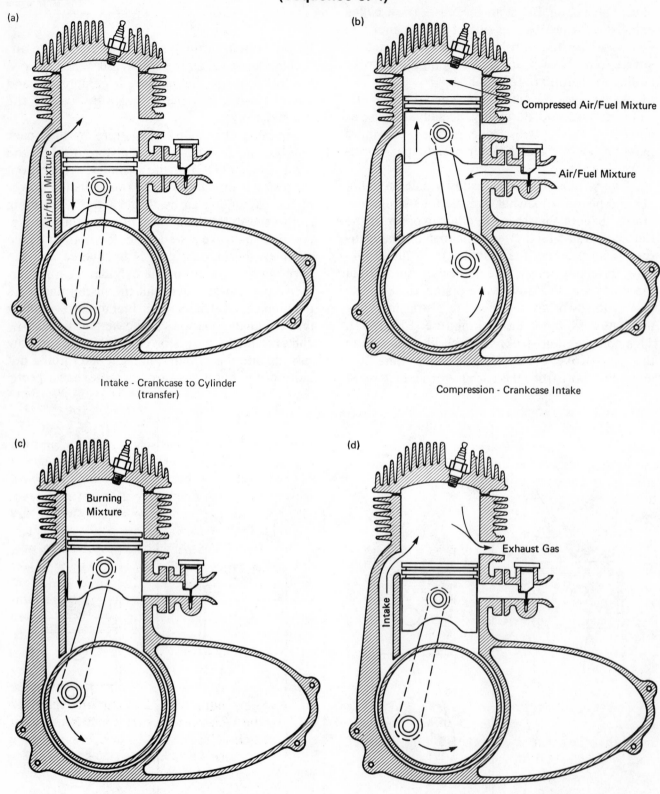

(a)

Air/fuel Mixture

Intake - Crankcase to Cylinder
(transfer)

(b)

Compressed Air/Fuel Mixture

Air/Fuel Mixture

Compression - Crankcase Intake

(c)

Burning
Mixture

Power — Crankcase Compression

(d)

Exhaust Gas

Intake

Exhaust — then Intake

Fig. 1–31 Two-stroke cycle, shows intake, compression, and crankcase intake, power, and exhaust, with intake starting.

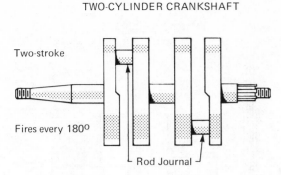

Two-stroke

Fires every 180°

Rod Journal

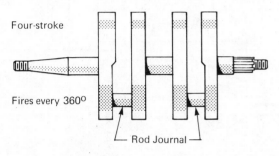

Four-stroke

Fires every 360°

Rod Journal

Fig. 1–32 Two-cylinder crankshaft, showing rod journals 180° and 360° apart

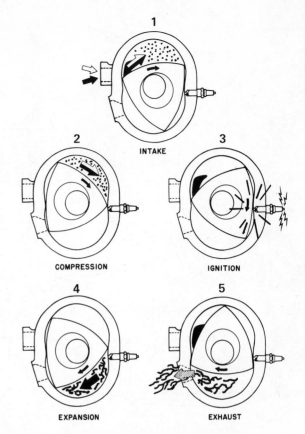

1

INTAKE

2

COMPRESSION

3

IGNITION

4

EXPANSION

5

EXHAUST

Fig. 1–33 Wankel engine cycles (Herbert & Ellinger, *Automechanics*, by permission of Prentice-Hall, Inc.)

As you can see, this piston has a power stroke every time it moves downward. This means that a two-stroke engine has twice as many power strokes for every 100 crankshaft revolutions as the four-stroke engine does. These extra power strokes, and the lack of a need for the whole valve train, are the key advantages of the two-stroke engine.

Disadvantages of the two-stroke engine include higher oil and fuel consumption. This type of engine burns more oil than the four-stroke model because the crankcase design for air-fuel compression requires greater lubrication. The two-stroke takes more fuel because the exhaust and intake cycles overlap. This allows some unspent fuel in the cylinder to exhaust without being burned effectively.

Twins and Multiple Cylinders. Making an engine with two cylinders rather than one does more than just increase the power output. Each time the crankshaft turns there will be two power strokes instead of one. If the pistons fire alternately, one will fire every 180° of crankshaft revolution in a two-stroke engine. This will increase the smoothness of the power output (Fig. 1–32).

For a given displacement—say, 200 cc—the twin will put out more power than the single and run at a higher number of revolutions per minute (rpm). These higher rpm are possible because the pistons and rods of the two smaller cylinders are each lighter than one big single.

The single has the advantages of being narrower (for woods and trail) and having fewer parts to break. Three-, four-, or six-cylinder engines represent just more and more of the two-cylinder advantages and disadvantages. They look impressive, however, and motorcycle corporation marketeers know it.

Wankel Engines. The Wankel rotary engine is now being introduced into motorcycling for many of the same reasons that it is being used in other vehicles. The Wankel design has fewer parts, puts out more power for its effective displacement, and is a smooth, low-vibration power source.

Here's how it works (Fig. 1–33). The rotor turns or rotates in the specially shaped rather tri-

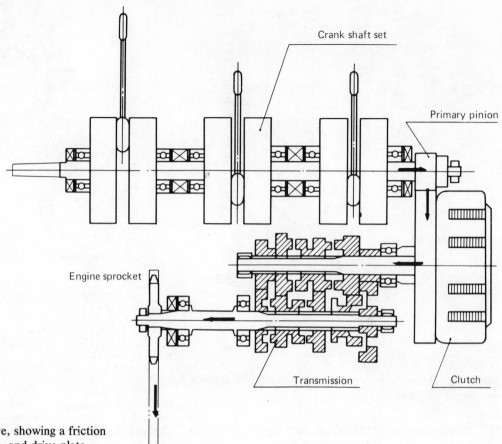

Fig. 1–34　The primary drive, showing a friction
　　　　　disc, friction face, and drive plate

angular chamber with each of its three sides in a different stage of the combustion cycle. During the first stage the rotor moves past the intake port. The increasing volume between that side of the rotor and the combustion chamber creates a partial vacuum that pulls in air and fuel by atmospheric pressure. As the rotor turns, the air-fuel charge is moved to another area of the chamber, compressing the mixture into a much smaller volume, just like the compression stroke of the piston engine.

The spark plug ignites the mixture, and the burning gases force the rotor to turn. As each face of the rotor passes the spark plug there is a power impulse, three power impulses per rotor revolution. The rotor turns the crankshaft by turning a cam on the crankshaft inside the rotor.

Drive Train

The engine's power is used to turn the rear wheel. The mechanical parts that connect the engine and the rear wheel are called the "drive train." On most bikes the first part of the drive train is a gear or chain reduction between the en-

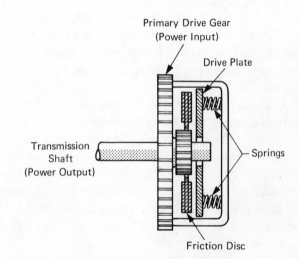

Fig. 1–35　A typical clutch, showing a friction disc, friction
　　　　　face, and drive plate

gine crankshaft and the clutch. This reduces clutch speed, but multiplies torque (turning force) (Fig. 1–34). Next in the power train is the clutch. Its purpose is to allow the rider to disconnect the engine from the transmission. This is necessary to be able to shift from one gear to another (Fig. 1–35). A clutch is a spring-pressure forced-friction disc and drive plate arrangement. When the

Fig. 1–36 Three-speed transmission gears (American Honda Motor Company)

spring pressure is forced off, the drive plate no longer turns the friction disc. Most clutches are multiple-disc types. The handgrip and cable control work the clutch on most bikes. Some clutches are operated automatically by centrifugal force.

Driving power flows from the clutch to the transmission or "gear box." To get the bike started down the road or up a steep hill a high gear ratio is needed. This is where the engine crankshaft turns many times to get the rear wheel to turn just once. A transmission usually has three, four, or more different gear ratios that the rider can select, allowing high torque multiplica-

tion for starting and also high speed for highway riding (Fig. 1–36).

Behind the transmission there is a linkage to the rear wheel. Most bikes have a chain-drive arrangement with a small sprocket on the output shaft of the transmission, a larger sprocket on the rear wheel, and a loop chain to transfer the turning motion of the transmission to the wheel. The difference in sprocket sizes allows for a further speed reduction (and torque increase). Sprockets can be changed to gain an overall gear ratio change.

A few manufacturers use a shaft to transmit power from the transmission to the wheel. This system is more expensive, has more parts, but requires virtually no maintenance.

Fuel System

The fuel system includes all those parts that store or regulate fuel in the motorcycle, from fill-up at the gas station until compression occurs in

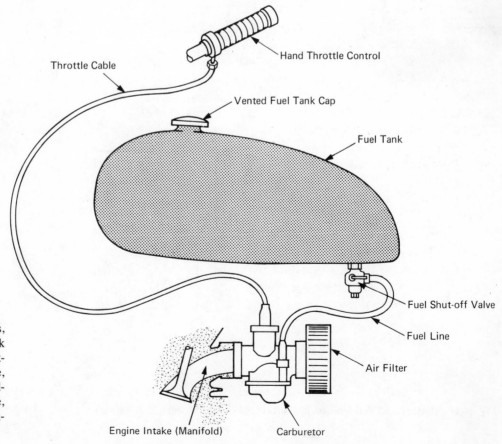

Fig. 1–37 Fuel system parts, showing fuel tank and vent cap, shut-off valve, fuel line, carburetor, air filter, intake passage, and throttle control

Throttle Cable

Hand Throttle Control

Vented Fuel Tank Cap

Fuel Tank

Fuel Shut-off Valve

Fuel Line

Air Filter

Engine Intake (Manifold)

Carburetor

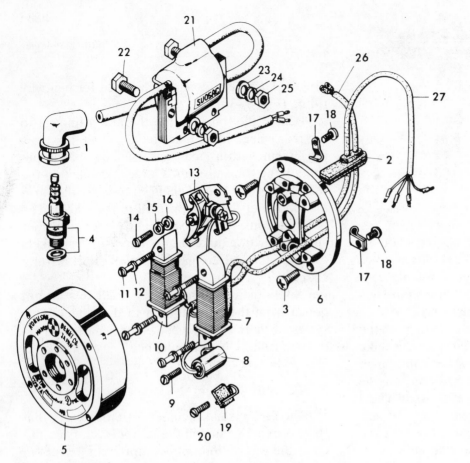

Fig. No.	Part Name
1	Plug cap
2	Grommet
3	Frame setting screw
4	Spark plug B-8
5	Flywheel
6	Frame
7	Ignition primary coil
8	Condenser
9	Condenser setting screw
10	Lighting coil
11	Ignition & lighting coil setting screw
12	Ignition & lighting coil setting spring washer
13	Contact breaker (point)
14	Contact breaker setting screw
15	Contact breaker setting spring washer
16	Contact breaker setting washer
17	Wire cord stopper
18	Wire cord stopper setting screw
19	Felt lubrication pad
20	Felt lubrication pad setting screw
21	Ignition coil
22	Ignition coil setting bolt
23	Ignition coil setting washer
24	Ignition coil setting washer
25	Ignition coil setting nut
26	Ignition coil primary cord
27	Lighting coil cord

Fig. 1–38 Magneto ignition system (Pabatco/Hodaka)

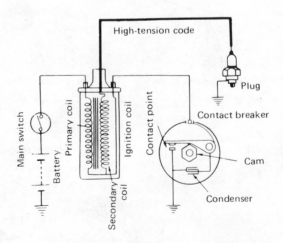

Fig. 1–39 Battery and coil ignition system (U.S. Suzuki Motor Corporation)

16

the cylinder. Major parts of the fuel system are the fuel tank and its cap, the shut-off valve, fuel lines, filters, carburetor and air filter, and the intake manifold from the carburetor to the engine (Fig. 1–37).

The tank stores the gas, its cap allows air to come into the tank as fuel is used. Most motorcycle tank shut-off valves have three positions: on, reserve, and off; reserve is provided so that you still have some fuel left when the engine slows down in the "on" position. Fuel lines extend from the valve on the fuel tank to the carburetor(s). The carburetor, controlled by the throttle grip, determines how much air and fuel the engine is going to get and what air-fuel ratio is going to be mixed. The intake manifold connects the carburetor to the engine with a passage for the air-fuel mixture to travel through. A valve or port at one end of the manifold controls when the mixture can get in. Air pressure (atmospheric pressure) pushes air into and through the carburetor, where it picks up gasoline, then is drawn into the cylinder to be burned.

Ignition

Something is needed to start the gas burning to make the piston go down to make the bike move. Motorcycle engines use an electrical spark that jumps across the spark plug gap inside the cylinder. The ignition system generates the high voltage that makes the spark fire at the right moment thousands of times a minute.

Currently there are three types of ignition systems in use. First is the magneto system that is often found on small bikes and competition bikes. It is simple, reliable, and doesn't require a battery since current is generated by the magnets and coils in the system. Most magnetos have magnets (usually a part of the motor's flywheel), coils, ignition points, a capacitor, and the high-tension lead and spark plug (Fig. 1–38).

The second type, the battery and coil ignition system, uses current from the battery to power the coil and produce the high-voltage spark (Fig. 1–39). A coil, points, condenser, and high-tension lead are parts in this system.

The third type is the electronic ignition system. The high voltage for the spark is developed by using a large capacitor for storage rather than the transformer type coils of the other two ignition systems. Resistors, thyristors, diodes, and transistors can also be parts in this new kind of ignition system.

Electrical System

Besides the electrical parts needed to operate the ignition system, the modern motorcycle has many electrical components to increase a riders' safety and enjoyment. These include head and tail lights, brake lights, warning lights, turn signals, buzzers and horns, radios, electric starters, and more to come. Such electrically operated accessories require a battery, generator, switches, relays, lots of wire and fuses, as well as a regulator and rectifier. The wiring diagram in Fig. 1–40 is typical of many of the new big bikes.

WHAT ELSE?

As complicated as all of the parts of the eight major motorcycle systems might seem, they can be readily understood if you read about, work with, and learn about one part of one system at a time. This book should help you to do just that. We think it would be best, of course, to start at the beginning and go through as we selected the order of our units. If you already have a motorcycle with a problem that's not discussed in one of the first units, we'll try to be understanding when you jump right into one of the middle units.

One thing certain is that motorcycling will change. A few guesses would include more shaft-driven bikes, more rotary-engine bikes in production, automatic transmissions becoming common, particularly on the large displacement machine, and disc brakes becoming common even on the small bikes.

Thus there is going to be an increasing need for trained motorcycle mechanics. As these machines become more sophisticated, mechanics need to sharpen their range of skills. Pollution controls and generally more complex mechanical and electrical systems will keep the better mechanics "in the classroom" wherever that may be, updating their skills from time to time.

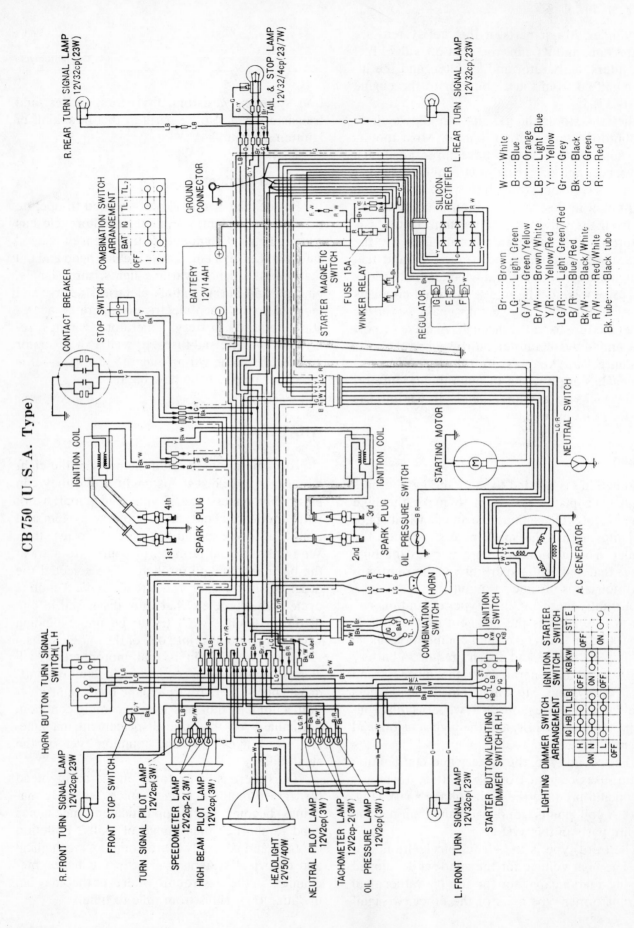

CB 750 (U.S.A. Type)

Fig. 1-40 Wiring diagram from owner's manual (American Honda Motor Company)

Riding Safely, Comfortably, and Politely

There are many facets of riding a motorcycle and many levels of expertise in each area. Each requires a basic dedication to safety and an interest in improving riding ability. This chapter assumes that you can get on a motorcycle and ride it, but want to advance both your safety and ability.

However, you should remember GUMPERSON'S LAW: "The worst possible thing that can happen, will happen—but only at the worst possible time" (Fig. 2–1). Also remember this paraphrasing of an old pilot's adage: "There are bold riders. There are old riders. But there are no old, bold riders."

These two quotations lead the cyclist to follow a fundamental premise: *Ride as if you're invisible.*

CONTROLS AND ADJUSTMENTS

Well, what *can* you do with Gumperson's law working against you? For one thing, you can modify and adjust the controls of your motorcycle so they are instantly available and easy to use. This is partially what a magazine writer means when he overworks the cliche "and all of the controls fall easily to hand." What he really

means is that a particular test bike happened to *fit* him pretty well. Fortunately, most cycles can be made to fit most people pretty well.

Handlebar Selection and Adjustment

Motorcycles come from the factory with handlebars designed to accommodate the average size person when he or she rides the machine as it was intended. Middle-weight street machines have medium width, medium rise handlebars. Motorcrossers have wide, flat bars with a center brace; road racers have low, flat bars or clip-ons.

Much of the design in handlebars is based on the assumption that the rider's back should parallel his calf. In addition, higher speeds require a lower crouch or more horizontal angle as illustrated in Fig. 2–2. Some provisions can be made to get closer to *your* ideal riding position by adjusting the handlebars and foot pegs.

To adjust the handlebars, simply loosen the clampdown bolts at the center and rotate the bars to the position that feels most comfortable to you. Be careful not to rotate them too far, especially if there are wires exiting from a hole in the center of the bars (Fig. 2–3).

If you decide to change the bars on your ma-

Fig. 2-1 Example of Gumperson's law

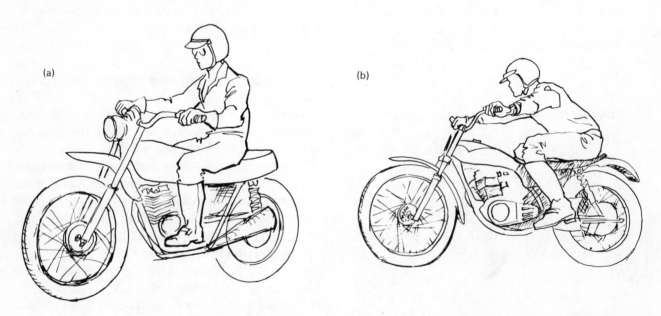

(a)

(b)

Fig. 2-2 Rider position: (a) rider upright and calf of leg vertical, or (b) rider in 45° crouch and calf also at 45°

chine, be sure to get the proper length cables and to position the control levers correctly at the handle end of the bars—not 6 inches toward the center or 2 inches from the end (Fig. 2-4).

Sometimes a motorcycle you're working on might have control wires routed through it to the switches at the levers. These wires are not difficult to reroute if you first probe through from the end with a string or wire as shown in Fig. 2-5. Another helpful hint is to enlarge the entry and exit holes with a drill, but don't go over 7/16 of an inch diameter or the bars will be weakened.

Fig. 2-3 Handlebar adjustment showing the wrench on bolt and bars about to be moved

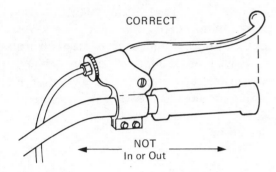

CORRECT

NOT
In or Out

Fig. 2-4 Control level position showing lever correctly adjusted

Control Levers

Safe riding dictates that you can get to your front brake lever rapidly and smoothly. Clamp it radially on the handlebar wherever it feels most comfortable and adjust the lever travel to give you enough braking action to prevent the lever from touching the throttle grip.

If you have small hands, both the clutch and brake levers can be positioned closer to the hand grip. On the more expensive levers, you can simply mount them in a vise and bend them the required amount if you apply gentle, even pressure as shown in Fig. 2-6. On some of the economy models with brittle levers, you can slit a faucet washer from your local hardware store and slip it over the exposed inner cable. Carry a few extras since these washers tend to wear out and occasionally fall off.

Be sure to maintain the proper clutch and brake action for your machine no matter which

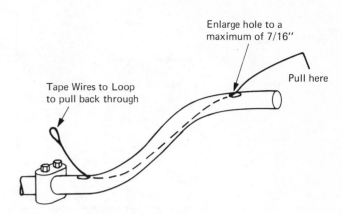

Enlarge hole to a
maximum of 7/16''

Tape Wires to Loop
to pull back through

Pull here

Fig. 2-5 Rerouting electrical wires in handle-bars.

cure for the small-hands problem you select. Often this means reducing some of the recommended free play.

Shifter Adjustment

The shifter can be moved up or down a few teeth on its spine, but avoid the extremes for two reasons. A shifter positioned so high that your foot leaves the peg to shift affects your stability and control dangerously during shifts. On the other hand, a low shifter is vulnerable to obstacles and could break off or damage the transmission in the event of a mishap.

A competent welder can shorten or lengthen the shifter for you if it is necessary. Again, avoid the extremes. A shifter that is too short is very difficult to operate, can blister your shifting foot,

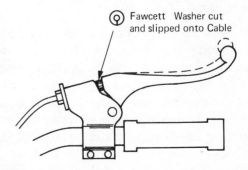

Fawcett Washer cut
and slipped onto Cable

Fig. 2-6 Faucet washer trick for adjusting levers closer to the handlebar

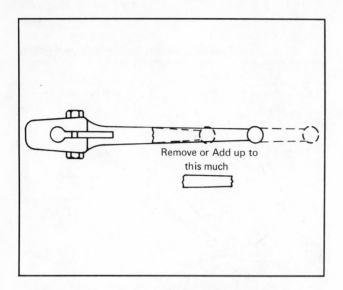

Fig. 2-7 Shift lever reworking, showing maximum and minimum amount to add or remove for rewelding

and even wear rapidly through your favorite motorcycle boots. An extended shifter can give the rider too much mechanical advantage on the shift linkage and damage it. Don't extend or shorten a shifter by more than one third of its original length (Fig. 2-7).

Rear Brake Pedal

The brake pedal can be modified for length and positioning much the same as the shifter. Once again, the one-third of the original length factor should be observed. Be careful, however, that any welding is thoroughly checked before reinstalling the pedal. A little reinforcement can help to insure that the brake pedal won't bend or break.

Accessories

Most of the controls and accessories on a motorcycle have some leeway in positioning and adjustment. The mirrors can be rotated and tilted. Often the horn button and kill switches can be positioned closer to your thumbs. The seat can be taken to an upholstery shop for removal of some of the foam padding if you're a bit short-legged for your bike.

Suspension and tire adjustments are often overlooked but can contribute greatly to safe motorcycle operation. Many of the final settings in this area are going to be your decision, but the recommended starting points can be mentioned here.

Tire Pressure. Most road machines call for 22 to 30 psi with a few pounds more in the rear than in the front wheel. Start with the recommended pressure for your machine. For every 40 pounds over 140 pounds your machine is to carry, increase the pressure by 1 psi. It is not difficult to stop at a gas station and put in a little more air when you're riding two-up, and it's a great deal safer. (Don't forget to let the extra air out again after your passenger has gotten off.)

Another consideration when carrying a passenger or a heavy load is the rear spring-rate setting. On many bikes the rear shock-absorber springs can be preloaded by a stepped, rotating collar. Twist this collar to compress the spring when you are carrying extra baggage or a passenger. You should have a special wrench in your tool kit with which to turn this collar. This task is illustrated in Fig. 2-8.

Clothing and Equipment. The most important safety accessory in motorcycling today is the crash helmet. There are three basic styles, each with its advantages and disadvantages (Fig. 2-9).

The half-coverage or "shorty" helmet was the early traditional helmet. It affords a good deal of protection for its light weight and offers better comfort, cooling, and ventilation than other mod-

Fig. 2-8 Rear shock collar adjustment, using special wrench to make adjustment

Fig. 2-9 Helmet styles, showing two helmets: the full coverage type and total coverage head gear.

els. The disadvantage is that you can't attach a decent face shield to the front of a shorty helmet.

The full-coverage helmet is the most popular motorcycle helmet for the street and trail rider. Protection from this full-coverage helmet is much greater because it covers a larger area. You can easily add face shields to it. The only disadvantage of a full-coverage helmet is its extra weight and its tendency to limit neck movement.

The third helmet, the total-coverage type, is seen more often on race tracks than on the street or trail. While these helmets offer the greatest amount of protection in the event of a mishap, they do limit lateral vision, decrease ventilation, and fog glasses.

There are many factors to consider before you select a helmet to meet your needs. Be sure that you get a helmet that allows you full neck motion while riding. If you feel the rear of the helmet dig or prod into the back of your neck when looking up from a riding crouch, shop around for another helmet with more rear cutaway.

Weight alone does not determine the quality of a helmet. If the helmet seems very heavy to you, check it against others of the same general design. Be sure that the helmet meets the required government standards; select one that won't make you "neck weary" after riding several hours.

Of course the fit of a motorcycle helmet is the main factor in rider comfort. Never buy a helmet without trying it on! If the helmet hints the least bit of being too tight, go to a larger size. A tight

new helmet can ruin your riding concentration and awareness by causing severe headaches. *Remember:* helmets don't wear-in like boots or leather jackets. Once you buy a tight helmet, you're stuck with it and all the headaches it causes, so avoid an "interference fit."

On the other hand, a helmet that is too loose doesn't offer the protection of one that fits properly. In addition, it can wobble on the rider's head, causing distorted vision through the face shield and other distractions.

Select a helmet that you can put on and take off easily and yet fits you comfortably. The helmet should be able to move slightly on your head until you cinch down the chin strap. After tightening the strap, there should be almost no helmet wobble. A *tight chin strap* is as important to your cranial protection as the fit of the helmet itself. If you over-tighten your chin strap and become uncomfortable, it's a simple matter to loosen the strap a bit. However, if you buy a helmet that's too tight, the only solution is a larger helmet.

Helmet manufacturers are not very consistent in sizing their helmets. One that is marked "Large" might fit you more tightly than another brand labeled "Medium."

If you have a serious accident and your helmet is involved, a new helmet should be purchased. The old one probably has some of the inner lining crushed and may have cracks in the shell. The inner lining does not return to its original shape after it has been dented.

Be selective. Your helmet will be with you through several motorcycles. It's the most important safety device you have, other than your own good judgment, so choose your helmet carefully.

Eye Protection. Some sort of eye protection is required by law for riding a motorcycle in most states. The simplest solution is a pair of glasses or sunglasses, but more specialized equipment is available. Almost any other protection in addition to or instead of glasses is better. However, this is a personal preference area and you should get whatever seems to enable you to see best and still be comfortable. Prescription or sun glasses should be of safety glass construction. Your optometrist can help here.

Goggles offer excellent eye protection while preserving that good old "wind in your nose" feeling while riding. Some cheaper varieties tend to distort vision, so if goggles are your preference select a set with minimum distortion.

Bubble shields were the first of the full-face shields. They protect the rider's face quite well but tend to distort vision around the edges of the bubble and are susceptible to wind loads at speed. If you turn to look at something while riding at higher road speeds you may be surprised by the "sail effect" of the wind on the side of your helmet and bubble shield.

A *flat face shield* has less distortion than the bubble shield, does not fog as readily, and is less susceptible to "sail effect." This is very popular for eye protection for cyclists and represents a simple, inexpensive solution. However, choosing a dark-tinted shield as your only shield can cause problems when you have to return home at night (Fig. 2–10).

Gloves. Every motorcyclist should have two or three pairs of gloves. Cold weather highway cruising calls for a pair of heavily insulated mittens or a pair of large leather gauntlet gloves worn over a pair of woolen gloves.

Fig. 2–10 Eye protection, showing goggles, bubble shield, framed flat shield, flat shield, and dark moulded shield.

Fig. 2–11 Footwear: typical riders' boots

Temperatures in the 50s and above generally require a pair of soft deerskin or pigskin gloves. You can hardly get a pair of leather gloves that are too soft from a comfort standpoint; however, the super-soft dress gloves tend to wear rapidly. You might look for the softest pair of workman's leather gloves you can find to fill the requirement.

Footwear. Ankle protection is a key item in selecting boots for motorcycling. Take time to select a boot that will protect your foot and ankle adequately in the event of a mishap. Anyone who has had an accident resulting in an ankle injury will emphasize this point to you. Heed the voice of experience.

The lace-up workboot or strap-over motorcross boots are the best protection you can get. Even the more stylish pull-on boots are much better than low shoes or loafers. Get boots with soft crepe-type soles to lessen vibration and help keep your feet warm. Keep away from high heels that tend to catch on rocks and logs. Holey, old tennis shoes and shower clogs hinder your ability to operate the foot controls of your motorcycle, making an accident more likely and offering virtually no protection during the accident they just caused. Anyone with a two-digit I.Q. or above will avoid unsafe footwear.

Learn the old "motorcycle cop" boot trick: Take your favorite scooter booties to a local cobbler and have him install double-thick soles on them. This helps isolate your foot from machine vibration and keeps your feet warmer too (Fig. 2–11).

Pants. There's nothing like a set of leathers to keep you toasty warm in winter and roast you in summer. Leather pants, unless you are racing or often tour in cold weather, would probably be an unjustified expense. Good, heavy denim dungarees or canvas hunter's pants offer decent protection, especially if worn over a pair of "long johns." Pick pants that fit snugly but not tightly so they don't flap, chafe or bind you on long trips.

Bermuda shorts or bathing suits permit you to feel the wind against your legs, but somehow the memory of that pleasurable sensation fades away as you pluck gravel from your calf after a minor fall.

Jackets. A leather jacket, on the other hand, is not so difficult to live with in hot weather. Leather offers the best protection you can get in the event of a slide, and now these jackets are made in brighter colors so motorists are more apt to see you. Whether cloth or leather, pick a brightly colored jacket to insure visibility.

If you lubricate your chain as often as you should, little drips of oil will be slung up on your back. A leather or vinyl jacket is easily wiped off, but a cloth jacket will wear these spots permanently. The oil isn't very harmful to the jacket, but makes it look a bit spotty.

Another important consideration in selection of a jacket is the collar design. Get a Mandarin or Nehru-style collar that has no pointed tips. Pointed tips on most jackets flap terribly while you're riding and can chafe your neck and face. Be sure the jacket sleeves fit well enough that they don't flap, yet are free enough to permit unrestricted movement.

Foul Weather Gear. Many companies manufacture clothing for people who must work in the rain. There are many high-quality rubberized rain suits consisting of both jacket (or poncho) and waterproof pants. Most of these are acceptable for short trips during a shower. Avoid the light, cheap vinyl or plastic rainwear because it tends to shred into ribbons the first time you reach 30 miles per hour!

Enduro riders have known for years that the heavy, waxed, Barbour or Belstaff style suits offer the best protection in wet going. Other companies are now manufacturing the same type of suit from synthetic materials. Whichever you choose will comfort you on those long, wet rides.

Other Accessories. The old stereotype Hell's Angel wore wrist straps and a star-studded wide belt in addition to his dungarees and engineer boots. You've read about the boots and pants, but what about the wrist straps and kidney belt?

Have you noticed how tired your left wrist can become after a long ride in traffic or on the trail? This results from the tendons straining whenever you pull in the clutch lever. A leather or elastic wrist band can ease the strain if worn properly. Make sure the band is gently snug yet does not hinder the blood circulation to your hand.

The old kidney belt has generally faded away with the advent of rear suspension on road machines. However, some riders find them helpful in relieving back strain on a long trip and still use them. Their original purpose was to protect the rider's internal organs, especially the kidneys, against injury from constant road shock and vibrations. These wide belts are available in leather, cloth, and elastic models and are recommended for long, rough trips on the road or trail.

GETTING STARTED

Just like a pilot, you should use a "pre-flight check list" before starting a motorcycle (Fig. 2–12). This list includes:

1. Gas level and quality
2. Oil level
3. Cable adjustment and condition
4. Brake adjustment
5. Chain adjustment and condition
6. Tire condition and inflation
7. Lights and horn
8. General (frame, oil leaks, etc.)

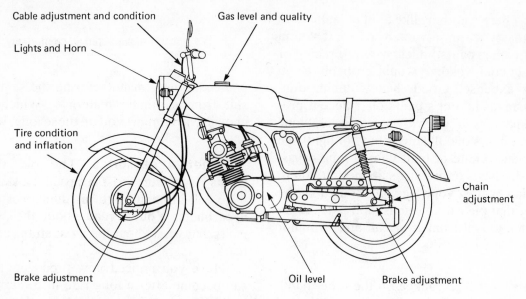

Cable adjustment and condition

Lights and Horn

Gas level and quality

Tire condition
and inflation

Chain
adjustment

Brake adjustment

Oil level

Brake adjustment

FRAME? — LEAKS? — TIGHTNESS?

Fig. 2–12 Before starting, examine these critical checkpoints!

Here are some questions to ask yourself during this check:

Have you got enough gas? Is it fresh? Is there water in it? Gas over three months old often is too stale to run an engine, and tanks left unfilled that long are often subject to condensation.

Is there a sufficient level of clean oil in the engine or oil tank?

Do the cables pull smoothly with the proper amount of adjustment? Are any of the strands of the inner cable frayed? Is the cable lubricated?

Does the rear brake work when the bike is rolled along manually? Is it adjusted properly?

Is the chain oiled? How is the adjustment?

What is the tire pressure? Do wheels and tires have any visible cracks or flaws?

Do all lights and turn signals work properly? Is the horn working well?

Is there anything on the motorcycle that is loose, bent, missing, or leaking that might cause unsafe riding?

If you've gotten through this check list and discovered no problems, you're ready to start the engine.

Warm Up

Motorcycles are generally air cooled. They take several minutes to reach proper operating temperature and for the lubricants to reach their work stations. Give your cold motorcycle at least 2 minutes running time before riding.

Getting Underway

A freshly started motorcycle often "clunks" badly when initially shifted into first gear. This is because the clutch plates are not completely freed from each other due to oil residue bonding them together. To ease this clash when engaging first gear, roll the bike forward as you shift to first gear. The clutch will generally free itself on the shift to second gear. To test it, pull the clutch lever and rev the engine slightly to insure the clutch is working properly.

Shift sharply but smoothly. There's nothing harder on the transmission than abusive shifting. Downshift when necessary to keep the engine running in its power range, because "lugging" an engine is also harmful.

Braking

You can brake more effectively with the motorcycle perfectly vertical while using both the front and rear brakes. The front brake is three times more effective than the rear brake because it handles 75 per cent of the braking load while the rear contributes only 25 per cent. Most riding instructors suggest applying the rear brake first to

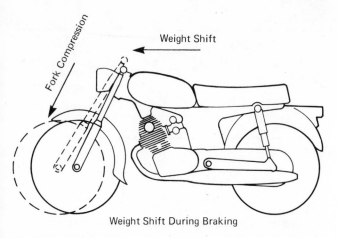

Weight Shift

Fork Compression

Weight Shift During Braking

Fig. 2–13 Weight shift and the resulting suspension change

insure keeping the rear wheel behind the front one. However, if you come to a situation where you need both brakes *instantly,* apply both brakes *instantly.* Afterwards, dedicate yourself to riding in a more careful manner so that you will never need both brakes instantly again. Remember that hard braking compresses the front forks. This results in less caster effect on the steering and less wheelbase. The bike will handle quicker and be less stable (Fig. 2–13).

Turning

Any turn, whether it's a sharp corner, a smooth curve, or a rough bend on a bumpy road, should be pre-evaluated, planned, and smoothly executed.

Plan the safest, smoothest line through the curve while avoiding pot holes, gravel, oil, water, or anything else that threatens. Do your braking *before* the turn, when the bike is still vertical, not after you've begun to lean into the turn. Harsh braking in a turn can cause a wheel to "lock up." Remember that the wheels *must* rotate in order for the motorcycle to maintain traction and execute the turn.

Look on a sequence of four turns as a pair of S-turns. Plan your entry and recovery toward a smooth, safe ride at every curve or pair of curves. One mistake is too many. Be conservative.

A police department riding instructor in Virginia discovered a significant rider tendency among his students. Right-handed students tend to turn more skillfully to the left, while left-handed riders tend to turn more skillfully to the

right. Try to develop your balance and coordination by practicing turns to your "weak side." You can never predict which way you'll have to go to avoid a mishap, so learn to turn in either direction equally well.

TRAFFIC

Be pessimistic in traffic. Remember Gumperson's law and pretend you're invisible. Be realistic, the 400-pound motorcycle is no match for a 2-ton car and offers virtually no protection for its rider. A minor accident that would be a "fender bender" if you were in a car, could cause you serious injury on a bike.

Keep an invisible barrier around you and your machine. Stay well behind the vehicle in front of you and avoid being "tail gated" yourself when possible. Use your extra visibility to advantage. Look through the windows of the car ahead of you to evaluate conditions ahead. Keep an eye on your own rear-view mirror to evaluate conditions behind you. Ask yourself as soon as you get behind a car: "Do his brake lights work or not?" Don't get the answer the hard way. Watch him slow down the first time from a very reasonable distance.

Avoid the center part of a traffic lane. The center of the lane collects the gas, oil, and coolant drippings from all the cars and trucks on the road. Traction tends to be better in either the right or left track sections of the lane.

There's a difference of opinion among "advisors" as to which section of the lane to travel in when riding. Some say to ride in the left track because you are more visible to the car ahead of you and motorists are less likely to attempt the old "squeeze play" by passing you in the same lane. Some riders say ride in the right track because it's easier to avoid trouble by riding to the shoulder of the road. Either way, avoid the oily section, especially for the first few minutes of a shower when it's icy slick.

Dogs have always posed a problem to motorcyclists. Some say the vibration frequency of some engines bother dogs' sensitive hearing. Oth-

Ye Olde Highway

Fig. 2–14   Correct pattern for group riding

ers say the size and novelty of a motorcycle encourage dogs to chase them. Whatever the reason, treat dogs respectfully when you are riding and remember their natural instinct is to *pursue* rather than attack. If you approach a crouching dog or a dog coming to chase you from ahead of you, head slightly toward the dog as you ride. This maneuver gives you a little extra room to turn at the last second and accelerate away from the dog. If your motorcycle will not outrun the dog, you should either avoid riding near the canine population centers or purchase a faster machine.

Highways and Open Roads

Higher speeds on the highway require a larger "safety zone" around your machine. When following another vehicle, stay at least 2 seconds behind it. This converts roughly into about one car length (20 feet) for each 10 miles per hour.

Prepare yourself for the "prop wash" or "air cushion" generated by big trucks. Avoid the direct impact of the air wake by staying almost a full lane away from oncoming trucks or the ones you are passing.

Group Riding

In many states it is illegal to ride directly beside another motorcycle in the same lane. When riding in a group, it is much safer to ride in a staggered pattern. This formation gives all of the riders an adequate "safety zone" fore and aft yet still allows them to ride as a group (Fig. 2–14).

Avoid the temptation to race or ride recklessly in a group. One "show off" or "hot dog's" antics are often infectious to the entire group, and

sometimes group riders find themselves trying to keep pace with an illogical rider. Let him go ahead as he pleases. You know the safety factor you are most comfortable with. *Stick with it.*

Passing

Overtake and pass other vehicles carefully. Check behind yourself very thoroughly to make sure that the car behind you isn't trying to pass both you and the slower vehicle ahead. *Always* give yourself plenty of room ahead. If the slower vehicle happens to be a large truck, prepare yourself for the wake or air stream it generates as you pass.

The laws for passing are the same for both motorcycles and cars. Remember to signal your intention to the cars behind you by using your left-turn blinker. As you pass the vehicle ahead of you, a short beep on the horn will alert the driver to let you by. Signal again with your right-turn signal as you pull back into the original lane. Execute your passing maneuver as politely as possible. For some reason one of the things an automobile operator resents is being passed by a roaring motorcycle. Give the driver a break. Don't rub it in. You'll be giving motorcycling a break, too.

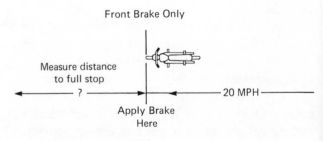

Fig. 2–15   Front brake stopping distance

Parking Lot Course

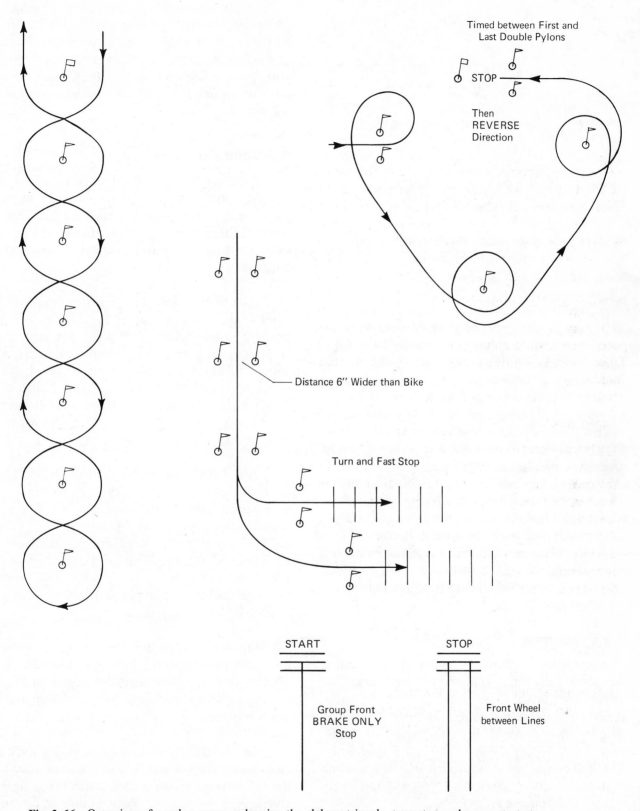

Fig. 2–16 Overview of a pylon course, showing the slalom, triangle, turn-stop and group start-stop

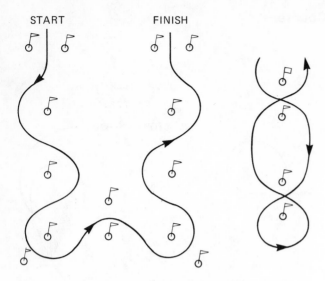

Fig. 2-17 Slalom and figure-8 drill patterns

Posture and Endurance

A bike that fits you and your riding style is important to your comfort on long-distance trips. The custom adjustments mentioned earlier in this chapter are critical factors that will determine whether you can cruise comfortably for 600 miles a day or whether you get backaches, sore arms, and neck aches after 3 hours in the saddle. These adjustments lead to correct riding posture; that is, lower legs parallel to your back.

Just as important, however, is your ability to relax as you ride. Don't "death grip" the handlebars until your knuckles turn white, or oversqueeze the tank with your knees. If you can't relax while riding on a trip, either you are riding too aggressively or your motorcycle isn't handling properly. Correct whichever problem exists.

Taking a Break

Operating a motorcycle on a highway requires that all of your riding skills be instantly available to get you out of jams. If you are overly tired, slightly intoxicated, emotionally upset, or otherwise mentally or physically unprepared for riding, *simply stop riding for awhile*. More importantly, though, become pre-conditioned so that when one of these situations *does* arise, you will not begin riding until you are ready.

If you feel yourself getting tired or drowsy, don't force yourself to continue riding. You'd be amazed how a 10-minute rest stop can make the next hundred miles much more pleasurable.

Carry your sunglasses along when riding long distances at night. Put your sunglasses on for the coffee breaks at those glaring, overlit, restaurants that adorn our highways. The sunglasses will fool your pupil a little bit so that they don't have to open up so much when you resume your nocturnal cruise.

Drills and Exercises

There are several good exercises and drill routines you can practice in order to improve your riding. Get your friends together and try some of these exercises in an abandoned parking lot some weekend (after you get permission, of course).

Front Brake Drill. Practice stopping with the front brake only. Set up a specific section and practice accelerating to 20 miles per hour, then stopping your bike with the front brake only. You should be able to stop in about 20 feet from 20 miles per hour by using the front brake only. Don't rush it though; be satisfied with 40 feet on your first day's try. If you can't get down to 20 feet, check your front brake (Fig. 2-15).

Tight Turning and Start-Stop Drills. These exercises are excellent ways to improve your slow-speed balance and coordination. There are several ways such a course can be set up; you can use tin cans if traffic cones are not available for markers. A suggested course is diagrammed in Fig. 2-16. Practicing several "start-stop" drills is an excellent way to improve your "downtown" traffic skills and techniques.

Slalom and Figure 8 Drills. These exercises help your maneuvering skills in slow traffic or on difficult surfaces. The diagrams shown in Fig. 2-17 suggest some configurations for slalom and figure 8 routines.

You should have someone timing your exercises with a stop watch. Try to improve your "lap times" through balance and control, not aggressiveness. Soon you will notice quite an advancement in your smoothness on the street, which will lead to safer, more controllable riding.

unit 3

Tools

The Rider-owner or best motorcycle mechanic in the world can't do a decent job without the right tools. Good tools are the means that enable you to transfer your knowledge into effective action. Knowing the different kinds of tools available and how to use them will help you become a faster, better mechanic. Most of the tools you will use are described in this chapter along with helpful hints about how to use them properly. Check the list at the end of this chapter for a suggested starter tool kit.

Screwdrivers

The screwdrivers used most often by the motorcycle mechanic are the electrical straight blade, mechanic's straight blade, Phillips head, and occasionally the hex head or Allen head (Figs. 3–1, 3–2). Blade sizes for standard screwdrivers are specified dimensionally (1/4″ × 1/32″) or are proportional to blade or overall screwdriver length. Shanks may be round or square, the square shank allowing you to use a wrench for additional turning power. The blade size should be chosen to fill just the screw slot (Fig. 3–3). Handles should be large enough for a comfortable grip, have no sharp edges, and be nearly unbreak-able. Occasional regrinding of the tip may be required for standard blades.

Pliers

Of the many kinds of general and special purpose pliers available, you should know about these:

Combination Pliers. Two-position pliers in 6- to 7-inch length with a wedge-type cutter for general and all-around work. (Fig. 3–4).

Interlocking Joint Grip. Eight- to 10-inch length with a 1 1/4- to 2-inch jaw opening for gripping larger work than combination pliers will handle. These pliers are often called "channel locks" after the company that developed them.

Diagonal Cutter Pliers. 6- to 7-inch length for removing cotter pins and cutting wire and small pieces of metal. Most mechanics call these "dikes."

Needle-Nose Pliers. Four- to 8-inch length, with or without cutter for small objects and restricted places. These are also used for bending wire.

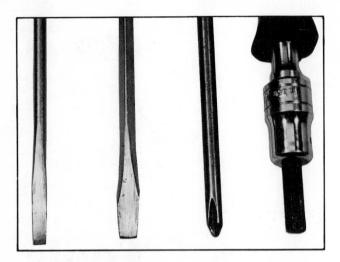

Fig. 3–1 Screwdrivers: from left to right, a standard thin slot, a standard slot, a Phillips, an Allen hex-type

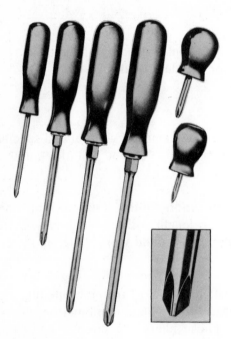

Fig. 3–2 Three or four sizes and lengths of screwdrivers are available. Close-up view at lower left shows cut of the Phillips tip

Fig. 3–3 Slot screwdriver blade should fill the slot cut in the screw head. Using wrong size driver will damage the screw head, the driver, or both.

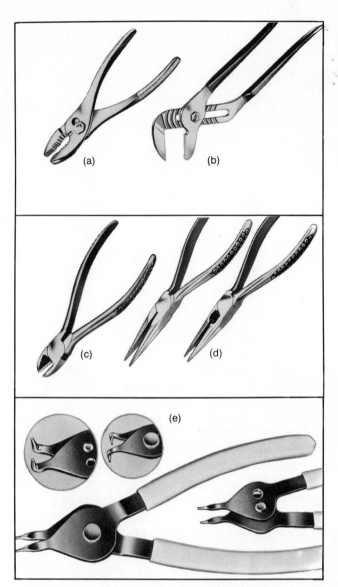

Fig. 3–4 Several types of pliers used in mechanical repair: (a) combination pliers, (b) interlocking pliers, (c) diagonal cut pliers or "dikes," (d) needle-nosed, and (e) snap-ring pliers.

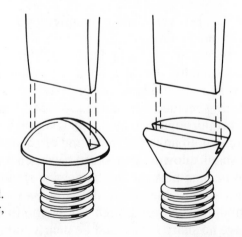

GENERAL TORQUE SPECIFICATION CHART

The following rules apply to the chart:

1. Consult manufacturers specific recommendations when available.
2. The chart may be used directly when any of the following lubricants are used:
   Never-Seez Compound, Molykote, Fel-Pro C-5, Graphite and Oil or similar mixtures.
3. Increase the torque by 20% when using engine oil or chassis grease as a lubricant.
   (These lubricants are not generally recommended for fasteners.)
4. Reduce torque by 20% when cadmium plated bolts are used.
   CAUTION: Tightening into aluminum usually will require less torque.

WHITWORTH STANDARD

GRADE OF BOLT	A & B	S	T	V	SOCKET OR WRENCH SIZE WHITWORTH	
MINIMUM TENSILE STRENGTH	62,720 P.S.I.	112,000 P.S.I.	123,200 P.S.I.	145,600 P.S.I.		
GRADE MARKING ON HEAD→	⬡	Ⓢ	Ⓣ	Ⓥ		
WHITWORTH	TORQUE (IN FOOT POUNDS)				WHITWORTH	
BOLT DIAMETER	U.S. DEC. EQUIV.				BOLT HEAD	NUT
1/4	.250	5	7	9	10	* 1/4	* 1/4
5/16	.3125	9	15	18	21	* 5/16	* 5/16
3/8	.375	15	27	31	36	* 3/8	* 3/8
7/16	.4375	24	43	51	58	* 7/16	* 7/16
1/2	.500	36	64	79	89	* 1/2	* 1/2
9/16	.5625	52	94	111	128	* 9/16	* 9/16
5/8	.625	73	128	155	175	* 5/8	* 5/8
3/4	.750	118	213	259	287	* 3/4	* 3/4
7/8	.875	186	322	407	459	* 7/8	* 7/8
1	1.000	276	497	611	693	* 1	* 1

U.S. STANDARD

GRADE OF BOLT	S.A.E. 1 & 2	S.A.E. 5	S.A.E. 6	S.A.E. 8	SOCKET OR WRENCH SIZE U.S. REGULAR	
MINIMUM TENSILE STRENGTH	64,000 P.S.I.	105,000 P.S.I.	133,000 P.S.I.	150,000 P.S.I.		
GRADE MARKINGS ON HEAD→	⬡	⬡	⬡	⬡		
U.S. STANDARD	TORQUE (IN FOOT POUNDS)				U.S. REGULAR	
BOLT DIAMETER	DEC. EQUIV.				BOLT HEAD	NUT
1/4	.250	5	7	10	10.5	3/8	7/16
5/16	.3125	9	14	19	22	1/2	9/16
3/8	.375	15	25	34	37	9/16	5/8
7/16	.4375	24	40	55	60	5/8	3/4
1/2	.500	37	60	85	92	3/4	13/16
9/16	.5625	53	88	120	132	7/8	7/8
5/8	.625	74	120	167	180	15/16	1
3/4	.750	120	200	280	296	1-1/8	1-1/8
7/8	.875	190	302	440	473	1-5/16	1-5/16
1	1.000	282	466	660	714	1-1/2	1-1/2

*Dimensions given on handles of U.S. Wrenches refer to actual size of bolt head or nut.

Dimensions given on Whitworth Wrenches refer to the shank or body diameter of the bolt, not the bolt head or nut size.

METRIC STANDARD

GRADE OF BOLT	5D	8G	10K	12K	SOCKET OR WRENCH SIZE METRIC	
MINIMUM TENSILE STRENGTH	71,160 P.S.I.	113,800 P.S.I.	142,000 P.S.I.	170,674 P.S.I.		
GRADE MARKING ON HEAD→	5D	8G	10K	12K		
METRIC	TORQUE (IN FOOT POUNDS)				METRIC	
BOLT DIAMETER	U.S. DEC. EQUIV.				BOLT HEAD	NUT
6mm	.2362	5	6	8	10	10mm	10mm
8mm	.3150	10	16	22	27	14mm	14mm
10mm	.3937	19	31	40	49	17mm	17mm
12mm	.4720	34	54	70	86	19mm	19mm
14mm	.5512	55	89	117	137	22mm	22mm
16mm	.6299	83	132	175	208	24mm	24mm
18mm	.709	111	182	236	283	27mm	27mm
22mm	.8661	182	284	394	464	32mm	32mm
24mm	.945	261	419	570	689	36mm	36mm

Fig. 3–5 Three principal torque specification charts

Snap-Ring Pliers. Small round tips to fit snap rings. Pliers may be straight or at 90° and may have interchangeable tips. The serious mechanic should have several sizes of both internal and external snap-ring pliers since the replaceable tip sets are too fragile for very hard work.

Occasional lubrication and using a tool large enough for the intended job will keep your pliers in good shape.

Sets

End Wrenches. End wrenches are made in a range of shapes, end types, and sizes. You will need to become familiar with metric sizes, and fractional inch sizes, and you may occasionally hit an English bike with Whitworth nuts and bolts (Fig. 3–5).

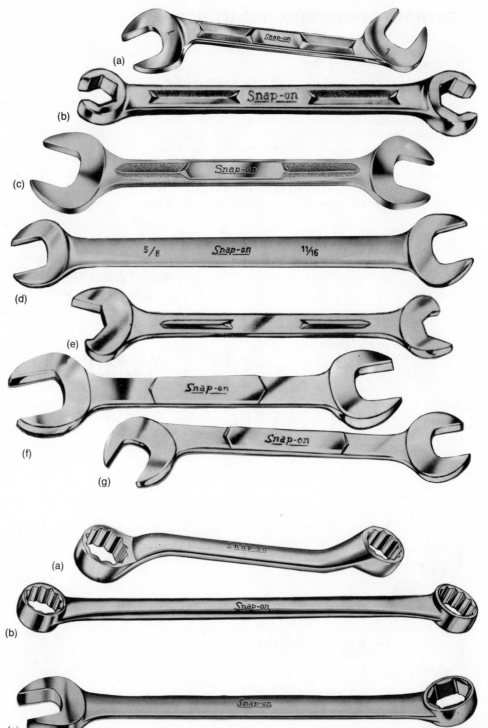

Fig. 3–6 Seven types of open-end wrenches in standard usage: (a) angle-head, (b) flare nut, (c) open end, (d) long slim, (e) open-end ratcheting, (f) short wrench, and (g) ignition wrench.

Fig. 3–7 Two standard box wrenches: (a) a double-hex offset box wrench, and (b) a long double-hex or 12-pt. wrench.

Fig. 3.8 Combination wrenches include (a) the 6-pt. box with flare end, (b) the 12-pt. box with flare, and (c) the combination flare and ratchet-end wrench

Open-End Wrenches. The wrenches shown in Fig. 3–6 normally have two different end sizes and are angled at 15°. These are used to remove nuts in limited access places. A complete set would run in size from 1/4 inch to 1 5/8 inches, or a fairly complete mechanic's set from 1/4 to 1 1/4 inches. A metric set from 6 to 32 mm would be very complete. Special angle 30° and 60° open-end wrenches are also available. A good starter set would include 10, 11, 12, 13, 14, 17, and 22 mm and 5/16″, 3/8″, 7/16″, 1/2″, 9/16″, 5/8″, 11/16″, 3/4″, 13/16″, and 7/8″ English sizes.

Box Wrenches. These are better to use than open-end wrenches as the box end is less likely to slip and scuff off the corners on nuts. Box wrenches are available in 6- and 12-point openings, in size ranges similar to open-end wrenches, and may have an angled or raised handle (Fig. 3–7).

Combination-End Wrenches. These have a box end and an open end at opposite ends of the same handle. Both openings are the same dimension. These combination wrenches are a good starting set of tools for the motorcycle mechanic or owner.

Two special end wrenches worth having are flare-nut wrenches for tubing fittings, as shown in Fig. 3–6b, and ratchetting-end wrenches for speeding assembly work as shown in Fig. 3–6e.

Torque Wrench. Torque wrenches are socket drive handles with some method of indicating the amount of turning force or torque being applied to the fastener. They are available in 3/8- and 1/2-inch drive sizes in the torque ranges needed by the motorcycle mechanic. Torques are indicated by direct reading dials, click type where a sound is emitted at the pre-set torque, and the less expensive beam type (Fig. 3–9). Torque wrenches can be purchased with scales in inch-pounds, foot-pounds, centimeter-kilograms, and meter-kilograms.

The dial-reading types are too bulky to fit in tight places. The click type is good if kept clean but loses accuracy when it gets grimy. A good starting wrench would be a 3/8-inch drive beam-type torque wrench with a dual scale 0 to 50 foot-pounds; 0 to 600 inch-pounds.

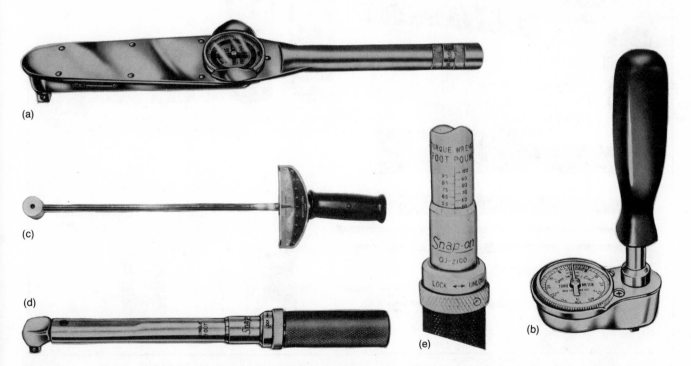

Fig. 3–9 Five styles of torque wrench include (a) a dial-type torque wrench showing foot pounds, (b) a dial-type showing inch-pounds, (c) a dual scale beam-type, (d) a beam-type with foot-pound scale, and (e) the click-type end showing foot-pound scale.

Fig. 3–10 Typical chain wrenches

Chain Wrench. This wrench (Fig. 3–10) is used to turn large or irregular shapes, as the chain will grip over a large surface area.

Socket Set. The socket set, one of the mechanic's most useful tool sets, consists of 6- and 12-point standard sockets, deep well sockets, a ratchet, extensions from 1 1/2 to 12 inches, and many other available drive and link parts (Fig. 3–11). The sockets fit into limited places, hold the fasteners firmly, and can be turned rapidly in either direction. Drive ends are available as screwdrivers and Allen wrenches.

Socket sets come in 1/4-, 3/8-, and 1/2-inch drives, referring to the size of the square tang inserted to turn the socket. Larger drives are available for heavy machinery. A good starting set for a motorcycle mechanic would be a 3/8-inch drive set, with both fractional inch and metric sockets from 1/4 to 7/8 inch and 8 to 22 mm in standard length with some deep wells.

Impact Driver. A 3/8-inch impact driver set (Fig. 3–12) with special sockets and screwdrivers can deliver a power rotary motion when struck with a hammer. The impact driver can help a mechanic "break loose" frozen nuts, bolts, or screws that resist turning with hand wrenches or screwdrivers. The impact driver is a *must* for motorcycle maintenance.

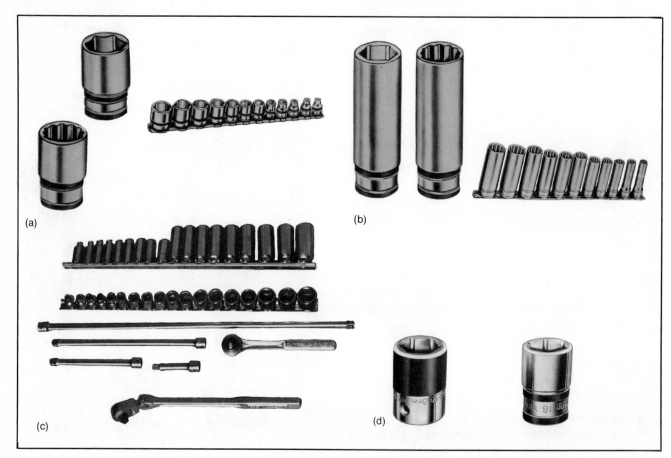

Fig. 3–11 Varieties of socket sets include (a) a standard socket set, with 6-pt., 12-pt. sockets: (b) 6- and 12-pt. deep well socket set, (c) a complete metric socket set, showing ratchet handles and extensions, and (d) close-up view of metric ferret sockets.

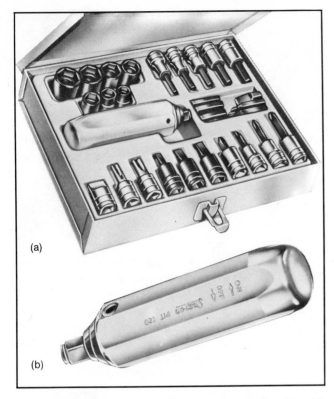

(a)

(b)

Fig. 3–12 Inpact driver set showing (a) complete kit with handle and various driver tips, and (b) close-up of the handle

Adjustable End Wrench. These wrenches (Fig. 3–13) are handy when no other wrench is available to fit a nut or bolt. They are made in 4-to 24-inch lengths with jaw openings ranging to 2 1/2 inches.

Hammers. As a motorcycle mechanic you will find occasion to use a variety of hammers (Fig. 3–14). The ball-peen hammer is the general machinists' hammer. It is used for driving punches, chisels, and impact drivers. Plastic tip or soft-face hammers are used where the finish or shape of parts such as aluminum cases and transmission gears would be marred by a steel hammer.

Files. A mechanic uses files to remove burrs on shafts, cases, and other parts, as well as to shape or straighten the edges of parts. Files vary in length, cut, shape, and edge. Cut refers to the number of teeth per inch and whether the teeth are single or double cut. Shape may be flat, round, or half-round. An edge is called "safe" when it is without teeth (Fig. 3–15). Handles should always

Fig. 3–13 The adjustable end wrench for square or hex head bolts

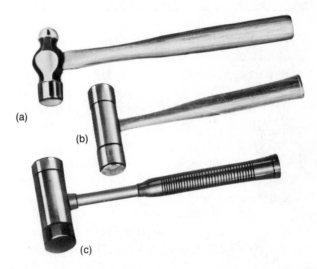

(a)

(b)

(c)

Fig. 3–14 Three common hammers: (a) a combination flat and ball-peen hammer, (b) a soft-face brass hammer, and (c) a combination brass and plastic-tipped hammer

(a)

(b)

(c)

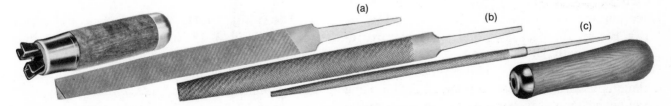

Fig. 3–15 Two types of handles and three styles of files: (a) a single cut flat file with a "safe" edge, (b) a half-round, and (c) a round file.

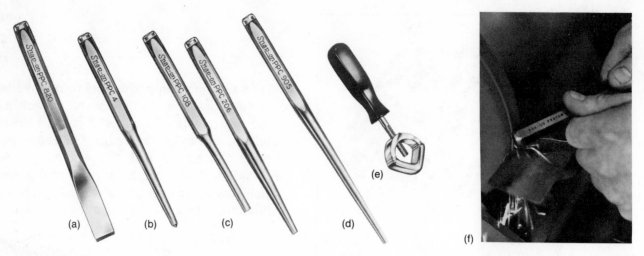

Fig. 3–16 Standard chisel (a) and several punches, including (b) a center punch, (c) two types of pin punch, (d) a starter punch, (e) a holder for either a chisel or a punch, and (f) grinding metal burrs off a chisel head after use.

be purchased and used with files because a bare file tang is sharp and will cause hand injuries. Files should be stored so they will not contact other files or metal; otherwise they will soon become dull. A file card or cleaner will make filing faster and the resulting metal finish smoother.

Chisels and Punches. Flat metal cutting chisels are used to cut bolts, nuts, pins, and other metal parts. Sizes range from 3/8- to 3/4-inch blade widths. Chisels need occasional sharpening by filing or grinding the blade to a 60° cutting angle and keeping the head round and free of burrs (Fig. 3–16).

Center punches are used to make a small identification for starting drill bits or marking parts during disassembly so that realignment is easy. Tapered punches are used to start driving out pins or bolts and to align parts during assembly. Pin punches with straight shafts are for driving through pins or bolts or maintaining part alignment. Chisel or punch holders are sometimes useful.

Saws. Hacksaws, jab saws, and hole saws are used by mechanics for frame and part modification and some types of disassembly (Fig. 3–17). Blades for hacksaws and jab saws are replaceable, with 18-, 24-, and 32-teeth per inch blades commonly used. The 32-tooth per inch blade is used to cut very thin metal. When using hand saws, apply pressure on the forward stroke only and keep the strokes down to 30 per minute to avoid overheating from the friction.

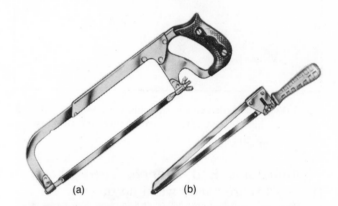

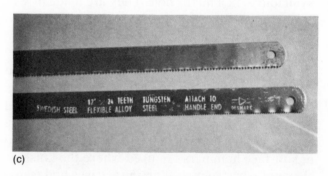

Fig. 3–17 In this figure, (a) shows the standard hacksaw, (b) a low-clearance hacksaw, and (c) two types of hacksaw blades.

Cleaning Tools. Wire brushes and gasket scrapers (Fig. 3–18) are often handy. The long-handled wire brush is a good all-around first choice. Good quality putty knives with flexible blades make good scrapers.

Screw Extractors. Screws, bolts, or studs that have broken off in cases or heads can be re-

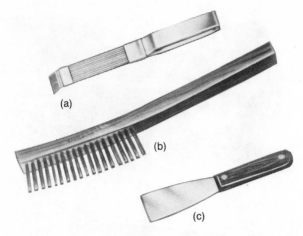

Fig. 3–18 A carbon scraper (a), (b) a wire brush, and (c) a metal or putty knife scraper are useful for cleaning tools.

Fig. 3–19 An occasional broken-off screw head makes the screw extractor kit useful in the pro or semi-pro cycle shop.

moved by drilling, then inserting a screw extractor (Fig. 3–19), and turning counterclockwise to turn out the remainder of the broken fastener. Careful drilling is critical. Unit 23 covers the complete process.

General Power Tools and Accessories

Electric Drill. 3/8-inch variable-speed reversible electric hand drill is a good first choice for the mechanic's power tool collection. The drill should have good electrical insulation and a fractional high-speed steel drill-bit set (Fig. 3–20).

Stone and Brush Hones (Fig. 3–21). These hones (a), (b), and (d) are used in cylinder bores

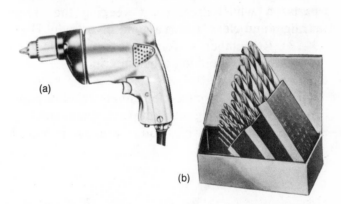

Fig. 3–20 The 3/8″ electric drill (a) is particularly useful. The compact bit set is shown in (b).

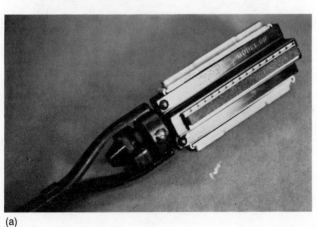

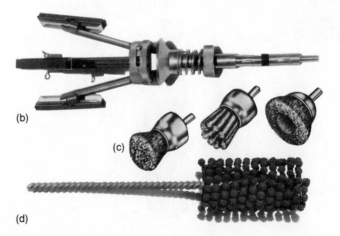

Fig. 3–21 Shaft mounted (a) and spring-type stone hones (b) are used to clean cylinder bores. Wire brushes (c) are used for cleaning, (d) is a brush hone used for cylinder deglazing.

after boring or when fitting new rings. Wire brushes (c) and stones are used for cleaning and smoothing or removing small amounts of metal.

Propane Torch. General heating for light bending, heavy soldering, and heating for press fits and removing parts are some uses you will find for this tool (Fig. 3–22). Fuel tanks are simply replaced. Accessories include soldering tips and various burning tips.

Bench Grinder. A bench grinder should have at least 6- by 1/2-inch stones, a ball-bearing shaft, and a 1/4-hp motor. Screwdrivers, punches, and other tools that require sharpening will use a 60-grit stone. A wire brush wheel on the other end of the shaft is great for cleaning valves and other parts. A wheel dresser for keeping the stone straight and clean is also a good investment (Fig. 3–23). Remember—safety glasses or goggles are a must when operating a bench grinder.

Hot Plate. A single-element electric hot plate is handy for heating press-fit parts, chain-treating grease, and coffee while you're working in a cold garage (Fig. 3–24).

(a)

(b)

Fig. 3–23 A 1/4-horse grinder (a) can be bench-mounted for use with stones, wire brush, or rotary grinder. A wheel dresser (b) keeps the stone straight and clean.

Soldering Gun. A soldering iron or gun for electrical wiring should be in the 150- to 250-watt heat range with replaceable tips. You should also have noncorrosive paste flux and good quality rosin core solder (Fig. 3–25).

Impact Wrench. For motorcycle work, impact wrenches are used primarily for disassembly as the soft metal cases and threads won't last long due to the easily applied high torques when assembling. A 3/8-inch drive compact model will be handiest. When compressed air is available, the

Fig. 3–22 The propane torch is used for metal bending and soldering.

Fig. 3–24 Hot plate makes a good warm-up device for chain grease, press-fit parts, or coffee.

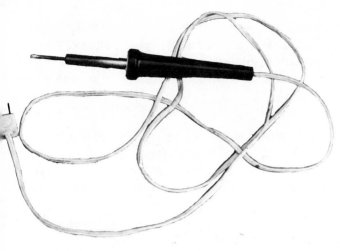

Fig. 3–25   Soldering iron with flux and solder is a "must."

air drive wrench, is a better choice because it's lighter and more compact (Fig. 3–26).

High-Speed Grinder. The rotary grinder is useful for port, piston, and head cleaning and modification. Look for one that has ball bearings and is capable of accepting 1/8-inch through 1/4-inch shafts (Fig. 3–27).

Impact Hammer. This is also known as an air chisel. It is used to cut sheet metal, frozen nuts, and welds. Special-purpose tips, such as rivet cutters and punches, are available (Fig. 3–28).

Test Equipment

The following equipment is listed in approximately the order of usefulness. To do a thorough tuning job you will find a need for each piece of this equipment eventually.

Tire Pressure Gage. Direct-reading gages are easier to read. Check your gage against a master gage to determine its accuracy. Dirt and hard knocks will change the readings you get (Fig. 3–29).

Fig. 3–26   Air-driven impact wrench

Fig. 3–27   High speed rotary grinder

Fig. 3–29   Dial-type tire pressure gauge

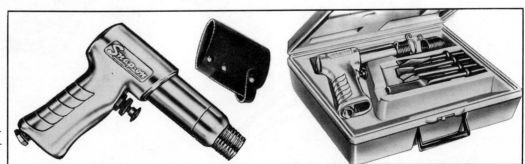

Fig. 3–28   Impact hammer or air chisel kit

Fig. 3–30 Typical compression gauge

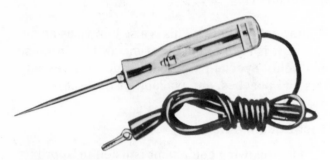

Fig. 3–31 Test light for electric circuits

Compression Gage. A compression gage with dual scales, psi and kg/cm², is most useful. It's easier for you to get an accurate reading by using the screw-in adapters for the various spark plug threads when kicking the bike through compression (Fig. 3–30).

Test Light. The test light is faster and handier than a meter for determining if voltage is avail-

able, has a sharp probe, and can get into small places. When necessary, you can even poke through insulation on a wire with it. Test lights are available with neon spark plug testing bulbs (Fig. 3–31).

Timing Light. The timing light is used to set the timing of spark plug firing. The neon type is less expensive but gives out less light. The power type needs to be connected to a 110-volt power source or should be equipped with clips for attaching to a 6- or 12-volt battery. It emits a bright light for easy timing (Fig. 3–32).

Volt-Ohm Meter. When a test light won't quite do it, you'll need a voltmeter to determine an accurate output. The ohmmeter will tell you the electrical resistance of a circuit—not bad for checking point conditions. Don't leave the meter in an ohm reading position as the batteries will run down. Also, don't try to read the resistance in a power-on circuit—the meter won't last long. Look for a meter that is protected by a fuse or circuit breaker (Fig. 3–33). A combination meter is usually cheaper than two separate meters.

Dial Indicator. A direct-reading meter, reading is usually in thousandths of an inch, for measuring shaft run-out, rim wobble, top dead center, etc. Screw-in, clamp-on, and magnetic bases are available (Fig. 3–34).

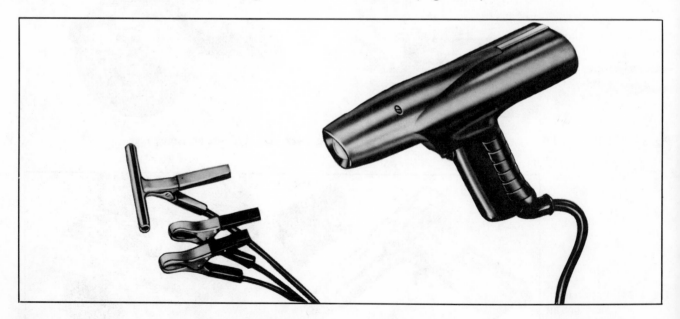

Fig. 3–32 Timing light for setting spark plug firing timing.

Fig. 3–33 A volt-ohmmeter for electric circuit testing

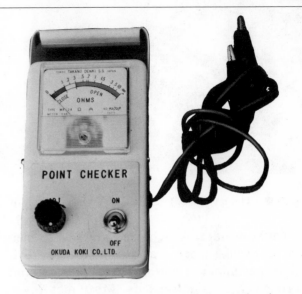

Fig. 3–35 Point checker meters small electrical resistance

Points Checker. This meter measures resistance with a single scale that reads from 0 to 10 ohms; the first 2 ohms are shown in tenths. Very small resistances can be read in ignition wires, through ignition points, and in other circuits where small differences are critical (Fig. 3–35).

Ammeter. Ammeters are used to measure generator or alternator output, starter drain, or current flow to a specific component. They are connected in series for measurement. A meter scale of 50 amperes will handle most bike applications. Some meters have induction pickups that do not require direct connection into the circuit (Fig. 3–36).

Fig. 3–36 Typical electric circuit ammeter

Carburetor Vacuum Balance Gauge. Some bikes have test ports in the carburetors or intake manifolds. When the port plug is removed and a vacuum gauge connected, the gauge readings indicate the carburetor adjustment. Multi-carb engines can be accurately balanced by using a vacuum gauge to adjust each carburetor to the same reading (Fig. 3–37).

Fig. 3–34 Dial reading meter for checking top dead center.

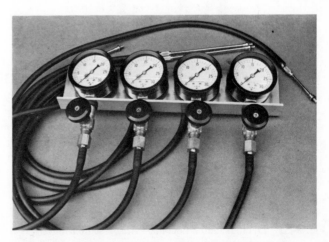

Fig. 3–37 Multi-carb engines can be finely balanced by using vacuum gauge like this

(a)

(b)

(c)

Fig. 3-38 Three types of tachometers: (a) mechanical, (b) electronic, and (c) photoelectric

Tachometers. A tachometer is used to measure the turning speed of a shaft or wheel in revolutions per minute (rpm) by electrical (ignition), mechanical, or video means. Most motorcycle tachs are the mechanical type powered by a speedometer-type cable driven by the engine (Fig. 3-38a). Electronic tachs convert impulses from the primary ignition circuit into engine rpm (Fig. 3-38b). Photoelectric tachs react to any bright spot (tape or paint spot) on a tire, wheel, gear, or shaft and give you a scale reading in rpms (Fig. 3-38c).

Decibel Meters. (Fig. 3-39) The measurement of sound or noise levels will become necessary as states pass laws governing maximum al-

lowable noise levels for motor vehicles. Initial laws have specific maximums around 86 to 90 dB at 50 feet, with the bike at high engine rpm in a lower gear. Most good mechanics agree that maximum power does not come with the most noise.

SPECIAL TOOLS AND EQUIPMENT

Twelve more specialized tools and pieces of equipment that are sometimes needed in repair are shown in Figs. 3-40 through 3-53.

Fig. 3-40 Chain breaker

Fig. 3-41 Tire irons

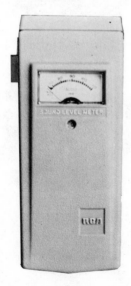

Fig. 3-39 Decibel meter becomes vital test instrument as noise level becomes a more important environmental concern.

Fig. 3-42 Mag flywheel puller

44

Fig. 3-43 Clutch hub puller

Fig. 3-44 Valve core tool

Fig. 3-45 Spoke wrench

Fig. 3-46 Hand-operated grease gun

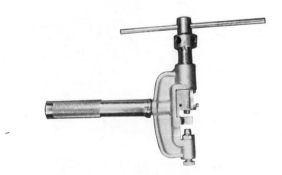

Fig. 3-47 Chain rivet tool

Fig. 3-48 Pin wrench

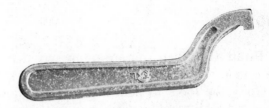

Fig. 3-49 Crown or shock spanner

Fig. 3-50 Seal installer

Fig. 3-51 Tubing bender

SHOP EQUIPMENT

If you intend to operate your own bike repair shop, you will need to invest in some of the larger equipment items. The following is a partial list of things to consider, perhaps in a good order of need:

1. Vise
2. Truing stand
3. Air compressor
4. Hydraulic press
5. Drill press
6. Gas and electric welding equipment
7. Motorcycle analyzer
8. Glass bead parts cleaner
9. Alignment board
10. Motorcycle lifts
11. Boring bar
12. Lathe
13. Spark plug cleaner
14. Valve shop
15. Dynamometer
16. Refrigerator

The last isn't for keeping liquids cold, but to help in cooling parts for press fits.

TOOL KITS

Road Kit. When you are riding any distance more than to the corner store, it pays to select carefully the tools to haul along in addition to those the bike manufacturer provided. Here are some suggestions if you can find room to carry them on your bike.

1. Combination-end wrenches 10, 11, 12, 13, 14 mm.
2. Box-end wrenches 17, 22 mm. American and English machine riders will have to adjust.
3. Impact driver with Phillips and common screwdrivers

4. Plug wrench
5. Tire irons and spare tube
6. Chain breaker and link kit
7. Chain lubrication
8. Set of spark plugs
9. Crescent wrench and small vise grips

Portable Tool Box. This is better defined as whatever you're willing to carry on your bike somewhere. Put in it whatever you have room for, starting back at the beginning of the hand tools, plus any power tools that don't have to be plugged in, unless you have a portable generator.

One Last Thought. When you spend your bread, remember that many of the better tool manufacturers replace their tools that break— free!

The Frame

The motorcycle frame provides a strong, rigid structure upon which to attach the components necessary to make up the machine. The size, weight, and type of frame contributes as much as any other factor to the "personality" of the motorcycle. Frame geometry determines, to a larger extent, the bike's handling characteristics. Also, the type of construction is a critical factor affecting frame stability and rigidity. Don't take the frame for granted. It's a very important part of your motorcycle and requires periodic inspection and maintenance.

NOMENCLATURE AND TYPES

Types of Frames

Tubular Frame. Single and double downtube swing-arm frames have emerged as the most accepted type, especially for motorcycles with engines over 200 cc. The tubular frame is light yet strong, and provides very good stability at highway cruising speeds. It also seems to have more "eye appeal" to most riders because of its leaner, racier look (Fig. 4–1).

Pressed-Steel Frame. The pressed-steel frame usually consists of two stamped-steel or sheet-metal halves welded together along a center seam. From a manufacturing standpoint this type of construction is more economical than tubular construction if many bikes of the same model are to be made. The drawbacks are that the pressed-steel frame is generally heavier, less rigid, and makes the motorcycle more difficult to repair. Of course, these problems are less critical in the 50- to 150-cc machines where the pressed-steel frames have been most popular (Fig. 4–2).

Engine-Based Frames. Often both the tubular and pressed-steel frames rely on the engine members instead of additional frame to add rigidity to the structure. While this design helps to reduce a machine's weight and cost, it often results in frame flex if the engine mounting studs are not properly torqued. With engine-based frame design carried to the extreme, as in the famous Vincent V twins, frame flex becomes a real concern. These machines have been likened to "riding a 140-mph ball joint." To a lesser degree, all frames that use the engine as a frame member may develop this problem if not properly maintained by

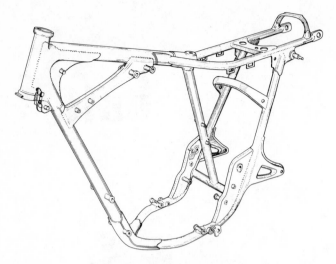

Fig. 4–1 Tubular type frame, exploded view (American Honda Motor Company)

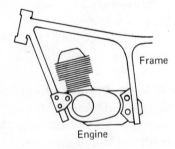

Fig. 4–2 Pressed steel frame (American Honda Motor Company)

Fig. 4–3 Engine-based frame

tightening the engine mounting bolts every month or so (Fig. 4–3).

Frame Components

Steering Head. The steering head is the tube at the top of the frame where the front fork assembly is attached (Fig. 4–4). The steering head incorporates two sets of ball bearings for easy

Fig. 4–4 Steering head, exploded view (AMF Harley-Davidson Motor Co., Inc.)

steering and a special adjuster nut for tightening the bearings as they wear. The steering head angle is very important because it affects the high-speed stability and low-speed maneuverability of the machine a great deal. A steep or near vertical angle results in quick slow-speed steering reaction, while a more "raked" angle yields more high-speed stability but sacrifices precise low-speed steering. Steering head angle is set during manufacture and is usually in keeping with the intended purpose of the bike. Smaller displacement trail bikes tend to have steep steering head angles, but higher-speed road machines and some racing motorcycles incorporate more "chopper-like" steering head angles for high-speed control (Fig. 4–5).

Triple Clamp. Triple clamp or fork-leg holders are two triangular brackets that mount the forks to the steering crown (Fig. 4–6). The handlebar mounts are usually incorporated into the design of the upper triple clamp along with provisions for mounting gages such as the speedometer and tachometer. The lower clamp sometimes incorporates a steering head lock or part of a steering dampening device.

Steering Dampening Devices. There are two popular types of steering vibration dampeners. The simpler consists of a set of fiber washers and metal discs that may be pre-loaded to re-

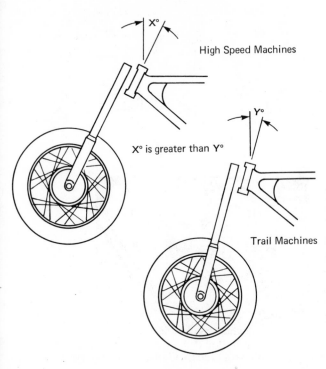

Fig. 4–5 Steering head angle, showing difference between high-speed angle and trail angle

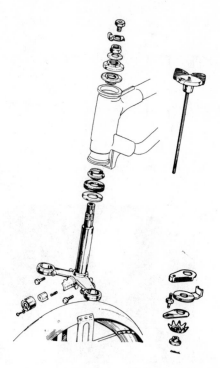

Fig. 4–7 Steering dampener, exploded view (American Honda Motor Company)

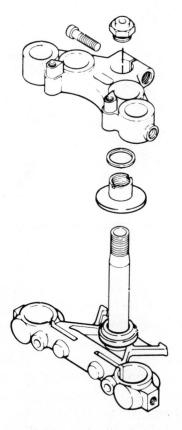

Fig. 4–6 Triple clamp, exploded view, (AMF Harley-Davidson Motor Co., Inc.)

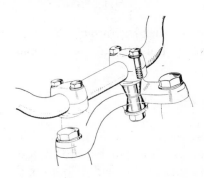

Fig. 4–8 Rubber mounted handlebars, phantom view, shows rubber bushing below center

strict turning motion (Fig. 4–7). A more sophisticated vibration dampener mounts between the lower triple clamp and the frame. This unit is basically a shock absorber that dampens the unwanted jolts and oscillations from the front wheel.

Handlebars, Clamps, and Cushions. There are literally hundreds of variations on the handlebar theme, but they generally fall into two sizes and classifications as far as mounting provisions are concerned. Handlebars are usually 7/8- or 1-inch diameter tubing. They are either fixed solidly to the upper triple clamp or mounted in rubber to help dampen vibration (Fig. 4–8). The clamping

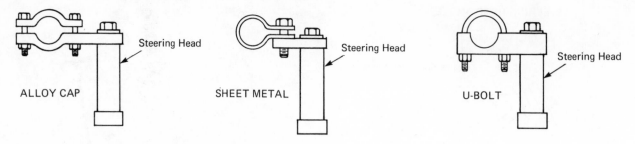

Fig. 4-9 Different handlebar clamps

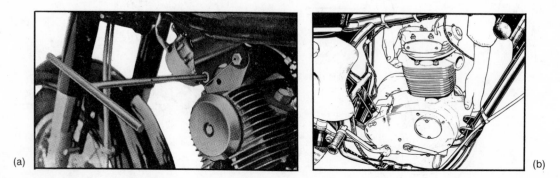

Fig. 4-10 Typical engine mounting provisions (a) (Honda Motor American Company) and (b) (Triumph Norton Incorporated)

devices on handlebars range from sturdy alloy caps to steel U-bolts to sheet-metal clamps (Fig. 4-9).

Mounting Provisions

Engine. Engines are usually attached to the frame in at least three places, and sometimes in as many as six places. Instead of bolting the engine directly to the frame tubes, there are metal tabs or mounts either bolted or welded to the frame. Usually the mounting bolts pass completely through the engine cases, adding stability to both the frame and engine. Some typical mounting schemes are pictured in Fig. 4-10.

Controls and Pegs. Another important set of mounts found on your motorcycle frame are those for the pegs and rear brake pedal. Often the foot peg mounts are adjustable for height or fore and aft positioning (Fig. 4-11). Sometimes the rear brake pedal is incorporated right into a cross brace of the frame for added strength to this important section (Fig. 4-12).

Rear Suspension. There are two important mounting points on the tail section of the frame

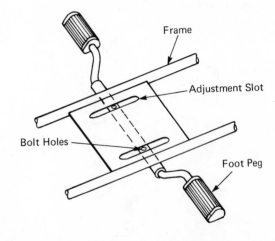

Fig. 4-11 Adjustable foot pegs, showing fore and aft adjustment

for the rear suspension. They are the swing-arm pivot mount and the top shock-absorber mount.

The swing-arm mount is usually bushed with a bronze, iron, or special rubber bushing, but some use tapered roller bearings (Fig. 4-13). This mount is very important because rear-wheel stability is almost totally dependent on the condition of the swing-arm mount. If the swing arm is free to wander laterally and flex on its pivot, dangerous handling will result. Figure 4-14 indicates

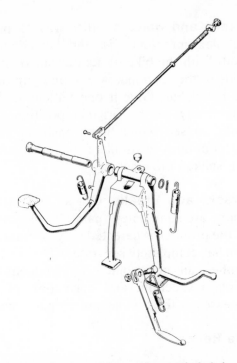

Fig. 4–12 Rear brake pedal mounting, exploded view, showing cross-tube mounting. (American Honda Motor Company)

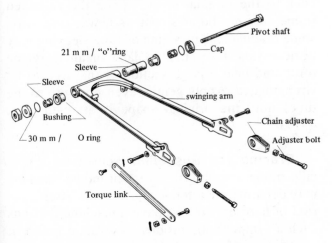

Fig. 4–13 Swing arm, exploded view, showing bushing in five from left. (Kawasaki Motors Corporation)

movement that can result from worn swing-arm bushings. Techniques for servicing the swing-arm bushings are described in Unit 5.

Tank, Fender, Seat. The frame is usually the base mount for other components such as the gas tank, fenders, seat, side covers, battery, oil tank, electrical components, center and side stands. You will find a myriad of engineering approaches to mounting these items, but most frames have them all.

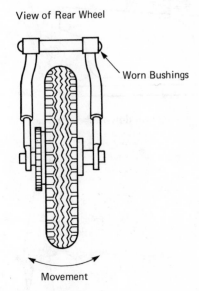

Fig. 4–14 Swing arm looseness

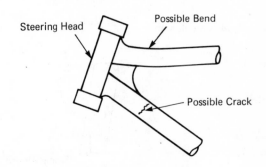

Fig. 4–15 Front down-tube crack area

The frame, hiding behind all the paint, glitter, and noise of the components it supports, is too often ignored. Give this base component the attention it deserves by periodic inspection and maintenance. The next section tells you how to do it.

Frame Service

Inspection. Certain areas of frames are more suspectible to fatigue and damage. A common one, especially on well-flogged dirt bikes, is the area between the front-down tube and the steering head. Another area to keep your eye on is the section just above the swing-arm mounting (Figs. 4–15, 4–16).

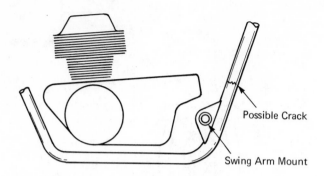

Fig. 4–16   Swing arm down-tube crack area

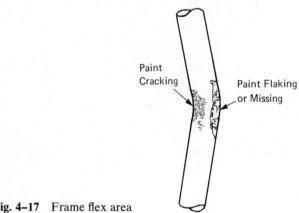

Fig. 4–17   Frame flex area

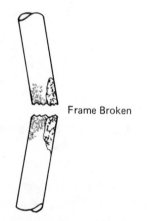

Fig. 4–18   Broken frame

Any place where you can detect chipping, flaking paint that hints of bending or flexing frame tubes, *be cautious!* Your frame tubes might be getting ready to break. Keep checking the suspicious section and reinforce or repair it as soon as you determine that bending or flexing is actually taking place. The problem area will look something like Fig. 4–17.

Have it fixed before it looks like the frame in Fig. 4–18.

Shake and Hold. Another way to pinpoint frame flex problems is the shake-and-hold method. With the bike off its kickstand, stand to one side of the machine, face it, and grip one end of the handlebar. Give it one violent shake, returning firmly to the original position. Watch carefully to see which joint bushing, axle, or mount continues to oscillate for a moment after you've shaken the machine.

Cracks and Breaks. Cracks and breaks in the frame are sometimes "painfully obvious" because the problem is detected only after the faulty section has completely separated. This sort of catastrophe can be avoided by frequent frame cleaning, inspection, and correction of frame weaknesses at the first sign of chipping paint.

Frame Repair

Straightening. Bent tube-frame sections can often be repaired by heating and bending them back to the original shape. Since the reshaped frame may not be as strong as it was originally, some bracing and gusseting or tube sleeving may be necessary. Use a neutral flame on an acetylene torch and heat a large section of the area to be strengthened. Apply gentle, even pressure to the tubes until the original shape is attained (Fig. 4–19).

Bracing and Gusseting. Sometimes a specific frame junction on a certain model machine may demonstrate a tendency to break after a period of hard use. If you have a machine that has such a symptomatic problem, correct it before it starts by reinforcing the weak area. A triangular

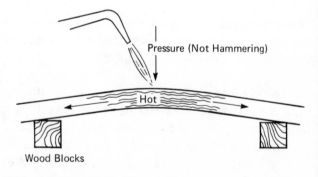

Fig. 4–19   Frame straightening

plate of steel welded into the junction of tubes at the steering head, or a plate welded between the two tubes at the rear of an Enduro bike, can prevent any mishaps that might arise. However, you should take this step only if the particular model you are working on has gained a reputation for a specific frame weakness (Fig. 4–20).

Break and Crack Repair. There are as many ways to repair cracked or broken motorcycle frames as there are welders. A good welder will say that his simple weld is as strong as the tube was originally. Naturally, that is not good enough for you, because your frame broke. What you need is not only repair, but reinforcement. There are several sound approaches to the repair.

Sleeving. A broken tube can be internally or externally sleeved to repair and reinforce it. Strive to retain the exact original frame geometry by perfectly matching the broken tube ends be-

fore welding. The steps for a complete sleeve job are illustrated in Fig. 4–21. You may use internal, external, or both types of frame repair on the same broken section.

Of course, depending on the nature of the break and the machine, you may elect to sleeve the frame only one way. Be sure to use fairly low

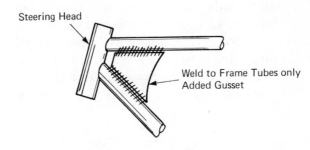

Fig. 4–20   Steering head gusset

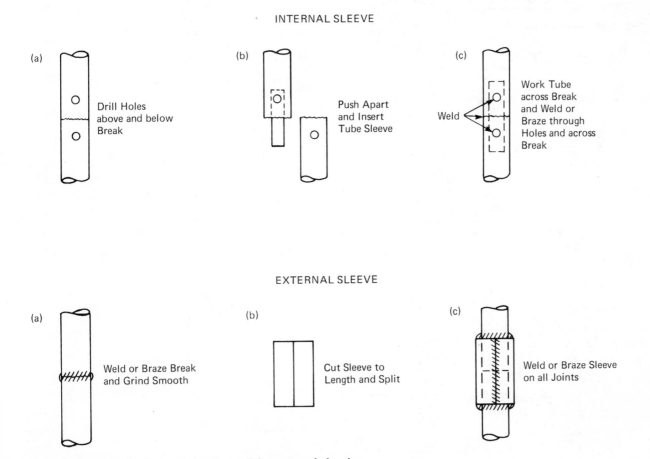

Fig. 4–21   Three steps for internal sleeving and for external sleeving

heat for this type of repair because the frame tubing tends to become brittle if overwelded.

Bends. While a straightened bend in a frame or swing-arm tube can be reinforced by external sleeving, it can also be braced with a simple rib section welded on (Fig. 4–22).

Brazed Joints. Some frames are constructed from a series of tubes brazed into sockets of joint sections. After a period of hard use, these brazed connections have been known to work loose. You can get these sections re-brazed, making them as good as new, if you clean and prepare the joint properly. Re-welding near brazed joints is not a good idea, because the brass tends to interfere with good weld puddling between steel sections (Fig. 4–23).

Pressed Steel Repair. A pressed-steel frame is repaired much like a "body and fender man" repairs sheet metal on a damaged car. The oxacetylene torch is used along with hammer and dolly to heat and form bent sections of the frame back to their original shapes.

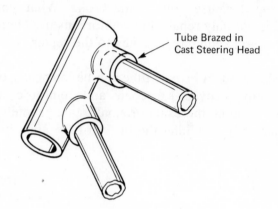

Tube Brazed in
Cast Steering Head

Fig. 4–23 Cast and tube joint

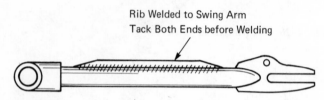

Rib Welded to Swing Arm
Tack Both Ends before Welding

Fig. 4–22 Rib or stiffener

Wheels and Suspension

WHEELS AND TIRES

Though most motorcycle wheels appear to be almost identical in construction, there are subtle size variations that enable designers to custom tailor wheels and tires to the intended purpose of the machine.

Sizes, Types and Application

The diameter of wheels and tires, measured at the bead, varies from as little as 16 inches up to 21 inches. The rims themselves may be of either steel or aluminum alloy.

Tire widths range from 2 to 5 inches and are accommodated by rims from about 1 1/2 to 4 inches wide.

Spokes are available in several diameters and range in length from 6 inches to more than a foot. Additionally, spokes may be "inners" or "outers" as well as "lefts" or "rights." That is, a single wheel may have as many as four different types of spokes.

Some manufacturers and specialty motorcycles use cast aluminum or magnesium wheels. The main reason for using this expensive type of wheel is that it is strong, light, and perfectly true, since it is finished on a lathe.

Figure 5–1 shows two types of wheels used on popular motorcycles.

The sizes of wheels and tires selected for a motorcycle usually depend on the bike's general size and weight class. Smaller motorcycles up to 200-cc street machines tend to use 17-inch or small 18-inch tires. Middle weight 250–500-cc street machines use 18-inch tires fore and aft, while heavyweights up to 900 cc use a large 18-or 19-inch tire on the rear and a 19-inch on the front. The big 1200-cc Harley reverts to a 16-inch tire bead diameter with a bulbous 5-inch cross section.

Enduro and Motorcross bikes lean toward the larger 21-inch front wheel assembly to ease rolling over obstacles. Smaller, slower trail bikes, get by with an 18-inch front tire, while dirt bikes of all types are generally backed up by an 18-inch knobby or trials universal.

Tread design and selection is based on the intended use of the machine. A full-fledged dirt bike used exclusively for Enduro, Motorcross, or trail riding, relies on rough knobby tires for traction in mud and loose dirt. On pavement, however, these tires lose their charm and their traction. Besides wearing rapidly (often in less than 1000 miles) knobby tires are poor on dry pavement and extremely unpredictable on wet pavement. Avoid using them on the street if possible. The dual-purpose street-trail machine is often found with trials universal or semi-knobby tread tires. This

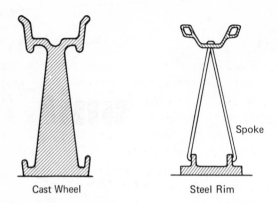

Fig. 5-1 Cross section of wheels (AMF Harley-Davidson Motor Co., Inc.)

tire is meant to feature the good traction of a knobby in the dirt while keeping the road maneuverability of a street tire. Although it is a good compromise, it does not perform as well as either a street or dirt tire when needed.

Street riders are deluged with a barrage of individual patterns of road tires. Some popular ones are shown in Fig. 5-2.

Fig. 5-2 Patterns for road tire tread, showing the common types

"Super tires" like the K81 and K87 Dunlop, Continental RB-H, and K111H and Avon Speed Masters have been designed for the large displacement multi-cylinder machines and seem to work well on them.

Some riders prefer rib tires on the front of their machines claiming more precise steering control. Generally, however, there is only a slight difference in handling; so, again, it is more a matter of personal preference. But *never* install a rib tire on the rear wheel. A slight application of power on a turn in less than perfect traction will often result in a mishap.

Theoretical Information

"I wunt ride on wunna them things! Hit one little pebble on them skinny tars and down she goes! No siree, I want four wheels under me."

You've heard it a hundred times, haven't you? But did you ever wonder why you *didn't* go down, even after striking large obstacles? The answer lies in the phenomena of the gyroscopic effect of rotating tires and wheels on the balance of the machine. The inertia of revolving tires tends to keep the motorcycle upright and headed in a straight line.

Spoke Patterns

Spoke patterns vary according to the size of the machine and the strength required. Smaller cycles generally use 36 spokes while larger machines have 40 spokes. The spokes are attached at various tangents to the inner hub and are fixed to the rim by threaded nipples. Wheels can be made stronger by altering the spoke pattern from the simple radial array to a criss-cross pattern. The patterns in Fig. 5-3 show various approaches to spoke patterning.

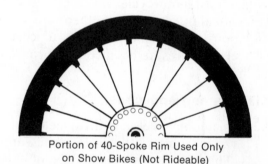

Portion of 40-Spoke Rim Used Only on Show Bikes (Not Rideable)

Fig. 5-3 Spoke patterns, showing array, cross 2, and cross 3

56

Hanging From the Spokes. Remember that your motorcycle is literally hanging from the top spokes of your wheels (Fig. 5–4). If the spokes are loose, absent, or incorrectly installed, serious consequences may follow. A series of loose spokes on one side of the tire will soon work the spokes loose on the other side of the wheel. If you discover loose spokes, tighten them immediately, according to the wheel-truing instructions on page 60.

← Turning direction

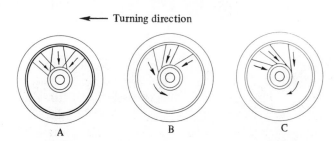

A   B   C

Fig. 5-4 Spoke force (Kawasaki Motor Corporation)

Repair and Adjustment Procedures

Daily Maintenance. Each day, before riding, check your tire pressure. In addition to being a riding hazard, improper inflation drastically reduces tire mileage. Superbike owners know well enough how low their rear tire mileage can be anyhow.

Flat-Tire Repair. Unfortunately, at some time every motorcycle is bound to have a flat tire. Repair procedures are basically the same, whether you're caught with a flat while out riding or have discovered the results of a slow leak at home in your garage.

1. Put the machine on its centerstand or prop it up somehow and remove the wheel.
2. Be careful with the accessory attachments such as mechanical and hydraulic brake linkage, speedometer cables, chains, and torque stays. Also note approximately where the chain adjuster was set so you can get "back in the ballpark" when reinstalling the wheel.
3. Completely deflate the tire by removing the valve core (Fig. 5–5a). Then stand on the tire with your heel to break the bead loose from the rim, as shown in (b).
4. Lubricate the bead area with a suitable rubber lubricant such as hand soap, soap suds,

brake fluid—anything but a petroleum product, which will deteriorate the rubber (c).

5. Now you're ready for the tire irons. Not screwdrivers, crowbars, wrench handles, or chisels—but properly prepared, special-purpose tire irons. Make sure that the business end of the tool has been ground or filed smooth so that there's no chance of ripping or cutting the tube.

6. After removing the valve stem retaining nut, slip a tire iron under the bead beside the valve stem. Simultaneously press the bead opposite the valve into the recession in the center of the wheel (d). Pry the bead of the tire over the lip of the rim (e).

7. Use another tire iron to take another "bite" a few inches to the right of the first (f). Now go a few inches to the left and pry again, being careful not to damage the tube. Continue around the tire until the bead is completely outside the rim (g).

8. Remove the tube carefully (h). Reinflate the tube and look for the leak, either by listening or submerging the tube in water. If the leak point is a cut or pinch rather than a puncture, the tube will be unreliable even when patched (i). In fact, you're always being a gambler when patching a punctured tube. The best approach is to use a new tube. Figure it this way: a new tube doesn't take up much more room on your touring machine than a tire patch kit and saves a lot of risk and grief. For a youngster's gravel pit bike, however, patching tubes saves money.

9. Locate the spot on the tire rim assembly where the leak occurred (j). Remove the nail, glass, wire, or thorn that may have caused the flat, and patch the inside of the tire casing if the inner surface looks as if it may cause more trouble in the future (k). If the leak is on the inner circumference of the tube, check for protruding spokes that can be filed down or a defective rubber rim strip that can be replaced.

10. Reinstall the tube after inflating it enough to give it a limp shape (Fig. 5–6a).

11. This time begin your tire-iron work *opposite* the valve after you've lubricated the rim, bead, and tire irons (b). Proceed gently and evenly around the bead until it is seated.

12. Make sure the tire, tube, and wheel are correctly aligned; that is, the valve stem should

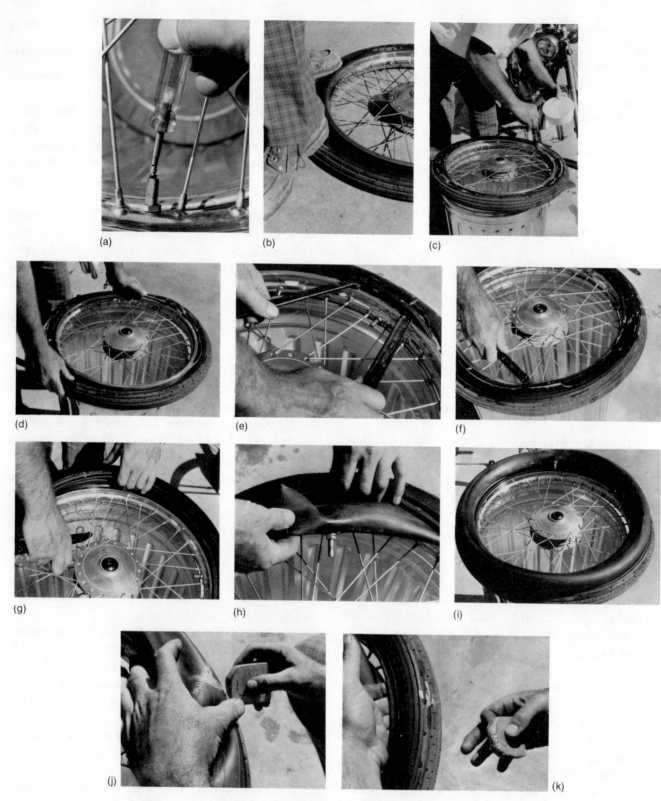

Fig. 5–5 Correct tire changing sequence: (a) Remove valve core, (b) break bead with heel, (c) lubricate bead, (d) place tire iron by bead and depress the opposite bead, (e) pry the bead over the rim, (f) pry the bore, using the second tire iron, (g) get bead completely outside of rim, (h) remove tube for repair. (i) Align the inflated tube on rim and tire to find flat cause and position, (j) mark the puncture position on inner tube, (k) mark puncture on the tire.

poke straight out of the wheel, not at an angle (c) and (d). If the tire has a dot mark that should align with the valve core for balance purposes, line it up properly. Many tires have no such marks. European and Japanese tires have a dot that lines up at the valve core on the rim. American tire manufacturers place a dot at the "heavy" spot on their tires, and this dot should be situated opposite the valve core.

13. Reinflate the tire being certain that the circumference of the tire coincides with the rim (Fig. 5–7a). There is a thin aligning seam around the tire that is used for this purpose. To correctly seat the tire, sometimes you must pump it up to

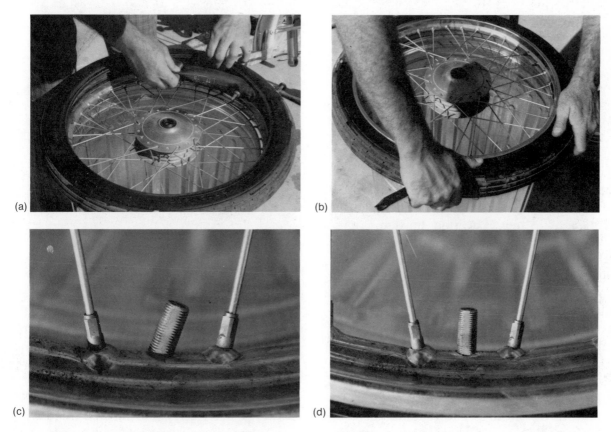

Fig. 5–6   (a) Re-install the partially inflated tube inside the tire, (b) re-install tire, starting opposite valve. Watch for crooked valve stem (c), be certain to get it in straight (d).

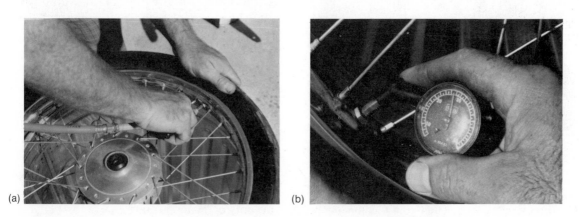

Fig. 5–7   Reinflate the tire (a), and check air pressure (b) in tube to be sure patch is holding.

60 or 70 pounds, then deflate it to the proper pressure (b). Other times you must break down the bead, lubricate it, and reinflate the tire to gain proper seating.

14. When replacing the wheel and tire assembly, be sure to adjust the axle alignment and chain tension correctly, and to re-attach all other fixtures securely.

Balancing Tires. Tire imbalance can cause quite a bit of discomfort to the rider and speed up the wear on bearings, tires, and other parts subject to vibration.

Motorcycle tires are generally static balanced only, but they may be spin-balanced at a shop that has a strobe-light balancer.

To static balance a motorcycle tire, first mount the wheel assembly on a wheel-truing stand. If you don't have access to a stand, loosen the brake adjustment, bearing tension, chain, speedometer cable, or other hindrances so the wheel will turn very freely on its own axle when elevated. Simply counterbalance the heavy spot on the wheel with motorcycle wheel weights (available at your cycle shop) attached to the spokes on the opposite side of the wheel until the wheel will remain at rest wherever it is set (Fig. 5–8). Heavy solder wound around the spoke can be substituted when wheel weights are not available. On a small machine, a wheel out of balance can lower the top speed by 5 to 10 miles per hour. On a large machine, poor wheel balance can contribute to high-speed wobble. In either case it pays to have precisely balanced wheels (Fig. 5–9a & b).

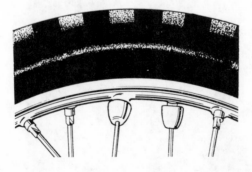

Fig. 5–8 Wheel weights (Triumph Norton Incorporated)

(a)

(b)

Fig. 5–9 Wheel balancing. Tire and wheel set on truing stand, showing the balance weights at 9 o'clock position (a) solid core solder wound on spokes to add weight (b).

Truing Wheels. A "true" wheel is one that is perfectly round with the axle in the center and has no radial run-out, lateral run-out or side wobble (Fig. 5–10).

As in balancing, wheels can be trued either on or off the bike. They may also be trued with the tire mounted or dismounted.

Only slight corrections (less than 3/8 inch) should be made with the tire mounted. Greater corrections call for tightening some spokes so much that a spoke end may eventually puncture the tube. Also, it is safer to correct only lateral run-out with the tire mounted. Remove the tire if any significant radial run-out is encountered.

The best procedure is:

1. Make sure that the axle is tight, that wheel-bearing play is minimal, and that all of the spokes are "snug," not loose.

2. Mark the high spots and low spots with chalk. Also try to indicate the extent or range of the entire "warped" area (Fig. 5–11).

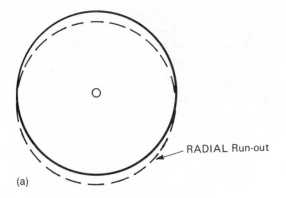

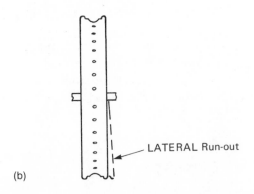

Fig. 5-10 Radial run-out (a), and lateral run-out (b)

Fig. 5-11 Chalking rim on bike. Note the thin white line on side of tire showing "high" area

Note that all of the spokes are attached to the center of the rim, but some are attached to the right side or left side of the hub. If the rim needs to be pulled to the left, loosen the right spokes and tighten the left ones a like amount (Fig. 5-12). At the "high spot" loosen the spokes (with a

spoke wrench) on the high side first, loosening more in the center of the high area. Decrease the amount of loosening as you get to the base line or true part of the wheel so that you are loosening only one-quarter turn at the last spoke. Tighten the spokes leading to the hub on the low side the same amount you loosened the corresponding high-side spokes. Repeat this procedure until all the spokes are tight and the wheel is true.

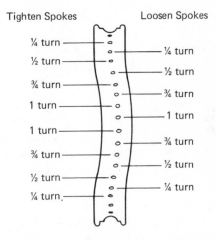

Fig. 5-12 Lateral truing technique, showing tightening and loosening sequence of spokes

Remember, however, for a freshly laced wheel or one that has severe radial and lateral run-out the best approach is to mount the wheel on a truing stand.

The first step is to eliminate radial run-out or "out of roundness" (Fig. 5-13).

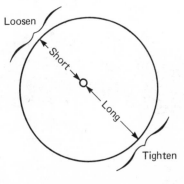

Fig. 5-13 Radial truing technique, showing tightening and loosening from side

Loosen the "short"-side spokes by using the tapering or graduated technique used for lateral run-out. Then tighten the long-side spokes, again tightening more at the extreme high point and gradually reducing the turns as you approach the "base line." Repeat this procedure until the wheel is perfectly round and all the spokes are tight. Now proceed to the lateral truing sequence outlined on page 61. Remember to *loosen the high side first* and tighten the same amount afterwards on the low side (Fig. 5–14).

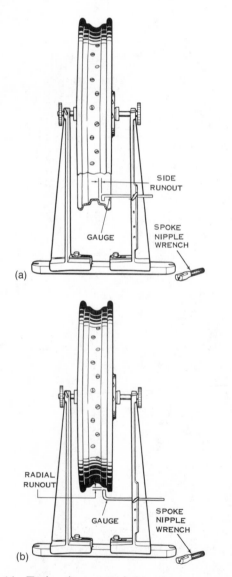

(a)

SIDE
RUNOUT

GAUGE

SPOKE
NIPPLE
WRENCH

RADIAL
RUNOUT

GAUGE

SPOKE
NIPPLE
WRENCH

(b)

Fig. 5–14   Truing rim on stand: (a)
(b)(AMF Harley-Davidson Motor Co., Inc.)

After the wheel is perfectly trued, grind off all protruding spoke ends flush with the nipple, clean out the metal filings left from grinding, reinstall the rim strip, and remount the tire.

Replacing a Rim. Replacing a rim can be a very simple, easy job if you follow certain steps to organize your approach to the task. Remember that there are both "inside" and "outside" spokes on each side of every wheel and that some wheels even have long and short inside and outside spokes. Spoke patterns vary according to the size and use of the machine; even spoke diameters vary with the size of the bike.

Before beginning the project, obtain any spokes you might need to replace broken ones. A spoke wrench, a screwdriver modified for spoke work (Fig. 5–15), and some masking tape are also handy.

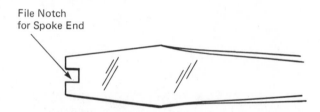

File Notch
for Spoke End

Fig. 5–15   Modified spoke screwdriver

The most reliable method for relacing a wheel is the "tape the spokes trick." Simply tape the spokes together at their various intersections or crossing points. Remove the nipples and lift the rim off. Replace any broken or damaged spokes and retape them in the proper position. Remember where the valve core hole goes and install the new rim the same way.

Another technique especially useful if you're building up a wheel from scratch is to install all of the inside spokes first (Fig. 5–16 a–f).

Lacing Wheels

If the rim only is being replaced (assuming the spokes are in good order), follow this practical shortcut: Tape spoke crossing points midway between hub and rim prior to unscrewing spoke nipples. After removing nipples, the hub with attached spokes can be lifted free of the rim. To reassemble, place the hub and spokes within the new rim and insert spokes in order through the

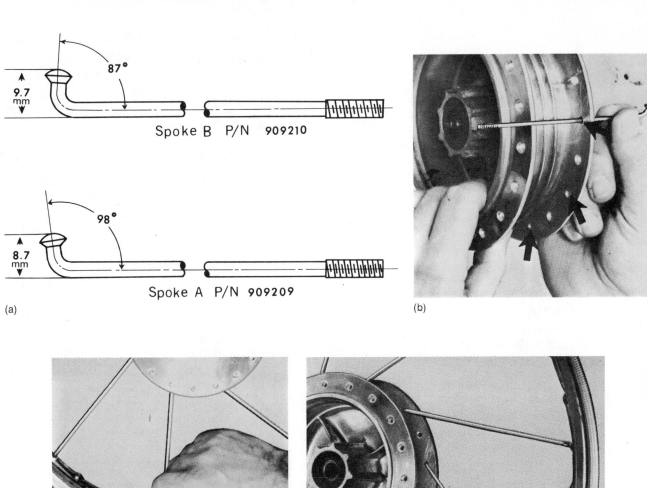

(a)

87°

9.7 mm

Spoke B   P/N   909210

98°

8.7 mm

Spoke A   P/N   909209

(b)

(c)

(d)

(e)

(f)

Fig. 5–16   Wheel lacing sequence

rim. (Be careful to insert the spokes through properly angled holes in the rim relative to the spoke itself). Starting from the valve hole in the rim, install spoke nipples and tighten each one until only four threads show at the bottom of the nipple. Again starting from the valve hole, proceed to tighten each nipple one turn, going all the way around the wheel. Continue in this manner until wheel tightens up, then true wheel as described in *Truing Wheels.*

Where hub or spokes require replacement, follow this method of lacing: Assuming the wheel has been dismantled and that the rim, hub and spokes are in good condition, lay out components on a workbench large enough to accommodate the wheel. Place 18 "A" spokes in one pile and 18 "B" spokes in another. Note that the hooked ends of the A and B spokes are bent with different radii (Fig. 5–16a). Holding the hub with one hand, insert an A spoke down through a non-chamfered flange hole (Fig. 5–16b). Repeat the process until nine A spokes are installed in the hub. Place hub face down on the workbench with the spoke heads seated against the hub and the spokes radiating outward. Set the rim over the hub with the valve hole facing you. Note that the holes in the rim are drilled offset up and down as well as sideways. Be sure that the spoke hole immediately to the left of the valve hole is angled upward and to the left. Insert the nearest spoke from the hub through the hole to the left of the valve hole and tighten on a nipple two or three turns. Working to the right, take the next spoke from the hub and insert it in the fourth hole in the rim to the right of the first spoke fastened in the rim. Tighten on a nipple a few turns (Fig. 5–16c). Repeat for each spoke, inserting them in every fourth hole in the rim until all nine spokes are mounted in the rim.

After the first nine spokes have been installed, turn the assembly over. Insert an A spoke through a non-chamfered hole in the topside flange and rotate the spoke to the right, crossing over two spokes on the opposite flange and inserting into the rim in the first hole left of a spoke from the opposite flange (Fig. 5–16d). Again, tighten on a nipple a few turns. Working to the left, install the remaining eight A spokes in every

other hole in the flange and rotate them to the right until located in holes just left of the lower flange spokes. Install nipples and tighten a few turns.

Install a B spoke up through any remaining hole in the top flange and rotate to the left, crossing two A spokes from the same flange and inserting into the rim as shown in Fig. 5–16e. Tighten on a nipple a few turns and repeat process until all nine spokes are installed. Turn the wheel over and repeat the above process on the other side (Fig. 5–16f). At this point, all spokes will be installed in the wheel assembly but the assembly will be quite loose. Starting with the valve hole in the rim facing you, tighten each spoke until there are about four threads showing below the bottom of the nipple. Finish tightening wheel up by turning each spoke nipple one turn at a time, working around the wheel from the valve hole. After tightening, true the wheel as described in *Truing Wheels.* Correctly tensioned, the spokes will emit a sharp "ping" when struck lightly with a screwdriver blade.

Balancing Wheels

Remove wheel assembly and temporarily lay backing plate assembly aside. Remove wheel bearing seals and clean grease entirely from bearings. Lubricate bearings with a few drops of cleaning solvent and mount wheel onto machine (without backing plate assembly). Allow wheel to stop with heaviest point down, mark center of heavy area with chalk. Assuming the mark made to be 0°, mark the wheel at 120° and 240° from the first mark around the circumference of the tire. Add weight at the 120° and 240° positions by coiling wire solder around the spokes adjacent to the marks. Solder should not be of the acid core variety and coils should begin around the spoke nipple. Do not extend coils longer than 2″ and keep coils at both positions equal in amount. Check progress often. When wheel will remain in any static position without rolling, balancing is completed and wheel may be remounted.

Tire and Wheel Accessories

Rim Locks. Under extremely hard use, tires tend to slip or rotate on the rims. To prevent this, some manufacturers use a cinch or rim lock to cinch the tire to the rim (Fig. 5–17a). These devices are often difficult to handle during tire changing, but can be dominated if you remember to install the rim lock just after the tube (b). Also be sure to move the rim lock toward the outside of the tire when prying the bead over the rim. Retain the rim lock stud with its nut on by a few threads to prevent losing it inside the tire. Check carefully before inflating the tire to be sure that the tube is not going to be pinched by the rim lock.

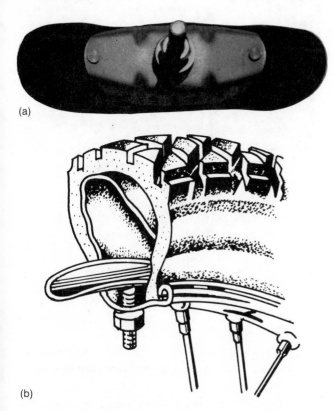

(a)

(b)

Fig. 5–17   Rim locks (Kawasaki Motors Corporation)

Instant Flat Repair. There are products on the market that will reinflate and temporarily seal a puncture. These products can save a cyclist some time if the cause of the flat is small enough to be blocked off by the sealant. Such products are not infallible life-savers in all cases, but they are good to have around for emergencies. The major drawback is that some cause tubes to stick to tires on the inside, often requiring that the tube be cut out of the tire.

Tire Balancing Fluid. Some companies manufacture a product that balances tires from the inside of the tube. The product works pretty well and is installed simply by pouring it into the inner tube. It requires a mile or two of riding to distribute it throughout the inner tube and accomplish its balancing function.

SUSPENSION SYSTEMS

There has been a slow but interesting evolution of engineering approaches to motorcycle suspension. Early machines simply had no suspension; wheels were rigidly mounted on the frame and had solid front forks much like a bicycle.

Front Suspension Systems

Springer Forks. The first stages of suspension development came at the front of the bikes. The riding characteristics of rigid front suspension were so hard at speed that something simply had to be done. Thus was born the "springer" front end (Fig. 5–18a). This system and variations of it endured even past the World War II era as the standard approach to front suspension on motorcycles.

Earles Type. Another old design is the Earles type or leading-link front suspension (Fig. 5–18b). This design was developed in Europe. Its most famous user is BMW. The leading link is a strong, smooth-riding front end though a bit slow in handling and awkward looking. Perhaps the esthetics of modern forks prompted BMW to offer the more modern slider forks on current models.

Telescopic Forks. One of the most significant developments in front suspension was the slider or telescopic front forks. This unit showed itself on foreign machines before Harley-Davidson and Indian bothered to change over to the better system. As a result, the light, quick-handling British machines with telescopic forks severely challenged American manufacturers for stateside sales. Soon the American manufacturers switched over to the telescopic units.

The early telescopic forks had short external springs usually protected by a rubber accordian gator or cover. Also, they only dampened on compression and would often rebound with a noisy "clunk." Even with such drawbacks, they were vastly superior to the springer front ends (Fig. 5–18c).

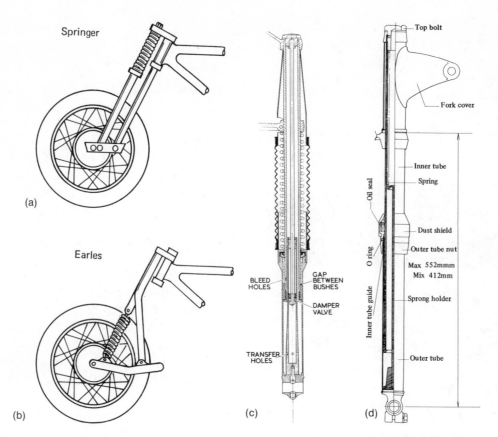

Fig. 5–18 Springer forks (a), Earles type forks (b), early telescopic forks (c) (Triumph Norton Incorporated) and (d) Cerianni type forks (U.S. Suzuki Motor Corporation)

Double-Acting and Internal Spring Telescopic Front Forks. The current state of the art in front suspension sees the nearly universal use of the double-acting internal spring telescopic front forks that are also known as Cerianni type, after the Italian company largely responsible for their popularity. This fork has a long, completely enclosed spring, a double-acting dampening device, and wipers rather than rubber accordian boots (Fig. 5–18d). Since this type of front suspension is most popular, we will study it in detail.

The typical front fork expanded in Fig. 5–19 consists of the upper tube or station, the lower leg or slider, a coil spring, dampening devices, "O" rings and seals, vents and plugs. The design and purpose of each of these items is explained briefly.

The upper or stationary tube section is clamped securely in the fork clamps or triple tree. This forms a secure base for fork operation and establishes the angle between the forks and the road. The top of these tubes are fitted with a threaded plug through which the fork may be

filled with fluid. This plug often contains a spring-loaded ball check valve to prevent bursting the slider seals.

A long, progressively wound coil spring is fitted inside the tubes and provides most of the suspension action of the forks.

The dampening action of the front forks is similar to that of a double-acting shock absorber. Different manufacturers use various approaches to the problem, but generally the dampening action utilizes a series of ports or orifices and check valves through which fluid is forced to pass. Figures 5–20 and 5–21 illustrate the action of a typical front fork.

The lower leg contains the fork seals, bushings, drain plug, and axle attachments. This lower leg, or slider, must fit the upper leg very precisely or fluid will escape and suspension action will be canceled (Fig. 5–22).

Rear Suspension Evolution

Rear suspension has had but two major changes in its evolution:

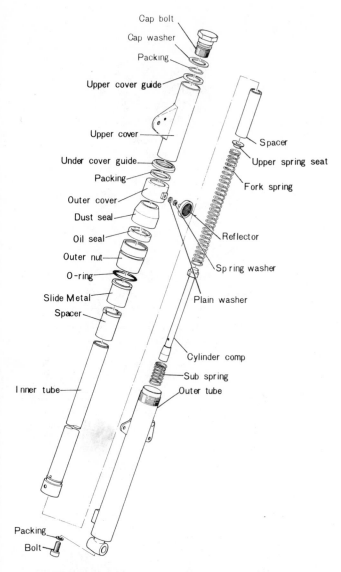

Cap bolt
Cap washer
Packing
Upper cover guide
Upper cover
Under cover guide
Packing
Outer cover
Dust seal
Oil seal
Outer nut
O-ring
Slide Metal
Spacer
Inner tube
Packing
Bolt

Spacer
Upper spring seat
Fork spring
Reflector
Spring washer
Plain washer
Cylinder comp
Sub spring
Outer tube

Fig. 5-19 Exploded view of front forks (Yamaha International Corporation)

Fig. 5-20 Telescopic fork dampening device, showing compression stroke (Kawasaki Motors Corporation)

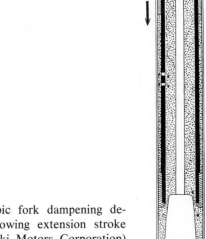

Fig. 5-21 Telescopic fork dampening device, showing extension stroke (Kawasaki Motors Corporation)

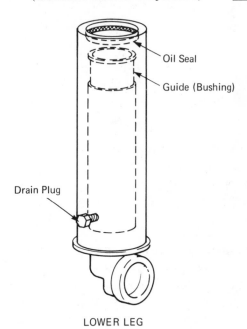

Oil Seal
Guide (Bushing)
Drain Plug

LOWER LEG

Fig. 5-22 Lower leg elements

Hard Tail. The hard-tail or rigid rear suspension was characteristic of early motorcycles that relied on the cushioning effect of the rear tire and the seat springs to absorb road shock (Fig. 5-23).

The first popular attempt at rear suspension was called the "plunger" system. This set-up used a set of small spring-shock absorbing devices between the rear wheel and the rigid rear section of the machine. Limited rear-wheel vertical travel helped to cushion road shock without

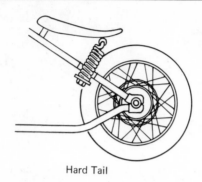

Hard Tail

Fig. 5-23 Hard-tail rear suspension with rigid rear wheel mounting

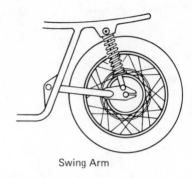

Swing Arm

Fig. 5-25 Swing arm suspension, showing frame, shock and overspring with swing arm

resorting to excessively large balloon tires. This plunger system was the forerunner of modern swing arm rear suspension (Fig. 5-24).

Fig. 5-24 Plungertype rear suspension (Triumph Norton Incorporated)

Swing-Arm Rear Suspension. The swing-arm rear suspension type is used almost universally today, so our discussion of rear suspensions is limited to this design. It consists of a pivoting fork, or swing arm, attached to the lower section of the frame just behind the transmission area, and a spring-shock absorber unit that vertically supports the top rear section of the frame (Fig. 5-25).

Repair and Service

There are several maintenance and repair procedures common to front forks. Each of these is covered in this section, beginning with the simplest and proceeding to the more complex procedures.

Changing Fluid. The front forks contain oil and, as you know, most oil needs changing occasionally. Several months of street riding or about 20 hours of dirt riding will usually contaminate the fork oil to the point where it needs changing. Fortunately, this often neglected maintenance step is a simple matter of opening a drain plug to let out the oil, closing the drain plug, then pouring new oil in through a fork cap hole. You can see how easy it is in the step-by-step series of illustrations in Fig. 5-26. Safety dictates stable elevation of the front wheel to eliminate spring compression.

Changing Dampening Rate. There may come a time when the front suspension of your motorcycle doesn't satisfy you, even after you have changed to fresh fork oil. The suspension may feel too soft and mushy or it may be too stiff and harsh. The problem could be in the viscosity or type of fork oil you used. Thicker oil will often stiffen a mushy set of forks, while thinner oil will usually soften the ride of harsh forks.

Use the same procedure to change the fork oil when switching to a different grade of oil. Remember, *never vary the amount of oil used,* only the viscosity rating (Fig. 5-27).

Alignment of Twisted Forks. A slight spill or bump can cause the front forks to twist, resulting in misalignment (Fig. 5-28). The sensation experienced in this instance is much like having bent handlebars. That is, to get the bike to go straight you must hold the bars either to the left or right. A quick, simple way to correct this problem is to

Fig. 5–26
Changing the chain fork oil: After elevating the front forks, open the drain plug (a), and allow fork oil to drain out (b). Remove fork caps under the handlebars. (c) Reinstall drain plug. After measuring new oil into a marked cup or bottle, pour new oil in forks (d). Carefully replace fork cap and accessories (e), then clean bike (f) and the area.

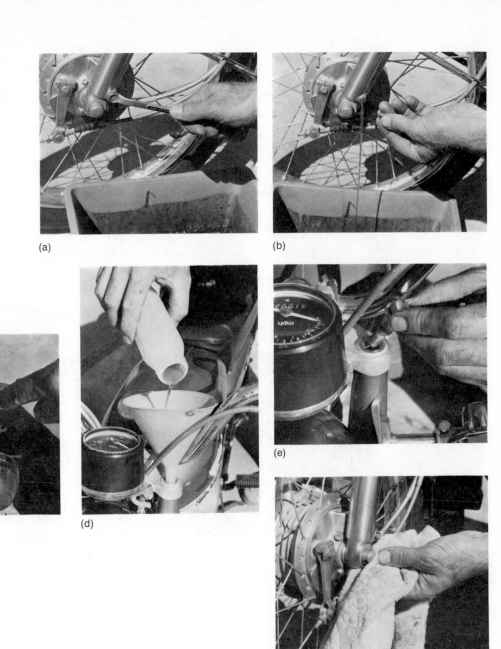

(a)

(b)

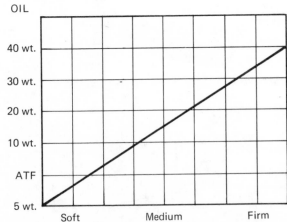

(c)

(d)

(e)

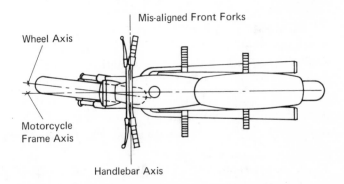

(f)

OIL

40 wt.

30 wt.

20 wt.

10 wt.

ATF

5 wt.

Soft   Medium   Firm

Fig. 5–27 Fork oil selection graph, showing relation of oil used to the type of ride that results

Mis-aligned Front Forks

Wheel Axis

Motorcycle Frame Axis

Handlebar Axis

Fig. 5–28 Mis-aligned front forks, showing wheel and handlebars out of alignment.

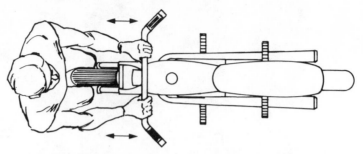

Straighten Front Forks

Hold Wheel with Knees — Pull Handlebars to Straighten

Fig. 5-29 Front forks can be straightened by standing over front wheel and twisting handlebars forcefully

Fig. 5-30 A box wrench is used to loosen triple clamp bolt

grasp the front wheel securely between your knees and twist the handlebars to align at a right angle to the wheel (Fig. 5-29). If the misalignment appears to be severe, you can loosen the triple-clamp fork pinch bolts a turn or so and retighten them after aligning the forks (Fig. 5-30).

Straightening Bent Tubes. Your upper fork tubes may become bent in an accident, but they can often be straightened again with a good hydraulic press and some "V" blocks. Be realistic, however, because straightening forks is an unreliable corrective approach if the forks are bent 10° or more (Fig. 5-31). If you do the work yourself:

1. Support the bent fork on "V" blocks with the apex of the bent section upward (Fig. 5-32).

2. Press the bend until it is straight, being careful not to permit the tube to rotate in the "V" blocks.

3. Release the press and rotate the tube to find the "high" spot again.

4. Press the tube straight again, or a bit "past" straight if the tube exhibits any tendency to spring back to a bent configuration after you've straightened it.

5. Gently repeat steps 3 and 4 several times if necessary until the tube is straight.

6. Examine the tube well after you have finished. If the fork is dimpled, dented, pock-

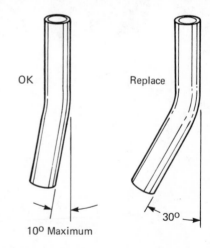

OK   Replace

10° Maximum   30°

Fig. 5-31 Fork evaluation—repair or replace?

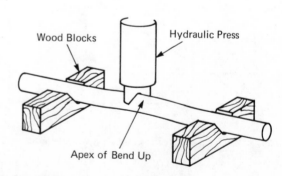

Wood Blocks   Hydraulic Press

Apex of Bend Up

Fig. 5-32 Fork straightening set-up

marked, but *straight,* it will work; but you'd better be prepared to change fork seals often because a damaged surface will accelerate wear of the front fork seals. If you have strong doubts—be safe—buy new tubes.

Replacing Seals. A fork seal is a part that must be replaced occasionally. It does a dirty, dusty, abrasive job, and eventually it just wears out. Fortunately, these seals are not very difficult to replace.

1. Remove the front wheel.
2. Remove the lower fork legs or sliders from the top tubes by taking off the retaining bolt, the attaching sleeve, or the circlip. Check your owner's manual to see which system your bike uses before removing the slider (Fig. 5–33).

Fig. 5–33   Removing lower slide, circlip style (U.S. Suzuki Motor Corporation)

3. Protect the slider with a rag and put it in a vise. Gently pry the seals out of the top of the slider, being careful not to damage the delicate outer flange of the seal retaining area. A screwdriver works pretty well most of the time, but a pair of pliers may have to be used to remove the seal completely.
4. Clean the seal retainer area thoroughly with solvent then, after the solvent dries, apply a thin film of sealer.
5. Tap the new seal into place gently and evenly, using a large socket, pipe, or seal installer to keep the seal from pivoting as you drive it home. Be sure the sharp rubber lip is pointed downward so that fluid rising to meet it under pressure forces the lip up against the tube for a better seal (Fig. 5–34).
6. Lubricate the seal lip with oil, then reas-

semble the forks. Be sure to fill the fork assembly with the correct amount and type of fork oil before riding the bike.

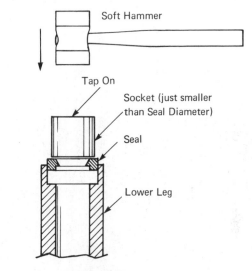

Fig. 5–34   Installing seal

Spring Shock-Absorber Assemblies

General Design. As you know, when a motorcycle is traveling in level forward motion and the rear wheel strikes a bump, a spring-type shock is rapidly compressed. What you may not know is that the compressed spring will attempt to return to its normal length, so it will rapidly rebound, causing the rear of the motorcycle to be jarred upward. The first spring oscillation is followed by many others and contributes greatly to poor handling. A hydraulic dampening device is needed to control this oscillating action. Designers have met this problem by combining the spring and shock absorber, or dampener, into a single unit.

The shock absorbers used on the rear of most machines are similar to the front forks in design and operation. They also use hydraulic fluid, a dampening device consisting of a piston, valves, and seals to suspend and regulate the ride of the rear of the motorcycle.

Figure 5–35 shows the basic components of a shock absorber and their functions, when at rest, in compression, and during rebound.

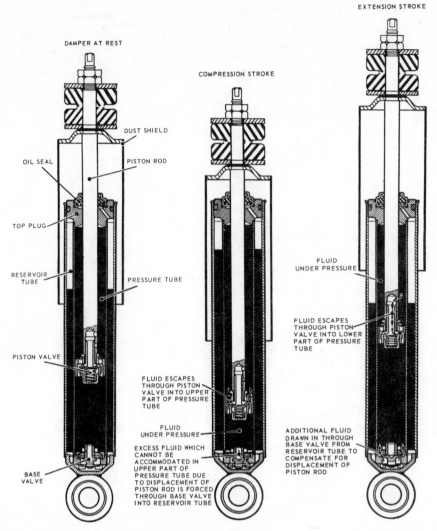

Fig. 5-35 Shock absorber functions (Standard Motor Company)

REAR WHEEL OSCILLATION PATTERN

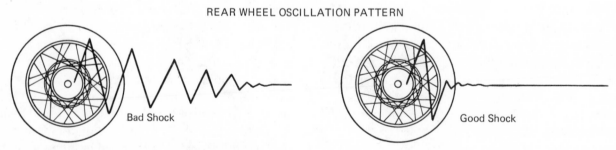

Fig. 5-36 Comparison of shock absorber oscillations

One end of the shock is mounted to the frame; the other end is attached to the swing arm near the rear axle. When the spring is compressed or rebounds, its action is hindered by the shock absorber. So, instead of a long, dangerous series of uncontrolled oscillations, the spring action is smoothed out and the machine soon returns to its normal level. Figure 5-36 shows the differences you may find between properly dampened and improperly dampened rear suspensioning.

Spring/Shock Details. The telescopic shock absorber has an inner cylinder, an outer cylinder, piston, piston rod, spring mounts, and sometimes dust covers. In addition, a series of valves, passages, and seals control the flow of hydraulic fluid inside the shock absorber. Figure 5–37 shows a typical telescoping shock absorber in three positions. The figure on the left shows the bike at rest or at normal loaded height. Note that the inner cylinder is completely filled with fluid, while the outer cylinder is only partly filled. The piston is near the midpoint of its travel to allow movement in both up and down directions.

The center figure shows shock action during compression. Note that the piston and rod have been forced down in the pressure tube. If the piston is to travel downward, the fluid must press through the piston valve into the upper section of the pressure tube. As the piston descends, some fluid is forced through the base valve into the reservoir tube. Shock absorber valves are calibrated to cause a certain resistance to the passage of fluid. They permit slow, smooth spring action, but resist or cushion violent spring oscillation.

The figure on the right shows the shock action during rebound. The piston is forced upward in the pressure tube, and the fluid trapped above is moving down through the piston by way of a different valve. Shock action on rebound is similar to that on compression. Some shock absorbers are calibrated to provide more resistance on rebound than on compression. Others may be custom calibrated by changing washers or by adjusting spring rates.

Spring/Shock Service. *Replacement.* Most shock absorbers are mounted by means of rubber grommets on studs that extend from the swing arm and frame. Some rubber lubricant, brake fluid, or soapy water can ease the installation of tight new shock grommets when replacing them (Fig. 5–37).

Adjusting Spring Rate. When riding with a passenger or carrying a significant load, you should compensate for the extra weight by stiffening the rear springs. This simple adjustment is accomplished by turning the spring retainer base a notch or two to shorten the spring. The number of positions for adjustment vary with the make of machine, so you should experiment to determine how much to adjust the springs for various weight loads on your machine. Should you need more or less spring rate than is available from the range of adjustment on your shocks, replacement springs or spring/shock units are available to meet nearly every conceivable need.

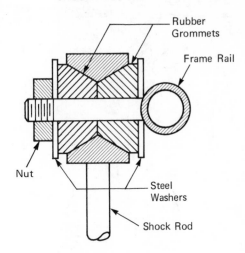

SHOCK ABSORBER MOUNTING

Fig. 5–37 Shock absorber mounting

Swing Arms. The stout swing arm found on today's motorcycles requires almost no maintenance itself, but places great demands on its bushings, which pivot on a cross shaft at the bottom of the frame. These swing-arm bushings should be lubricated periodically and inspected for looseness. There should be almost no detectable lateral movement when you try to move the swing arm sideways. If there is excessive movement, order a new set of swing-arm bushings and replace them, using the following sequence: (Fig. 5–38a–e)

1. Remove the rear wheel.
2. Disconnect the lower shock mounts and the chain guard if necessary.
3. Remove the swing-arm pivot shaft by using a drift (a).
4. Clean the swing-arm bushing area with a solvent.
5. Drift out the old bushings (b).
6. Press or carefully tap in the new bushings, being sure to align the grease holes if they are present (c).
7. Ream or hone the bushings to a proper fit if necessary (d).
8. Lubricate the shaft and reinstall it. Use a

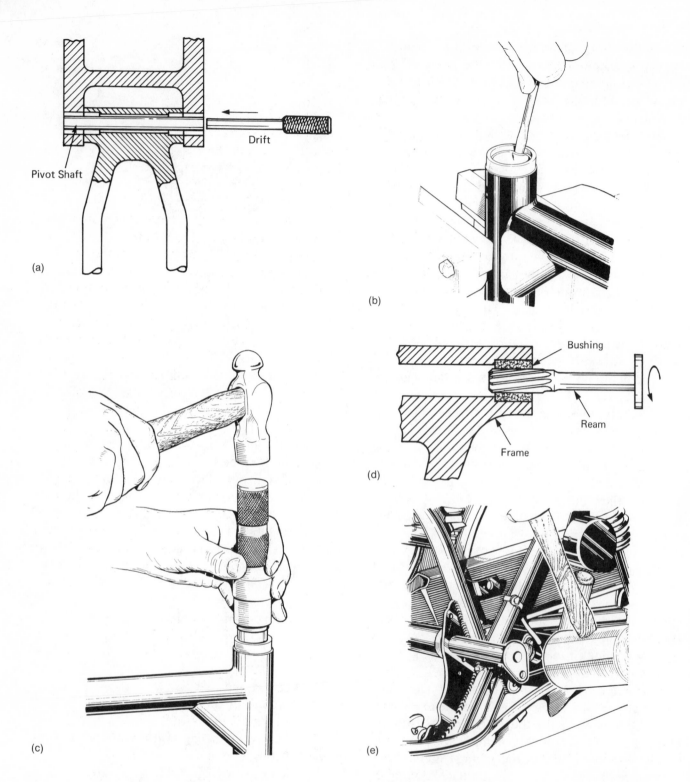

Fig. 5–38 Swing arm shaft removal (a), removing swing arm bushing (b), replacing swing arm bushing (c), ream bushing for exact fit (d), and (e) installing swing arm shaft (Triumph Norton Incorporated)

mallet or press it in with a clamp or hydraulic press (e).

9. Reinstall the wheel, shocks, chain guard, etc.

Suspension Geometry

A motorcycle's handling characteristics are very sensitive to several factors. Of course, the overall size and weight of the machine have the most pronounced effect on its handling. The ponderous touring machines meet the need of the high-speed, long-distance highway traveler while the local commuter rider takes advantage of a smaller machine's nimbleness in traffic.

Front wheel size, as described earlier, can be chosen to meet one of three needs:

1. 21-inch wheels roll over logs and obstacles easily.
2. 18- and 19-inch wheels compromise "rollability" with lower overall height, weight, and greater strength.
3. 16- and 17-inch wheels are used generally on smaller motorcycles where height must be kept minimal.

A low center of gravity is essential to good handling. It's easy to see that a top-heavy machine would be difficult to straighten up if leaned over too far.

Of course, ground clearance becomes a critical factor in the quest for a low center of gravity. Avoid extremes when selecting a machine unless the machine is to be used for only one purpose where an extreme center of gravity or ground clearance is required.

Wheel base affects handling from the standpoint of turning ability and reaction time. Long wheelbase machines are generally slower and more predictable in turns and more stable at high speeds, while short machines tend to react more quickly and are capable of tighter slow-speed maneuvering. Wheelbase may be increased by lengthening the swing arm.

Rake angle is an angle described by an imaginary line through the center of the steering head and an imaginary line through the vertical. The rake angle contributes to the caster effect, or straight line stability, of a motorcycle. Increased rake angles tend to enhance high-speed, straight-line stability while detracting from low-speed ma-

neuverability. Conversely, lower rake angles tend to quicken low-speed handling while causing the machine to be skitterish at extreme high speeds (Fig. 5–39).

Trail is similar in its effects to rake angle; however, it is a linear measurement rather than an angular one. Trail refers to the distance between that imaginary point where the rake-angle line intersects the road surface and the center of the front tire contact patch. Once again, as increased measurements are obtained, high-speed stability is improved and low-speed handling is sacrificed.

Motorcycle engineers have experimented for decades with suspension geometry. Despite what you read in magazines, they have made a great deal of progress. Don't look for radical suspension changes as a cure-all for handling problems. Work to perfect what has been designed into your machine.

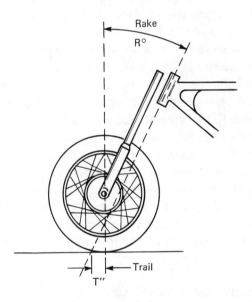

Fig. 5–39 Rake angle set for trail distance

Brakes

A 600-pound motorcycle-rider combination zipping along the road at 70 miles an hour represents a powerful force of kinetic energy (energy stored up in a moving vehicle). A great effort is required to halt this mass that is traveling at high speed. Fortunately, we are able to convert such kinetic energy to heat by means of the braking system. The main job of a braking system is to rapidly convert kinetic energy into heat through friction and dissipate that heat into the surrounding air. With leverage gained by mechanical linkage, or the power boost gained from a hydraulic system, the cycle rider is able to force a braking shoe or disc of friction material against a steel drum or brake disc to stop his or her machine.

THEORY OF BRAKE ACTION

Stopping a motorcycle depends on the efficiency of the braking system as well as the traction available between tires and terrain. If you apply the brakes too hard for available traction, you will skid as your wheels lock up. The quickest stopping takes place just before "lock up" on any kind of terrain. Sliding a tire to a stop wastes time and rubber—not to mention how dangerous it can be.

Most motorcycles tend to "nose dive" as the brakes are applied. When the forks are compressed, the trail specification is reduced and the overall wheelbase of the bike is lessened. These changes mean quicker, less stable handling, so be prepared for a different reaction rate from your machine when the forks are compressed during and just after braking (Fig. 6–1).

Brake Linings

Brake linings are made of asbestos that has been impregnated with special compounds to bind the asbestos fibers together. Some linings are woven of asbestos threads and fine copper wire. Other ingredients are added to brake lining compounds to produce improved characteristics such as water resistance, durability, fade and glaze resistance.

Brake Fade and Glazing. When brake linings become overheated they lose a lot of their frictional properties. When this occurs, even intense lever pressure will fail to produce a fast, even stop. Overheating also leads to brake linings becoming glazed; this lessens brake effectiveness greatly (Fig. 6–2).

The interaction between the shoe and drum is very important to efficient braking. The softer,

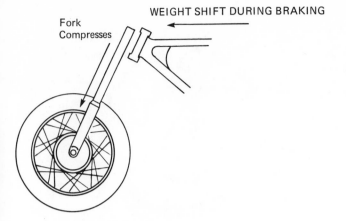

WEIGHT SHIFT DURING BRAKING

Fork Compresses

Fig. 6–1 Weight shift, showing how front end compresses when brakes are applied

Fig. 6–2 Unglazed lining on top, glazed lining below

high-friction material of the shoe lining is forced against the smooth, hard surface of the drum, resulting in extremely high friction, then heat. Tight contact at the rotating drum quickly wears away some material from the stationary brake shoe. This worn material comes off as powder or dust. As this dust breaks off from the lining it forms tiny wedges between the shoe and drum, which create more friction and heat, and result in better braking (Fig. 6–3).

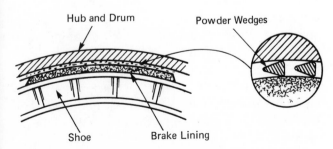

Hub and Drum   Powder Wedges

Shoe   Brake Lining

Fig. 6–3 Wedging action of brake lining particles

Brake Configurations

Three basic brake configurations are found on motorcycles. These are single leading shoe, double leading shoe, and disc brakes. Each has its own special use and strong points.

Single Leading Shoe. The single leading shoe brake has a single brake cam and two brake shoes with stationary pivot points (Fig. 6–4, 6–5).

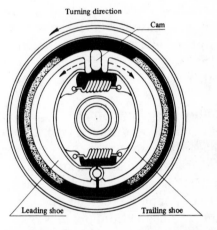

Turning direction   Cam

Leading shoe   Trailing shoe

Fig. 6–4 Single leading shoe (rear brake) (Kawasaki Motors Corporation)

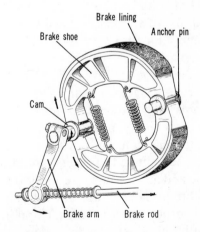

Brake lining

Brake shoe   Anchor pin

Cam

Brake arm   Brake rod

Fig. 6–5 Single leading shoe cam action (American Honda Motor Company)

The front or leading shoe is "wedged" into the drum as the brakes are applied because the rotation of the drum tends to pivot the shoe on its pivot point and turn it into the drum. This action results in a "self-energized" brake because the more the brakes are applied, the harder the brake shoe is forced into the drum.

The trailing shoe, on the other hand, is pivoted *away* from the rotating drum. The advantage of a trailing shoe is that it becomes a leading shoe when the motorcycle is rolling backward, or when it is stopped on an uphill grade. Trail and Enduro bikes use single leading-shoe brakes front and rear because of this characteristic. Most street machines use single leading-shoe set-ups on the rear to ease the bikes' roll-back tendency when stopped at a light on a steep uphill grade. In addition, they are simpler, lighter, and cheaper than other types of brakes.

Double Leading Shoe. Bigger, faster machines demanded advances in brake designs to keep pace with powerful new engines and better handling frames and suspensions. The full-width, double leading shoe front brake emerged as the answer to stopping problems for most of these machines. Since the front brake is responsible for about 75 per cent of the stop, it needs a more efficient system to handle all the weight that shifts forward during braking.

All that's needed to re-engineer a single leading shoe brake into a double leading shoe system is the addition of another cam and some linkage to actuate and adjust it (Figs. 6–6, 6–7).

Let's examine the double leading shoe backing plate and shoe set-up in Fig. 6–6. Each shoe has its own engagement cam and pivot points. These cams and pivot points are opposite each other so that each shoe can be "self-energized" by the rotating drum. Naturally, it is critical that each shoe be adjusted to engage the drum at the same time and at the same rate. Poor double leading-shoe brake balance adjustment can result in jerky, dangerous stops and erratic braking action.

In both the single leading-shoe and double leading-shoe arrangements, the backing plate must have a firm anchor to lock it to the frame. There is always a torque stay strap or a locking lug to prevent backing plate movement during braking.

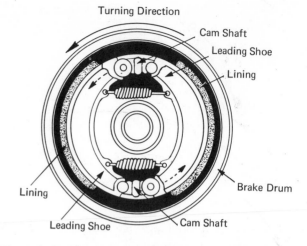

Fig. 6–6 Double leading shoe twin cams (front brake) (Kawasaki Motors Corporation)

Fig. 6–7 Double leading shoe cam linkage, showing front brake arms 1 and 2 and panel 3 (American Honda Motors Company)

Disc Brakes. Disc brake systems employ a round, solid steel plate or disc attached to the rotating wheel. Two fiber brake pads or "pucks" are located in a caliper assembly that is attached firmly to the fork or swing arm. When the brakes are applied these pads are squeezed together against both sides of the disc, creating the friction and heat needed to stop the bike. The disc brake is superior to the drum brake because it is fade resistant, smoother operating, self-cleaning, and easier to service (Figs. 6–8, 6–9).

Most disc brakes employ a "floating caliper" where the caliper can slide on its bracket. This enables the caliper to move sideways during engagement to insure firm contact by both brake pads even though only one pad is activated (Fig. 6–10).

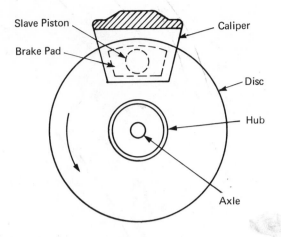

Fig. 6–8 Disc brake, side view

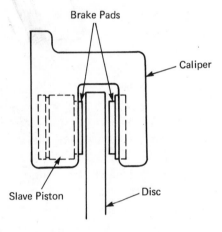

Fig. 6–9 Disc brake, front view

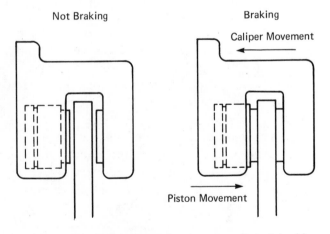

Fig. 6–10 Floating caliper, showing normal and braking positions

Each of these items plays an important role in stopping your motorcycle. You should know the parts in this system and how they operate.

Levers, Pivots, and Adjusters

A lever assembly helps the operator gain mechanical advantage over the braking or clutching system of a bike. About a 6-to-1 mechanical advantage is gained at the lever (Fig. 6–11). It is important to keep the pivot lubricated to ease operation. The adjustor simply provides a quick, easy way to compensate for stretch that develops in the cable over time.

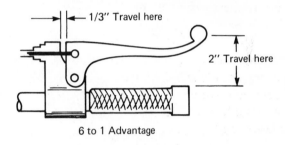

Fig. 6–11 Mechanical advantage provided by brake lever

The cable is basically a steel wire inside of a flexible rubber covered steel tube. It provides a flexible coupling between the operator and the brake. If the outer tube is held stationary at the ends, motion can be transmitted via the inner cable even if both have to go around corners and be flexing while the inner cable works.

The cable is attached to a brake lever that is splined to the brake activating cam. Once again, mechanical advantage of about 6-to-1 is gained between the lever and the cam.

Strong retracting springs are connected between the brake shoes to return the brakes to a disengaged position. Lighter springs are used to return the levers and pedals to their ready positions. These springs are shown in Figs. 6–6 and 6–7.

MECHANICAL BRAKE CONTROL SYSTEMS

Mechanical brakes operate by means of levers, pivots, adjusters, cables, springs, and cams.

HYDRAULIC BRAKE CONTROL SYSTEMS

Just as levers can be used to increase mechanical advantage, a hydraulic system can accomplish the same task. A force applied to a small piston in a hydraulic system over a long distance can be converted to a much stronger force over a short distance. This increase in force takes place when the original force from a smaller piston is applied through a liquid medium to a larger piston (Fig. 6–12).

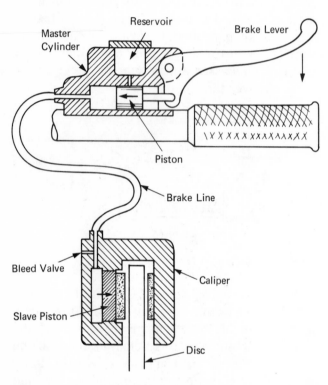

Fig. 6–12   A typical hydraulic brake system

A motorcycle braking system uses this principle to increase hand pressure on a lever to the great energy required to clamp two pads together on a disc to stop the machine. To accomplish this, the hydraulic brake system uses a master cylinder, brake line, and a slave cylinder in the caliper assembly.

The *master cylinder* is the central unit in which hydraulic pressure is developed. Pressure from the rider's hand on the lever is transmitted to the master cylinder piston. As this piston is forced forward in the master cylinder, it pushes brake fluid ahead of it. Since the brake line and caliper piston are filled with fluid, the piston is acting upon a column of fluid. As hand-lever pres-

sure increases, pressure on the caliper piston increases the pressure of the pads against the disc. These pressures build up throughout the system and result in quicker stopping.

BRAKE SERVICE

As with any other working part of the motorcycle, the brakes require periodic adjustment, cleaning and replacement. We can't over emphasize the importance of good workmanship when servicing motorcycle brakes.

Adjustment

Single and Double Leading Shoe. Adjusting the free travel in a single leading-shoe brake should begin by loosening all the slack in the cable at the hand lever. Take up the slack at the brake-control lever at the wheel. Readjust the hand lever for proper free play at the handlebars (Figs. 6–13, 6–14). Adjust the rear brake by tightening the nut on the brake rod until pedal free play is correct (Fig. 6–15). Remember to readjust the rear brake after making any chain adjustment or a rear-wheel alignment.

Double leading-shoe brakes have the same adjustment features as a single leading shoe with one addition. There is also a brake-balance bar or connector link between the two cam levers. It is very important that this bar be adjusted so that both brakes contact the drum simultaneously and with the same force. This is accomplished by lengthening or shortening the ends of the rod until both shoes contact the drum at the same time (Fig. 6–16).

Disc Brakes. The main adjuster on a disc-brake system is the rotor-caliper positioning adjustment. This is a threaded adjuster that positions the caliper to reduce or increase the amount of "float" it uses before the braking action begins. This adjuster should be positioned to allow about 3/4 inch travel of the hand lever (Fig. 6–17). Check the fluid level in the reservoir that is part of the hand lever assembly. If it is low in fluid, inspect the system for wetness or leaks. Sponginess in the lever or front brake feeling may be caused by air in the disc slave cylinder. This air is removed by "bleeding" or allowing some of the brake fluid to escape along with the air.

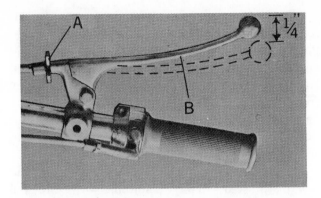

Fig. 6–13 Cable adjuster A, and brake lever B. Dotted line shows free play (Pabatko/Hodaka)

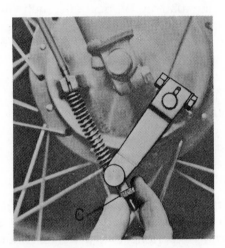

Fig. 6–14 Cable slack adjustment (Pabatko/Hodaka)

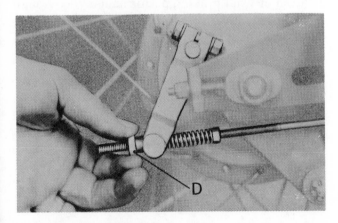

Fig. 6–15 Adjusting rear brake with adjuster knob D (Pabatco/Hodaka)

To bleed the disc brake slave cylinder, follow this procedure:

1. Ensure that the master cylinder is filled with fresh disc brake fluid.

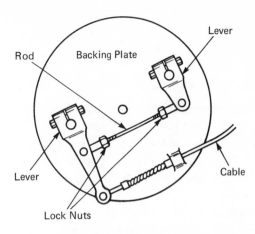

Fig. 6–16 Connecting rod adjustment with lock nuts

Fig. 6–17 Disc brake threaded caliper adjuster

2. Apply light hand lever pressure to the hydraulic brake system.

3. Open the slave cylinder vent valve slightly, allowing the air and some fluid to escape. Use precautionary measures to keep the brake fluid off of the brake disc, brake pads, and painted surfaces of the motorcycle.

4. Close the valve *before* releasing the hand lever pressure.

5. Repeat this sequence until no air escapes with the brake fluid. Do not allow the master cylinder reservoir to become less than half full.

6. A final filling of the reservoir and wiping down of the bike of stray fluid completes the procedure.

81

Repair Techniques

The best repair technique for brakes is simply to replace worn parts with new ones. The most frequently worn parts are the brake shoes and springs. It is a good idea to replace springs along with shoes even though the old springs still function.

Often brake cams are not properly contoured at the factory, but you can get better braking action by smoothing the rough edges of the cams (Fig. 6–18).

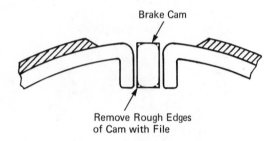

Brake Cam

Remove Rough Edges
of Cam with File

Fig. 6–18 Contouring brake cam

The drum-hub assembly can be reused even if it has been scored or scratched a little, but it should be replaced if it is severely gouged or drastically "out of round." In an extreme emergency, motorcycle hubs can be turned on a lathe, but this practice is *not* recommended (Fig. 6–19).

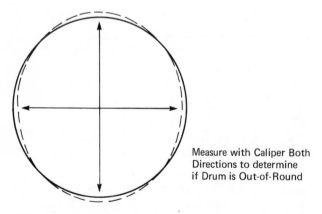

Measure with Caliper Both
Directions to determine
if Drum is Out-of-Round

Fig. 6–19 Out of round drum — hub. Solid line shows round, dashed line shows out-of-round contour

Disc brakes are relatively easy to service. After removing the rotor and retaining clips, the old pads can be removed very quickly. You simply slip the old brake pads out and slip new ones in. Be sure to keep grease, brake fluid, and dirt away from the fiber lining of the brake pads. Check carefully and if you detect any leak in the hydraulic system the unit should be honed and the piston seals replaced.

Honing a disc-brake cylinder insures that the new piston seal will have a suitable surface to seal against. This honing should be done only with a special disc-brake hone. Refilling and bleeding will then be necessary.

A small dab of lubrication, such as white grease, should be applied wherever there is metal-to-metal movement in the brake system. The cam-shoe area and shoe-to-backing plate area are the most important areas. But don't overdo it — a very thin film of lube is all that's needed.

When any brake part is replaced, make fresh adjustments after you reinstall the assembly on the bike.

Approximate Stopping Distances

Many manufacturers give stopping distances for their machines. Most of these figures are derived from experienced lightweight riders who stop well-adjusted motorcycles under ideal conditions. However, these statistics give some indication of what braking performance you should expect. Some average stopping distances that are considered normal are shown in Table 6–1.

Table 6–1 AVERAGE STOPPING DISTANCES FOR AVERAGE RIDERS

Type of Bike	60 mph	Speed 40 mph	20 mph
Disc Brake Road Bike	175′	65′	20′
Drum Brake Road Bike	185′	70′	20′
Drum Brake Trail Bike	200′	75′	25′

Inspection

If the bike you are working on requires much more stopping distance than indicated in Table 6–1, you should inspect the braking system more closely.

Your manual should outline the specific method for removing the brake assembly on your bike, but there are also axles, torque stays or stopper arms, and control linkages to remove. Pay special attention to spacers and clips, because *they must be reinstalled exactly as they were removed.*

While removing the wheel, inspect the cable ends, linkages, and pivots for wear or lack of lubrication. Remove the backing plate and blow out the excess dirt and grit with an air nozzle. Inspect the springs, shoes or pads, brake cam, pivot, and drum-hub assembly for wear or damage (Fig. 6–20). Special care and attention must be emphasized when working on any brake component.

Fig. 6–20 Worn parts, showing stretched spring, worn brake pad, and shoe

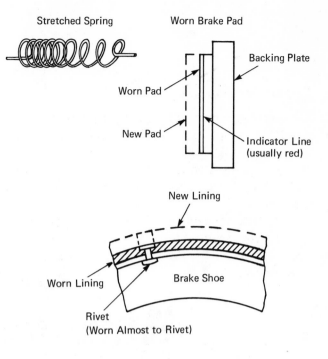

Measurement and Measurement Systems

WHY MEASUREMENT?

Did you ever wonder why two identical bikes may perform so differently, even though both seem to be tuned identically? With the same timing, valve adjustment, gearing, jetting, and rider weight, why will one bike outperform the other? Most likely the answer lies in the clearances and tolerances with which the engine and transmission were assembled. The measurement, tolerances, and clearances used when an engine is assembled are major factors in performance and reliability.

When an engine is designed, every part has its size stated in distances, radii, bore, thread size, or other dimensions with a numerical value. These dimensions are the ideal or designed size. When the part is manufactured however, it is not always the exact size stated by the designer. Instead, it can be within a narrow range of allowable sizes — say, plus or minus 1/1000″. This range is referred to as a tolerance. Since machining parts to an exact size would be very expensive, they are machined to a tolerance instead (Fig. 7-1).

These dimensions for a part are stated in fractions of an inch, thousandths of an inch, and millimeters. The designer also decides how much distance, or clearance, is needed between two moving parts to allow for lubrication and for expansion when the parts become heated (Fig. 7-2). Too little clearance or too much heat expansion forces lubrication out, causing metal-to-metal contact to occur, which often results in seizure (Fig. 7-3).

The designer could increase piston clearances to a point where seizure would be impossible, but this would cause poor sealing, and result in a loss of power and piston slap. A thousandth of an inch can make a difference in both power and reliability.

The performance difference discussed at the beginning of the chapter could have been the result of many different problems, most of them relating to measurement. Of course, running too fast, too hard, too soon are also critical factors. Designers often specify close clearances between moving parts so that some desirable wear-in or break-in is possible. Until that initial mating occurs, clearances are relatively tight and require moderate driving (Fig. 7-3).

What's Measured?

Almost every dimension of every part is designed and manufactured to precise tolerances. In the motorcycle world measurements are given in

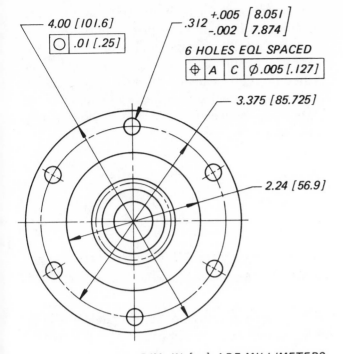

4.00 [101.6]

◯ .01 [.25]

.312 +.005 −.002 [8.051 / 7.874]

6 HOLES EQL SPACED

⊕ A C ∅.005 [.127]

3.375 [85.725]

2.24 [56.9]

DIM. IN [ ] ARE MILLIMETERS.

UNLESS OTHERWISE SPECIFIED:
±.01 [.25] TOL ON MACH DIM.
±.03 [.75] TOL ON CST DIM.

Fig. 7–1 A drawing of a machined part, showing the specified dimensions and tolerances (AC Spark Plug Div. of General Motors Corporation)

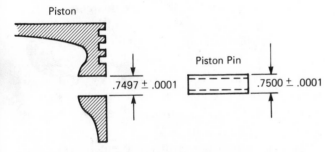

Piston

Piston Pin

.7497 ± .0001   .7500 ± .0001

Fig. 7–2 Mating part dimensions, showing part of piston and piston pin dimension and tolerance

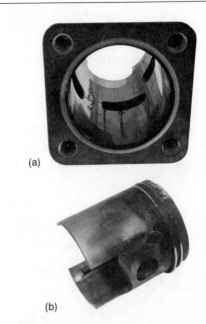

(a)

(b)

Fig. 7–3 Examples of piston seizure: (a) a cylinder with scoring marks, (b) a piston burned where seizure has occurred

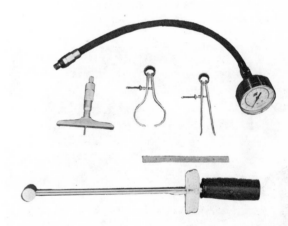

Fig. 7–4 Measuring instruments, showing a compression gauge at top: below (left to right) a depth micrometer, outside and inside calipers: and, at bottom, a scale and a torque wrench

either metric or the English standard system. In many cases, measurements are given in both systems, allowing the mechanic to use the kind of measuring equipment he has available. Where this is not the case, the mechanic must be able to convert the measurements from one system to another.

Distances, such as length, diameters, or thicknesses are measured with scales, calipers, micro-

meters (Fig. 7–4). Pressures, tensions, and torque settings are measured with spring type scales such as the torque wrench. Vernier scales on instruments, such as calipers or micrometers, allow even greater accuracy in measurement, by indicating fractions of basic measurement units. Instruments such as depth gages and telescoping gages provide a means of measuring internal dimensions that normal measuring instruments can-

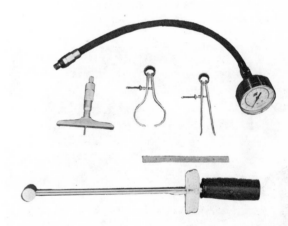

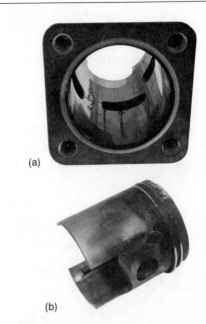

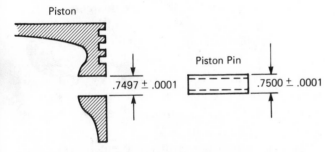

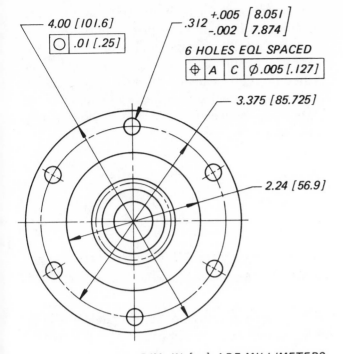

not measure directly (Fig. 7–5). Other measuring instruments used in motorcycle diagnosis and repair include: dial indicators, feeler gages, wire gages, and screw-pitch gages (Fig. 7–6). The performance and condition of parts or groups of parts can be measured with instruments such as compression gages or electrical meters. These various measuring tools allow the mechanic to determine the condition of the different parts of his machine.

Fig. 7–5   A telescoping gauge showing gauge used to measure inside diameter of cylinder

Fig. 7–6   Measuring instruments, showing feeler gauge at top, a wire gauge, dial indicator, and a screw pitch gauge

RELATIONSHIPS

A mechanic should consider the relationship of the size of fasteners to the parts they connect. Various sizes of fasteners, such as studs and bolts, are chosen for their ability to apply a certain force to hold parts in place. This force depends on both the size and quality of the bolts and nuts. The quality of many kinds of bolts is indicated on their heads by marks or designs (Fig. 7–7). A good mechanic comes to understand the relationship between the size of a bolt and its torque capacity.

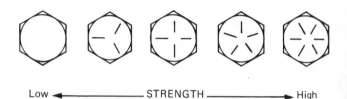

Low ◄——————— STRENGTH ———————► High

Fig. 7–7   Bolt head marks, showing plain to 6-line bolt

Another indication of a mechanic's ability, perhaps an even more important one, is how well he or she is able to apply the principles of measurement. If you can use all of the measuring tools discussed in this chapter, you're in top gear and have the ingredients that mark the difference between a successful mechanic and a shade tree butcher.

Inches or Centimeters

Really good motorcycles are designed both in inches and centimeters or millimeters (hundredths or thousandths of a meter). So let's face it—you'll probably have to work in both systems. At this time, however, most motorcycles use the metric system rather than the English system of measurement. Let's compare the two systems (Table 7–1 and Table 7–2).

A common conversion problem is torque. If your torque wrench says inch-pounds or foot-pounds, but the book says kilograms and centimeters, what do you do? These conversions are easy (Table 7–3).

MEASUREMENT TOOLS

One of the most useful tools in the mechanic's box is a 6-inch steel rule. A Metric-English version, available from the parts shop, stationery or hardware store, is indispensable. The graduations should be as fine as 1/32 of an inch or in millime-

Table 7-1

Length		
Metric:	English:	
1 Millimeter (MM)	= 0.0394 Inches	
1 Centimeter (CM)	= 0.3937 Inches	
1 Decimeter (DM)	= 3.9371 Inches	
1 Meter (M)	= 39.3707 Inches	

Volume		
1 Cubic Centimeter	(CC) = 0.061	Cubic Inch
1 Liter (1000 CC)	(l) = 61.023	Cubic Inch
3.785 Liter	(l) = 1.00	Gallon
33.818 Cubic Centimeter	(CC) = 1.00	Ounce Liquid

Weight	
1 Gram (G)	= 0.0022 Pounds
1 Kilogram (KG)	= 2.2046 Pounds

Pressure:	
2.927 Kilograms/ Square Centimeter (KGC²)	= 1 Pounds/Square Inch (P.S.I.)

Table 7-2

Conversion Factors

Length:
To convert inches to MM multiply by 25.4
To convert inches to CM multiply by 2.54
To convert feet to meters multiply by .3048
To convert millimeters to inches multiply by .0394
To convert centimeters to inches multiply by .3937
To convert meters to feet multiply by 3.280

Volume:
To convert ounce liquid to CC multiply by 29.6
To convert cubic inches to CC multiply by 16.393
To convert gallons to liters multiply by 3.785
To convert cubic feet to liters multiply by 28.317
To convert cubic centimeters to ounce liquid multiply by .0338
To convert cubic centimeters to cubic inches multiply by .061
To convert liters to gallons multiply by .264
To convert liters to cubic feet multiply by .0353

Weight:
To convert grams to ounces multiply by .0352
To convert grams to pounds multiply by .0022
To convert kilograms to pounds multiply by 2.205
To convert ounces to grams multiply by 28.409
To convert pounds to grams multiply by 454.55
To convert pounds to kilograms multiply by 0.454

Pressure:
To convert pounds per square inch to kilograms per square centimeters multiply by .0703
To convert kilograms per square centimeter to pounds per square inch multiply by 14.22

Mileage (gasoline):
To convert one mile per gallon to kilometers per liter multiply by .4249

Table 7-3

Torque Conversions

To convert inch pounds to gram centimeters multiply by 1155
To convert inch pounds to kilogram centimeters multiply by 1.155
To convert foot pounds to kilogram centimeters multiply by 13.84
To convert gram centimeters to inch pounds multiply by .0009
To convert kilogram centimeters to inch pounds multiply by .866
To convert kilogram centimeters to foot pounds multiply by .072

ters. A rule that's somewhat flexible is even more useful.

The vernier caliper (Fig. 7-8) can make both inside and outside measurements up to 6 inches with an accuracy of 1/1000 of an inch. This accuracy is accomplished by a principle Pierre Vernier, a French mathematician, invented. His system has the number of lines on the vernier scale differing from the number of lines on the regular scale of the rule by one unit (Fig. 7-9).

It's easy to see that for each thousandth of an inch that you open the slide, the next mark on the vernier scale will align with a mark on the base scale. Simply add the vernier scale number to the number indicated on the base scale at zero (0). This gives your precision measurement to the closest thousandth. The correct reading for the first setting between the jaws of the caliper would then be 1 inch and 402 thousandths (written as 1.402 inches or 1.402″).

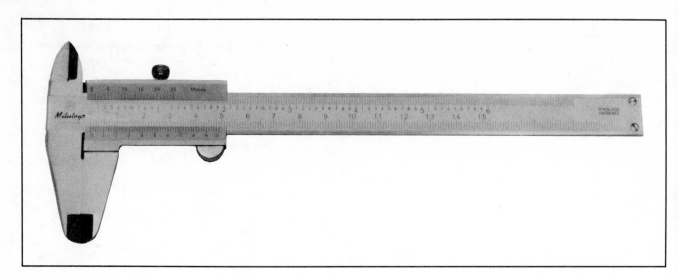

Fig. 7–8 Vernier caliper

With a little practice you can develop good consistency and accuracy when using the vernier caliper. A small magnifying glass helps to determine which number on the vernier scale lines up with a number on the base scale.

Another measuring tool, the dial indicator — with its many holding and positioning devices — is one of the easiest instruments for a mechanic to use and provides accuracy to 1/1000 of an inch. The set-up in Fig. 7–10 shows the dial indicator used as a height gage from a smooth surface. Its common uses in motorcycle mechanics include setting two-stroke timing, truing crankshafts and, occasionally, truing wheels.

Micrometers, ranging in sizes from 1 inch to 4 inches capacity, comprise the set normally used by motorcycle mechanics. Large micrometers are also available of course. Measurement with a micrometer is based on the principle that an internal thread with exactly 40 threads per inch will allow the barrel to advance at a rate of 25/1000 of an inch per revolution (also written as 0.025″). Twenty-five accurate graduations are then radiated around the thimble scale of the micrometer to allow the reading of measurements to an accuracy of 1/1000 of an inch. The 1- to 2-inch micrometer pictured in Fig. 7–11 shows a reading of 141/1000 of an inch or 1.141″.

Feeler gages are measuring tools made from precisely ground thin metal strips. If you can slide a flat feeler gage in between two parts, you have an indication of this clearance. That is, you know

there is at least the thickness of the feeler gage between the two parts. Wire-type feeler gages rather like probes are used in situations where the two

Fig. 7–10 Dial indicator, showing indicator used as a height gauge

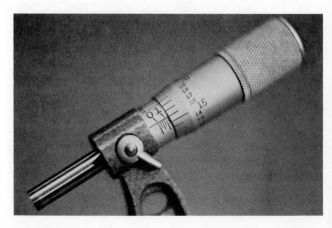

Fig. 7–11 Two-inch micrometer, showing a reading in thousandths of an inch

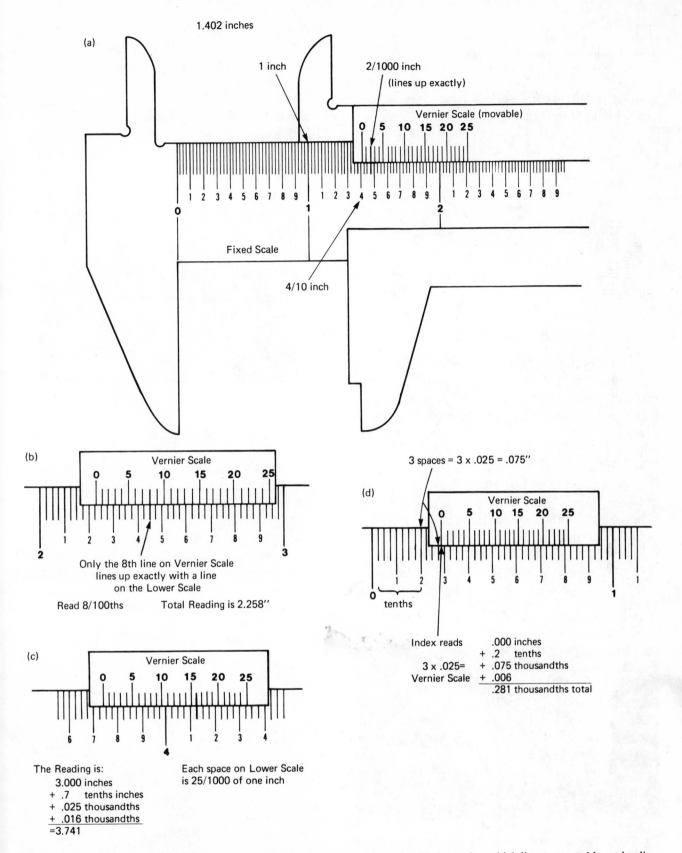

Fig. 7–9 Vernier reading sequence: (a) read number at 0 on movable scale, (b) determine which line on movable scale aligns exactly with line on fixed scale, (c) add inches + tenths + whole 25th (if any) + number on movable scale, (d) read second example

contact points are not surfaces, but may be only small high spots (Fig. 7–12).

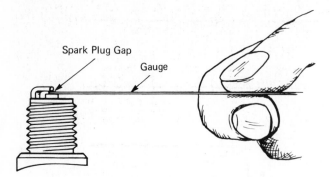

Fig. 7–12 Wire gauge

Telescoping gages are tools that are used to take an internal dimension in a tight spot, then transfer it outside where it can be measured accurately by a micrometer. The telescoping gage is placed in position, such as a cylinder bore as shown in Fig. 7–5. It is then expanded to contact both surfaces. The expanded gage is locked on that dimension and is carefully drawn out of the cylinder bore. The distance across the telescoping gage is then measured accurately with an outside micrometer. When measuring a cylinder, this process is repeated several times in different directions and at different levels to get an accurate idea of the dimensions of the cylinder (Fig. 7–13).

Fig. 7–13 Taking a measurement with a telescoping gauge and micrometer

Plasti-gauge is a measuring device that is relatively inexpensive, but it is rarely used in motor-

cycle-engine rebuilding. To determine the clearance between an insert bearing and the crankshaft journal, a small piece of Plasti-gauge is broken off the strip and placed across the journal surface. The bearing cap is then put into place and the bolts tightened to the correct torque. When the bearing cap and bearing are removed, the width of the Plasti-gauge is measured and the clearance is determined (Fig. 7–14).

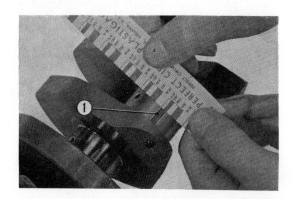

Fig. 7–14 Plasti-gauge measurement showing paper gauge being compared with dark flat Plasti-gauge in bearing cap (American Honda Motor Company)

Volumes can be accurately measured by using many different devices and materials. For motorcycles, a simple baby bottle seems to serve most purposes such as measuring the amount of oil for the front forks or pre-mixing oil with gas for two-strokes. These bottles are available at many stores and are graduated in both cc's and ounces (Fig. 7–15). Sometimes extreme accuracy is required, as in measuring the volume of a combustion chamber. These instances require a chemist's burette or a graduated cylinder.

Fig. 7–15 A baby bottle, showing ounce and cc scales

If accurate measurement of the weight of an object is necessary, the proper measuring instrument would be either a shadowgraph or a balance scale. These scales (Fig. 7–16) measure weights down to 1/10 of a gram. When necessary, conversion can be made to ounces with the comparisons given in Table 7–1.

Fig. 7–17 Taking a compression reading

Fig. 7–16 A beam balance used here to weigh piston in left pan. Weights are shown in right pan with set of weights in box in front

Pressure Checking Devices

A quick look at various manufacturer's specifications will show that pressures are an important measurement for the motorcycle mechanic. A compression gage is one of the most important tools available for assessing an engine's basic mechanical condition. Normal procedure is to loosen the spark plugs one turn, then spin the engine over to blow out carbon at the inner surface of the plug before any compression reading is taken. After the dirt is blown away from the outside, the spark plug can be removed from the cylinder head. The correct adapter is chosen to make sure the gage fits properly in the spark plug threads. With the compression gage in place, the engine is then kicked through at least five times and a pressure reading is taken (Fig. 7–17). This procedure is accomplished with the choke and throttle fully opened, and with the engine at normal operating temperature. In multi-cylinder engines this procedure is followed for each of the cylinders, making sure that the spark plugs are re-

moved from the cylinders initially so that correct readings are obtained. After the first compression gage readings are taken, a small amount of oil (approximately a teaspoonful) should be placed in each cylinder, then the engine turned through several times. New compression readings should be taken for each cylinder and the difference from the original readings if any, noted. If the oil increases compression pressure above 25 psi, we may assume that the rings are worn and need to be replaced. If a four-stroke engine's compression (both wet with oil and dry) is much lower than shop manual specifications, the mechanic should look at the valves. Low compression pressures might also be caused by blown head-gaskets, damaged pistons or cylinder walls, or stuck or broken rings.

The most frequently used pressure gage should be the tire gage. Tire pressure plays a very important role in handling, tire wear, and overall motorcycle performance. Gage pressures are given in pounds per square inch (psi) or kilograms per square centimeter (kg/cm^2). The conversion factor is: 14.25 psi = 1.0 kg/cm^2. Tire pressure should be checked daily and increased for heavy-load or high-speed driving conditions.

The valve-spring tension gage is used to measure the force on this spring (Fig. 7–18). The required condition of a spring may be stated in different ways. The specifications may require a certain length of free height, or the resistance of a spring at a stated height may be required. Valve springs are often measured for resistance at both installed and open heights. An example is the

Fig. 7-18   Measuring the valve spring, showing pressure applied to spring in tester

Fig. 7-19   Timing marks, showing T (top dead center) and fire (F)

specification of 80 pounds seat pressure required to compress the valve spring to a 1.50-inch installed height. See Unit 11 for the actual application of this measuring tool.

Arcs

The measurements of rotation, angles, and arcs are shown in degrees of a circle, one full rotation equaling 360°. In a motorcycle engine the crankshaft is indexed at "zero" when the piston reaches the top of its travel. The amount of turn in one direction or another is given in degrees. The position of the crankshaft at the precise time of ignition is often stated in "degrees before top dead center." This is called "timing advance." Determining the degree of advance is accomplished by measuring the difference between index marks on the rotating crankshaft or attached flywheel and a stationary mark on the engine case (Fig. 7-19). Degree scales are commonly used to set engine ignition timing, camshaft timing, and port timing on two-stroke engines. Degree scales are also found on machinery such as lathes, and valve grinders, where they are used to indicate the angles at which various parts should be machined.

Torque

Torque is the amount of rotational or twisting force that can be exerted by an engine, in-

strument, or other rotating object. In the English measuring system, the common measurements or specifications are in inch-pounds or foot-pounds. The length in inches indicates the distance from the center of rotation; the force in pounds indicates the pressure exerted at that distance from the center of rotation (Fig. 7-20). In the metric system the specifications are given in kilogram-centimeters or kilogram-meters.

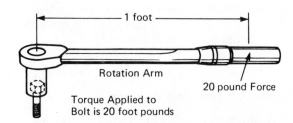

Fig. 7-20   Torque, showing length of rotation arm and the force applied to arrive at torque

The force exerted by an engine is specified as a given torque at a given rpm of the engine. The force exerted by a fastener is specified in a torque applied to that fastener. A common example of this is a cylinder head that is tightened with all of the head bolts or fasteners applying a retaining force or torque of the same specification. The manufacturer might specify that all head bolts be torqued to 25 foot-pounds. Torques for fastening most components of a vehicle are often specified.

Three common styles of torque wrenches are the dial indicator type, the pre-set click type, and the beam type. These are shown in Chapter 3 in Figure 3-9. Air impact wrenches are also capable of applying high torque. There is usually an adjustment on these for pre-setting the amount of torque desired. Forgetting to adjust this torque will often result in broken bolts or stripped threads. Other wrenches are also designed to apply a certain torque within a given range. A smaller wrench with a short handle will obviously apply lower amounts of torque than the same size wrench with a longer handle, or a larger wrench with a longer handle. Adding some kind of extension to a wrench of a given design destroys the designer's intended torque range for that wrench.

PROTECT YOUR INVESTMENT

A mechanic needs to calibrate his equipment, care for it, and store it correctly to insure that it will continue to give accurate measurements. For instance, calibrating a 1-inch micrometer is accomplished by closing it until the spindle just touches the anvil, then observing that the reading is zero. Of course, a micrometer should not be stored this way. The anvil should *never* touch the spindle during storage. Calibration of a pressure gage is accomplished by measuring it against a known standard, such as a master pressure gage, to see if both gages read exactly the same for a given pressure.

Many instruments, such as scales or rules, are not designed to be recalibrated. Therefore, they must be used and stored carefully. This includes lubricating the moving parts where necessary and applying silicone spray or wax to prevent rust on unfinished metal parts. Common sense should be employed when using or storing measuring instruments. They should be used only to do the job that they were designed for. Never substitute a measuring tool for some other device just because it's handy.

It is particularly important to clean measuring tools before returning them to their proper storage place. Clean, dry storage insures more accurate readings. Also, returning them to their proper storage place will insure that you will know where to find them the next time you need them. A special storage cabinet or box is "a must" for a measuring instrument if it is to retain its accuracy. Measuring tools are some of the most expensive equipment a mechanic ever purchases; they should be treated with the proper care. Accurate calibration, careful storage, and proper usage are necessary ingredients to protect your investment.

Two-Stroke Engine Upper End

THEORY AND ANALYSIS

Everyone notices the contrasting sounds of two-stroke and four-stroke engines. What causes the throaty, mellow tones of a four-stroke and the ring-ding buzzing drone of a two-stroke? Why do they have different riding traits? Why does a two-stroke puff a little smoke when you open the throttle? To begin to hint at the answers to these questions, it's important to explain the operation of both types of engines. Since the two-stroke is simpler in construction, it's the one to look at first.

The two-stroke features simple construction by using the piston, cylinder, and crankcase to serve dual roles in developing power (Fig. 8–1).

Not only is the piston used as the primary driven member on the power stroke, it also serves as a sliding control valve in the two-stroke engine.

The cylinder barrel is used to seal and guide the piston so it can absorb the power of the expanding gases, but it also has passageways cast into it to channel gases into and out of the engine (Fig. 8–2). Sometimes the barrel is actually two pieces—a steel liner is shrunk or cast into a set of aluminum fins. The cylinder head is used with a gasket to provide a tight lid for the engine. The head may have extra spark plug holes, sunburst fins, or other features (Fig. 8–3).

Piston rings are used to seal the clearance gap between the piston and cylinder. Three popular types of piston rings are used in two-strokes today (Fig. 8–4).

A wrist pin is used to transfer motion between the piston and the connecting rod. This pin also provides a joint or hinge that enables the rod to change angles as the engine rotates (Fig. 8–5). The wrist pin is usually held in place very tightly in the piston, and clips are added (as a safety measure) to prevent it from sliding out (Fig. 8–6). The wrist pin connects the piston to the upper end of the connecting rod. The eye of the rod has either a bronze bushing or a small needle bearing for the pin to ride in, so it can hinge more easily.

PRINCIPLES OF TWO-STROKE OPERATION

Port Control Systems

The motorcycle engine captures the power of rapidly burning gases by making this force push the piston down the cylinder bore. It's easy to trace the steps involved and account for each port's activity during the different phases of operation. Refer to Figure 8–2.

Inlet Phase. During the crankcase inlet phase, an air-fuel-oil mixture is inhaled into the

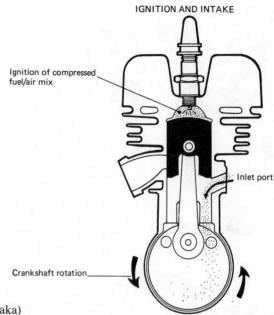

IGNITION AND INTAKE

Ignition of compressed
fuel/air mix

Inlet port

Crankshaft rotation

Fig. 8–1 Two-stroke compression and intake (Pabatco/Hodaka)

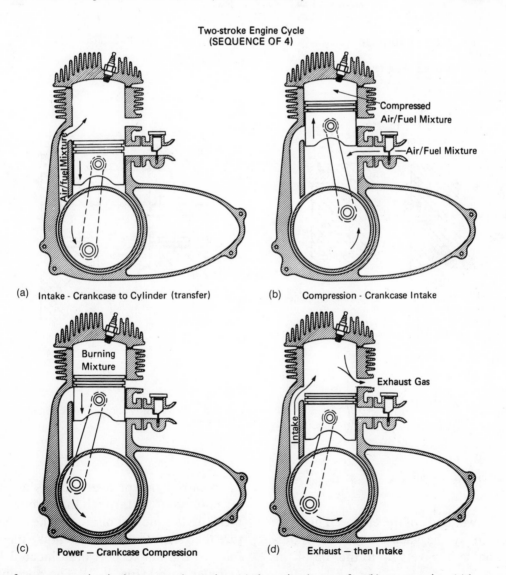

Two-stroke Engine Cycle
(SEQUENCE OF 4)

Air/fuel Mixture

Compressed
Air/Fuel Mixture

Air/Fuel Mixture

(a) Intake - Crankcase to Cylinder (transfer)

(b) Compression - Crankcase Intake

Burning
Mixture

Exhaust Gas

Intake

(c) **Power — Crankcase Compression**

(d) **Exhaust — then Intake**

Fig. 8–2 Transfer port operation in the two-stroke engine: (a) shows intake transfer, (b) compression, (c) burn, and (d) exhaust

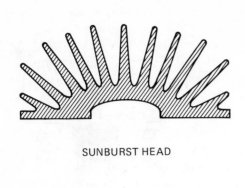

SUNBURST HEAD

(a)

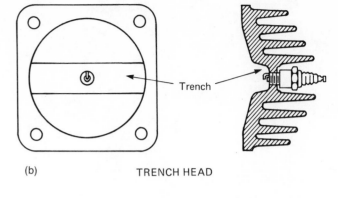

(b)　　TRENCH HEAD

Trench

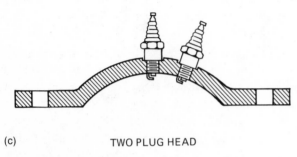

(c)　　TWO PLUG HEAD

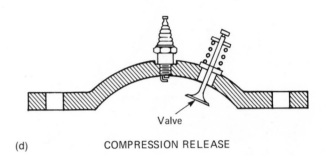

(d)　　COMPRESSION RELEASE

Valve

Fig. 8–3　Four popular cylinder head features

Cross Section

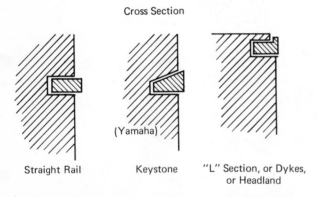

Straight Rail　　(Yamaha) Keystone　　"L" Section, or Dykes, or Headland

Fig. 8–4　Two-stroke piston ring types

Fig. 8–6　Typical circlip or snap ring

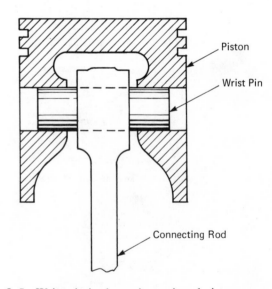

Piston

Wrist Pin

Connecting Rod

Fig. 8–5　Wrist pin is shown in sectioned piston

crankcase or "lower end" of the engine. This mixture is drawn in by the vacuum created underneath the piston as it travels up to the top of the bore.

Atmospheric pressure forces a rapidly moving column of air through the carburetor where it picks up the fuel-oil mixture. The column of mixture then travels through an intake passage (manifold) to the intake port area located low on the cylinder barrel (Fig. 8–7). The opening and clos-

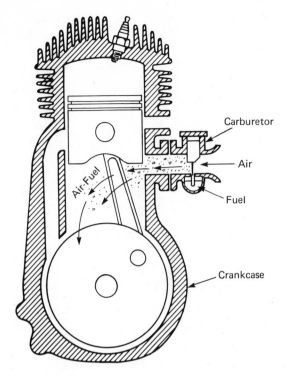

Fig. 8–7   Inlet phase of fuel mixture from carburetor
to crankcase

Reed Valves. The reed valve system employs a set of thin "flapper" valves that are opened by vacuum and closed by pressure (Fig. 8–9). As the piston travels up the bore, a vacuum is created below it, but the piston port intake system is not usually exposed to this vacuum until the skirt edge of the piston opens the port. In a reed valve system, however, there are holes in the piston that let the mixture pass right through the piston without waiting for the lower edge of the piston to open the port. This method allows the crankcase chamber to be filling up during almost the entire upward stroke of the piston. It also helps retain the mix in the chamber rather than "blow back" any of the charge because the reed valve is a one-way valve. In other words, the reed valve permits the mixture to pass into the crankcase from the carburetor, but does not allow it to return (Fig. 8–10).

ing of the port is controlled by the lower edge of the piston skirt on most engines. The port opens as the piston travels upward and closes as it comes down (Fig. 8–8). This is the conventional method of controlling intake port opening. Engines that use it are referred to as "piston port" engines.

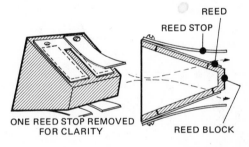

Fig. 8–9   Reed valves and block (Kawasaki Motors Corporation)

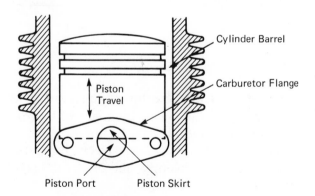

Fig. 8–8   Piston port induction

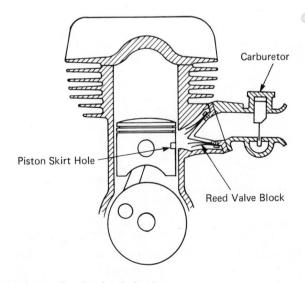

Fig. 8–10   Reed valve induction

Other ways of controlling the mixture fed into the crankcase chamber generally attempt to fill the crankcase chamber more thoroughly by exposing the intake system to intake vacuum for a longer time.

Rotary Valve. A rotary valve system controls the intake port by using a partially cutaway rotating disc to open and close the port at strategic times (Fig. 8–11). This design performs better generally than conventional piston porting. The carburetors are mounted on the sides of the engine to give more direct flow to the rotary valve (Fig. 8–12). The rotary valve cut allows the air-fuel-oil charge to enter the vacuum of the crankcase chamber during the entire or any desired portion of the upward stroke of the piston (Fig. 8–13).

The crankcase then becomes an interim storage chamber for the fresh air-fuel-oil mixture. Oil in the mixture settles out onto the roller, or the ball bearings on the crankshaft and connecting rod, providing lubrication for these moving parts. It is generally desirable to make the crank chamber volume as small as possible to lessen the tendency for the mixture to compress in the crank-

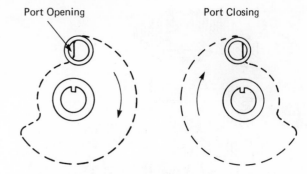

Fig. 8–13   Rotary valve operation showing relation of valve to port on opening and closing

case. A small chamber improves the flow of gas through the transfer ports to the combustion chamber, because a small volume of gases is easier to move up the transfer ports than a large volume.

Transfer Ports. There are many different configurations for transfer ports, but all serve the same purpose — to transfer the air-fuel-oil mixture to the cylinder. Some engines have as few as one port, while other engines have as many as seven. These small passages go from the crankcase to the middle of the cylinder wall. Some are cast right into the cylinder barrel; others are grooved into the cylinder wall (these are known as finger ports). On all ports that enter the cylinder it is necessary to bevel or "chamfer" the edges so the rings and pistons pass the edge of the port easily. It's important to match the transfer port passage in the crankcase to the transfer port opening in the cylinder barrel also (Fig. 8–14).

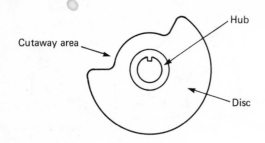

Fig. 8–11   Rotary valve disc

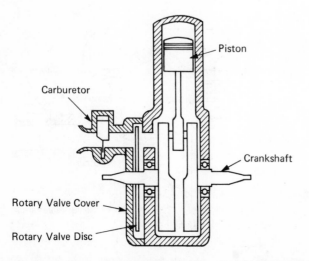

Fig. 8–12   Rotary valve in crankcase, showing placement of valve in relation to crankcase

Ignition and Power Strokes

Ignition. Just before the piston reaches the top of its travel, the spark plug ignites the fresh charge and starts it burning. By the time the piston reaches the top, the charge has begun to burn rapidly, explodes violently, and drives the piston down on the power stroke.

It is very important that the ignition spark occurs at *precisely* the right time — too early and the piston must fight to reach the top against a flame front it can barely overcome — too late and the piston is already moving down the cylinder while the flame front follows it weakly, rather than driving it strongly.

transfer ports creates a swirl of the intake charge that helps to push the exhausted gases out as shown in Fig. 8–14. In addition, the column of gas in the exhaust system already moving out from the previous power/exhaust stroke and the resonance of that chamber help to "pull" the exhaust from the cylinder.

So efficient is this system that some of the fresh charge is often drawn into the exhaust port area, also which insures that the mixture to be compressed is relatively uncontaminated with leftover exhaust. Unfortunately, this fresh mixture has to be wasted, resulting in relatively poor fuel efficiency and a higher output of unburned hydrocarbons.

This concludes the discussion of the theory of operation for the two-stroke engine used on most motorcycles today. A thorough understanding of the theory of operation is necessary in order to diagnose effectively and maintain the two-stroke. Be sure to review this section before "tearing into" the engine.

FORMULAS

When working with engines, it is convenient to know several formulas.

Displacement. Displacement refers to the volume of mixture that is drawn into the cylinder with each downward stroke of the piston. Naturally, the larger the displacement, the greater the volume of fresh mixture and, subsequently, the greater the power that is produced.

$$D = \pi R^2 S$$

where D = Displacement

π = 3.1416

R = Radius of Cylinder (1/2 bore)

S = Stroke

Compression Ratio. Compression ratio is the numerical relationship between the volume in the cylinder at the beginning of the compression phase and the volume in the combustion chamber at T.D.C. So compression ratio tells how much the mixture is squeezed down or compressed. As

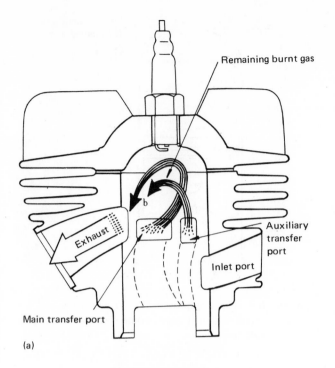

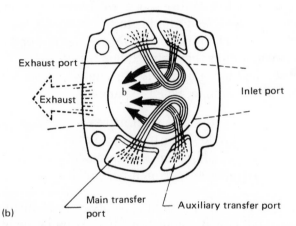

Fig. 8–14 Transfer port (Yamaha International Corporation) (a), and (b) exhaust port

Another way to express the reasons why precision ignition timing is so necessary is: On most engines the combustion that takes place is only significant for the first 26 degrees of crankshaft rotation after T.D.C. It is imperative, therefore, to fire the flame front early enough so that it's doing its hardest work precisely during those critical 26 degrees.

Exhaust. The exhaust port on a two-stroke engine begins to open just as the piston's top edge passes the upper edge of the port. Under the high pressure of combustion, the gases rush out to exhaust as the port starts to open. The design of the

a rule of thumb, the higher compression ratios are associated with high performance, but they sacrifice some reliability and longevity. Manufacturers compute compression ratio by two methods, with the piston at the base of the cylinder or just past the exhaust port as shown in Figs. 8–15 and 8–16. The European system considers the entire volume of the cylinder when computing compression ratio. This method is questionable since part of the charge is forced out of the exhaust port or down the transfer port as the piston rises. A more accurate method of determining compression ratio considers only the volume of the charge *above* the exhaust port.

Total volume 110 cc to combustion chamber
Volume 10 cc = 110 to 10, or 11 to 1.
Total effective volume 76 cc to combustion chamber Volume 10 cc = 76 to 10 or 7.6 to 1.

As you see, the second method gives a more realistic approach to figuring effective compression ratios.

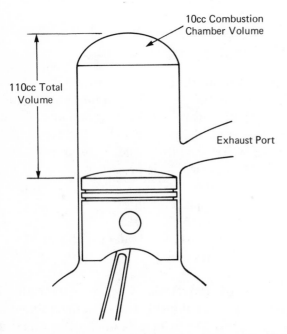

Fig. 8–15 European compression ratio: shows total volume to chamber volume

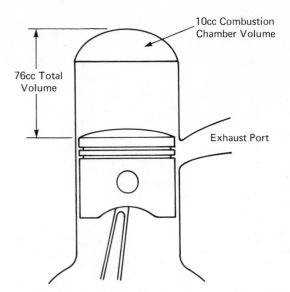

Fig. 8–16 Japanese compression ratio: showing volume above exhaust port compared with chamber volume

Expansion Rate. When working on an engine, you will need to refer to the factory specifications for clearances. There are some general expansion rates that help explain the necessity for these clearances and why they must be so precise. For example, when expanding,

iron and steel increase
0.0003″ per inch per 50° F
aluminum increases
0.0006″ per inch per 50° F

Notice that aluminum expands *twice* as fast as iron. That is why the piston expands much faster than the cylinder. Therefore, it is important to assemble pistons and barrels with the proper clearance to avoid seizure at high temperatures and piston slap at low temperatures.

WHY TOP ENDS FAIL

With a strong background knowledge of the functions and operations of the two-stroke engine, let's take a look at the five major causes of top end failure. We will start with engine enemy number one—dirt—and go on to adjustment problems, clearances, lubrication, and rider abuse. These are the main causes of piston, ring, and cylinder problems in two-stroke engines.

Dirt. A trip to a windy desert will soon prove to the visitor that wind-blown sand will eventually grind rocks smooth and erode anything exposed to it. The same thing can happen in an engine if fine dust becomes mixed with the air-fuel-oil mixture. The grit or dirt wears away the metal of the cylinder wall, piston rings, and skirt until the piston loses its sealing ability (Fig. 8–17). Instead of the combustion power being applied to the piston top, the power leaks past the rings. Instead of the piston developing a strong crankcase vacuum on its upward stroke, it fails to draw a good charge into the crankcase (Fig. 8–18). The engine becomes harder and harder to start and develops less and less power (Fig. 8–19).

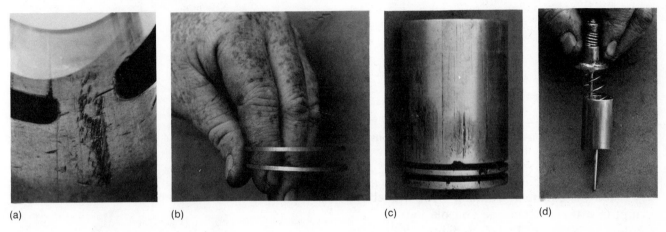

(a) (b) (c) (d)

Fig. 8–17 Abrasive dirt wear on parts: shows wear cause caused by excessive dirt entering the engine (a) cylinder wall wear, (b) worn rings, (c) piston wear, and (d) damaged carburetor slide

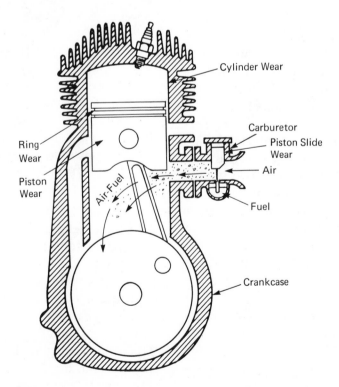

Fig. 8–18 Abrasive dirt wear places

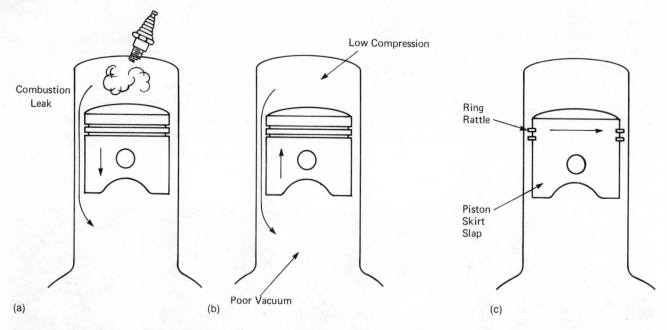

Fig. 8-19 Worn piston-cylinder problems (a) combustion leaks, (b) compression vacuum leaks, and (c) piston slap and ring rattle

When an engine is running with the above symptoms, there is but one consolation—it's not too late to repair it. Unless repaired, the piston would soon break a skirt or a ring, possibly destroying the entire engine.

Spark Plugs. Though an engine may foul the plugs, too cold a spark plug is not dangerous to the two-stroke upper end. Using too hot a plug is another story. A hot plug develops high local temperatures in the combustion chamber that can cause a hole to burn right through the piston. This is why it is recommended that you consider using a hotter spark plug very carefully, even if you have a plug-fouling problem in your two-stroke. Eliminate all other possible causes before risking a hotter plug as a solution. And when you do install a hotter plug, move up only one heat range at a time and keep checking the plug often. Little globules of molten aluminum are prophets of holey pistons and indicate that you have gone too hot in plug selection.

A bike with no compression that has been ridden hard with a hot plug is a sure suspect for a ventilated piston. Pull the cylinder head and you'll generally find a piston like the one shown in Fig. 8-20.

Fig. 8-20 Holed piston showing hole melted in piston during operation with hot plug

Timing. Accurate timing is very critical on a two-stroke engine. Timing that is either too advanced or too retarded can damage upper-end components.

Early or advanced timing causes the piston to fight against an already violently burning combustion charge (Fig. 8-21). This battle can be heard as a "ping" or rattling sound under load. Operating an engine that pings can cause cracked pistons and rings eventually, if the high temperature doesn't burn a hole in the piston first. Some-

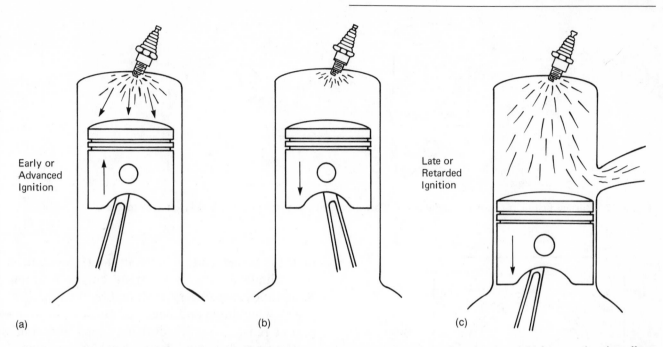

Early or
Advanced
Ignition

Late or
Retarded
Ignition

(a)   (b)   (c)

Fig. 8–21 Advanced or retarded timing: (a) early combustion pushes against upcoming piston and (b) late combustion allows power to exhaust (c) as piston moves ahead of combustion flame

times an engine will seem to "really scat" with advanced timing, but it won't scat for long if pinging is allowed to continue. Instead, it will scatter.

Retarded timing on a two-stroke is also dangerous. The charge is ignited too late in the cycle, and the piston never gets the proper combustion force applied to it, so the engine seems lazy. In addition, the charge continues to burn longer and over a greater area, causing engine temperatures to rise drastically. These extremely high temperatures can cause piston fatigue and ring land failure and seizure.

Lean Mixture. Lean-mixture symptoms are often similar to hot-plug symptoms; that is, a hole may burn right through the top of the piston. The cause is a little different however.

The perfect air-fuel ratio is around 14 to 1 (by weight). This means that with 14 parts air and 1 part fuel, all of the oxygen oxidizes all of the fuel under ideal conditions. Where there is too much oxygen, such as in an 18-to-1 air-fuel mixture, those four other parts of oxygen begin looking around for something to oxidize. When they find

the piston, they begin to oxidize the aluminum crown of the piston head. This results in aluminum oxide dust exiting with the exhaust. Soon the piston runs out of aluminum to contribute to those four hungry parts of oxygen and simply quits — with a big hole burned through the top of it (Figs. 8–22 a & b).

Clearance. Remember our formulas for expanding aluminum and iron? The different expansion rates of these metals are the reasons for precise clearance specifications in two-stroke engines. Typical two-stroke engines require about 0.001″ of piston-wall clearance per inch of cylinder bore. This clearance compensates for the piston which expands faster than the cylinder barrel so that there is minimum clearance at normal operating temperatures, thus minimum leakage and power loss.

If a clearance is too small, the piston will expand and scuff or score the cylinder wall (Fig. 8–23). The rings cannot seal the cylinder wall effectively then because of the vertical grooves worn in the wall's surface. Compression and com-

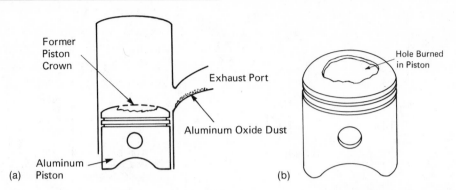

Fig. 8–22 Burned piston, (a) showing metal piston crown burned away, (b) piston burned from lean mixture

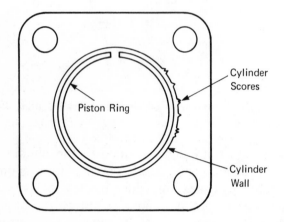

Fig. 8–23 Overhead view of a scored cylinder: note the space between the cylinder wall and ring caused by scoring

bustion gases escape past the rings via these grooves, causing poor performance.

If scoring continues and the piston gets too hot, "seizure" will occur. A seizure is the locking up of the piston in its bore; it is caused by excessive heat and insufficient clearance (Fig. 8–24). In

fact, the piston can become an interference fit in the cylinder, instantly stopping engine rotation. Sometimes a seizure is predicted by the bike simply slowing down and becoming lazier for no apparent reason. You're cruising along and rpm's just begin to drop, and there's a substantial loss of power. At times, though, there's no warning at all—the engine seizes, the rear wheel locks, and you slide to a stop. Two-stroke riders who stay alert never discount the possibility of a seizure and are prepared to pull the clutch lever and release the clutch if the engine locks up for any reason at all. If the engine seems to run all right after cooling off for a while, you can be sure you just experienced a seizure.

One way of safeguarding against seizures is to polish the high spots off the piston and measure for adequate clearance (Fig. 8–25). This procedure is covered in the service section.

Fig. 8–24 Seized piston showing scores and seized rings

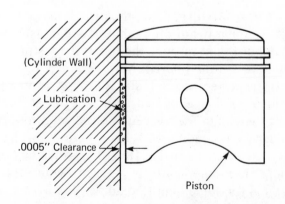

Fig. 8–25 Normal piston-to-wall clearance, showing piston, cylinder wall, lubrication, and clearance

Loose Clearance. Loose clearances are equally dangerous and can lock up an engine also, particularly if parts break and lodge in the wrong places. The problem stems from the need for the piston to go straight up and down without any wobble or rattle. If the piston rocks in the bore, the skirts may crack and break off, damaging the lower end of the engine. Inspect suspected pistons for cracks in the skirt area (Fig. 8–26).

Fig. 8–26 Cracked, broken piston, showing broken skirt and crack on the top

Even if the skirts don't crack, a rocking piston prevents good ring-sealing action, so blow-by is permitted and lower-end vacuum is weak. All these conditions cause poor performance and hard starting.

Excessive clearance may be caused by normal wear (after high mileage), poor air filtration, or excessive honing before assembly.

Lubrication. Another cause of upper-end failure in two-strokes is improper lubrication.

If a two-stroke engine is run without oil or with too little oil, it will seize in a very short time. The proper oil is required in the correct quantity, to insure a smooth film between the moving metal parts to prevent excessive friction and heat as shown in Fig. 8–25.

The wrist pin can scuff and gall from improper lubrication; so always inspect it carefully if you suspect a lubrication problem.

Too much oil can cause problems also. Fouled plugs, too much smoke, gummed up rings, a plugged exhaust system, excessive carbon deposits, and poor performance can result from a higher percentage of oil in the mixture than recommended. It is not necessarily a safeguard or "extra insurance" to run an engine with more oil

than it needs. Ring grooves may then fill with deposits, causing stuck rings. This leads to ring breakage. Dykes or "L" section rings are especially susceptible to this condition (Fig. 8–27).

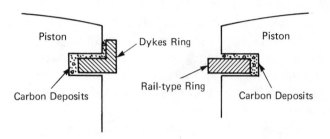

Fig. 8–27 Stuck rings, showing dykes and rail-type rings with carbon packing

Many mechanics spend hours tuning motorcycles with restricted exhaust systems and are then baffled by the poor running of the machine until they finally discover that the real problem is a blocked exhaust pipe.

The exhaust system, especially the exhaust port, can be choked off by carbon deposits that result from too much oil. Sometimes the condition is so bad that the exhaust port becomes almost entirely closed off by deposits (Fig. 8–28).

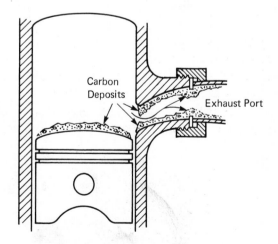

Fig. 8–28 Choked exhaust port showing carbon build-up

Wrong Lubrication. Manufacturers and racers have experimented for years in search of "miracle" lubricants. According to most oil company advertising, however, the search seems unnecessary. Pay attention to the manufacturer's handbook on the machine, or seek advice from your dealer about which brand of lubricant to use in a given machine. Also, be sure to find out what to avoid. For instance, unless a machine is used exclusively for high-speed all-out racing, don't even consider using a castor based oil. These lubricants gum up and curdle just like milk unless very specific procedures are followed. A mistake may cost you an engine.

Engine oil that doesn't have the proper base of crude oil or the right additives may cause seizure on one extreme and excessive fouling and deposits on the other. Both top-end maladies have already been discussed.

Oil that has too high a viscosity rating does not flow through small oil-injection lines easily; so be sure to avoid using heavy oil in these systems. This caution is especially critical in cold weather.

Rider Abuse. Rider abuse can damage the top end of a two-stroke engine even though all other factors are at the optimum setting. Rider abuse falls into two general catagories: (a) flogging or aggressive abuse, and (b) lugging abuse.

Flogging. Constant open throttle for long periods of time can cause excessive heat build-up and seizure or scuffing. A two-stroke engine likes to be "breathed" on occasion rather than held at one constant throttle setting. If mysterious scuffing or seizure occurs despite proper lubrication, spark-plug range, mixture, and timing, the rider should learn to alter his riding habits to include "breathing" the engine every minute or so. By closing the throttle partially on occasion, a richer mixture enters the engine, providing momentary additional cooling and lubrication.

Lugging. Operating a two-stroke engine at low rpm, causing it to work hard against heavy loads without downshifting, can be detrimental to pistons, rings, and cylinder walls. Lugging an engine, as it's called, encourages pinging, heat build-up (seizure and scuffing), carbon deposits, broken rings, and cracked pistons. Since the two-stroke engine likes varied rpm operation, try to keep it singing in the mid-range area most of the time when riding, but not at one monotonous throttle setting.

Two-Stroke Service and Repair

TESTING FOR TOP-END PROBLEMS

A test ride will tell you more about the condition of a motorcycle engine than its rider can convey to you verbally. When diagnosing a problem, try to get a test ride. If the bike has rattling noises in the cylinder, poor response at low rpm's and is hard to start, you can begin to suspect top-end problems. A dirt bike that looks like it has had many laps around the local gravel pit and a street machine with neglected air filters could be prime candidates for top-end problems.

Compression Test

If the test ride indicates a top-end problem, or if the bike won't start at all, a compression test is in order. There are a few precautions to take before beginning the test. Be sure to retorque the cylinder head nuts and check the throttle for proper opening. Carefully remove the spark plugs, after cleaning the dirt away from them so that no grit falls into the plug holes. Insert the compression gage snugly into the spark-plug hole and crank the engine through five or six times (Fig. 9–1). Always open the throttle during the compression test to allow plenty of air to enter the engine. This assures a more accurate reading.

Note the reading on the compression gage and write it down. Add about a teaspoonful of oil to the cylinder through the plug hole, then kick the engine over a couple of times to distribute the oil around the rings. Repeat the compression test and note the reading again.

Compare your first and second readings to the compression specified for that engine.

If the first reading is more than 100 pounds, the engine should start. If it won't, something else is probably wrong.

If the second reading is 20 per cent higher than the first, you can suspect excessive top-end wear.

If both readings are low, the problem may be a drastically worn top end, defective gasket, cracked or damaged piston or rings, or a badly scored cylinder.

If the compression reading is too high, you can be sure of finding excess carbon built up on the piston and in the combustion chamber.

Whatever your diagnosis, be certain that you *clean the cylinder and base before starting to disassemble the engine* (Fig. 9–2). This important step prevents any dirt from entering the crankcase, which would ruin the rod bearing. It surely would be a shame to ruin the lower end during a top-end overhaul.

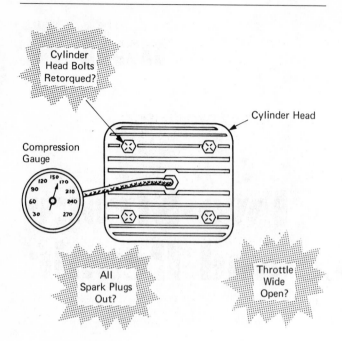

Fig. 9–1 Compression test checklist

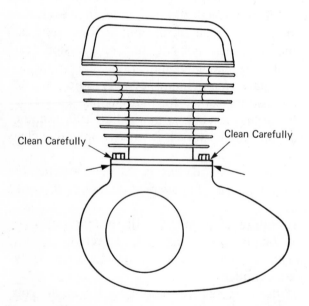

Fig. 9–2 Cleaning the cylinder, showing points where dirt must be removed thoroughly before disassembly

Disassembly

On most two-strokes, top-end service doesn't require engine removal because there is usually enough room to lift off the head and cylinder. Be-gin the task by removing the spark plug, the exhaust pipe, and the carburetor. Carefully loosen the cylinder retaining nuts, 1/4 turn at a time for the first turn or so, to avoid warping the head or cylinder. Remove the cylinder head and gasket if one is used on your machine. Treat the gasket gently, because it can probably be used again.

Using the kick starter, rotate the engine until the piston reaches the top of the cylinder. Now gently lift the cylinder barrel until the spigot section is slightly out of the engine case. Slip a rag or two under the barrel to catch any carbon, dirt, or broken rings that may fall out as you lift it off the rest of the way (Fig. 9–3). Lift the barrel straight away from the case—don't twist it or you may break something. If the cylinder-base gasket stayed intact, leave it alone. If not, scrape the old one off the case and replace it.

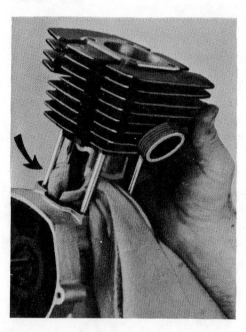

Fig. 9–3 Removing cylinder (Pabatco/Hodaka)

Situate the rags in the lower end to completely protect it; then begin to remove the piston. With needle-nose pliers, or a small screwdriver, remove the circlips from the piston (Fig. 9–4). Support the piston with one hand and push the pin out with a wooden dowel or soft drift punch (brass). Sometimes heating the piston with a butane torch will help the pin slide free more easily. If not, a piston-pin extractor must be used. See Unit 11, page 131 for how to use it.

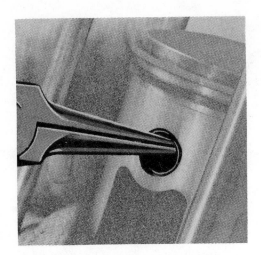

Fig. 9–4 Removing circlip (Pabatco/Hodaka)

Cleaning the Carbon

In a two-stroke engine that has been run for some time, you will notice carbon deposits that have built up on the piston crown, cylinder head, and exhaust port. Smaller deposits have built up in the ring lands of the piston. All of this carbon should be removed when servicing the top end.

Scrape carbon away from the exhaust port with an old kitchen knife or dull screwdriver. Be careful not to scratch the cylinder wall or port opening. Use an old piston ring to scrape carbon from the ring lands, but be careful not to scratch away any aluminum while you're doing it. Scrape clean the top of the piston, but don't polish it. Service the cylinder head by scraping the carbon from the combustion chamber and running a tap through the spark plug threads if they're dirty. Be sure not to damage the gasket-sealing surface when scraping carbon off the head. This is probably also an excellent time to clean carbon from inside the exhaust pipe and muffler baffles.

Clean parts in a good solvent and dry them with clean rags and an air hose if possible. A light honing with either a spring hone or a brush hone will deglaze the cylinder for better ring sealing.

Seizure Treatment

If piston seizure has left aluminum deposits on the cylinder wall, apply a few dabs of muriatic acid (hydrochloric acid) with a small brush. After four or five minutes, rinse off the acid with water. Repeat this procedure until the acid dissolves the aluminum away. Regular battery electrolyte will

also work, but be careful not to damage cylinder walls (Fig. 9–5). Hone the cylinder as above, clean it, and inspect if for score marks or other damage.

Fig. 9–5 Removing aluminum from cylinder wall

Honing the Cylinder

The purpose of honing is to refinish the cylinder wall surface to the correct *size, texture,* and *trueness* for proper piston operation. Of course, your honing may have as its objective less than all of the above factors. For instance, light honing may be performed in order to deglaze the varnish-like deposits that eventually build up on cylinder walls.

Types of Hones. Parallel stone hones such as the Sunnen, Jr. and Midget series are the common types found around a motorcycle shop (Fig. 9–6). Various stones are available to alter the cutting rates and surface finish of the hone job. Generally, "roughing" stones are replaced by "finishing" stones for the final passes. The smoother finishing stones insures a smooth texture for the cylinder walls and minimize wear during break-in.

The most common hones for the home mechanic are the spring-type stone hone and the brush hone shown in Unit 3. These hones are relatively inexpensive and do a good job of deglazing the cylinder for back-yard ring replacement jobs.

Fig. 9-6   Parallel stone hones

Fig. 9-7   Honing the cylinder, showing cylinder in vise with electric drill operating the spring type hone

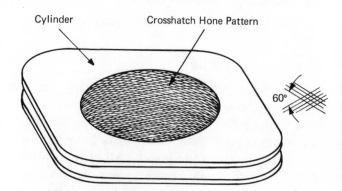

Fig. 9-8   Cross-hatch pattern

Whichever hone you choose, use it only with a *low-speed* drill. Never hone with the drill operating at more than 500 rpm. If you can locate a 250-rpm drill or a speed reducer for your higher-speed drill, your hone job will be better.

Honing Techniques. Major hone manufacturers provide extensive directions with their parallel stone hones, so we'll discuss only spring and brush hones.

Mount the cylinder in a vise and clamp it securely so it can't rotate if the hone should snag it. Mount a spring-type expanding hone in a slow-speed drill. Spray some honing oil or solvent on both the hone and cylinder walls. Start the drill and begin stroking the hone through the cylinder, being careful not to allow the honing stones to snag the spigot extension of the cylinder (Fig. 9-7). Supply enough honing oil to prevent the stones from loading up with cuttings and oil. Stroke fast enough to produce the classic 60° crosshatch pattern (Fig. 9-8). The crosshatch angle is controlled by how fast you stroke the hone up and down as it rotates in the cylinder.

A honing brush is much easier to use. There is almost no danger of damaging the hone or the cylinder barrel. However, the little hone "berries" on the bristles of the brush hone sometimes catch in a port and are propelled back at the hone operator or a bystander. One of these honing "berries" could put out an eye; *be careful to wear eye protection when using any hone* (Fig. 9-9).

Fig. 9-9   Using a brush hone, showing cylinder in vise, drill, brush hone, and hand-operated oil applicator

Brush hones remove almost no metal from the cylinder, so using a slow-speed drill is not quite so critical. Light engine oil and automatic transmission fluid are cheap, readily available honing fluids that work well with honing brushes. The brush is used just as the spring hone. Remember to stroke it fast enough to provide about a 60° crosshatch pattern.

Sometimes a bike that was running well will just carbon up eventually and need a new set of rings. The procedures of decarbonizing and deglazing plus the addition of new gaskets and rings will improve the running of any two-stroke. How much it improves depends on the piston-to-wall clearance. The importance of piston-to-cylinder wall fit in a two-stroke cannot be over-emphasized. It is better to use precision expanding gauges and micrometers rather than strip feeler gauges to check piston-to-wall clearance to guarantee accurate readings.

Measuring Piston-Wall Clearance

Measure the piston skirt at the bottom of the skirt with a micrometer (Fig. 9–10). Check the

Fig. 9–10 Measuring a piston skirt

cylinder bore at the bottom also (Fig. 9–11 a and b). The difference in these two readings is the piston-to-wall clearance (Fig. 9–12). Compare the actual clearance to the recommended clearance specification in the shop manual. If clearance is less than the maximum allowable clearance, a new set of rings, checked for proper end gap, should be all that is necessary (Fig. 9–13).

If the cylinder wall to piston clearance is less than double the recommended specification, a new piston of the same size as the one to be replaced should help tighten the clearance down to an acceptable level. Deglaze and use new rings to complement the new piston.

If piston-to-wall clearance is more than twice as much as the manufacturer's maximum specification, buy an oversize piston set and have the cylinder rebored by a competent machinist. Make sure all port edges are carefully beveled with a

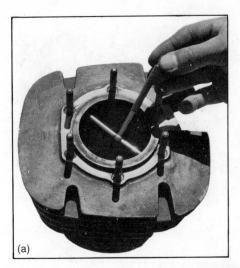

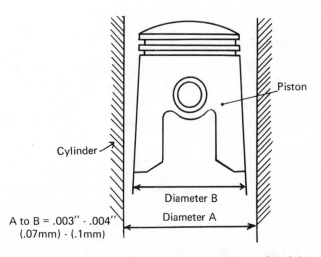

Fig. 9–11 Measuring the cylinder bore, showing (a) snap gauge in cylinder bore and (b) micrometer on snap gauge

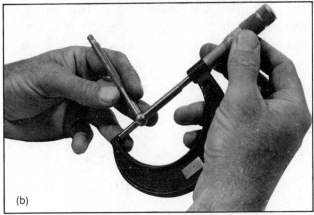

A to B = .003″ - .004″
(.07mm) - (.1mm)

Fig. 9–12 Piston to cylinder clearance (Pabatco/Hodaka)

Fig. 9–13 Measuring piston ring end gap (Pabatco/Hodaka)

fine file before final honing (Fig. 9–14). Check the end gap on the oversize rings before reassembly, as shown in Fig. 9–13.

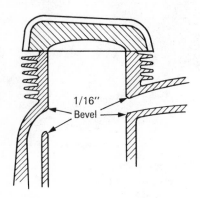

1/16″
Bevel

Fig. 9–14 Beveled cylinder ports

Reassembly

Install the rings onto the piston gently. Be sure that the end gap is correctly situated on the anti-rotation peg (Fig. 9–15). Sometimes the rings are backed by thin wire expanders which should be installed first, although some mechanics have left them out without ill effect.

Note the arrow on the top of the new piston. It should point forward; that is, toward the exhaust port. After aligning the pin holes in the piston with the one in the rod, oil the rod bearing and push in the pin. It helps if you install one of the new circlips in the piston beforehand so you can shove the pin through to it. Insert the other circlip with a pair of needle-nose pliers and be sure it is firmly seated in its groove.

Install a new base gasket if necessary and use a light coat of grease on each side of it to help seating. Move the piston to the top of its stroke and realign the rings over their pegs after squirting a little engine oil on them. Slip the lightly lubricated cylinder over the piston, being careful not to rotate it while slipping it down over the piston. Compress the piston rings with your fingers to start them into the lower taper of the cylinder. The reassembly sequence is shown in Fig. 9–16. Don't force anything—you'll break it!

If the barrel doesn't slip over the piston and rings easily, you've probably rotated a ring over its locating pin, as shown in (b) Fig. 9–15. Reposition the ring, then the barrel should slip over the piston if you've checked the piston-wall clearance and ring end gap properly.

Reinstall the cylinder head and tighten the retaining nuts to the torque recommended in the service manual. Use a torque wrench—don't guess! Carefully reinstall the carburetor, exhaust system, and spark plug, using new gaskets wherever necessary.

Break-In

Give the bike a good static tune-up first and check the general adjustments.

Break in a fresh top-end job gently, but don't lug the engine. If the break-in period is a controlled one, the rings will seat with a minimum of

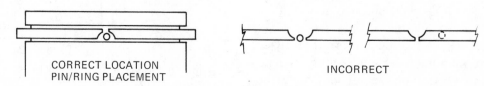

CORRECT LOCATION
PIN/RING PLACEMENT

INCORRECT

Fig. 9–15 Positioning piston ring; showing correct and incorrect pin-ring relationship

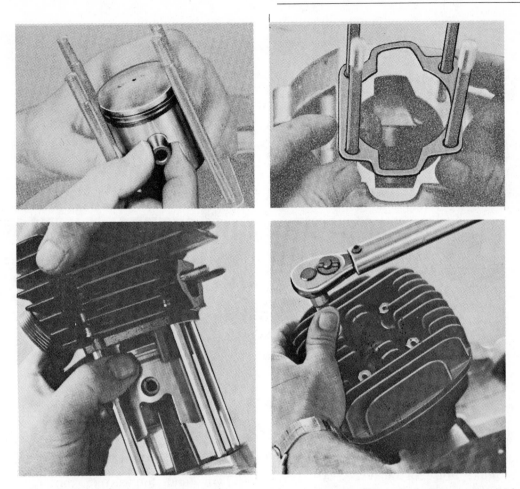

Fig. 9-16 Reassembly sequence: (a) installing piston to connecting rod, (b) installing cylinder base gasket, (c) installing cylinder, (d) using torque wrench to tighten cylinder head nuts (Pabatco/Hodaka)

wear to themselves and the cylinder wall. Hard riding during break-in causes excessive cylinder, piston, and ring wear which causes excessive piston slap, ring rattle, and wide end gap. You don't want these conditions—they're what you just spent all that time and money to correct. If the bike hasn't been ridden for a month or two, put in fresh oil and fuel. Start the bike up and ride it through at least one tank of gas, remembering these three break-in rules:

1. Don't overheat the engine.
2. Don't lug the engine.
3. Don't over rev the engine.

Retorque the cylinder head nuts and check the carb and exhaust fasteners too.

Now you are probably ready, after that first tank of gas is gone, to ride your two-stroke a little harder and enjoy the extra power it's putting out.

Four-Stroke Upper End

The deep, throaty sound of a large displacement four-stroke motorcycle differs from the high-pitched buzz of a two-stroke for several reasons. The intake noise of most two-strokes nearly matches the exhaust in loudness. However, the four-stroke noise is almost all exhaust note. A two-stroke engine has a firing pulse on each revolution, resulting in a higher-pitched tone than a four-stroke, which fires only once every two revolutions.

The riding characteristics of the two types of engines also differ considerably. A two-stroke engine favors high rpm and fairly aggressive riding tactics. A four-stroke is content to run at low to moderate rpm, giving good torque and hardly ever fouling spark plugs.

It's generally conceded that the new two-strokes generate much more horsepower per cc, yet are lighter in weight than a similar sized four-stroke. The weight difference is caused by the many extra parts required to make up the cam and valve train, which will be examined in detail after a short review of how a four-stroke engine works.

BASIC FOUR-STROKE DESIGN

Basic Piston Engine Configuration

Two- and four-stroke motorcycle engines have similar crankshafts, pistons, rods, and cylinders which make up some of the basic components of both engines. Both have a power stroke, that is, the explosive burning of a compressed air-fuel mixture in a cylinder (Fig. 10–1a). The objective of all other phases of an engine's activity lead to or clean up after the power stroke. Let's take a look at the phases required in a four-stroke.

Intake. To fill the cylinder with a fresh charge of gas-air mixture, a valve must open as the piston travels down its bore, drawing the fresh mixture into the complete volume of the cylinder. This intake valve opens as the piston starts down and closes as the piston starts back up so none of the fresh mixture is lost (Fig. 10–1b).

Compression Stroke. With the cylinder volume filled with the fresh air-fuel mixture, the pis-

114

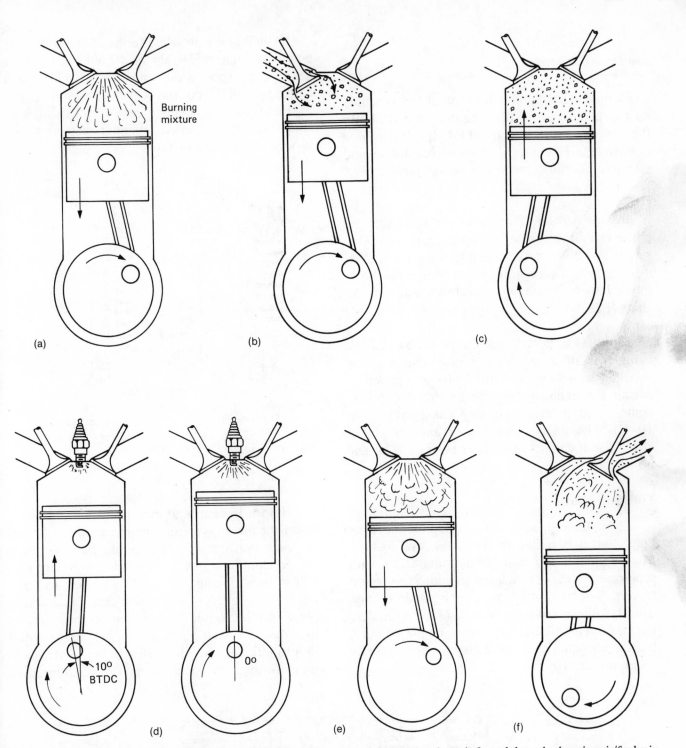

Fig. 10-1 Firing sequence in a typical 4-stroke engine: (a) on power stroke the piston is forced down by burning air/fuel mixture, (b) on intake stroke, the intake valve opens and mixture enters cylinder as piston goes down, (c) on compression stroke the piston rises with valves closed, (d) on ignition stroke the piston is at 10° BTDC and TDC, (e) on power stroke combustion occurs and valves close, (f) on exhaust stroke the exhaust valve (smaller) opens and gas goes out

ton now comes up to squeeze the fresh mixture into a "bomb"-like charge in the combustion chamber (Fig. 10-1c).

Ignition. The sparking of this compressed charge is not a "stroke" but, it is a critical factor in how well the four stroke engine runs. The spark plug is fired just before the piston reaching its top position (top dead center or TDC). By the time the piston reaches TDC the fuel charge is burning well enough to insure complete and effective combustion on the power stroke (Fig. 10–1).

Power Stroke. The power stroke is the one phase when the engine is generating power. This power results from the violently burning air-fuel mixture which forces the piston down the bore, moving the rod that applys this force to the crank-shaft (Fig. 10–1).

Exhaust Stroke. After the power stroke the cylinder is filled with burned gases that must be expelled somehow. Another valve is opened to permit the exhuast gases to exit as the piston comes up on its last stroke in 4-phase cycle (Fig. 10–1f). The piston now begins another set of strokes so it can get to its next power stroke and do its job.

Top-End Parts

The cylinder is sometimes called the barrel or "jug" and it is bolted to the crankcase section. Most cylinders are made of aluminum fins with replaceable steel or iron liners in which the piston travels. Some cylinders are simply made of cast iron, but these are a bit heavy. Other cylinders are made of aluminum with a chrome-plated bore, but the chrome flakes off. This type is not easily rebored (Fig. 10–2).

Cylinders are attached to the lower end cases either by long studs that also hold the cylinder head or by short studs that are attached to a flange around the bottom of the cylinder (Fig. 10–3). Either system seems to work, but if the long studs are overtightened, cylinder distortion and loss of power may result.

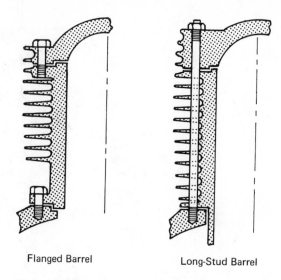

Flanged Barrel   Long-Stud Barrel

Fig. 10–3 Typical cylinder hold-downs.

Piston. In nearly all motorcycles on the road today the piston is an aluminum casting. A few of the high performance engines do have stronger forged aluminum pistons. Pistons are nearly perfectly round, being only slightly oblong to compensate for different expansion rates at different places on the piston. The dimension measured at the pin section will usually be several thousandths of an inch smaller than the measurement through 90° away from the pin direction.

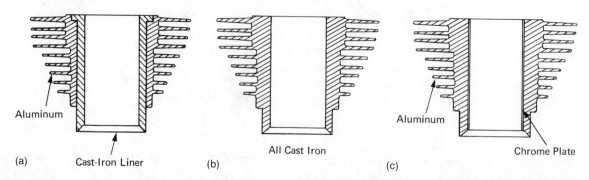

Aluminum   (a)   Cast-Iron Liner   (b)   All Cast Iron   Aluminum   (c)   Chrome Plate

Fig. 10–2 Three types of cylinder barrel: (a) iron-lined aluminum, (b) cast iron, and (c) chrome-plated aluminum construction

They are tapered slightly for the same reason. These tapered and cam-ground pistons insure less wear and quieter engines when the engine is starting cold (Fig. 10–4). The crown or top of a piston may have various configurations. Most are slightly domed or flat, while others have a tall "pop up" section for increased compression in hemispherical combustion chambers (Fig. 10–5).

Four-stroke pistons often have notches cut or cast into the crowns to insure that the pistons and valves don't hit one another.

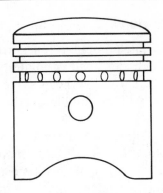

Fig. 10–6 Piston design showing two top compression ring grooves and the oil groove with drilled holes

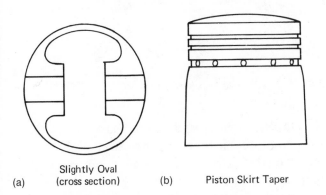

Slightly Oval
(cross section)

(a)   (b)   Piston Skirt Taper

Fig. 10–4 Piston dimensions, showing oval shape of piston from top and taper of skirt

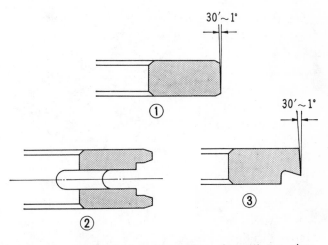

Fig. 10–7 Sectional view of a piston ring: (1) top view, (2) oil ring, and (3) second ring with bevel (American Honda Motor Company)

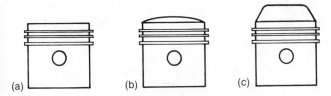

(a)   (b)   (c)

Fig. 10–5 Piston crown shapes showing (a) flat piston (b) slightly domed type, and (c) pop-up top

Rings. The popular ring set-up for four-stroke engines has two straight rail compression rings at the top and a wider cast iron oil-control ring at the bottom (Fig. 10–6). Most compression rings are chrome-plated, but some are plain cast iron. Holes drilled into the piston at the oil ring land enable the oil-control ring to relieve itself of extra oil that it scrapes from the cylinder walls. The oil-control rings have openings that allow oil from the cylinder walls to pass through the holes in the ring land. The second compression ring often helps oil control also. Sometimes the lower edge of the ring is beveled to enable it to wipe away some of the oil from the wall (Fig. 10–7).

Pin and Retaining System. Pistons are attached to the connecting rods by wrist pins or "grudgeon pins," as the English call them. These pins are centered and retained in the piston by snap rings or locking clips. The English refer to these items as "circlips" (Fig. 10–8).

Fig. 10–8 Piston pin retaining clips showing three common types of clips

The Cylinder Head

The three most popular four-stroke motorcycle engine cylinder head configurations in use today are the pushrod overhead valve, the single overhead cam, and the double overhead cam.

Pushrod Overhead Valve. Activated by pushrods coming up from a case-mounted camshaft, the rocker arms of this type of cylinder head act upon the valves, opening them at the proper time (Fig. 10–9).

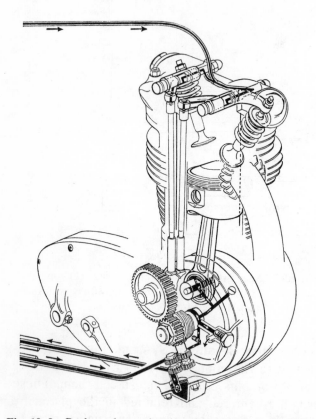

Fig. 10–9   Push rod overhead valve (Triumph Norton Incorporated)

Single Overhead Cam. The camshaft in this type of head mounts above the valves so that pushrods are eliminated. Extra drive mechanisms (chains, sprockets, and idlers) are required, but are justified since the performance of overhead-cam engines often surpasses that of the pushrod overhead-valve engine. The rocker arms simply

ride with their follower end on the cam, and the adjuster end activates the valve (Fig. 10–10).

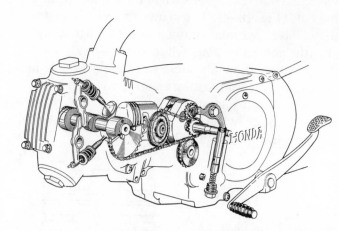

Fig. 10–10   Single overhead cam (American Honda Motor Company)

Double Overhead Cam. Dual Overhead Cam motorcycle engines are rare, perhaps because of the extra expense and weight with little gain in performance capability over the single overhead-cam design. The cylinder head contains two camshafts, one for exhaust valves and one for intakes. The valves are adjusted by little spacers placed under the caps which ride over the valve tips. Thicker spacers reduce clearance, while thinner spacers increase valve clearance (Fig. 10–11).

Ports. The passages or holes through which the intake and exhaust gases flow are called ports. Most engines have one port per valve all the way from each carburetor to each intake valve, and one exhaust port per exhaust valve all the way to the exhaust pipe. Twin-cylinder motorcycles (Fig. 10–12) with only one carburetor have a single carburetor port that branches into two cylinder ports. Ports that branch into two ports are known as siamesed ports.

Valves. A valve is a very important part of the cylinder head because it is the door that opens and closes at exactly the proper time to draw in the fresh fuel mixture in or to expel the burnt exhaust. Though a one-piece item, a valve has several sections with different names (Fig. 10–13).

Seat Inserts. Since most heads are made of somewhat soft aluminum, a hardened steel valve-

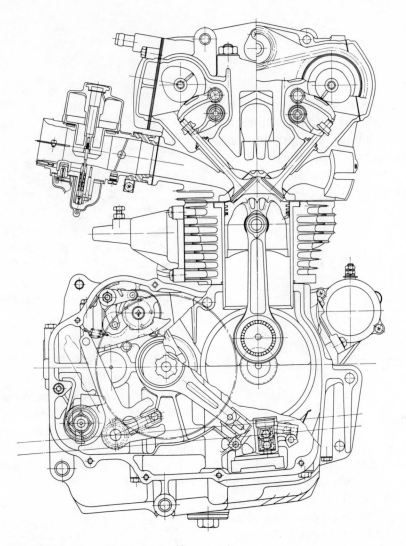

Fig. 10–11 Dual overhead cam (American Honda Motor Company)

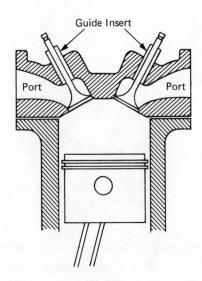

Fig. 10–12 Ports in cylinder head

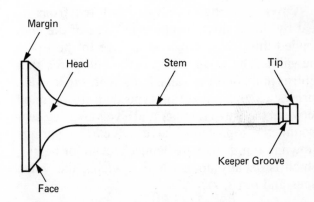

Fig. 10–13 Valve parts showing margin, face, head, stem, keeper groove, and tip

119

seat insert is necessary to absorb the pounding shock of the valve face as it seals the cylinder. These seat inserts are installed with an extremely tight press so they don't fall out during operation. If badly pitted or worn, the seat insert is a replaceable item that requires special tools and training to repair or replace (Fig. 10–14).

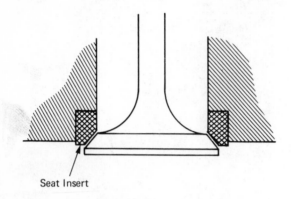

Seat Insert

Fig. 10–14   Valve seat insert

The soft aluminum of the cylinder head also requires that a better metal be used to guide the valve. The bore through which the valve stem operates must stay tight for good oil control and accurate valve seating. For these reasons the valve guide, made of an iron or bronze pipe, is inserted into a larger hole with a tight press fit. In Fig. 10–12 you can see the valve guide as it is installed in the head. Note that the lower section of the guide protrudes slightly into the port.

Valve Springs. The valve is lifted from its seat by the positive mechanical force of the cam applied through mechanical linkage to the tip of the valve. The valve spring is the only force that returns and holds the valve in its seat. Most valve springs are the coil-spring type that are retained between the valve retainer and a valve-spring seat around the top of the valve guide. The springs shown in Fig. 10–15 are being checked for height, which is usually done when servicing the valve faces and seats.

Camshaft. The camshaft is geared to rotate at only one-half of engine speed since the valve

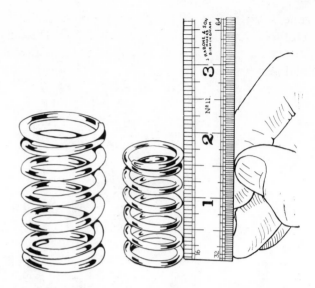

Fig. 10–15   Valve springs (Triumph Norton Incorporated)

needs to be opened only every other revolution. The profile or "lobe" on the cam determines how high and how long the valve stays open. Mild, reliable street engines need moderate lift and duration, while racing jobs need higher lifts and longer durations. These sacrifice reliability for performance. Like the valve, the cam is a one-piece unit with several sections that have different names (Fig. 10–16).

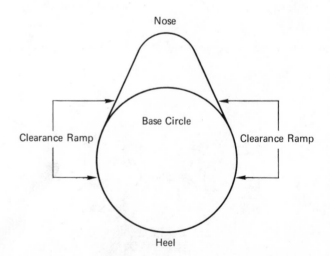

Nose

Base Circle

Clearance Ramp

Clearance Ramp

Heel

Fig. 10–16   Camshaft lobe, showing base circle, heel, clearance ramp, and nose

As previously stated, cams may be mounted in the engine cases or in the cylinder head. There must also be some provision to drive the cam. In overhead cam engines, a chain-sprocket system is generally used to drive the cam, while pushrod overhead engines use a gear drive for the cam. Overhead cam design incorporates a spring-loaded tensioning device also, which keeps the cam chain operating properly (Fig. 10–17).

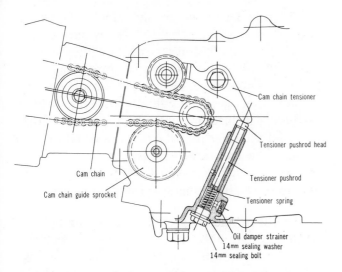

Fig. 10–17 Cam chain tensioner (American Honda Motor Company)

A cam may be mounted in several places, some requiring more linkage to the valve than others. The pushrod type overhead valve engines requires the most cam-valve linkage, which includes a tappet or lifter, pushrod, rocker arm, and adjuster (Fig. 10–18).

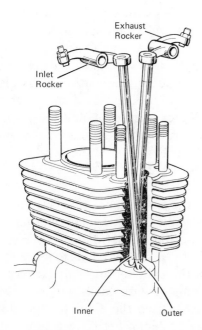

Fig. 10–18 Push rod linkage (Triumph Norton Incorporated)

In order to allow for expansion of these metal parts, a certain amount of clearance is required between the parts in this system. Clearance is obtained by adjusting a nut and stud assembly at the end of the rocker arm or by adjustable length tappets as in Harley "V" twins (Fig. 10–19).

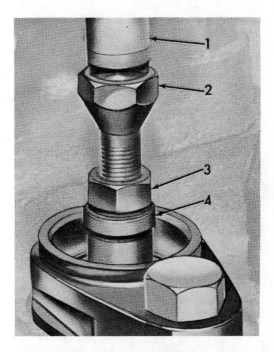

Fig. 10–19 At top, the push rod (1) seats in the tappet adjusting screw (2), which fits onto the lock nut (3) on the tappet (4)

Overhead cam engines require much less clearance than overhead valve engines, partially because there are fewer parts to expand in the system.

Spark Plug Hole. A threaded hole must be provided in the cylinder head so a spark plug can be installed. Spark plug holes may be 10, 12, or 14 mm in diameter and vary in depth according to engine design. Threaded into aluminum, these fragile holes are often abused, resulting in damaged threads. Fortunately, this damage can usually be repaired with an insert.

Lubrication Provisions. Usually there are internal passages for the delivery and return of oil to the moving parts of the cylinder head. These passages must be sealed properly or oil leakage will result (Fig. 10–20).

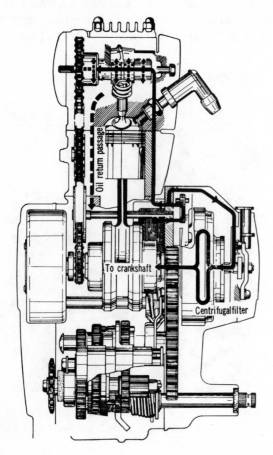

Fig. 10–20   Pressure lubrication diagram (American Honda Motor Company)

Top-End Problems

You should be able to isolate top-end problems in a four-stroke either to the head and valve area or to the piston and cylinder area by noise isolation and a compression test.

Let's consider some problems that occur in the piston and cylinder area first. Note that these problems are identical to those that occur in two-stroke upper ends.

Normal Wear. Even the best air filters available for motorcycles cannot filter out *all* the dirt from the incoming air. Eventually the abrasive action of dirt and grit will wear away metal from pis-

ton rings and cylinder walls. With meticulous attention to air-filter condition, engine lubrication, and ignition and valve adjustment, a carefully ridden street machine can get 20,000 miles or more from its original upper end.

Excess Dirt. See those velocity stacks on your buddy's street screamer? They sure do funnel in plenty of air, don't they? Well, they're sucking up plenty of dirt and grit to grind away at the innards of his engine. He can expect rapid wear to pistons, rings, and the cylinder wall. Most likely his bike will lose power and have excess "blow by" past the rings in just a few thousand miles of riding. One trip down a dusty road with no air cleaner can spell disaster for a formerly healthy engine. *Use* air cleaners and maintain them.

Ignition. The chapter on ignition timing (Unit 21) tells you that the time at which spark occurs is critical to the performance of the machine. Ignition timing affects engine temperature also. Timing that is very advanced or retarded causes very high piston temperatures. A spark plug with too hot a heat range can cause the same problem. These high piston temperatures can lead to a burned piston crown or a seized engine. Keep ignition adjustments and spark plug selection in the recommended factory range or be prepared for upper-end disaster.

Mixture. As with any other variable, there are hazards to avoid when setting and resetting the air-fuel mixture. A lean charge creates high engine temperatures with excess oxygen around to burn the red hot engine parts such as pistons and valves. A rich mix causes deposits of unburned carbon, dilutes engine oil, and fouls spark plugs. Follow the recommendations in the carburetion section (Unit 15) to avoid the results of either extreme (Fig. 10–21).

Clearance. An engine that is set up with tight piston-to-wall clearances may overheat and seize up some hot day. This dangerous condition occurs when the piston expands to more than the diameter of the cylinder and stops its travel immediately. This seizure locks the rear wheel and sometimes causes the rider to "go down." To avoid this problem, break in a new motorcycle carefully and check the clearances thoroughly be-

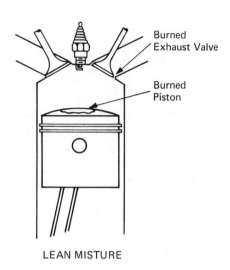

Fig. 10–21   Rich and lean mixture problems

fore reassembling upper ends. An engine that has been assembled with too much clearance can cause problems too. Loose pistons will rock in their bores, resulting in poor ring seal and possibly cracked skirts. Valves require a certain clearance in their guides to operate properly also. Too much clearance leads to rapid wear and bell mouthing the guide (Figs. 10–22, 10–23).

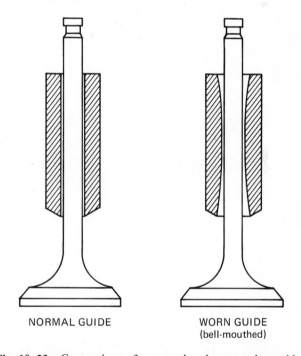

Fig. 10–23   Comparison of a normal and worn valve guide

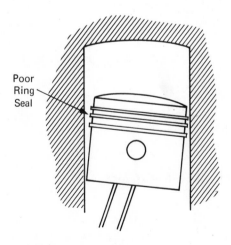

Fig. 10–22   Cocked piston, showing poor ring seal due to worn, cocked piston

Lubrication. Obviously the lack of lubrication will cause quick and extensive engine dam-

age. Improper lubricants can also harm engines. If oil is too thick, it won't reach the critical areas of a cold engine fast enough and rapid wear will result. If oil is too thin, it won't have sufficient viscosity to permit the pump to maintain the proper oil pressure. Use the weight and type of oil the manufacturer recommends, and avoid extremes in oil viscosities to insure long, reliable engine life.

Rider Abuse. The two general types of rider abuse are "flogging" and "lugging." Both damage engines.

A rider flogs his machine by constantly over-reving the engine, shifting too fast and too hard, and using drag race take-off techniques. Since a street engine wasn't built for this kind of treatment, its cast pistons may crack, or they may contact a floating valve. At high rpm broken parts tend to break other parts around them. "Valve float" is the biggest danger to a flogging rider. Weakened valve springs, changing valve clearances, and worn guides contribute to valve float at high rpm. The valve springs simply cannot return the valve to its seat in time to get out of the up-coming piston's way. There's a collision — possibly a broken piston and valve, or a totally ruined engine. The harder a bike is ridden, the more frequent checking and careful maintenance it must be given.

"Lugging" is another story. The rider who lugs his engine is the fellow who putts around town at 1800 rpm in high gear with two up, resorting to a down shift only when chain snatch and engine bucking make it imperative. A motorcycle engine is made to operate efficiently at higher rpm than the family station wagon, so keep it buzzing freely in the ranges the factory recommends. While there's no need to keep the tach needle on the red line, don't force it to do hard work at low rpm. For normal riding, a good shift point would be about 50% of red line rpm or when the engine sounds "half-way wound up."

Lugging leads to excess carbon, overheating, and bearing wear. In addition, it damages the chain, the sprockets, and the clutch assemblies.

Four-Stroke Upper-End Service and Repair

The first step in any repair job should be to identify the real existing problem and its cause. Spend a few dollars for the specific shop manual for your machine. The specifications and the procedural information it contains will speed the repair process considerably. The successful repair is one that not only fixes the damage, but lessens the likelihood of its recurrence. Therefore, the good mechanic begins his task with a thorough diagnosis.

The question that immediately presents itself—along with the machine—is: "Will it run?" If not, then are the ignition and fuel systems operating properly? Is the valve adjustment correct? Is the fuel fresh? If all of these check out, then it's time for a compression test to determine the basic engine condition (Fig. 11-1).

CHECKING ENGINE CONDITION

Compression Test

A simple compression test is performed when you try to start the engine with the kick starter. If you notice that there is virtually no compression resistance to kick through, especially when you already suspect a compression problem, there's a good chance your gage readings will be low. Re-move the spark plug and insert the gage into the plug, hole being careful not to damage the soft aluminum spark plug threads. With the gage in place, *open the throttle* and kick the engine through about five times, or engage the electric starter for a 2- to 3-second burst (Fig. 11-2).

If the engine shows less than 90 to 100 psi compression pressure, you should look further into the upper end for your troubles. Begin by squirting about a teaspoonful of clean engine oil into the cylinder and rotating the engine several times to distribute the oil around the rings. Now you're ready to take another compression reading with the rings temporarily sealed. If your readings jump up to 120 to 190 psi, you know a re-ring job is in order. If the reading remains extremely low, however, you know that compression is probably escaping through the head gasket or valves. In either case, if you have taken a careful compression test, with the valves adjusted properly and throttle open and you still get low readings, you know the top end should be disassembled and repaired.

Cylinder Leakage Tester. Another type of compression test employs the cylinder leakage tester. This device pumps air into the cylinder and isolates the problem by tracing down the es-

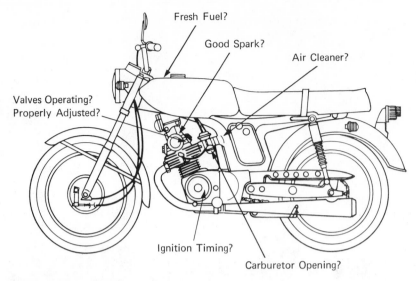

Fig. 11–1   Motorcycle diagnosis checkpoints

Fig. 11–2   Compression reading, showing gauge in spark plug hole with a good reading

Fig. 11–3   Cylinder leakage test gauge

caping air. *Note: Never use any sort of leakage tester on a two-stroke engine*—the crankshaft end seals will surely blow out (Fig. 11–3).

Noises

Sometimes the compression readings are good, but the engine is noisy. Often these noises come from cam chains, primary chains, rattling clutch hubs, or loose valve adjustments. Eliminate these areas of potential noise by inspection and adjustment before dismantling your machine for an upper-end overhaul.

The tone of the noise is usually a hint of what is causing the problem. Ticking and light tapping noises indicate that the offending part is small, perhaps a rocker arm or a valve. Heavy slapping and clunking suggest heavier parts, such as pistons, rods, crankshafts, and clutch assemblies, as the offenders. These heavy slapping noises may also come from cam or primary chains slapping against engine cases. Constant grinding or "whirring" noises indicate the problem is occurring at a rotating shaft rather than a reciprocating part. Hissing or puffing sounds suggest compression loss through leaking gaskets. Such leaks must be caught early and corrected before the sealing surface is damaged by blow-by, which mean remachining or replacement.

ENGINE REMOVAL

When all diagnostic tests are completed and a top-end overhaul is in order, there is yet another decision to make before actually beginning. Should you remove the engine, or leave it in the frame? Many bikes require that the engine be out of the frame in order to remove the head. Fortunately, most bikes have plug connections for the electrical systems and other features. These make engine removal and reinstallation simple. If you decide to leave the engine in the frame, be sure to clean away any dirt on the upper frame rails and the gas tank area so the dirt won't fall into the engine while you're working. Generally, a cleaner job can be done on a bench than in the frame, so let your available facilities dictate the approach you take.

After thoroughly cleaning the entire motorcycle, remove the engine in approximately this order of work steps and you'll stay out of trouble:

1. Disconnect the battery and wires. Where wires don't have plugs, trace the wire to its end and tape a label on it to help you remember where and how to re-install it. *Never snip wires* and reinstall them with splices!

2. Drain the engine, the primary, and the transmission oil.

3. Remove the carbs from the engine but leave them attached to their cables. Wrap each in a rag and place them so they are protected until reinstallation.

4. Remove the exhaust system—be careful of rusted bolts and nuts. (A little penetrating oil applied several hours before beginning this task works wonders).

5. Remove the rear chain, or primary chain if the bike has a seperate transmission.

6. Double-check to insure that the only connections between the engine and the bike are the mounting bolts and plates. Make sure you remove all cables, lines, tubes, wires, ducts, covers, panels, and straps that connect the engine to any other part of the machine.

7. Remove the mounting plates and bolts, then slip the engine out. Be careful! Engines are heavier than they look and often can be removed only from a particular side of the frame.

Cylinder Head Removal and Inspection

Having removed the engine from the frame, the next task is to situate it on a stand or fixture to steady it enough to work on it. A simple wood frame made from two-by-fours usually works well (Fig. 11–4).

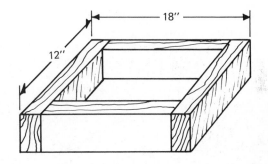

Fig. 11–4 Engine support fixture made of 2 × 4s

Begin by removing any electrical components on the head such as the points plate after you have marked its location with a lightly scribed line.

On overhead-cam engines, first remove the timing assembly, cam covers, cam-chain tensioner, cam sprocket, and camshaft. After these components have been neatly stored away, wire up the cam chain as shown in Fig. 11–5.

Fig. 11–5 Cam chain is wired up to keep it from falling into case

Now you can loosen the head stud nuts one-half turn at a time each until they will spin off. Remove the head, being careful not to disturb the cam chain wiring or mar the head gasket surface.

Cylinder Head Service

Now that you've removed the cylinder head, clean it with solvent and give it a general inspection for cracks or other damage. Fill each port, one at a time, with solvent to check each valve's seepage (Fig. 11–6).

The valves that leak worst will require the most reseating effort. If they don't leak at all, they probably don't really need service at this time.

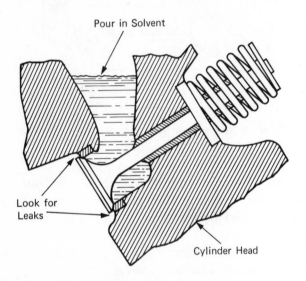

Fig. 11–6 Checking for valve leaks

Valve Spring Removal. Most bikes require a special motorcycle valve-spring tool. However, your local welding shop can usually make one for you out of a "C" clamp if necessary (Fig. 11–7). Compress the valve springs just enough to free the keepers. Then gently unclamp the spring and store the keepers, retainers, washers, and spring until later (Fig. 11–8). If the end of the valve is mushroomed or peened over, file the edges until it slips freely through the guide (Fig. 11–9). Test the valve springs for height with an accurate scale (Fig. 11–10). If you can detect at the valve seat more than four or five thousandths of an inch of

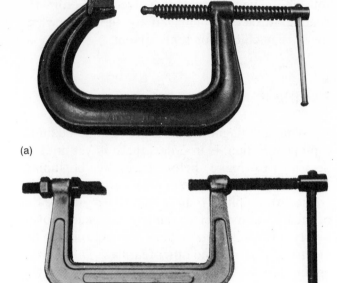

Fig. 11–7 Valve spring tools: (a) a C-clamp and (b) a valve spring compressor

Fig. 11–8 Valve spring removal showing compressor on spring

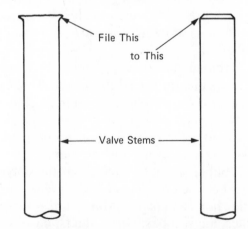

Fig. 11–9 Mushroomed valve stem showing mushroomed stem at left and a filed stem at right

Fig. 11-10 Checking valve spring height (Triumph Norton Incorporated)

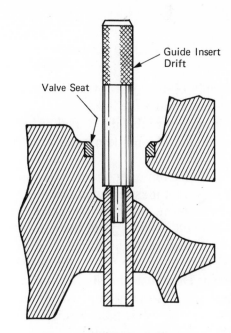

Fig. 11-11 Drifting out the valve guide

Guide Insert Drift

Valve Seat

wobble in the valve guide, the guide should be replaced. These guides can be replaced by using a special drift to remove the old guide after heating the head in an oven to about 350° to 400°. The same drift can be used to install a new guide. A special valve guide removal technique for stubborn guides is shown in Unit 23 (Fig. 11-11). Inspect the valve seat and valve face for burning or pitting. Sometimes motorcycle valves can be lapped in with an abrasive compound and will seat perfectly. Often, however, a new valve is required and it must be lapped into the old seat. These steps are required to lap a valve to its seat:

1. After cleaning the seat and the valve, *sparingly* apply some lapping compound to the face of the valve.

2. Insert the valve in the guide, being careful not to contaminate the guide area with compound (Fig. 11-12a).

3. Using either a suction-cup stick on the head or a piece of small hose on the stem, rotate the valve against the seat. Lift the valve 1/4 inch occasionally to help the lapping compound work (Fig. 11-12b).

4. Check the contact pattern made on the seat and face. There should be a dull gray pattern completely around both the valve and the seat.

5. Clean the seat and valve thoroughly with solvent or soap and water. Again, be careful not to get any compound in the guide (Fig. 11-12c).

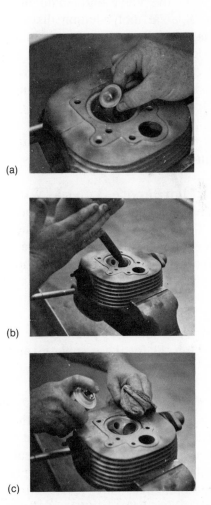

(a)

(b)

(c)

Fig. 11-12 Valve lapping sequence: (a) inserting valve in guide, (b) lapping the seat and valve with a hand tool, (c) cleaning the seat and valve with solvent

6. Apply oil to the seat face, stem, and guide before reassembling the head.

7. Check your job with Varsol or kerosene in the ports to see if more lapping is required.

If the seat is in poor condition, it too must be refaced or sometimes replaced and the new seat refaced. It is more common to replace the valves in a motorcycle than to grind them as is done in automotive head reconditioning.

Be sure to clean the valve thoroughly before replacing it. Don't use abrasive on the valve stem area since any material ground away will increase the clearance between the valve and guide and cause the guide to wear faster.

Lubricate the valve and guide before reassembling. Special molybdenum disulfide grease for engine rebuilding will insure minimum wear when the engine is first restarted. If the engine uses valve seals, slip them over the valve stems before installing the springs and retainers.

Check your valve job by pouring Varsol or kerosene into the ports and seeing if the valves seep any fluid. If so, disassemble that valve assembly and lap it until the valve seals properly.

Spark Plug Service. You may want to repair a damaged spark-plug hole while you have the head off. Thread inserts are an easy, cheap way to fix damaged plug holes. The procedure is to run a special reamer-tap through the old hole until a new, larger set of threads are cut. A coiled wire insert is installed in the new threads that duplicates the original threads. Break off the "tang" with a pair of needle-nose pliers and you're done. Refer to Unit 23 for the complete thread insert sequence.

Piston and Cylinder Service. As you know, the piston is designed to operate in the cylinder with a little clearance to allow for heat expansion and lubrication. If there's too little clearance, the engine will seize up; too much and piston slap, eventually breakage, may result. Most motorcycles call for 0.001″ to 0.003″ of piston-to-wall clearance. You can generally assume that most pistons use about 0.001″ clearance per inch of cylinder bore. Your manual gives you the exact specification. You can measure your existing piston and barrel using a micrometer and snap gauge to determine clearance.

Before you measure these parts, however, the machine should be clean, so give it a good washing. The steps involved in removing the head on most models will vary considerably—some even require removing the engine from the frame. Follow the instructions in your manual relative to engine and cylinder removal.

Once the head is reworked and carefully stored, you can inspect the tops of the pistons for excessive carbon, burns, or damaged piston crowns. Carefully remove the cylinder assembly from the engine, following these precautions:

1. Never pry cylinders with a screwdriver—tap them with a soft rubber or plastic-tipped hammer.

2. Stuff clean rags into the crankcase to protect the lower end as soon as you have lifted the barrel an inch or so.

3. Lift the barrel straight up—don't rotate or twist it.

With the barrel off, the piston can be removed from the connecting rod. In nearly all pistons there are retaining clips to remove before the pin can be extracted. These clips can usually be removed with a good pair of needle-nose pliers. Don't scratch the piston or damage the clip if you must use a small screwdriver to pick out the clip. Be careful that the clip doesn't fly out and hit you in the eye as it springs out of the piston (Fig. 11–13).

Fig. 11–13 Removing circlip (Triumph Norton Incorporated)

Sometimes gentle finger pressure will enable the piston pin to slide right out and free the piston from the rod. Other times, however, the piston must be heated gently with a torch, or a piston-pin extractor must be used (Fig. 11–14). A C-clamp and the proper size sockets might be used to press out the pin.

Fig. 11–14 Heating piston, showing propane torch being used to heat and expand piston

Piston-to-Wall Clearance Measurement.
Pistons are tapered somewhat because high temperatures cause the top of the piston to expand more than the skirt area. For this reason pistons are measured in the skirt area rather than across the crown (Fig. 11–15). Also, pistons are cam ground; that is, they are oval-shaped because they expand more in the direction of the pins.

To get the proper piston measurement, measure it at its largest diameter. You must measure the piston near the bottom of the skirt perpendicular to the pin.

By using a micrometer it is possible to obtain piston-size readings that are accurate to less than a thousandth of an inch. With either an inside micrometer or a telescoping gage, it is then possible to get an accurate reading on the cylinder size. The difference in these two figures is the piston-to-cylinder-wall clearance.

A cheap and easy, though less accurate, way to determine piston-wall clearance is to use long, thin feeler gages (0.0015″ to 0.005″). Slip the clean piston into the clean cylinder along with the feeler gage placed perpendicular to the pin (Fig. 11–16).

Try to fit larger or smaller feeler gage stips until you find one that will just pull free with your fingers. That gage represents approximately the amount of piston-wall clearance you have. Carefully inspect the piston-pin bearing or bushing area of the connecting rod. If the bearing feels gritty, or the pin appears scored, replace both. If the piston pin rocks or binds severely in its rod bushing, both the pin and the bushing should be replaced (Fig. 11–17).

Now that you've determined the actual piston-to-wall clearance and looked up the recom-

Fig. 11–15 A micrometer is used to measure skirt of piston

Fig. 11–16 Feeler gauge measurement of piston to wall clearance

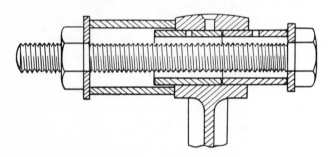

Fig. 11–17 Use the new end bushing to push out the old, using a threaded bolt about 4 inches long (Triumph Norton Incorporated)

mended factory specifications you have several options:

Option 1: Reinstall the old parts.
Option 2: Replace the rings only with a new ring set of the same size.
Option 3: Replace the piston and rings with a new set of the same size.
Option 4: Rebore the cylinder, then install proper oversize pistons and rings.

Option 1. If the clearance specifications are within recommended factory tolerances, you're safe to simply reassemble the upper end after cleaning and lubricating the parts.

Option 2. If the clearances are toward the loose side of factory recommended tolerances, deglaze the cylinder with a hone, then install new rings (Fig. 11–19).

Fig. 11–18 Deglazing the cylinder with a brush hone, showing hone in drill with jug in vise on table

Option 3. If the piston is worn considerably and replacing it with the same size new piston would decrease the clearance to factory tolerances again, you can save the cost of a bore job (up to $20.00 a hole) by this simple replacement. Again, you must deglaze the cylinder and use new rings (Fig. 11–20).

Fig. 11–19 Deglazing with a spring stone hone

Option 4. To update an engine to peak performance, a bore job is called for. This requires remachining the cylinder with a boring bar or special hone so it will accept a larger piston. Always buy the new piston first and take the piston and cylinder to the machinist who is to do the job. Without the piston, he can only guess how far to bore and hone the cylinder. If he has the piston he can measure exactly.

Reassembly. It's a good idea to clean the fins and spray them lightly with some flat black high-temperature exhaust paint. This helps the engine cool better. Check the piston-ring end gap before installing rings on the pistons. If the gap is tight, carefully make a light cut or two across the ends of the rings with a fine file. Remove just enough metal from the end of the ring so the gap will be at or slightly larger than factory specifications. Follow the manufacturer's recommendation for locating the end gaps on the piston (Fig. 11–20).

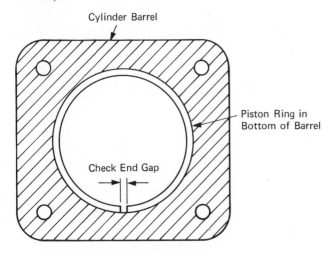

Fig. 11–20 Checking ring end gap showing ring in bore and end gap with dimension

After assembling the piston, pin, and rod, be sure that the pin clips are securely seated in the piston before reinstalling the barrel. Also, don't forget to put on the base gasket before you put on the barrel (Fig. 11–21).

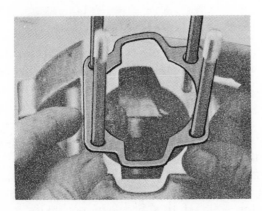

Fig. 11–21 Base gasket installation, showing gasket being slipped on studs

Installing the cylinder assembly over the pistons requires special care and patience. *Don't force anything.* The base of the cylinder is tapered to allow the rings to slide into the barrel more easily. Use some clean light oil on the piston rings and cylinder when reassembling them to guard against scoring when the bike is first started (Fig. 11–22).

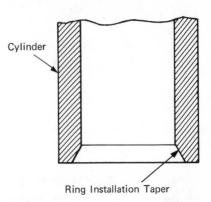

Fig. 11–22 Barrel ring installation taper, showing taper at base of cylinder

Follow the manufacturer's instructions for retorquing cylinder head studs—aluminum heads distort easily if you don't. Many mechanics take several passes at this first, torquing the nuts to half, then three-quarters, and finally to full torque setting. Be sure to follow the recommended sequence when torquing the head.

If you're working with an overhead-cam engine don't forget to keep the cam chain suspended throughout the installation of both the barrel and the head. Refasten the cam chain only after the cam is properly reindexed according to the technique recommended in the factory service manual (Fig. 11–23).

Buttoning Up

Reinstall the carburetors, points, plates, covers, and accessories that should be in place before the engine is put back into the frame. Leave yourself access to the valve adjustment and the points, however, and set them as well as you can before

Fig. 11-23 Cam indexing (1) Woodruff key, (2) "O" mark, (3) cam chain

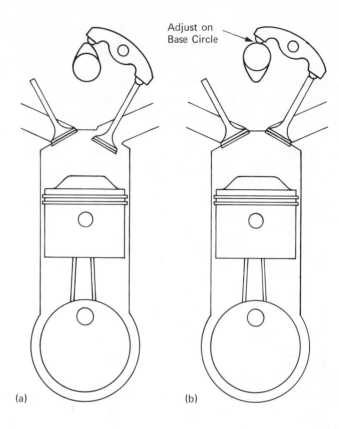

Adjust on Base Circle

(a)   (b)

Fig. 11-24 Locating the cam on the base circle

you start the engine. Poor timing and bad valve adjustment can ruin the "breaking in" of a rebuilt engine.

Sure-Fire Valve Adjustment. If adjusting valves is still a mystery to you, remember one thing: "The crankshaft rotates twice while the cam rotates once." It follows, then, that if you rotate the engine with a box end wrench on the bolt head end of the crank until a valve is all the way down, the same cam follower will be at the center of its base circle with one more revolution of the crank. When the cam follower is on the base circle in the proper place to adjust valves—it doesn't matter if the valve is an exhaust or intake valve—you will have the valve in the proper place on the cam for adjustment (Fig. 11-24).

Check the valve adjustment settings with a feeler gage. Set them as close to factory specifications as you can, but don't wear out the adjuster nuts doing it.

Retime the engine statically, carefully following the directions given in the ignition chapter in this book, then you should be ready to reinstall the engine.

Remounting the Engine. Make sure the engine cases, mounting plates, bolts, and nuts are clean before you remount the engine. Dirty mounting areas are bound to loosen up after a few hours of riding, and no one wants their engine to fall out—especially after top-end overhaul! Re-

member, when you reconnect the wiring, carburetors, exhaust system, and fuel system that these are all delicately tuned sections of the motorcycle. Keep everything clean. Take time to reinstall *all* nuts, bolts, brackets, clips, gaskets, and retainers properly. Sure, you're eager to try out your newly rebuilt top end, but don't hurry the final stages of this job and risk damaging what you've just improved.

Break-In

This same principle of careful restraint holds true also for the break-in procedure. Disregard the old tale: "Break 'em in fast, they run fast. Break 'em in slow, they run slow." Any engine that's flogged right after it is rebuilt is destined for a short life and poor performance. Since no ring manufacturer has control of the exact finish and crosshatch angle of a cylinder, the new rings require a certain period of time to seat against the cylinder wall. If this break-in period is a controlled, leisurely one, then the rings can seat without too much wear either to the wall or the rings.

This careful approach insures good seating and keeps the final ring end gap smaller. A violent break-in period will make the rings and cylinder wear too fast causing excessive end gap.

Having given the bike a good static tune-up, start the engine on a good set of plugs and fresh oil. Listen for any distinct metallic noises that weren't there before. If you hear strange noises, turn off the engine and correct the problem.

Again with the engine warming up, check the timing with a strobe light and adjust the timing if necessary. After the engine has warmed up, check the carburetion adjustments for cable synchronization, idle mixture, and idle speed (Fig. 11–25).

By now the machine should be ready to take for a break-in ride, assuming, of course, you've adjusted the chain, control cables, and other items on your "pre-flight" checklist. Be careful as you dab the shift lever into first gear. Often a clutch that hasn't been run for a while is sticky and will stall the engine. Instead, coast the bike along a bit in neutral and dab for first while you're

rolling. Pull in the clutch and rev the engine a bit to free the sticky plates. Remember three important points during your initial break-in ride:

1. Don't overheat the engine.
2. Don't lug the engine.
3. Don't over-rev the engine.

After an hour or two of gentle riding, change the oil, reset the valves, and double-check the timing. Look for seeping gaskets, fuel leaks, loose bolts, etc. After the engine cools down, retorque the cylinder head and all other nuts and bolts you worked on.

Changing the oil a couple of times in the next thousand miles or so will carry away any microscopic particles that sluff off during the break-in period and will help insure the success of your four-stroke top-end overhaul.

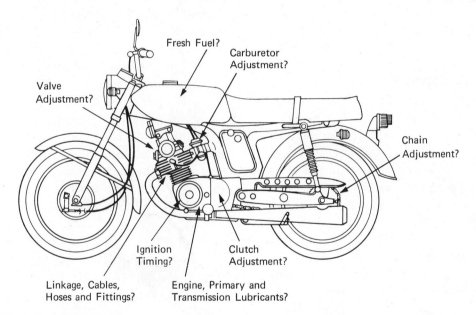

Fig. 11–25 Final check for adjustments, fuel, and oil

Single Cylinder Lower End

GENERAL THEORY

All two-stroke or four-stroke motorcycle engines have one thing in common — the crankshaft. They use this same basic device to convey the powerful energy released by burning gasoline and convert it into useful rotary motion. Combustion pressure literally "turns the crank." The heart of every engine is its lower end — the crankshaft and parts associated with it that convert linear motion into rotary motion. The crank has come a long way from the hoist used to raise a bucket of well water. In the modern motorcycle the crank operates at speeds measured in thousands of rpm, it deals with forces measured in thousands of pounds, and at temperatures in the hundreds of degrees. The lower end must have great strength and rigidity to handle these forces without bending or breaking. The crank assembly depends on highest quality bearings, tightest fits and clearances, and the best lubrication in the entire engine to do its job smoothly without rattling apart or burning up from friction.

When we look at the engine as a cranking device, the parts (Fig. 12–1) function as follows. The piston is acted upon by the pressure of expanding gases in the combustion chamber. The piston is free to slide in the straight, linear cylin-der. The piston transmits its linear motion to the small end of the connecting rod through a pivot joint made up of the wristpin and the wristpin bearing. The other end of the connecting rod, the big end, has another pivot joint where the rod is connected to the crankshaft throw. The small end of the rod undergoes linear (piston) motion and the big end of the rod undergoes rotary (crankshaft) motion. The rod undergoes an angular combination of linear and rotary motion. The crankshaft receives angular pushes from the rod at the crankpin or rod bearing. The crankpin is rigidly mounted in two flywheels. The crankpin-flywheel assembly rotates on the main bearings and puts out useful rotary force, torque, through the main shaft. The crankshaft main bearings are supported by the engine crankcase that also serves to enclose the crankshaft assembly and mount the cylinder.

This basic design is the same for all piston engines, but manufacturers have refined and added many different features to this basic design. Most single-cylinder engines use a "built up" crankshaft (Fig. 12–2). This type of crank is made of a crankpin and a pair of flywheels that are pressed together. The crankpin is a tight interference fit in the two flywheels. In most cases, the main shafts are integral with the flywheels, but sometimes

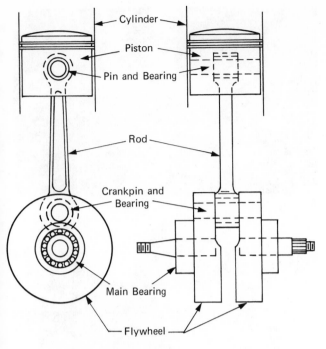

Fig. 12-1   Lower end components

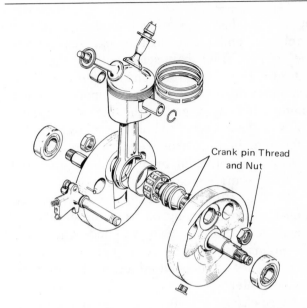

Fig. 12-3   A typical bolt-up crankshaft (Norton Triumph)

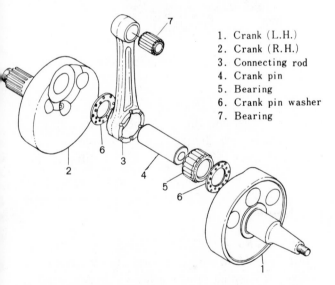

1. Crank (L.H.)
2. Crank (R.H.)
3. Connecting rod
4. Crank pin
5. Bearing
6. Crank pin washer
7. Bearing

Fig. 12-2   A typical built-up crankshaft (Yamaha International Corporation)

they too are pressed in. In some models, the crankpin is tapered, the flywheels are taper-bored, and the assembly is secured by large crankpin nuts (Fig. 12-3). Built-up crankshaft assemblies usually employ roller-type connecting-rod bearings, since disassembly of the crank permits installation of a one-piece rod. This type of bearing uses the hardened crankpin as its inner race and the big end of the one-piece rod as the

outer race. Some designs use bronze thrust washers at the sides of the rod. Engines have oil passageways drilled into the crankshaft to provide lubrication directly to the big-end rod bearing (Fig. 12-4). Crank mainshafts are designed with some means of fixing a gear, or sprocket, or magneto flywheel at each end. Tapers, keyways, splines, and threads are the most common ways of securing the shaft to the gear or sprocket it drives.

Main bearings are usually ball or roller type. A crankshaft mounted in roller bearings will have

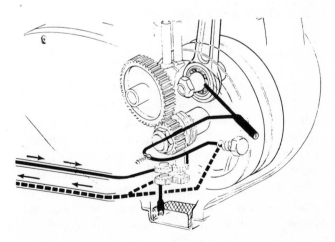

Fig. 12-4   Oil passages in crank (Triumph Norton Incorporated)

137

either a washer or bearing provided to restrict crankshaft end play. Most crankcases support one or two crankshaft seals outside the main bearings. In a two-stroke engine, the crankcase functions both as main bearing supports and as a compression chamber for the fuel-air mixture. Crankshaft seals serve to hold this pressure in the cases and, in four-stroke engines, are used to keep engine lubricating oil in the sump and out of the primary drive area.

All four-stroke engines have a crankcase drain plug for emptying oil from the crankcase. Some two-strokes are also provided with crankcase drains that are very convenient for draining the cases of accumulated oil and fuel, and occasionally water.

Crankcases are split either horizontally (Fig. 12–5a) or vertically (Fig. 12–5b). Whichever way they do split, they are well secured by a number of bolts or screws and sealed to prevent leaks. Many engines are designed with a gasket between the crankcase halves, but others are designed without a gasket and depend on carefully mated sealing sufaces and a sealing compound at the joint. Alignment studs or pins hold crankshaft main bearings in proper alignment when the crankcase halves are assembled. Locating pins are also used to locate bearings and to prevent them from spinning in their bores in the crankcase.

DIAGNOSIS AND SERVICE

We are really getting to the heart of things when we decide that it is necessary to "pull down" the lower end of an engine. Breather and seal repairs notwithstanding, a lower-end overhaul is about the most important work we can perform on an engine. For this reason we should be sure that the decision to "split the cases" is the correct one. Many a crankcase has been disassembled because of a loose primary chain or clutch hub nut. The major nature of a lower-end overhaul well warrants a little extra diagnosis time prior to "digging in." The same reasoning applies to the teardown. A little extra time taken

(a)

(b)

Fig. 12–5   Split cases: (a) horizontal, and (b) vertical

to inspect parts as they are removed will insure that the cause of the malfunction is not overlooked. It is very disheartening to have an engine spread all over the work bench and still not know what is wrong with it, or what to fix.

Diagnosis

Oil Leaks. Crankcase oil leaks are the most minor lower-end malfunctions. They may occur as a slight seepage, or as a heavy stream gushing from the engine that covers everything on the bike with a disgusting coat of sludge. To repair any oil leak successfully and permanently, the mechanic must first identify the source (Exactly where is the oil getting out of the case?) and the cause of the leak (Why is it coming out there?). This usually requires that the engine be thoroughly cleaned, since oil leaking from one place on an engine may be blown over a large area making it impossible to see just where the leak really is. Once the engine is cleaned, the mechanic can run it, and see exactly where the oil starts to leak out. It could be from a seal or a gasket. Oil has even been known to seep down the threads of a bolt and leak out from under its head. Don't rule out porous castings either.

Just finding the oil leak may be hard enough, but the mechanic must also find the reason for the leak. Replacing a leaking seal may not repair the leak. Shafts and housings must be carefully inspected for nicks and scratches that could ruin the new seal, just like the old one. Gasket surfaces should be checked for surface distortion, nicks, and scratches to be sure that the new gasket won't leak or blow out like the old one.

There is a reason for everything that goes wrong with the motorcycle, and the experienced mechanic who removes a leaking seal, and finds no apparent reason for the leak, will become suspicious. A pinched breather hose may be the culprit, and it may not be necessary to replace the seal at all. The breather system should always be suspected any time oil is found seeping from every gasket, seal, crack, and crevice of the engine. The crankcase may simply be overfilled with oil. Or it may be "wet sumped" with gasoline. This common malady is the result of leaving the petcock turned on for some time after the engine has stopped running. Fuel will often leak out of the carburetor float bowl through the intake port and into the lower end. After a long time the lower end may fill up completely. Since liquid gasoline doesn't compress very well, and has to go somewhere to make room for the piston on its downstroke, it will usually blow out all the lower-end seals when an attempt is made to start the engine.

Two-Stroke Crankcase Leaks. Two-stroke engines depend on their crankcase seals to hold lower-end pressure and the vacuum used to pump fuel and air up the transfer ports to the top end. If these seals leak, performance suffers due to poor lower-end compression. In addition to poor performance, the engine may draw transmission oil through the seal on the engine's primary drive side, resulting in plug fouling and excessively smoky exhaust. If the magneto-side seal leaks, the engine may suck air and run lean and hot, and even seize or hole a piston. The crankcase center seal and cylinder base gaskets may also leak air, resulting in serious engine damage.

There are several crankcase leak-testing kits available for two-stroke engines. They consist of

a means of sealing the intake and exhaust ports, a pump, and a pressure gage. First, the intake and exhaust ports are sealed. Then the pump and gage are attached to the engine at the spark-plug hole. The engine is pressurized to about 6 psi, and the leakage rate is recorded. If the leakage rate is excessive, soapy water is brushed around areas suspected of leaks such as seals, head gasket, base gasket, crankcase seam, and last but not least, the test equipment may be checked for leaks. Once the leak has been located, the mechanic can take steps to replace the seal or gasket.

Noises. Pounding, rattling noises are usually the first indication of worn out lower-end bearings. These bearings operate under very heavy pounding loads. Excessive clearances and resultant up-and-down play in rods or main bearings will result in harsh pounding sensations that can be felt throughout the machine. Left unattended, these loose bearings could shatter and lock up the crankshaft. It is important to localize the source of any abnormal engine noise. There are many other parts in the engine that could make noises similar to a loose or scored lower-end bearing. A mechanic's stethoscope is very useful in localizing engine noises. Lacking a stethoscope, a long screwdriver can be held to the engine, (Fig. 12–6) the handle to the ear, and the tip moved around the engine to find where the noise seems loudest.

The speed, regularity, and engine loading at which noises occur often provide hints as to their sources. Sometimes just listening and feeling the engine as it is kicked through will produce the noise in such a way that you can tell exactly where it is. But diagnosing the source of engine noises just by listening is sometimes impossible. What we need is some real physical evidence. The search for evidence begins with the engine oil. Remove the crankcase drain. Are there bits of metal in the oil? What kinds of metal? Remove the spark plug. Is there any metal on the plug? Two-strokes will often breathe little bits of lower-end bearings up the transfer ports and into the combustion chamber. Main-bearing problems can often be spotted and clearly identified without splitting the crankcase, with the engine still in the

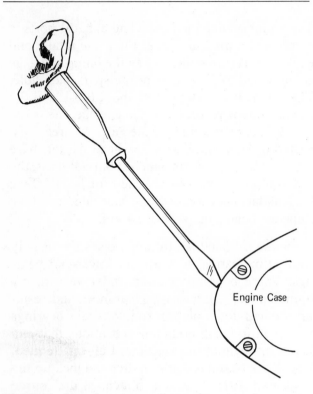

Fig. 12–6   Listening to a running engine

Fig. 12–7   Checking crankshaft end play

When the top end is off and inspected, and if there is no sign of our elusive noise yet, we then perform the age-old test. We grab the end of the connecting rod and push it up and down (Fig. 12–8a) feeling for tell-tale up and down looseness in the big end bearing. Check rod side clearance and the condition of thrust washers (Fig. 12–8b). The slightest detectable "up-and-down" play in the big end or main bearings will result in loud noise and rapid self-destruction of the engine. Side play is usually okay though.

frame. Remove the engine side covers and gain access to both ends of the crankshaft. Push the crankshaft up and down (Fig. 12–7a). There should be no detectable movement. Pull it in and out. Is there excessive end play? Rotate the crankshaft (Fig. 12–7b). Is there any grinding? Are there any tight spots? Does the main-bearing outer race turn in the crankcase? It should not.

If you've pulled off the side covers and still can't find the source of your noise, the next thing to do is pull down the top end. Make a careful inspection as the engine comes down. Examine the wear patterns on all parts; they will provide information as to what happens when the engine is running. A part that is worn abnormally may indicate the source of the engine noise. Don't forget to check piston clearances, cylinder distortion, and wrist-pin fit, because many suspected lower-end noises have been found in the top end. Worn and broken cam chains, tensioners, and sprockets will also produce loud noises from the lower end. Take careful note of the condition of the pushrods and lifters; these parts are also sources of a great deal of lower-end noise.

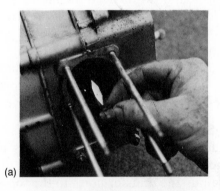
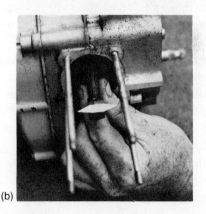

Fig. 12–8   Rod play up, down and side

Use a wristpin and a pair of parallels (ground pieces of machined steel) (Fig. 12–9) to determine whether the connecting rod is straight or bent.

If the main bearings, rod bearings, or a connecting rod must be replaced and the engine removed from the frame, the crankcases will have to be disassembled.

ness with 400- or 600-grit emery cloth. Lubricate the shaft and the new seal with light grease. A seal running dry would last only a few minutes. Slide the new seal over the end of the crankshaft. Threaded or splined shafts can easily cut the seal lip during this operation. To avoid this, many manufacturers provide seal protectors (Fig. 12–11), special assembly tools that are installed over the rough crank and provide a smooth shaft over which to slide the new seal as it is installed.

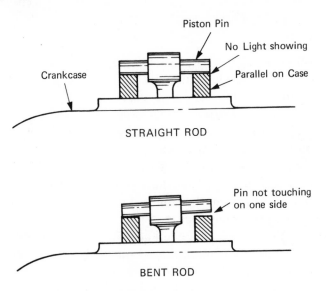

Fig. 12–9 Checking for a bent rod

Service Procedures

Seal Replacement. Many engines are designed so that crankcase seals can be replaced without removing the engine or disassembling the crankcases. An outer spoke can be ground to make a very serviceable seal remover (Fig. 12–10). Insert the hook under the lip of the seal and

Fig. 12–10 Seal removing tool: a spoke that has been ground and bent to shape

pull it out. Use care not to scratch the shaft when it goes through the seal. Inspect the seal for wear and signs of damage. Inspect the shaft for burrs or scratches that would wear the delicate sharp edge of the seal lip. Polish out any scratches or rough-

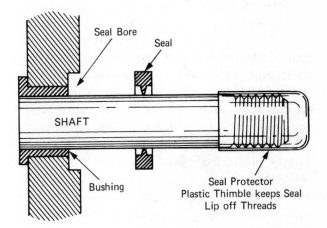

Fig. 12–11 Seal protector

Use a round seal driver to drive the new seal squarely home in its bore in the crankcase. If a special driving tool is not available, a large deep-well socket may be used to drive the seal home by its outer edge.

Many two-stroke engines have a smooth collar on the crankshaft where it goes through the seal. The collar can be slid off the end of the crankshaft to provide easy access for pulling the seal. This collar should be inspected for scratches and smoothed up just as the crankshaft. There will always be an O-ring on crankshafts that employ this type of collar. The O-ring prevents leakage between the crankshaft and the collar and should be replaced at the same time as the seal.

Overhaul Preparation. A lower-end overhaul is a big job and demands adequate preparation. Once it is determined that the engine is coming out, and down, it is time to stop, clean up, arrange the work area, and plan the operation.

Before the job is started, read the service manual and become familiar with the recommended engine removal and disassembly procedures. Be sure that all necessary or special tools are available. Have at hand enough parts containers to keep the job neat and organized. Have at hand paper and pencil to list the new parts that are required and to record fits and clearances that are measured during disassembly.

Engine Removal. Removing and replacing a motorcycle engine is an easy job. It is often rushed and done sloppily. There are probably more odd parts left over from engine removal and replacement than from the overhaul, especially strange little things like cable guides, cable clips, ground straps, tab washers, and the like. The key to a good job here is organization. Label parts if necessary. Keep units together (all exhaust pipe fittings in one box, all carburetor fittings in another box, etc.). Return nuts, bolts, washers, clips, plates, etc., after the part or engine is removed to their original positions and screw them together loosely. Then reinstallation will be easier, and no one will be able to tell that the engine was out. There will be no question where a fastener belongs.

Follow the sequence of operations given in the manufacturer's service manual. Many engines can be removed only from one side of the frame. Others must be partially disassembled before they can be removed. The service manual for the model provides all of this specialized information.

Once the engine is out, it is most easily worked on in an engine stand, if one is available. A vise-mounted engine fixture is the next best thing to a floor-type stand. Many mechanics prefer to work on the bench with a wooden box or platform to steady the engine (Fig. 12–12). At any rate, some device is in order to steady the engine because this makes disassembly work much easier and surer. It is difficult, often destructive, to try to work on an unsteady engine.

Preparing for Case Splitting. Before the crankcases can be disassembled, a number of

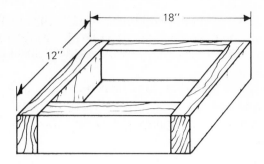

Fig. 12–12 Engine support, showing 2 × 4 fixture

other assemblies must be removed from the engine. The service manual will detail the sequence of disassembly for these parts. Usually the top end, primary drive, shift linkage, cam drive, and alternator or magneto assemblies must all be removed. Here again, parts should be stored in small containers and in groups (clutch parts, magneto parts, etc.). List the parts that must be replaced as you notice them. Don't forget the circlips, tab washers, etc.

When no parts are left attached across the two case halves and all the case bolts and screws have been removed, you are ready to split the cases (Fig. 12–13). Recheck for hidden fasteners.

Fig. 12–13 Horizontal case ready to split: bolts, nuts, and accessories have been removed

Splitting the Cases. Motorcycle engine crankcases split in two ways: horizontal split or vertical split. Just looking at the engine, it will be obvious which way the crankcases come apart, but *do* read the manufacturer's service manual. Every engine is designed to be split by a specific procedure. Failure to adhere to the specific details of the recommended procedures will almost always result in damaged or ruined crankcase halves or rods. Here are some general rules and techniques.

Determine which side of the crankcase is to be removed. Try to avoid disturbing the transmission shafts and gears that should remain in the other case half.

Horizontal-split cases are usually split in line with all shafts in the engine and transmission. A common procedure is to invert the assembly and lift off the lower case half, leaving all the shafts in the top case half (Fig. 12–14). Use a rubber mallet to tap the case halves apart gently. Never pry the cases apart with a screwdriver or chisel. If horizontal cases won't tap apart, then some bolt or screw or clip on some shaft is still in place and is holding the cases together. Continued beating and prying will only ruin the crankcases. If cases don't come apart after normal tapping, stop a minute and take a careful look to be sure there is no overlooked fastener holding them together.

ing tools that pull the crankcase halves off the main bearings, much the same as a gear is pulled from a shaft (Fig. 12–15). Some manufacturers recommend heating the crankcase bearing boss with a propane torch to relieve the interference fit of the main bearing, then tapping the cases apart with a soft mallet (Fig. 12–16).

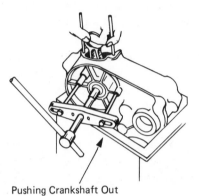

Pushing Crankshaft Out

Fig. 12–15   Using a crankcase bearing separator

Fig. 12–14   Separating the horizontal split case

Horizontal split cases are by far the easier type to work with. A few taps of the mallet and the bottom pops off, and there everything is—ready for examination.

Such is not the case with vertical split crankcases. Bearings are often an interference fit (have zero or negative clearance) on their shafts and in their cases. The result is an assembly that must be pushed, pulled, or carefully tapped apart. Many manufacturers provide special crankcase-separat-

Fig. 12–16   Tapping the case apart; vertical and horizontal are done in the same way, carefully!

This operation requires patience and careful, even tapping around the case, because the crankcase must be tapped off squarely. If it gets cocked too much, it may jam in place and subsequent hammering may distort and ruin it. If a crankcase starts to move and then sticks tight, reheat it and try to tap it down square again. Then get another start. Tap transmission shafts with the rubber mallet to keep them in the other case half, and to keep the upper case coming along evenly. When the case is free, lift it off and replace any shims that may have been dislodged on the shafts. The crank and transmission shafts can then be tapped out of the other case half individually. Usually bearings must be drifted out of vertical split cases (Fig. 12–17). Again, heat is used to expand the aluminum crankcases and relieve the interference fit.

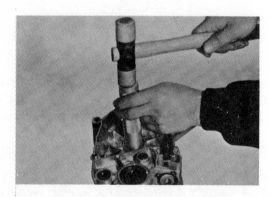

Fig. 12–17 Bearing removal (Yamaha International Corporation)

Cleaning. Clean all parts in degreasing solvent: Varsol, or triclorethane, or one of the commercial degreasers. A recirculating solvent tank is the most convenient means of cleaning parts, but a drain pan and parts brush do the job just as well. A wire brush will loosen stubborn dirt and burned oil. Remove all traces of dirt, grit, metal shavings, etc. Loose dirt will ruin a newly rebuilt engine in no time. When parts are clean, dry them with clean rags or low-pressure compressed air. Oil the bearings lightly and the other steel parts that might rust.

Inspection. During the cleaning process, make a careful visual inspection of all parts. The purpose of the teardown inspection is to determine the full extent and cause of engine damage.

Obvious damage, heat discoloration, galling, and cracks are the main reasons for parts replacement. Patterns of destruction tell the story of every engine failure. A careful inspection of wear patterns in an engine can provide information about the cause of engine failure. The cause of an engine failure must be corrected or the failure is sure to recur. Remember, failure is always the *effect,* not the cause.

Examine piston wear patterns. Polished spots show areas of extreme cylinder-wall pressure (Fig. 12–18). Normal piston wear occurs as matte gray areas at the front and rear of the skirt—the piston's primary and secondary thrust surfaces. Uneven side wear at the skirt or on top of the piston indicates improper lower-end geometry, resulting in piston side thrust. Examine the wristpin fit in the piston and in the connecting rod small end bearing. Examine the small end bearing for heat discoloration, scratches, galling, or excessive clearance. In most cases, the wrist pin should be a tight push fit in the cold piston, and a light sliding fit in the small end bearing.

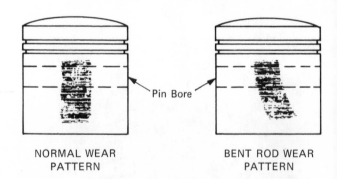

NORMAL WEAR PATTERN · Pin Bore · BENT ROD WEAR PATTERN

Fig. 12–18 Piston wear pattern

Examine the connecting rod for cracks or discoloration. Check the rod for straightness with the crankshaft rod assembly in the engine cases. Use a wristpin and pair of machinist's parallels as shown in Fig. 12–9. The connecting rod big end bearing should have no up-and-down play at all. Check side-to-side clearance against manufacturer's specifications. The lightly oiled big end bearing should turn freely with no scratching or hissing sounds. Main bearings should also be in perfect condition with no detectable play, scoring, or tightness. They must, of course, be absolutely clean.

Check that the crankshaft assembly is true. Install the assembly between centers as shown in

Fig. 12–19. Use the dial indicator to measure fly-wheel and shaft runout. The manufacturers' specifications listed in the shop manual will give maximum allowable deflections.

Examine the surfaces of the mainshaft and crankcase main bearing bases for evidence of a turning outer race. A bearing race that is spinning in the case or on the shaft will polish or score the case bore surface.

When the full extent of engine damage or wear and the cause of failure has been determined, the list of parts to be replaced or reconditioned can be completed.

Fig. 12–20 A Suzuki Crankshaft Kit

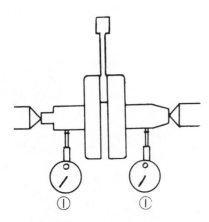

Fig. 12–19 Crankshaft assembly runout (Yamaha International Corporation)

Replace Defective Parts. Seals, O-rings, gaskets, lock tab washers, and spring snap rings should be replaced as a matter of course during a lower-end overhaul. The small cost of these items is cheap insurance, considering the expensive damage that can result from their failure.

Parts that are obviously broken or weakened should, of course, be replaced with new parts. Parts worn past their size tolerances should also be replaced. Large expensive parts that are only slightly damaged often need not be replaced, but may be reconditioned.

If the lower-end rod bearing is damaged, it is usually necessary to replace the rod, crankpin, rollers, cage, thrust washers, and expansion plugs. These parts are often available as a set (Fig. 12–20).

Reconditioning. Crankcases and crankshafts are the most commonly reconditioned parts in the lower end. They are by far the most expensive parts and, therefore, often worth the effort.

Broken or cracked crankcases present the appearance of total financial disaster to many riders, but sometimes they might be salvaged by a skilled welder who uses special welding equipment (Fig. 12–21). The machining operations that are almost always required after the welding should be entrusted only to a competent shop. The extent of damage determines whether a set of crankcases are worth repair or not. Whereas a cracked transmission casing may be easy to repair, it is impossible to reconstruct a set of engine cases from a basketful of aluminum shrapnel.

Fig. 12–21 Welded case, showing completed weld on left side

Crankcase bores that secure main bearings and transmission bearings become scored occasionally or enlarged by a spinning outer race. This enlargement ruins the bearings interference fit in the bore. A new bearing would continue to spin in the case and continue to wear the bore. Cases worn in this way (Fig. 12–22) need not always be discarded. Bearing mount (Lock-tite) cements are available for securing bearings in loose bores. Such cement provides an inexpensive solution, provided that the bearing bore is not worn more than 0.002 to 0.003 inch oversize.

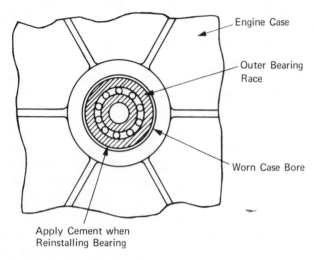

Fig. 12–22   Bearing installed on worn case bore

Crankcases with damaged sealing surfaces should be cleaned up with a draw file (Fig. 12–23). Case surfaces that are slightly distorted can be lapped together with coarse, then fine, grinding paste to insure a leak-tight joint (Fig. 12–24).

Crankshaft threads are often damaged during forceful disassembly of the crankcase. Although damage can usually be avoided by replacing the nuts on the ends of shafts before striking them and by using soft hammers, the advice often comes too late. A properly sized thread-restoring die is usually all that is necessary to reclaim the damaged crank (Fig. 12–25). Often the shaft is mushroomed so much that the die cannot be started. The best tool available for repairing this condition is a thread-chasing file (Fig. 12–26). Teeth on the thread-chasing file are arranged in standard thread patterns. The file can be used to reduce the shaft diameter while retaining the thread.

Crankshaft keyways and tapers are often ruined by a loose magneto flywheel. The Wood-

Fig. 12–23   Draw filing a case, showing a large single cut file being drawn across case

Fig. 12–24   Lapping a case

Fig. 12–25   Chasing threads: die is placed in diestock on crank-thread end, with the crank in a vise

Fig. 12–26   A thread-chasing file

ruff key (Fig. 12–27) only locates the flywheel—it does not secure the wheel to the shaft. The wheel is secured to the shaft by the tight taper fit of the

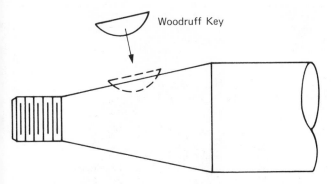

Fig. 12–27 Woodruff key and its position or keyway in shaft

shaft in the flywheel. If the flywheel is not tight on the tapered shaft, it will shear the Woodruff key and spin on the shaft. This will score and gall the tapered surfaces of the shaft and flywheel, and often ruin both the shaft and flywheel keyways.

Scored tapers can be repaired by lapping the flywheel onto the shaft using a fine lapping compound (Fig. 12–28). Grinding the parts together increases the contact area that is needed for a tight, nonslip fit of the flywheel on the shaft. After lapping the shaft, the bore must be meticulously cleaned. Any grinding compound that remains will surely cause engine damage. A drop of Locktite cement will provide additional insurance that the flywheel will not spin again.

Fig. 12–28 Lapping a flywheel and shaft

Distorted keyways can be cleaned up with a small file. If both slots have been widened, a slightly larger Woodruff key may be necessary for a snug fit. Sometimes keyways are damaged beyond repair. A machinist will be able to cut new keyways in both the shaft and the flywheel. The cost of replacing the flywheel and crankshaft should be weighted against this expensive repair cost.

Top-End and Transmission Parts. While the lower end is apart, chances are that the top end and the transmission are also disassembled. This provides an opportunity to inspect these assemblies. Consider replacing any parts that are worn past their tolerances, or that are close to their tolerances or show abnormal wear.

Reassembly. Before you begin to reassemble the lower end, be sure that the assembly area is extremely clean. Small particles of grit and dirt can severely damage lower-end bearings. Read the assembly procedures in the manufacturer's service manual carefully and completely. Identify each part and its sequence in assembly before beginning.

The first step to pressing the crankshaft assembly apart for parts replacement is to inspect the ends of the crankpin. Some crankpins are fitted with expansion plugs or pins. These are small tapered pins in the ends of the main crankpin and are found in some European bikes like Bultaco and CZ. These smaller pins must be drilled out. If the crankpin is a one-piece unit, however, it can be removed without the extra drilling step. Using about a 20-ton press, and suitable fixtures as recommended in your shop manual, press the pin out of the top flywheel. After removing the rod, bearings, cage, and thrust washers, press the pin out of the second flywheel. Press the new crankpin into one flywheel. Wipe the crankpin clean and lightly oil it. Assemble the thrust washers, cage, rollers, and rod onto the crankpin. Insure that the bearing and crankpin form a light "running fit." The rod should spin freely but show no radial or lateral play. Align the flywheels, then press on the second flywheel about 1/16 inch (Fig. 12–29). Remove the assembly from the press. Use a wristpin or other suitable straight edge to check flywheel alignment as shown. Correct any flywheel misalignment by tapping with a brass or lead hammer. Reinstall the assembly in the press and continue to press home the second flywheel.

Fig. 12–29 Crankshaft reassembly sequence: (a) press crankpin into first flywheel about 1/16″, (b) check pin for squareness to flywheel, (c) straighten and press the pin into flywheel, (d) assemble thrust washers, cage, rollers, and rod on pin, (e) align flywheels and start second flywheel on pin 1/16″, check flywheel alignment with straight-edge, (f) correct adjustment by tapping with soft hammer, (g) press second flywheel to rod and check side clearance using feeler gauge

Use a feeler gage to set the rod end clearance to manufacturer's specifications. Once the flywheels have been pressed together to the proper rod end clearance, the crank assembly is ready to be trued.

Crank flywheels may be out of alignment as shown in Fig. 12–30. A set of centers and an indicator, as shown earlier in Fig. 12–19, are absolutely necessary for accurate crank truing. After inspecting the centering bores in the ends of the crankshaft, mount the crankshaft lightly between two centers. Make sure it spins freely, with no noticeable end play. Flywheel misalignment, as shown in part C of Fig. 12–30, should be checked and corrected first. After removing the crankshaft from the centers, use a soft metal (brass) hammer to tap the flywheels until they are within 0.001″ to 0.002″ of being perfectly parallel. Remount the crankshaft assembly in centers and recheck the alignment. Next, use a wedge or C-clamp to cor-

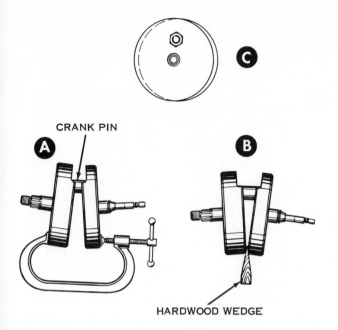

CRANK PIN

HARDWOOD WEDGE

Fig. 12–30 Crank flywheel misalignment

vice manual directions for the manufacturer's specific reassembly procedure. Many manufacturers provide special tools to pull the crankshaft or main bearing into the cases (Fig. 12–31). But many manufacturers still require that the cases be heated and tapped onto the shafts and bearings. This technique requires patience and evenness in tapping on each case. If a bearing becomes cocked in its bore, it may stick and it will be difficult to get the crankcase on or back off. Tap evenly around the edge of the crankcases, rotate the shafts to insure that they don't hang in their bearings. Follow the manufacturer's specifications when tightening and torquing case screws or bolts.

rect a flywheel that is out of parallel. This is shown in parts (a) and (b) of Fig. 12–30. Don't expect the crankshaft truing process to be an easy affair the first time. A mechanic cannot overstress the "patience necessary" to true a crankshaft. Careful, accurate checking and rechecking are required. Making adjustments on the order of a thousandths of an inch with a 4-pound lead hammer takes a little practice.

When the crankshaft rod assembly is trued, it is ready to receive the main bearings. Main bearings are often an interference fit on the mainshafts. If this is the case, heat the bearing in a pan of oil to 400° F. This will expand the bearing to a light sliding fit so that it can be slid onto the mainshaft easily. The crankshaft main-bearing assembly is now ready to be installed in the crankcases.

Before reassembling the crankcases, be sure that all seals, gaskets, locating pins, and transmission shafts, shims, and bearings are in place. Oil all moving parts lightly and apply any sealants recommended by the manufacturers.

Horizontal split cases are usually assembled with the upper case inverted on the workbench, holding all the engine shafts. The bottom cover is simply laid on and bolted down. This bolting down should follow the manufacturer's torquing sequence and specifications.

Vertically split cases are not so easy to reassemble as the horizontal split type. Refer to ser-

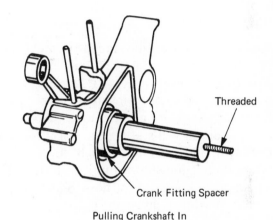

Threaded

Crank Fitting Spacer

Pulling Crankshaft In

Fig. 12–31 Pulling the crank assembly and main bearing into the case

Before final assembly, be sure that all shafts turn freely without binding. Check the shifting operation if possible. When the lower end and crankcase have been assembled and checked, install the assemblies that were removed to gain access to the lower end.

When the alternator or magneto, shifter, primary device, clutch, and top-end assemblies have been installed, adjusted, and carefully checked for proper operation, the engine is ready for reinstallation into the frame. Careful checking and adjustment will insure that the engine will start up right after it has been installed in the frame. This on-the-bench tune-up prior to frame installation should include valve adjustment, cam drive adjustment, ignition timing, and clutch throwout adjustment. The service manual will detail the specific order for installation procedures. Be sure that every fastener is installed just as it was removed. Be sure that locking washers and nuts are doing their job—a loose engine mount or axle can be disasterous on a motorcycle at speed. Be sure that all cable guides and clips are located correctly. Check the routing of all wires and cables; these must not be bound, pinched, or stretched. Check carefully for carburetor and exhaust leaks that could destroy your newly rebuilt engine. Top up the engine and transmission oils. Be sure that the fuel supply is fresh, the battery charged, and the bike ready for starting.

Starting and Break-In

A newly rebuilt engine, tuned on the bench, with fresh fuel and good spark, should start within the first two or three kicks. If it doesn't, something is wrong. Check to insure that the gas is fresh and spark is getting to the plugs. An engine in good condition will start right up if it has gas, compression, and spark in the right time.

When the engine starts, run it at a brisk idle and check for oil pressure or flow. Some engines are provided with oil pressure lights; some with return lines to the oil bottles. If the engine is a two-stroke equipped with an oil injection pump, disconnect the pressure line and check to see that there is a flow of oil into the engine. If engine oil is not being injected or circulated as it should be, shut the engine off immediately. It cannot run long on just its assembly oil. Locate and correct the lubrication failure. Maybe that's why the engine broke in the first place!

Once the mechanic is sure the engine is running and lubricating itself, he will listen to the engine running. He will listen to be sure it sounds and feels right—not too loose and not too tight. He will adjust the carburetor and see that the engine revs up and idles down smoothly and evenly. He will make sure that it is not running too hot. He will certainly listen for any noises that may have been the reason for the overhaul.

A lower-end overhaul is worth at least 5 or 10 miles of road test and break-in, during which the engine is run under light loads and at varying speeds. Any problems that might arise from an engine overhaul will usually show up in the first few miles of operation. Check the engine for vacuum, exhaust, and oil leaks. Check all controls for proper operation. Check top-end compression, and perform a crankcase leakage test on the engine to insure that it is in first-class condition. Recheck the ignition timing and valve adjustment after the engine has cooled from the test ride. Be sure that it starts snappily even when it's cool. Change the engine oil and filters soon after an overhaul to rinse out any dust or lint that might have entered during assembly or any small bits of metal that have scraped loose as new engine parts "settled in."

MultiCylinder Lower Ends

There are many advantages to using multiple cylinders to achieve a given displacement in a motorcycle engine. More power can easily be produced from a displacement range by the multiple cylinder approach. As a bonus, since power pulses are smaller and occur more frequently, the engine runs much more smoothly. The disadvantages show themselves in the extra costs and added weight involved in a multiple cylinder engine.

ENGINE DESIGNS

There are many approaches to designing multicylinder engines. The most popular and simplest is the twin or two-cylinder engine.

Conventional two-stroke twins use a 180° crankshaft, so that one piston is coming down while the other is going up. With two evenly spaced power strokes for each crankshaft revolution, the two-cycle twin is as smooth as a four-cycle four-cylinder machine (Fig. 13–1).

In-line four-stroke twins have a built-in dilemma. If they use a 180° crankshaft, the power pulses occur 180° apart with 540° of the cycle idle. If they use a 360° crankshaft, the power pulses occur evenly spaced 360° apart, but the pistons must go up and down together. This piston action leads to harsh engine vibration and balance problems (Fig. 13–2).

Some Japanese manufacturers have attempted to improve the four-stroke twin by adding extra counterweight shafts to cancel out the engine's tendency to vibrate (Fig. 13–3).

Four-Stroke V-Twins

The V-twin is an old basic design that has been used by the major American manufacturer since motorcycling's early times. The design is narrow and compact—just right for fitting into a motorcycle frame which a rider must straddle. The 60° angle between the cylinder bores dictates that a long stroke and a small bore be used (Fig. 13–4). Though an old design, the V-twin makes up for its lack of sophistication with large displacement and high quality components.

Horizontal Opposed Engines

Volkswagen has successfully used a horizontally opposed engine in their famous "bug" to change the world's transportation pattern in the last three decades. This excellent engine design is found in another German product, the BMW motorcycle. The crankpin locations enable the two

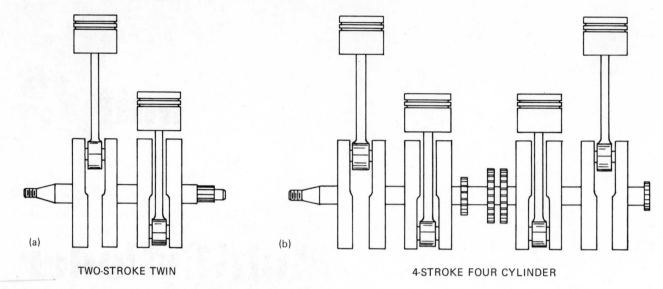

TWO-STROKE TWIN

4-STROKE FOUR CYLINDER

Fig. 13-1 Two stroke (a) and four-stroke multicylinder (b) lower ends

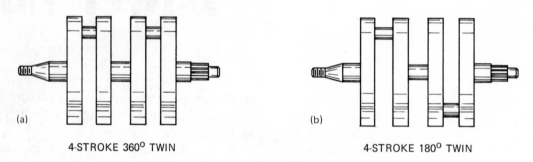

4-STROKE 360° TWIN

4-STROKE 180° TWIN

Fig. 13-2 Four stroke twins (a) 360° and (b) 180°

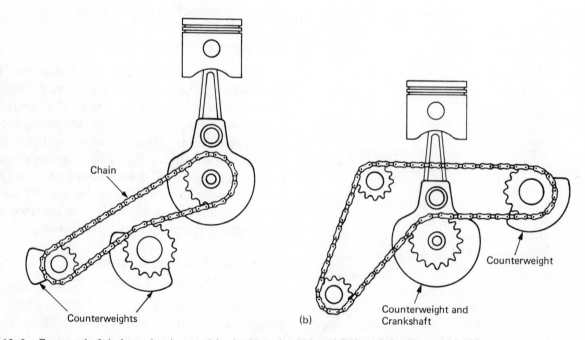

Chain

Counterweights

Counterweight

Counterweight and Crankshaft

Fig. 13-3 Countershaft balanced twins used in the Yamaha 500 and 750 and the Kawasaki 400

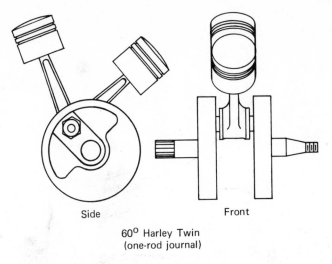

Side   Front

60° Harley Twin
(one-rod journal)

Fig. 13–4 The 60° twin Harley-Davidson

pistons to balance out each other's tendency to cause the engine to vibrate. The BMW engine lends itself to an automotive type of drive train arrangement with a dry, single-disc clutch and shaft-type final drive (Fig. 13–5). The Honda GL 1000 is a further refinement using a 4 cylinder, overhead cam horizontal engine.

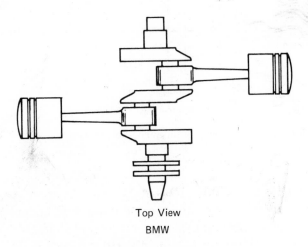

Top View
BMW

Fig. 13–5 The BMW opposed twin

Crankshafts

The reciprocating motion of the pistons is converted to rotating motion by the crankshaft. This desirable function makes it one of the very important parts of the engine.

There are two types of crankshafts: "built-up" and "one-piece." The built-up crankshaft is a group of wheels and shafts that are pressed together. The one-piece crankshaft is cut or forged from only one piece of metal, although accessory pieces such as flywheel weights may be bolted to it (Fig. 13–6).

Built-Up Crankshafts. In order to take advantage of roller bearings for use on connecting rod journals, some multicylinder crankshafts are built up from their various components. Virtually all two-stroke engines use this design. [The oil mist easily penetrates a roller bearing but could not properly lubricate an insert-type bearing.] In order for the crankshaft to be sturdy enough to withstand the pounding loads it receives, it must be pressed together with a very tight fit. A strong hydraulic press is required to accomplish this.

Let's take a look at the components as they are assembled (Fig. 13–7). The crankshafts are the centrally located bars around which the flywheels and crankpins rotate. They locate the assembly and provide a strong basis for crankshaft operation. In multi-cylinder crankshafts, it is important that the individual shafts be aligned perfectly or vibration and short bearing life will result (Fig. 13–8).

The crankpins take quite a pounding from the rods. The pins are made from specially hardened polished steel and are pressed between the flywheel sections of the crankshaft. It is very important that their press fit be tight and straight for long, reliable bearing life.

Flywheels. To keep the crankshaft assembly rotating although no power is being applied by the piston, some of the crankshaft's rotating energy is stored in a flywheel. Once a heavy wheel is spinning, it tends to keep spinning. The spinning enables the piston to go through its exhaust, intake, and compression phases using the power stored in the flywheel.

Outside Ends of the Crankshaft. The outside ends of the crankshaft are specially made to accept components driven by the crank. One side is called the drive side because the power flows to

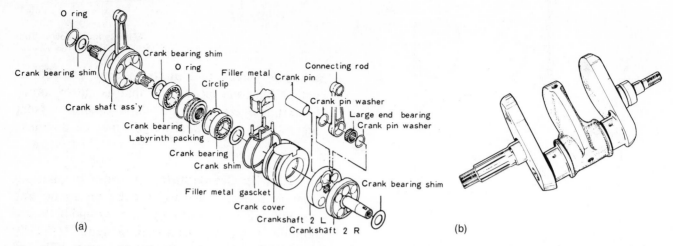

Fig. 13–6 Built-up Yamaha (a) and one-piece BSA (b) crankshafts (Yamaha International Corporation and Triumph Norton Incorporated)

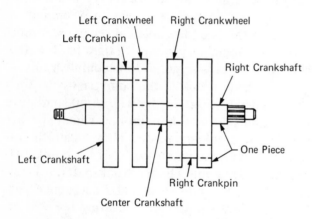

Fig. 13–7 Major built-up crankshaft components

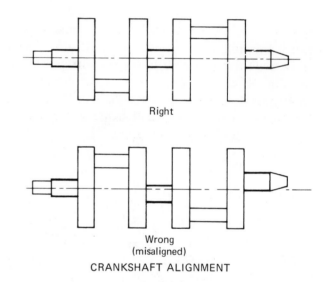

CRANKSHAFT ALIGNMENT

Fig. 13–8 Aligned and misaligned crank pins

the clutch and transmission through that side. The other side is called the "timing" side because ignition components, alternators, oil pumps, and other accessories are mounted there. The crankshaft ends are specially tapered or splined to handle these duties.

One-Piece Crankshafts. Some crankshafts are made from a single piece of metal. The metal may be cast, forged, or machined from a billet, but this crank does not come apart as a built-up crank does. Nearly all automobiles use this type of crankshaft.

The shaft has parts that perform certain functions as illustrated in Fig. 13–9.

The connecting rods on a one-piece crankshaft are split at their big ends and clamp onto the rod bearing journals over a pair of precision insert bearings. These assemblies are precision fit to

maintain a 0.001″ to 0.0025″ oil clearance between the bearing and the rod journal. Oil is pressure-fed through drillings in the crankshaft to the rod bearing journal (Fig. 13–10).

On many one-piece crankshafts the flywheel consists of a large annular iron ring that bolts around the center of the assembly. During removal and installation the flywheel ring must be cocked slightly to pass over the counterweights (Fig. 13–11).

A sludge trap is often located inside the rod journal section of a one-piece crankshaft. This trap can be removed for cleaning when the crankshaft is removed from the engine. The trap operates centrifugally; as the crankshaft rotates the

154

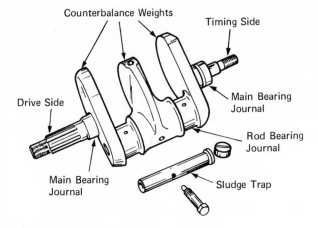

Fig. 13–9 Crankshaft parts and positions

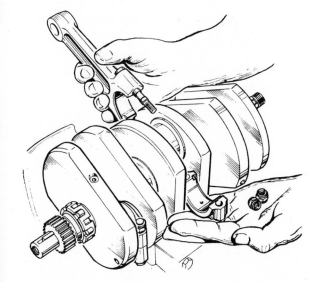

Fig. 13–10 Split connecting rods on solid crankshaft (Triumph Norton Incorporated)

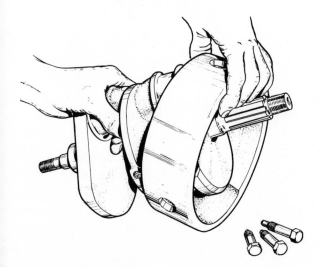

Fig. 13–11 Flywheel removal (Triumph Norton Incorporated)

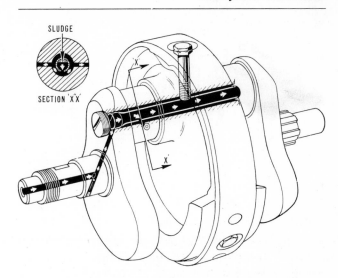

Fig. 13–12 Crankshaft sludge trap (Triumph Norton Incorporated)

heavier dirt particles are spun outward and are retained in the trap (Fig. 13–12).

DIAGNOSIS AND SERVICE

Diagnosing lower-end problems in a multicylinder motorcycle engine follows the same sequence as diagnosing a single. See the diagnosis section of Unit 12 for some background in diagnosing single-cylinder engines before delving into multis.

The big diagnosis differences lie in specifically locating the noises, because now we no longer have simple upper-end and lower-end noises; we have right, center and left noises to contend with also. This is where our mechanic's stethoscope comes in handy. Isolate as much of the problem as possible before tearing down the engine.

When pressure-testing the lower end of a two-stroke multi, treat each cylinder as you would a single. If you detect excessive lower end leakage, be prepared to replace the crankshaft seals. It is possible that the seals may be leaking inside as well as outside (Fig. 13–13).

Signs in the Oil. When changing the oil on your four-stroke, keep an eye on the amount of

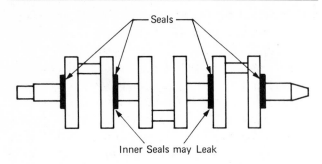

Fig. 13-13   Seal positions in a 2-stroke 3-cylinder lower end

shiny metal flakes you find in the oil. In a brand new bike you might expect a slight bit of metal flake to come out with the oil due to normal break-in wear. However, if excessive engine lower-end noises are associated with drastic increases in the metal flake content of the oil, prepare for the worst. In all likelihood you have a lower-end job on your hands.

Service Questions. Before removing the engine for a lower-end job ask yourself again: "Am I sure, absolutely and positively, beyond any shadow of a doubt, that the problem is in the lower end? Have I exhausted all other possibilities? Have I performed all the tests and diagnostic procedures that are possible with the engine still in the frame?" If the answers to these questions are yes, then remove the engine. Have your service manual handy because the information given here is not meant to replace the shop manual for a particular model but rather to help you understand the theory behind its directions.

Removing an engine can be a challenge. Some engines can be removed only from one side of the bike. That is to say that some frames are designed with special bevels for clearance to remove the engine on only one side.

Be Organized! Remember again that thousands of basket cases begin as sloppy disassembly jobs. One woodruff key that was lost, or a misplaced spacer that was left out, has disabled many a machine and soured many a young mechanic. Before turning out that first bolt, find enough small boxes, bags, muffin tins, or whatever storage aids you need to help organize the fasteners and small parts.

Loosen the bolts, nuts, and screws incrementally by the pattern recommended in your manual. Store each part or fastener removed in the same sequence as you removed it so that the parts will be in proper order when you reassemble the engine. Be sure to keep things like the connecting rods and caps in sets with their pistons, rings, and bearings. Keep the cam followers in order so you can replace them onto the same lobe of the cam.

Servicing One-Piece Crankshafts. After splitting the crankcases carefully, using the procedures outlined in the manual, you are ready to remove the connecting rods from the crankshaft. Again, be sure to keep the rods in order and mark each cap and rod so that it is replaced exactly as it was removed. Examine the bearings for scratches and embedded dirt. Check the crankshaft journals for scores or scratches. English crankshafts can be reground at a crankshaft shop to correct most scratches and scores, but a badly damaged Honda four-cylinder crankshaft must be replaced (Fig. 13-14). Whichever course of action your manual calls for, do it.

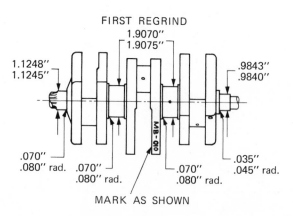

Fig. 13-14   Regrinding instructions for typical one-piece crankshaft (Triumph Norton Incorporated)

Don't try to save money by ignoring a damaged crankshaft. That's like putting off a heart operation in favor of a face lift. Get the crankshaft to proper specifications for straightness, diameter, and bearing clearance even if it means buying a new one.

Check the clearances of your crankshaft with Plastigage. This clever testing device consists of a thin strand of compressible plastic. You put a strip of it between the bearing and the shaft before tightening the rod cap or main bearings to the lowest specified torque. See how much you've squashed the plastic strand. Be careful not to turn the crank or move the rod as you remove the cap or main bearing shells. Compare the new width of the strip with the widths on the Plastigage envelope. The matching will tell you the bearing clearance (Fig. 13–15).

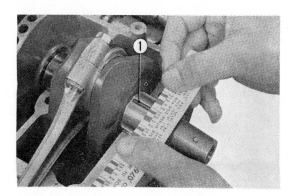

Fig. 13–15 Using plastigauge to check clearances: (1) press gauge (American Honda Motor Company)

When you have the engine torn down to the crankshaft and have precisely fitted the bearings, it is an excellent time to have the engine balanced, especially a twin. If you were fond enough of your machine to disassemble it and service the crankshaft, you probably want to keep it for awhile. Those next few years will be much more pleasant if you treat the crank, rods, and piston assemblies to a precision electronic balance job. Check the local high-performance shops to find a high-performance balancing expert in your area.

What he will do is accurately match the weights of the pistons and both ends of the rods. After determining a balance factor for your engine, he will make up bob weights for your crankshaft and spin it at about 700 rpm. His electronic balancing machine will indicate how much weight to add or subtract to the crankshaft's counterweights for a perfectly balanced engine.

Servicing Built-Up Crankshafts. There isn't much difference between the steps required to service a single-cylinder built-up crank and a multi-cylinder built-up crank. Of course, you have a few more shafts and wheels to true in one assembly, and that requires quite a bit of patience. Be sure to read Unit 12 carefully again if

you have any doubts about the basic principles of reassembling a built-up crankshaft.

Since many multi-cylinder machines use this type of crankshaft, with some cases splitting horizontally and others vertically, follow your manual closely for disassembly instructions. Once you have removed the crankshaft, mount it on V-blocks or between the centers of a lathe or truing stand. Radial runout should be measured with a dial gage at the right- and left-hand main journals and also at the center ball bearings. If any reading exceeds the manufacturer's specifications (usually about 0.002″) the crankshaft should be trued (Fig. 13–16).

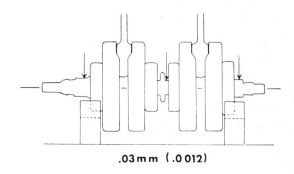

.03mm (.0012)

Fig. 13–16 Measuring crankshaft alignment (Yamaha International Corporation)

Note the direction in which the wheel is out of true. Lay the crankshaft assembly on V-blocks and tap the offending crankwheel in the proper direction to correct the runout. Check the crankshaft, then repeat this technique until all crankwheels are true to within 0.002″.

If the crankshaft needs new rod bearings and pins, or otherwise must be disassembled, you could be in for a problem. Some cranks require special jigs and press fixtures for crankshaft work and reassembling the cases. Check your manual carefully. If you don't have the right equipment, don't attempt the job! Take it to a qualified shop in your area for this part of the work. Always get the center crankshaft oil seals replaced when reassembling the crankshaft, even if the old ones don't seen worn. Lubricate everything well with some good two-stroke oil and don't forget to keep things *clean* during reassembly.

Lubrication

If you've bought many parts for your motorcycle, you will certainly be aware of the high cost of metal components relative to the cost of rubber or plastic parts. Metal parts, especially engine and transmission parts, are made from very expensive materials that are then subjected to expensive operations like machine work and heat treating. Finally, these metal parts are precisely fitted together by expert engine assemblers who use high-quality bearings, gaskets, rings, seals, nuts, and bolts.

With these factors in mind, you should be inclined to take better care of your crankshaft and connecting rods than your tail light lens or plastic front fender. What can you do, you ask, to maintain and protect your beloved crankshaft and other expensive engine and transmission components? The answer lies in proper lubrication, tuning, and considerate riding tactics to insure longer life to your engine's internal parts.

Since we cover tuning and riding elsewhere in this book, let's concentrate on lubrication in this unit. Of the three factors necessary for long engine life, lubrication is probably the most important.

Heat and friction are engine's worst enemies. Friction is the resistance between two surfaces that move against one another. If no lubrication is used, the engine parts would get hot enough to melt at their rubbing surfaces and the working parts would literally weld themselves together. In a motorcycle engine, friction cannot be eliminated but it can be greatly reduced by proper lubrication.

KINDS OF LUBRICANTS

Most lubricants used in motorcycles are made from crude oil, the source of gasoline. During the distillation process, crude oil is heated and vapors are given off. These vapors are condensed in various ways to produce different types of petroleum products. Grease and oil are the most frequently used lubricants on a motorcycle, though many dry lubricants and self-lubricating materials are also employed.

Heavy greases are used in steering-head bearings, wheel bearings, and wherever water resistance and adhesion are important. Formerly, most ball- or roller-bearing greases were fiberous, which helped them stay in the bearing at high speeds and temperatures. Now most high-quality wheel-bearing greases are less fiberous and may be used as standard chassis grease in the swing-arm bushings, clutch throw out, and other chassis areas (Fig. 14–1).

Chain "oil" is a special heavy grease diluted with a solvent and sprayed into the links of a chain. The solvent quickly evaporates, leaving the grease to lubricate the chain by repelling water and clinging to the chain at high temperatures and speeds.

Fig. 14–1 Fiberous and non-fiberous grease

Oil and Additives

The engine is the part of the motorcycle with the heaviest lubrication demands, of course. Two-stroke and four-stroke engines each take two different approaches to lubrication, so we will study four different systems later in this unit. All motorcycle engines discussed so far have used motor oil to lubricate their internal parts. Powered lubricants, self-lubricating materials, or other unconventional substitutes for oil have not been used successfully to date in mass-produced motorcycle engines.

Studying the nature of motor oil leads to an understanding of oil's success as a lubricant. Add to this a study of the new additives that oil companies have developed, and you will see why oil is still the best way to lubricate an engine. In addition to lubricating and removing heat from the engine, the oil also serves to absorb shocks between the bearings and it seals spaces between the cylinder wall and piston, which helps to prevent blow-by. With detergent additives, the oil also cleans the metallic parts it contacts, holding any contaminants in suspension until the next oil change.

Antiscuff additives help to prevent the galling or scratching of internal engine parts. Oxidation

inhibitors help to prevent some oils from burning, while anticorrosion and antirust compounds help the oil protect engine parts from the elements. Pour depressants and viscosity index improvers help to regulate the thickness or viscosity of oil over broad ranges of temperatures. All things considered, today's oils are for superior to those of ten years ago and are the key to long engine life in today's machines.

Dry Lubricants

Many dry lubricants now on the market do an excellent job in special circumstances. Since a dry-lubed chain won't pick up as much dust as an oiled one, many desert riders prefer powdered graphite to chain oil for dusty conditions. The graphite lubes are mixed into a very thin solvent and, therefore, will penetrate deeply and quickly. They are perfect for quick control cable service, freeing stiff locks, and similar duties. Molybdenum disulfide in liquid, spray, grease and solid carriers is an important new lubricant to consider for difficult lubrication areas such as the drive chain.

Lubrication Breakdown

Lubricants should be replaced periodically because of their very nature. They tend to cling to surfaces and trap dirt particles that settle in them. Some lubricants, such as chain and engine oils, require frequent replacement. Other lubed parts areas, such as wheel bearings and steering-head bearings, last much longer without service.

Manufacturers have studied how long an area can go without service and recommend the proper lubrication intervals in the riders' handbook for each machine. They also recommend what types of lubricants to use. Their recommended service intervals assume that you are following their recommendations.

Lubrication breakdown can occur from several causes. Contamination is probably the most frequent since dirt finds its way into most lubricants. Eventually other materials or solvents may dilute a lubricant so that it begins to loose its effectiveness. In a four-stroke engine, oil may also suffer from accumulating acids, raw gasoline, and water, which break down both the oil and the additives in the oil. Guard your machine against deteriorating lubricants by servicing the machine at *least* as often as the riders' hand book recommends.

Power Train Lubrication

Two-Stroke Pre-Mix. The simplest form of engine lubrication is the old style oil-gas pre-mix approach. Gasoline is mixed with oil at about a 20:1 ratio, and this mixture is burned in the engine as fuel. As the gas-oil-air mixture is pumped into and out of the crankcase, some oil settles out onto the roller or needle bearings on both ends of the rod and at the ends of the crankshaft (Fig. 14–2). Some of the oil also settles on the cylinder walls where it lubricates the piston and rings.

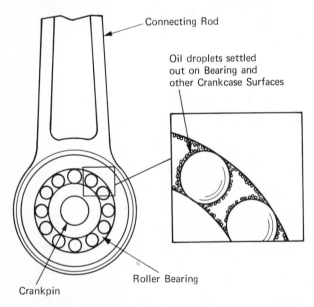

Fig. 14–2 Connecting rod, big end bearing, and crankpin with oil settled out

There is one great advantage to the pre-mix lubrication system—it has no parts. Thus it is just as reliable as the person who is responsible for mixing the fuel for the machine—which, unfortunately, is also one of pre-mixing's great disadvantages. If one fails to include oil in the gas tank certain total disaster for the engine will result. There are other disadvantages to the pre-mix system. The oil settles out of the mixture on occasion. It is inconvenient to carry extra oil on any long-distance outing. Many gas stations don't sell the proper oil for motorcycles, not to mention the inconvenience of having to mix the fuel every time you need gas.

Oil Injection. With these inconveniences in mind, the Japanese two-stroke manufacturers popularized oil injection systems in the mid 1960s. Their systems featured large oil reservoir tanks and pumping systems that proportioned the oil as the engine needed it. Many two-stroke road machines can cover more than 500 miles before the oil tank needs to be replenished. There is only one drawback: the oil tank *must* be refilled, because if it runs dry the engine will surely "self destruct." Professional mechanics never cease to be amazed at the number of engines that are destroyed by such rider carelessness. They are also amazed at the number of machines that are returned for warrantee repair with seized engines, dry oil pump and lines, yet have a full tank of fresh oil. Suspicious, eh? DON'T LET YOUR TWO-STROKE OIL RESERVOIR RUN DRY!

Port Injection Systems. Some oil injection systems pump oil into the intake port just downstream from the carburetor (Fig. 14–3). The

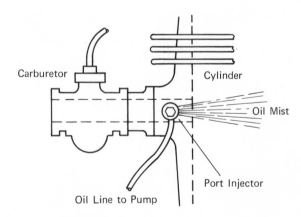

Fig. 14–3 Port injection

amount of oil being pumped into the engine depends on rpm and throttle setting. Naturally, a wide open throttle at high rpm signals the pump to deliver the greatest amount of oil to the incoming gas-air mixture. Lower engine rpm and a smaller throttle opening requires less oil for the engine lubrication needs, so the pump delivers less. At idle, when lubrication demands are minimal, the pump delivers a very small amount that is equivalent to about a 100:1 gas-oil mixture. This lean mixture doesn't harm the engine at all; in fact, it helps to keep the spark plugs clean and reduces unpleasant oil smoke.

C.C.I. or Direct Bearing Lubrication Systems.

Developed by Suzuki, C.C.I. is a abbreviation of "Crankcase/Cylinder Injection" lubrication. This system supplies the correct amount of oil under pressure directly to the critical points of the engine. Rather than simply routing one oil line to the port, oil is supplied under pressure through two oil lines and is completely separate from the gasoline supply. Each oil line is divided at a junction, and one of these split lines serves an outside main bearing and cam-rod bearing, while the other serves the cylinder wall and wristpin. A large center main crankshaft bearing shares oil with the clutch and transmission on a gravity feed basis (Fig. 14–4).

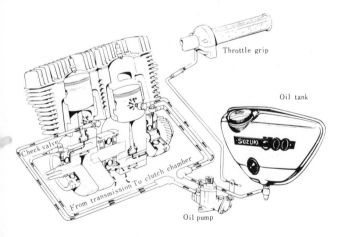

Fig. 14–4 CCI lubrication system (U.S. Suzuki Motor Corporation)

Four-Stroke Lubrication Systems

Four-stroke motorcycle engines use either the wet sump or dry sump lubrication system. Traditionally, the smaller machines have wet sump systems while larger ones use dry sump. Part of the

reason for this is that wet sump oil systems increase the overall engine height, raising the center of gravity and decreasing ground clearance. On a machine with a small engine, there is room for an oil reservoir under the crankshaft. On most bikes with big engines, there is no vertical room to spare, so the oil reservoir is placed elsewhere.

Wet Sump. Most four-stroke engines, including the one in your car, use a wet sump lubrication system. The heart of this setup is a single oil pump and an oil reservoir at the bottom end of the engine. The pump draws oil from the reservoir and pumps it through lines and passages to the areas where oil must lubricate the various moving parts of the engine (Fig. 14–5).

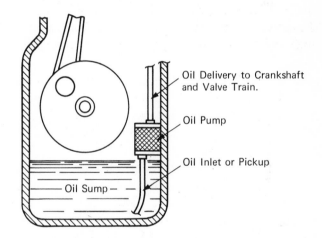

Oil Delivery to Crankshaft and Valve Train.

Oil Pump

Oil Inlet or Pickup

Oil Sump

Fig. 14–5 Wet sump oil system

Dry Sump. In a dry sump system, oil is fed by gravity from a reserve tank to a high-pressure pump. The pump forces the oil through passages and lines to areas where it lubricates various components of the engine. Gravity returns the oil to a small sump at the bottom of the engine. A scavenger pump, often simply another set of chambers in the pressure pump, returns the oil through a one-way check valve to the oil tank reservoir. The scavenger pump is designed to return the oil to the tank much faster than the feed pump supplies it to the points of lubrication. Since the sump is always being pumped dry, imaginative engineers called this system "dry sump" (Fig. 14–6).

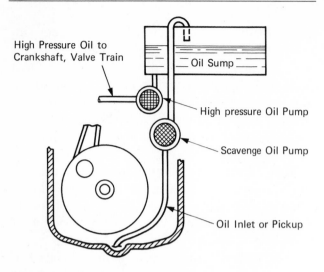

High Pressure Oil to
Crankshaft, Valve Train

Oil Sump

High pressure Oil Pump

Scavenge Oil Pump

Oil Inlet or Pickup

Fig. 14–6   Dry sump oil system

Common Sump. Whether a wet or dry sump system is used, it is possible and often practical to lubricate the engine, transmission, primary drive and clutch with the same oil supply. Some manufacturers have taken this approach on models designed in recent years. Earlier engineers believed that heavy, thick oil was required to lubricate transmission gears, that another weight was required in the primary drive and clutch area, and yet another weight for the engine. Some redesigning of the components themselves and new overall designs of engines have led to common sump lubrication system that seems to be the trend in four-strokes for years to come (Fig. 14–7).

Primary Case, Transmission, and Ring and Pinion Lubrication

Of course, two-stroke engine designers must isolate their transmission and primary drive areas from the crankcase for two reasons: two-strokes don't run well with excessively large crankcase chambers, and a gas-oil mixture would not properly lubricate the transmission, clutch assembly, or primary drive. Many four-stroke engines also isolate the primary drive section and transmission case from the engine oil. In these instances special oils are used to lubricate these mechanisms.

Primary Case Lubrication. Some older motorcycle engine designs call for seperate lubrication of the primary drive chain. These machines are often nonunit construction; that is, the engine and transmission are in separate cases, joined by a primary drive chain. This chain should run in a shallow oil bath to insure long life and smooth operation. A small filler plug is provided on the primary case so the oil level can be "topped up" frequently with lubricant. Keep a close eye on the primary case oil level if you have one of these machines because they are notorious "leakers." The manual recommends the type of lubricant to use.

Transmission and Ring and Pinion Lubrication. Where gears mesh and turn against each other, a thicker, more viscous lubricant is usually needed. Some older machines went overboard, however, calling for 90 and 140 weight gear oil in the transmission. Did you ever try to shift a bike

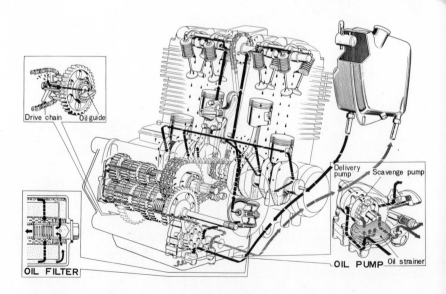

Drive chain   Oil guide

Delivery pump   Scavenge pump

OIL FILTER

OIL PUMP   Oil strainer

Fig. 14–7   Common sump lubrication system (American Honda Motor Company)

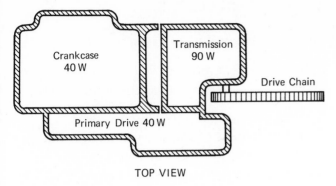

Fig. 14–8 A typical example of separate oil reservoirs

with 90 weight oil in the transmission on a freezing day? It's sluggish, to say the least!

Most manufacturers now recommend transmission oils of about 40 weight. This viscosity more than meets the lubrication demands of the transmission and certainly makes shifting easier on cold mornings.

Ninety weight oil is still required in the rear end of shaft drive machines, however. With the spiral bevel gears found in this final drive system, there is a good deal of sliding tooth contact that is cushioned by the thicker 90 weight oil.

There isn't much mystery to how the transmission and rear end gears are lubricated. They stay wet with oil, just like a paddle wheel does on a Mississippi River sternwheeler. The teeth of the lower gears dip into an oil bath on each revolution, transmitting lubricant to other gears and

splashing it onto shafts and bearings as required (Fig. 14–9).

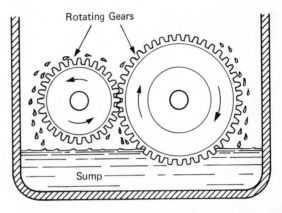

Fig. 14–9 Gear lubrication, showing how gears pick up oil from the sump as they rotate

Chain Lubrication. The aerosol-powered chain lubricants on today's market, though relatively expensive, are clean and convenient. They penetrate the rollers of the chain with a solvent-thinned grease. As the solvent evaporates, the grease solidifies inside the chain where it's needed (Fig. 14–10). Lubricating the chain with a high-quality lubricant should be considered a mandatory task *every time you use a tank of gas.*

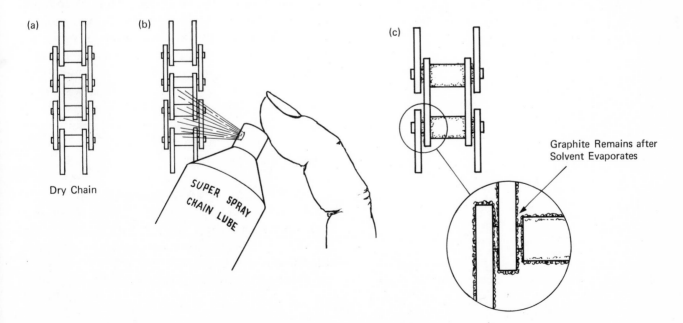

Fig. 14–10 Chain lubrication: (a) dry, (b) being sprayed, and (c) with solvent vaporized, leaving heavy grease

Sure, some bikes have automatic chain oilers, but chain life is really lengthened with this small extra service.

Chassis. The frame and its associated pivots, cables, linkages, and sliding components require lubrication too.

Some machines provide grease fittings for swing arms, steering heads, and other moving parts. Other manufacturers require disassembly of the component to lubricate it, as is the case with most steering head bearings.

The swing arm is an especially important area to lubricate, because neglect here can quickly lead to worn bushings and their associated handling problems (Fig. 14–11).

The cables are your link between the brake and clutch and your hands. Don't strain your hands and invite riding problems by forgetting to lubricate these important items. Try to follow all of the important service procedures in the following paragraphs to insure smooth reliable riding on your machine.

VIEW OF REAR WHEEL FROM TOP

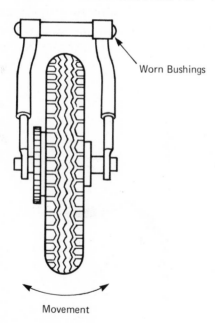

Worn Bushings

Movement

Fig. 14–11 Swing arm wear

SERVICE PROCEDURES

Engine Lubrication – a Pre-mix

Before preparing a batch of gas-oil mixture, be certain of:

- the ratio of oil to gasoline required
- the accuracy of your measuring instruments
- the freshness of the gasoline
- the cleanliness of the containers and components.

A baby bottle is an excellent measuring instrument to use when mixing gas and oil. It is graduated on one scale in ounces and in order to get your mixture ratio, all you need do is remember that 1 gallon has 128 ounces. Table 14–1 is helpful in determining how much oil to use per gallon of gasoline if your math is a bit shaky.

When doing the actual mixing, put half of the gasoline in the mixing can first. Then add the oil and shake the can thoroughly for a minute or so. Add the rest of the gas and shake it again. Sometimes, if you fill a can to the brim and then add oil, there isn't enough room to agitate the gas-oil mixture for thorough blending.

Oil Injection Systems

Filling and Priming. Properly adjusted, an oil injection system is essentially trouble-free if it is kept filled.

Sometimes, however, it may run too rich and exude excessive smoke. This excessive smoke is generally caused by improper control cable adjustment. The cable from the throttle junction block must be adjusted properly to regulate the oil delivery from the pump. Sometimes a shim adjustment at the oil pump is also required. Whatever the case, follow the service manual closely because you are involved in a critical area when adjusting the oil pump.

Priming or Bleeding the Pump. If the oil pump has been removed or allowed to run dry, you must bleed the system before you start the engine. This step typically involves loosening the oil delivery line at the pump and holding the throttle open with the engine turned off to allow

Fig. 14–12 Draining dry sump oil: a cardboard flume can be taped to bike to drain oil away from frame

manufacturer suggests intervals, but they should be considered maximums. Halving recommended manufacturers' oil change intervals would probably be a worthwhile investment.

On a wet-sump system always warm up the entire machine by a half-hour ride before changing the oil. Hot oil flows out more freely and carries out more dirt and contaminants. The day you plan to change your oil, get out a flat drain pan, the proper wrenches for your drain plugs, the new oil, and a funnel. It's easier to get the oil drain plug out with a six-point socket and a long breaker bar if you have a stubborn plug like the Honda 350's. Drain the oil into the pan, replace the plug, then fill the crankcase to the proper level with new oil.

On a dry sump system, you must drain both the oil tank and the sump. Again, warm the engine thoroughly before draining the oil. Protect the bike's paint and chrome by taping a piece of cardboard under the tank while it drains (Fig. 14–12).

the oil to run from the reservoir to the pump. Carefully follow the manufacturer's directions in the service manual for the specific steps involved in bleeding your oil pump.

Oil Changes

Periodically the oil in the engine, primary case, and transmission should be changed. The

Oil Filters. As more bikes are designed to use oil filters, the industry will probably select the self-contained spin-on automotive style filter. Presently, a canister type is used which requires a little more trouble to service. To change the oil filter, place a drain pan under the front of the en-

Table 14–1   GAS-OIL PREMIX RATIOS

Amount of Oil to Mix
(cubic centimeters and ounces)

		CC	Oz.	CC	Oz.	CC	Oz.	CC	Oz.	CC	Oz.
Mix	40	95	3.2	189	6.4	284	9.6	379	12.8	474	16
Ratio	35	109	3.7	216	7.3	326	11	432	14.6	542	18.3
	30	127	4.3	252	8.5	379	12.8	506	17.1	630	21.3
Parts	28	133	4.5	269	9.1	405	13.7	542	18.3	678	22.9
Gas	26	145	4.9	290	9.8	438	14.8	583	19.7	728	24.6
to	24	157	5.3	317	10.7	474	16	630	21.3	790	26.7
Part	22	172	5.8	343	11.6	518	17.5	690	23.3	858	29
Oil	20	189	6.4	379	12.8	658	19.2	758	25.6	947	32
	18	210	7.1	420	14.2	630	21.3	841	28.9	1054	35.6
	16	237	8	474	16	710	24	947	32	1184	40
	14	269	9.1	541	18.3	811	27.4	1083	36.6	1353	45.7
		1		2		3		4		5	

Gallons of Gasoline to Mix

gine, turn the center bolt on top of the filter counterclockwise to loosen it. Remove the canister and discard the old filter inside it, keeping the springs, spacers, and washers in proper sequence. If necessary, carefully replace the large rubber O-ring between the canister and the engine. Be sure to clean the canister and parts before reassembly.

Greasing Joints. There are two tricks to lubricating the straight type of grease fittings found on many motorcycles. The easiest approach is to buy a special pointed end for your grease gun (Fig. 14–13). You simply probe the small hole in the grease nipple with this point and push the plunger.

If you have the conventional type of automotive grease gun for American-style fittings, you can often grease your motorcycle by putting one layer of cotton cloth over the fitting before lubricating it. The layer of cotton helps form a seal around the nipple, encouraging the grease to go into the proper area. Another approach is to change the fittings to standard automotive Zerke fittings so you can better lube your bike without special grease guns or rags.

Cables. Occasionally, the cables on a bike need a thorough lubrication. The "baggie trick" is a tremendous way to lubricate the cable thoroughly and helps to make the controls work very smoothly, giving the rider better control of his machine. This method, shown in Fig. 14–14, induces a flow between the inner and outer section of the cable to assure complete lubrication. A 10W-40W oil can be used and should seep through the cable in a couple of hours or sooner. If it doesn't seem to go through, hang the cable overnight and you'll find that by morning the oil has all seeped through.

Foam-Type Air Cleaners. While you have clean oil at hand, clean and oil the foam-type air cleaners if your bike uses them. Soak them in solvent first, then gently squeeze out the solvent, as you would squeeze out a sponge. Slightly compress the filter in your hand and pour oil over it as it expands. Shake off the excess oil and replace it on the bike.

Periodic cleaning and lubrication not only of the air filter, but the rest of the machine as well, will insure many long happy miles of cycling for you and your loved ones. It even works for people you don't like so much.

Fig. 14–13   Pointed end grease gun, showing close-up view of special point

Fig. 14–14   Baggie trick for lubing bike cable (Triumph Norton Incorporated)

Fuel Systems

Yogi Berra once said: "You can observe a lot just by watching." This statement is especially true of the nature of burning gasoline. Have you ever noticed that an open container of liquid gasoline burns rather slowly and just on its surface? Have you experienced the violent combustion associated with burning gasoline vapors? Don't conduct your own backyard experiment if you haven't, but ask yourself why gasoline behaves like it does. You'll soon arrive at the conclusion that the vaporization of gasoline has a lot to do with its burning rate (Fig. 15–1).

As you know, burning is simply a more common term for "oxidation." Oxidation refers to the fact that what really takes place during burning is a chemical reaction where the molecules of a material combine with oxygen. This oxygen usually comes from the atmosphere, which is about 20 per cent oxygen, but it may come from another source as in the case of the oxyacetylene welding torch (Fig. 15–2).

Your motorcycle uses the oxygen from the atmosphere, combining it with partially vaporized gasoline in order to have a suitable combustible air-fuel mixture for the engine.

Your carburetor's job is to mix air and fuel in the proper proportions and in the proper amounts for the engine to operate efficiently from idle to red line rpm. The carburetor can do this by sup-

plying about a 14-to-1 air-fuel ratio (by weight) throughout the operating range of the engine. If you were to compare the *volume of air* to the volume of gas handled by the carburetor, you would come up with about a 8000-to-1 ratio. That represents about 62 gallons of air to one tablespoon of gasoline.

HOW CARBURETORS WORK

Since the carburetor handles 8 thousand times more air than fuel, let's look at how the air passes through it. The air is drawn into the cylinder by the piston as it descends in the cylinder bore. Incoming air can be drawn through the carburetor only because there are no leaks anywhere else, hopefully (Fig. 15–3).

Some writers explain that atmospheric pressure forces a column of air through the carburetor and fills the cylinder, which is actually true. However, you're better off thinking of the engine "sucking" a column of air through the carburetor, because good cranking suction or vacuum is necessary for the engine to start and operate properly.

The intake phase is responsible for drawing air through the carburetor, now how is the gasoline introduced and mixed? Simply put, the mov-

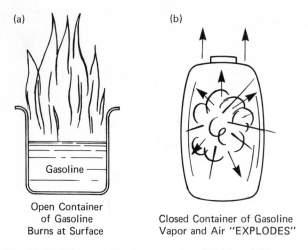

Fig. 15-1 How gasoline burns as (a) a liquid, and (b) a vapor

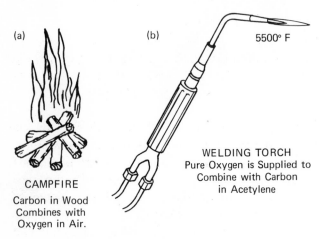

Fig. 15-2 Atmospheric combustion is shown in (a) versus artificial combustion as shown in (b)

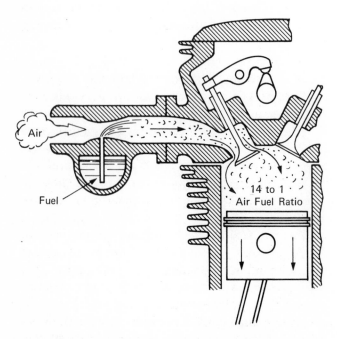

Fig. 15-3 Carburetor supplies fresh fuel-air mixture

ing column of air draws the gas from a little reservoir in the carburetor and disperses it into tiny droplets for quicker vaporization and better combustion in the engine.

Venturi Effect

No section on carburetion would be complete without the classic old-fashioned bug sprayer to demonstrate how a moving column of air can draw liquid up a tube, then disperse it into tiny droplets. Unfortunately, many readers may be familiar only with aerosol pressurized push-button cans of bug spray. However, the blame for the general misunderstanding of motorcycle carburetion cannot be laid entirely upon the aerosol can industry (Fig. 15-4). The rapidly moving column

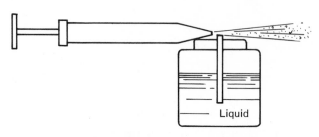

FUEL, LEAVING THE DISCHARGE JET IS VAPORIZED IN THE SAME WAY AS LIQUID IN A BUG SPRAYER

Fig. 15-4 Common liquid vaporization

of air causes the same phenomenon going through a carburetor as it does when traveling across a hand-pumped bug-sprayer spout. The difference is that the carburetor mixes gasoline rather than bug spray with the air. The carburetor further helps to draw the gas into the air because of the Venturi effect of the shape of the air passage. The constriction of the air-flow passage increases air velocity at the gasoline discharge nozzle, which provides a better draw on the liquid and better mixture of the air and fuel (Fig. 15-5).

An air column traveling through a tube maintains a constant speed as long as the tube size is constant. Any restriction in the tube causes the air to speed up through the restricted part if the air is going to maintain a constant speed in the rest of the tube. A physical law states air speed increases air pressure decreases.

The restriction built into a carburetor to provide the air speed increase and pressure decrease is called a Venturi. Venturi effect is therefore the pressure decrease and speed increase caused by

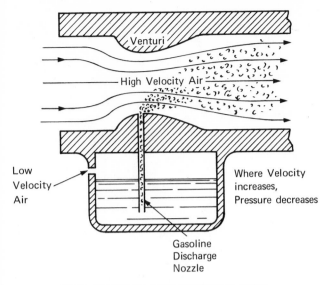

FUEL FLOWS TO LOW PRESSURE AREA

Fig. 15–5 Fuel vaporization in a carburetor

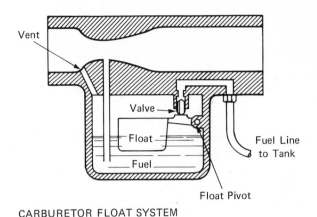

CARBURETOR FLOAT SYSTEM

Fig. 15–6 Carburetor float system

the restriction or Venturi. Normal air pressure on the surface of a fuel supply stored in another part of the carburetor will force the fuel into the low pressure area created by "Venturi effect." The difference in pressure created, along with a sized opening the fuel must flow through determines the amount of fuel mixed with a given flow of air through the carburetor.

Carburetor Subsystems or Circuits

There are five or six separate sub-systems or "circuits" in a carburetor. Each of these circuits has a specific job to do and can be studied independently. They are the float bowl, the idle circuit, the mid-range circuit, the accelerator pump, the power circuit, and the choke or enrichening circuit. Most motorcycle carburetors don't have an accelerator pump, and some race jobs even omit the idle circuit and choke. After you have read and become acquainted with the basics in this chapter, study the manual for your model to become familiar with those particular carburetor features.

Float Bowl System. The float bowl system provides a constant level reservoir from which the other carburetor circuits can draw fuel. Usually the float chamber is a simple metal bowl affixed to the bottom of the carburetor. It contains a hollow float that opens and closes a needle valve, depending on the level of fuel in the bowl itself (Fig. 15–6). The level of the fuel must be correct

under all conditions. If it's too high, the engine runs rich and fouls or floods out. If it's too low, the engine may run dangerously lean.

High-Speed Power Circuit. This system has no moving parts. It consists of the air intake horn, main jet, and discharge tube. This circuit ingests all the air and fuel the engine possibly can take when this circuit is employed. The only means of adjusting the air-fuel ratio at wide open throttle (WOT) is to change the size of the main jet at the bottom of the discharge tube. Too large a jet leads to rich running, plug fouling, and sluggish performance. Too small a jet causes an engine to run lean and hot, risking seizure or piston burning (Fig. 15–7).

Idle Circuit. The idle circuit also has no moving parts. Its job is to supply a 12 or 14-to-1 air-fuel ratio to the engine in the 1000 rpm range so the engine will idle smoothly when the machine is at rest. The idle circuit consists of a throttle stop, an idle jet and passages, a discharge port, and idle air-fuel mixture adjusting screw, and the main air passage of the carburetor at closed throttle (Fig. 15–8).

An engine needs very little air-fuel mix to run at idle. A very small amount of air passes under the slide and across the idle discharge port. This port releases the fuel in a precisely metered amount. The precise metering is accomplished by a spring-loaded needle-pointed adjusting screw, which is used to restrict or open the idle fuel pas-

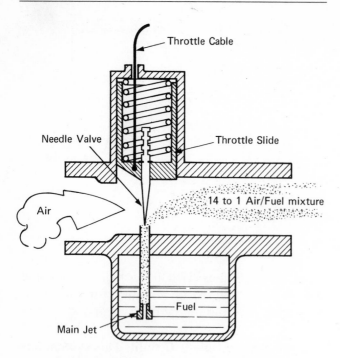

VARIABLE VENTURI SLIDE TYPE CARBURETOR
Throttle Slide is in fully-raised high-speed position.
Needle Valve is fully raised, allowing Main Jet
to be completely Open.

Fig. 15–7   Main jet Venturi operation

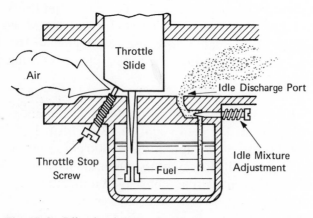

Fig. 15–8   Idle circuit operation

sage, depending on its position. A rule of thumb for setting the adjustment screw is to turn it all the way in (clockwise) until it lightly bottoms, then back it out (counterclockwise) 1 1/2 turns (Fig. 15–9).

The throttle stop screw resembles the idle mixture adjusting screw but has a blunt rather

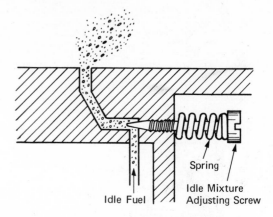

Fig. 15–9   Idle mixture adjustment screw and port

than a sharply pointed end. This blunt end wedges against the throttle slide, causing it to rise or fall very slightly. It provides a positive stop or rest to position the slide at its lowest travel (Fig. 15–10). This screw holds the throttle slide open just enough to insure that a proper idle rpm is maintained.

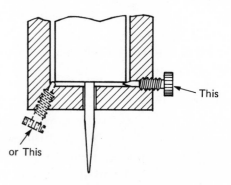

THROTTLE SLIDE STOP SCREW

Fig. 15–10   Idle stop screw

Mid-Range or Intermediate Throttle Circuit. Since a carburetor spends most of its time operating at part throttle, the mid-range circuit must be more sophisticated than the idle or full-power systems. The intermediate throttle circuit provides approximately a 14-to-1 air-fuel mixture to the engine at all throttle settings between idle and wide open. In other words, this circuit must vary the amounts (but not the ratio) of fuel and air that it supplies to the engine to meet the demands the rider dictates by his or her use of the throttle. The amount of mixture is controlled by means of a rising slide that allots the amount of air and a tapered needle in a hole that allots the amount of gasoline (Fig. 15–11). This tapered needle fastened to the base of the slide rides in a brass needle jet. As the needle rises it allows more gasoline to pass through the needle jet into the intake air stream.

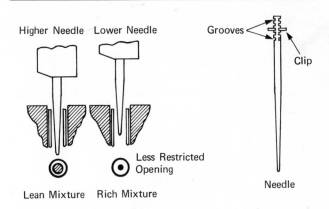

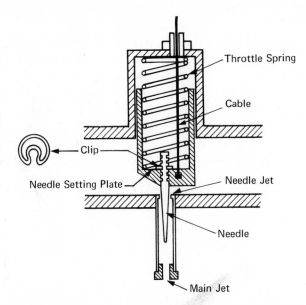

Fig. 15–11 Midrange circuit, showing slide, needle and jet

Fig. 15–12 Needle position adjustment

The air-fuel ratio is adjustable for the mid-range circuit. Adjustments can be made by raising or lowering the position of the needle in the slide. Lowering the needle restricts the jet more, which allots a leaner mixture. Raising the needle brings it farther out of the needle jet, which allots a richer mixture (Fig. 15–12). Adjustment is provided with a clip and multiple groove arrangement at the top of the needle.

Needle positioning notches are numbered from the top. The top notch is called position number one. Five notches or more are usually available on the needle jet.

Choke Circuits. There are several approaches that carburetor manufacturers take for enriching the air-fuel mixture for easy starting. We will deal here with the three most popular types: the air restrictor choke, the enrichening valve, and the tickler system.

Air Restrictor Choke. If an engine can draw both air and fuel through the carburetor and you restrict the air, more gasoline is going to be drawn into the intake passage. This condition is desirable when starting a cold engine and subsequently warming it up. Some manufacturers restrict the

air at the air filter intake, but most restrict it with a butterfly valve right at the carburetor. Closing the air restriction choke allows more vacuum to be applied to the fuel, which is then drawn from the float bowl into the engine.

Enrichening Valve. Many manufacturers use a separate passage, much like the idle mixture passage, to enrich the air-fuel mixture for starting and warm-up. The passage is larger than the idle passage and is located between the throttle slide and the engine. With the slide closed, vacuum draws fuel directly from the enrichening port when the control valve is open. The control valve is operated either by a lever on the carburetor or by a small lever and cable assembly on the handlebar (Fig. 15–13).

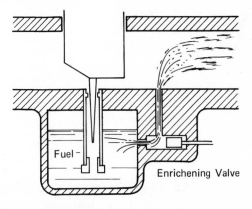

Fig. 15–13 Enrichening valve operation

Tickler System. Some carburetors have a small button over the float chamber. The button is actually the top of a rod that can depress the float, allowing the float valve to open and permit extra fuel to enter the float chamber. The button is depressed by the rider for a few seconds before starting the bike. The excess fuel entering the float chamber temporarily "floods" the carburetor with extra gasoline so that a very rich fuel to air mixture is available for starting (Fig. 15–14).

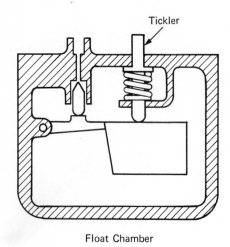

Fig. 15–14   Tickler for starting, showing button and spring return

CARBURETOR TYPES

The most common type of carburetor used on motorcycles is the variable Venturi or slide-type carburetor. This carburetor design controls the amount of gas-air mixture available to the engine by means of a cylindrical slide that is raised and lowered in a bore perpendicular to the air intake passage. The slide holds a tapered needle that regulates the amount of fuel being mixed with the incoming air. A simple cable pulls the slide up in its bore, compressing a spring that returns the slide to idle position after the throttle is released (Fig. 15–15).

Vacuum-Controlled Variable Venturi Carburetor. The vacuum-controlled carburetor is similar to the slide type except that a vacuum is used to raise the slide rather than a cable. In addition, a butterfly valve is used on the engine side of the carburetor to which the throttle cable is attached. It is possible for the rider to open the

throttle butterfly valve too fast and so wide that it would stall the engine, but with a vacuum-controlled carburetor the slide will rise only enough to satisfy the engine's demands. You can see that this approach to carburetion helps to eliminate stalling problems due to opening the throttle too fast.

The vacuum-controlled slide may be made of rubber or metal. The slide senses the engine's demand for air-fuel mixture by the degree of manifold vacuum routed to the throttle bore, thus activating the slide. Figure 15–16 shows what takes place in a vacuum-controlled carburetor.

Butterfly Valve Carburetors. On some carburetors a disc or butterfly valve is used to control the amount of fuel mixture available to the engine. As the throttle shaft and attached disc is turned, it opens and closes the carburetor bore. The fuel passages are placed a little differently on this type of carburetor and no needle valve is used. Instead, an intermediate range jet and an air fuel mixture passage are used to provide for the engine's midrange demands. Figure 15–17 shows the operation of a butterfly type carburetor.

CARBURETOR DIAGNOSIS AND REPAIR

Carburetors are simple mechanical devices. They normally use nice, clean, filtered air and clean, fresh, filtered gasoline. Don't touch the carburetor until you've checked the ignition timing, the spark plugs, the intake and exhaust, valve adjustment, the cam chain, fuel freshness, air cleaner, and engine compression. The diagnosis procedures in this section assume that all of these areas have been investigated and that carburetion has been isolated as the trouble spot. If an engine operation problem develops, needlessly working over a carburetor when something else is wrong with an engine will soon find the mechanic with an engine that has two problems instead of just one.

Starting Problems. If carburetion problems are really preventing your bike from starting, the engine is either getting too much air and no fuel, or too much fuel and not enough air. The spark plug will tell you which problem exists because it will either be wet with gas or bone dry.

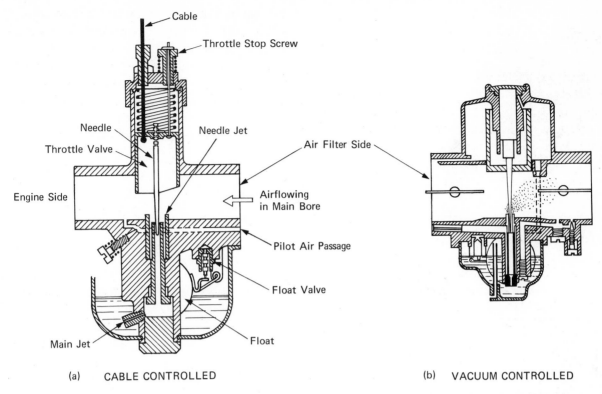

Fig. 15–15 Cable controlled (a) versus vacuum controlled (b) carbs

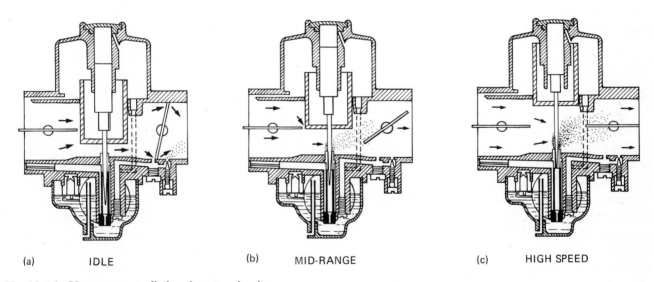

Fig. 15–16 Vacuum controlled carburetor circuit

If the spark plug is dry, there are several areas to examine and repair if needed.

Vacuum Leaks. A damaged connector hose, flange, or gasket can leak air to the engine, bypassing the carburetor completely. If air isn't taken in through the carburetor it can't draw fuel to the engine. Any suspected vacuum leaks can easily be corrected with new gaskets or connector hoses. Sometimes a connector hose can be tem-porarily sealed with plastic electrical tape until you can get the parts to fix it permanently (Fig. 15–18).

Blocked Fuel Passages. Is gas getting to the carburetor? To check this, disconnect the fuel line at the carburetor, then briefly open the pet-cock to the ON position. If gas flows, the restric-tion must be inside the carburetor. A part that of-ten clogs up is the fuel inlet needle and seat

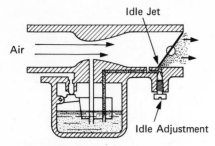

Air →

Idle Jet

Idle Adjustment

With butterfly valve nearly closed, the idle jet is used. An adjustment needle is provided to regulate the idle mixture fuel-air ratio.

IDLE

Air →

As the butterfly valve is moved toward closed, the vacuum at the main jet may be weak to draw fuel into the passing air, so an intermediate jet is provided.

INTERMEDIATE

Air →

Carburetor showing butterfly valve completely open for high speed operation.

HIGH SPEED

Fig. 15–17   Disc or butterfly throttle valve carburetor circuit

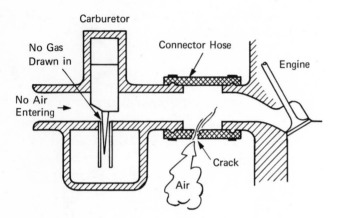

Fig. 15–18   Illustration of a vacuum leak situation

assembly. Carefully remove the float bowl, float, and needle. Reconnect the fuel line, then turn the fuel ON again to check for blockage. If you haven't found the fuel restriction yet, remove the carburetor and check the float level according to the manual. Sometimes a low float-level setting will cause fuel starvation. With the carburetor disassembled, blow compressed air through the idle passages, enrichening circuit, and main jet needle valve passage. (*Be sure to wear eye protection when using compressed air for this process.*) You should be able to determine which passages are clogged. Follow the techniques outlined later in this section for carburetor overhaul procedures.

Excess Fuel or Flooding. A common problem in hard-starting bikes is too much fuel. Of course, too much fuel floods the spark plugs and eliminates any chance of the engine starting until the plugs are dry again.

Several conditions can cause flooding. Check for a clogged air cleaner, stuck choke, stuck enrichening valve or tickler, a very high float level, and whether the float needle and seat are blocked open.

Running Problems. If the engine will run at all, a carburetor problem is rather easy to isolate by using the "three-carburetor system." Consider the carburetor as three carburetors—a small idle carburetor, a mid-range carburetor, and a high-speed carburetor.

If the problem occurs from zero to 1/8 throttle, work on the idle circuit. If the problem occurs from 1/8 through 7/8 throttle, work on the mid-range circuit. If the problem occurs at wide-open throttle, work on the main power circuit.

Carburetor Synchronization. Most street twins and multis have more than one carburetor. These carburetors must work together—*exactly together*—if the engine is to run smoothly. There are two steps to getting the carburetors to work together: synchronize the throttle slides and synchronize the idle adjustments.

Throttle slides can be synchronized by adjusting the cables at the carburetor until the slides rise exactly together. You can determine if the slides are rising together by putting your fingers on them while someone slowly twists the throttle on. A slide that lags can be hurried by adjusting the cable at the top of the carburetor. The adjustor may require the use of a wrench but can often be turned by hand (Fig. 15–19).

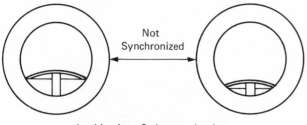

Looking into Carburetor Intakes

Fig. 15–19 Carburetor slide synchronization

Idle settings can be synchronized approximately by setting both the mixture and speed screws at the recommended initial settings. For instance, you can gently turn the idle mixture screws until they bottom then back them out 1 1/2 turns. Again these can usually be turned by hand but may require a screwdriver. Idle speed screws can be turned in until they just contact the throttle slides. From this base setting, most bikes will idle well, but a finer adjustment can be obtained. On twins, disconnect one of the plug wires and adjust the carburetor on the "live" cylinder by turning the idle mixture screw to obtain the highest rpm. Back out the throttle speed screw until the engine is barely running. Repeat the process on the other cylinder, then reconnect both spark plugs. If the idle speed is too high, unscrew the idle speed screws in steps, 1/4 turn each, until proper idle speed is obtained. Idle adjustment is not nearly as critical as slide synchronization, so don't wear out the screws and destroy the idle mixture needle by "overtuning" the idle settings.

Carburetor Overhaul. Occasionally a carburetor may need rebuilding. This is especially true of carburetors that have not been used for a long time or ones that are served by rusty fuel tanks with dirty fuel. You should have several items on hand before beginning the task: screwdriver set, small adjustable wrench, steel 6-inch ruler, two small cans of carburetor and choke cleaner, rags, small-diameter wire (.010 to .015″), a 1/2 pint pan or jar, a gasket kit, and possibly a new slide.

The carburetor being rebuilt in the sequence in Fig. 15–20 is typical of most motorcycle carburetors. Follow the shop manual for the specifications and settings on the machine you are servicing.

Air Filters

Recent air filter developments have doubled the engine life on motorcycles. Air cleaners used to be nothing but thick wire mesh units that weren't very effective. The change to foam, paper, and fiberglass air filter elements has been a great stride forward. Now air cleaners are far more effective and easier to service.

Paper Filters. Filters made of porous paper work very well. The size of the pores in the paper are controlled at the factory so that the paper filter traps harmful dust while permitting plenty of air to enter the carburetor. The paper is fanfolded in the case to obtain the greatest amount of surface area in the limited available space.

Foam-Type Air Cleaners. Foam-type air filters are often referred to by the name Filtron after the company that helped develop them for motorcycles. These elements are made of a porous synthetic foam that also has its porosity controlled during manufacture. The air going through a Filtron must pass through these pores that have been oiled to help trap dust particles. The foam air filter is easily serviced by washing it in gasoline, the re-oiling it with 20 or 30 weight oil.

Wire Mesh Air Cleaners. Older motorcycles and some minibikes use wire mesh air filters. Since the size of the openings between the wires cannot be accurately controlled, these air filters are rather inefficient. For better engine operation why not convert to a foam or paper air filter if you have wire mesh now.

Tanks, Valves, and Lines

Most gas tanks are made from mild steel and, though heavier, are more durable than the aluminum or fiberglass tanks found on racing bikes. Gas tanks are generally taken for granted, but there are some things you should know about caring for them. The cap should be vented and have a good gasket to prevent leakage. Some riders use two cap gaskets if a cap starts to leak.

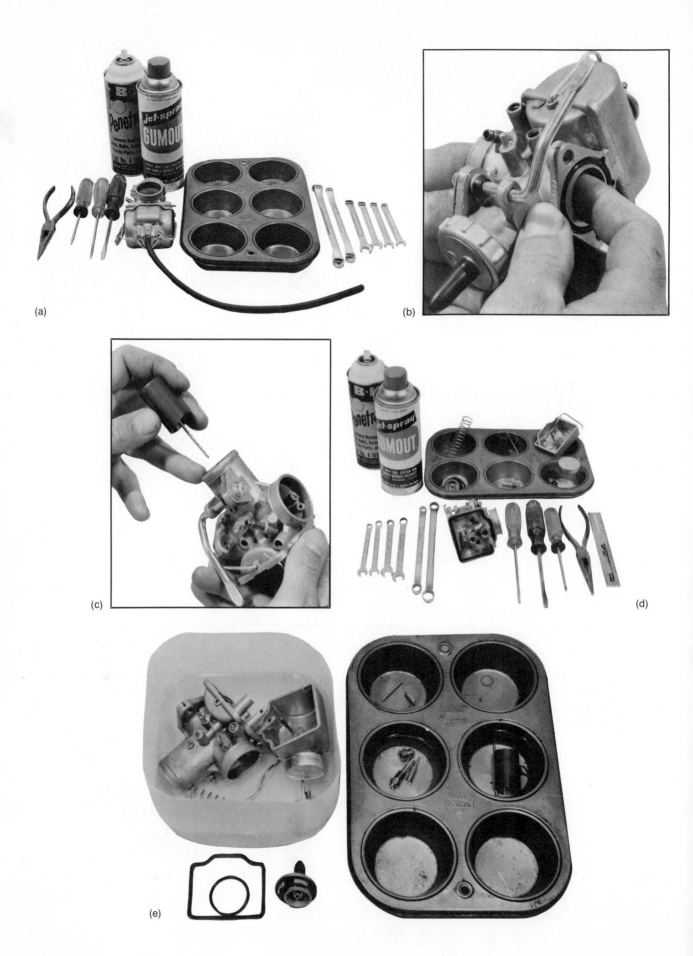

(a)

(b)

(c)

(d)

(e)

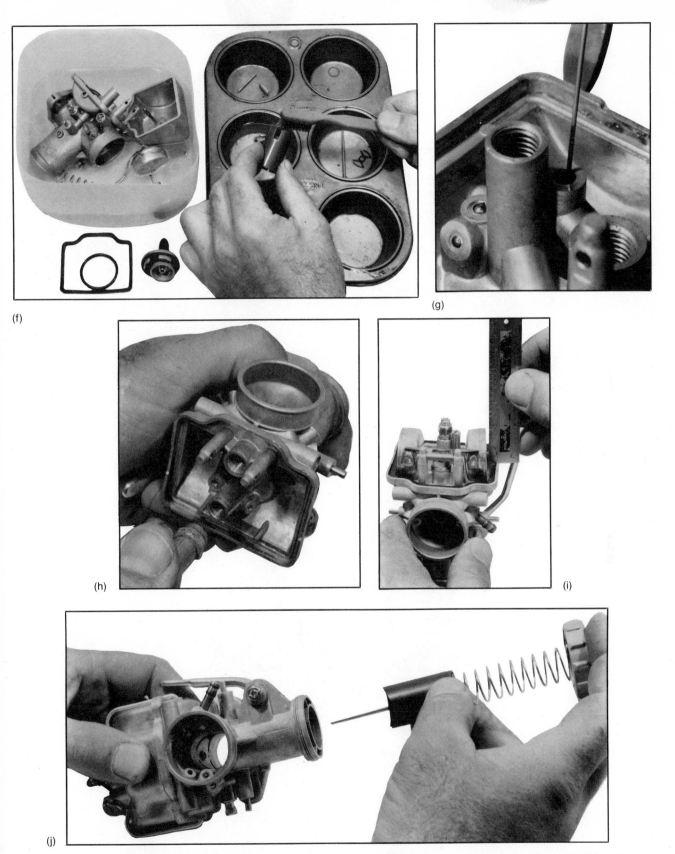

(f)

(g)

(h)

(i)

(j)

Fig. 15–20 Carburetor overhaul sequence: (a) materials, (b) checking slide for wear, (c) disassembly, (d) parts laid out, (e) soaking parts in cleaner, (f) scrubbing and rinsing parts, (g) wiping out parts with fine wire, (h) blowing out passages with air, (i) adjusting the float setting, and (j) reassembly

Always store a bike with its gas tank filled. This prevents condensation from forming inside the tank and rusting it. If you have an extra tank to store, put a quart of 40 to 50 weight oil in it and slosh the oil around until all interior surfaces have been oiled. Dump the oil out before using the tank again, but don't worry about the little bit that remains; it won't hurt a thing.

The sediment trap and filter screen need cleaning two or three times a year. (Fig. 15–21.) Stop by the dealer and get a new gasket before you remove the fuel strainer for cleaning. There is nothing quite as frustrating—or dangerous—as a leaking fuel strainer gasket when you want to ride your bike.

Once you have the carburetor, air filter, and gas tank in good shape, you might treat your machine to an "in line" fuel filter. These little filters work well, especially on trail bikes where gas is often carried around in a dirty old can. An inexpensive in-line fuel filter could prevent your getting stranded in the woods someday (Fig. 15–22).

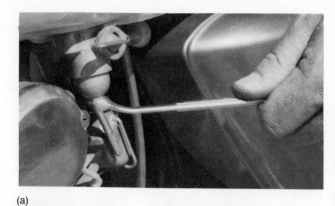

(a)

(b)

Fig. 15–21 Sediment bowl service: (a) removing bowl, and (b) examining bowl

Fig. 15–22 In-line fuel filter installation

unit 16

Exhaust Systems

A motorcycle exhaust system has three important functions: routing exhaust gases, enhancing the power curve of the engine, and muffling exhaust noise. Exhaust systems, too, have seen tremendous developments through the years and have evolved to a point where they are producing more power with less and less noise.

The physical location of the exhaust system is a major design consideration for any motorcycle. Some manufacturers develop a street-trail combination bike simply by producing high tucked-in exhaust pipes for an existing street model (Fig. 16–1).

There are advantages and disadvantages to high pipes or low pipes on a street-based motorcycle. The obvious advantage of high-mounted pipes is that they won't strike rocks and stumps when you are buzzing along a woods trail. The disadvantage is that high pipes usually have sharp bends near the exhaust port, which hinders the flow of exhaust gases and reduces power (Fig. 16–2). The more gracefully curved street pipes often result in a 5-horsepower increase over high pipes in a 650-cc machine.

The power curve that is generated by a four-stroke motorcycle engine is affected by its exhaust system. Large diameter, short exhaust tubes generally produce more top-end power. Small diameter, longer pipes produce more low-to-

mid-range power. Combining the primary pipes of a four-stroke into a single collector broadens the torque curve and gives another variable to tuning.

Two-stroke exhaust tuning has a few more variables involved, but follows certain general rules of thumb. High rpm torque curves on perky racing engines can be complemented by expansion chamber exhaust systems with large center chambers and long, thin stingers. Lower rpm torque curves are improved by straighter expansion sections and larger, shorter stingers (Fig. 16–3).

Silencing is the most important aspect of any motorcycle exhaust system as far as the nonriding public is concerned. Indeed, straight pipes and unmuffled expansion chambers have alienated many people from cycling. Most bike manufacturers offer stock exhaust systems that have had hours of dyno-tuning and sound-level testing. They have selected just about the right combination for most purposes.

EXHAUST SYSTEM DESIGN

Four-Stroke Types

Four-stroke exhaust systems fall into two major categories: siamesed or collector type, and the far more common independent headpipe and muffler type.

Fig. 16–1   Side view of combination street-trail pipes

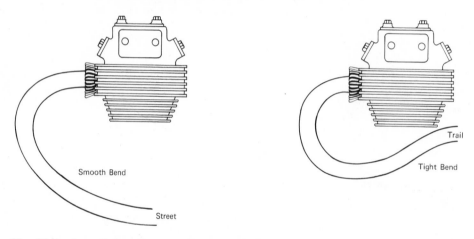

Fig. 16–2   Smooth bends versus tight radius bends

The balanced, racy look of many pipes and mufflers have enticed designers of four-cylinder motorcycles to include a lot more chrome and bulk than is actually necessary. However, the four pipes and mufflers do an excellent job of silencing the engine and still generate respectable power output. A typical "four-into-four" system is shown in Fig. 16–4. Here each exhaust pulse is truly "independent" of pulses from neighboring cylinders, thus the name "independent pipe exhaust system" is applied.

Siamesed or Collector Systems. In an effort to lighten and simplify their exhaust systems, early woods riders "siamesed" the exhaust pipes of their four-stroke twins into one collector pipe and muffler. They noticed an immediate increase in low-end and mid-range torque. Most of them

didn't know that they were increasing the velocity of gases through the collector pipe and actually generating pulses that helped to "extract" the exhaust from the ports at certain rpm. In siamesed and stock pipes the power increase was usually in the 2000- to 4500-rpm range (Fig. 16–5).

Exhaust tuning soon evolved into a science that enabled builders to enhance the overall purpose of the machine by designing an exhaust system to produce more power in a given rpm range. No longer were pipes simply "siamesed" or joined into a single pipe. Now motorcycle exhaust header systems were being made to feature individual runner pipes blending at reducing cones into collector pipes (Fig. 16–6).

The advent of the four-cylinder four-stroke engine brought on the success of the four-into-one exhaust system. It has already proven itself

(a)

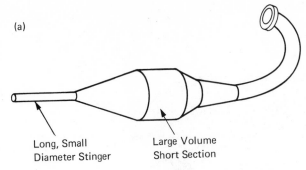

Long, Small
Diameter Stinger

Large Volume
Short Section

High Engine RPM Expansion Chamber

(b)

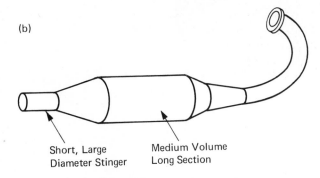

Short, Large
Diameter Stinger

Medium Volume
Long Section

Medium Engine RPM Expansion Chamber

Fig. 16–3 Expansion chamber: (a) high engine rpm and (b) medium engine rpm

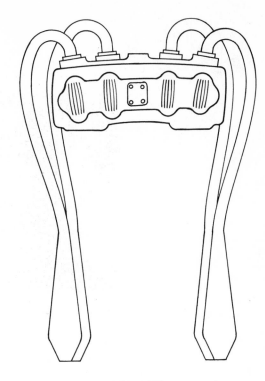

TOP VIEW
4-Cylinder Engine Exhaust

Fig. 16–4 Four into four, showing individual pipes going to individual mufflers

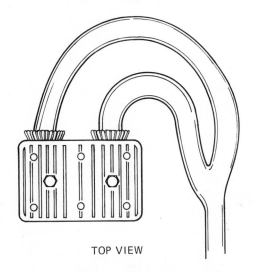

TOP VIEW

Fig. 16–5 Siamesed exhaust pipes: a top view of a twin cylinder engine with exhaust pipes merging into one alongside of engine

Equal Length Runner Pipes

Collector

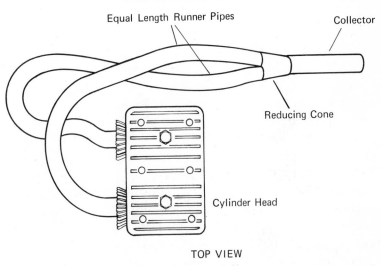

Reducing Cone

Cylinder Head

TOP VIEW

Fig. 16–6 Two-cylinder header showing the individual runners, the reducing cone, and collector pipe

at drag strips, road courses, and on the street (Fig. 16–7).

Two-Stroke Types

So far, two-stroke tuners have not met with any great success using collector-type exhaust systems. For this reason, the ring-ding fraternity has stuck with individual pipe exhaust systems both for competition and the street.

Street systems use a conventional baffle type of muffler expansion chamber combination that has been factory tuned for good performance with low noise levels. Two-stroke muffler systems are

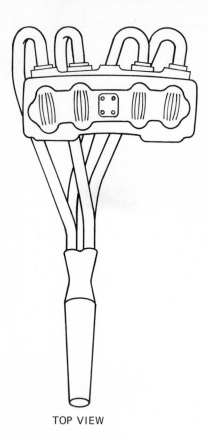

TOP VIEW

Fig. 16–7 A four-cylinder header

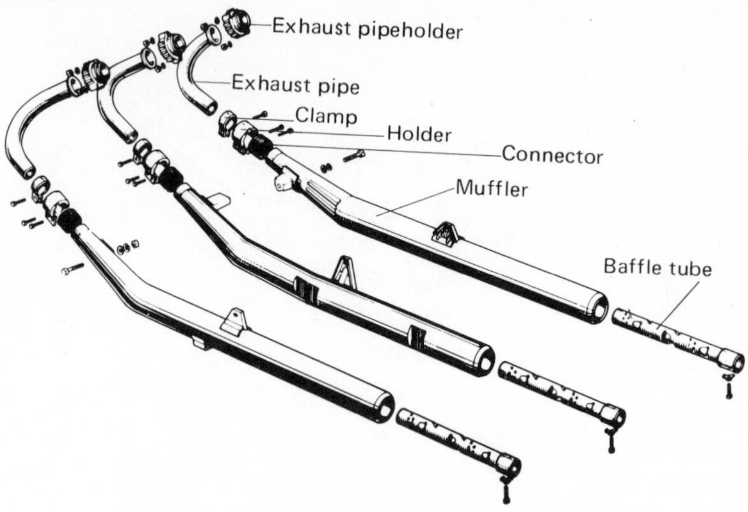

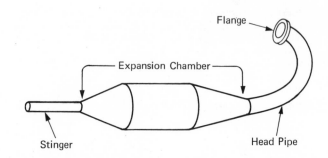

Fig. 16–8 Two-stroke street exhaust system (Courtesy Kawasaki Motors Corporation)

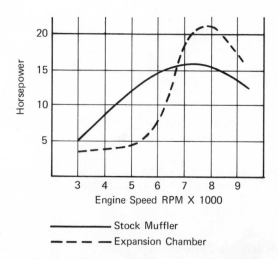

Fig. 16–9 Expansion chamber: a typical expansion chamber configuration showing flange, head pipe, expansion chamber, and stinger

so well designed that most of the noise you hear comes from the intake passage rather than the exhaust. A typical two-stroke street exhaust system is shown in Fig. 16–8. Notice that the muffler insert tubes can be removed for cleaning, they will be discussed in the service section of this unit.

Competition two-stroke exhaust systems and many after-market mufflers follow the expansion chamber configuration (Fig. 16–9).

The stinger section is often a fiberglass-packed muffler that helps keep down the decibel level. The sizes and lengths of various parts of the expansion chamber affect how the engine runs. The usual result is that expansion drastically increases power in a very narrow rpm range while greatly sacrificing power at other rpm ranges (Fig. 16–10).

Muffler Design. Exhaust system engineers have advanced to a point where they are designing quite efficient silencers for today's motorcycles. They now avoid the use of the old straight-through fiberglass-packed muffler in favor of the internally baffled chambered type (Fig. 16–11).

Fig. 16–10 Performance curve comparing stock muffler versus expansion chamber effectiveness

182

The straight-through muffler would seem to be more efficient to the casual observer, but it isn't necessarily better. Since exhaust gases flow at the outside of the air column as well as the inside, it is important that turbulence caused by holes in the straight through muffler tube be avoided. The jagged edges of the perforated inner tube between the exhaust and the fiberglass packing generates surface turbulence that causes decreased flow and lost power.

Some Accessory Silencers. Spark arrestors of the swirl type redirect the exhaust gases past a baffle in a swirl pattern so they exit through a ring-type slot to the atmosphere. These little devices work well where a very narrow, very quiet unit is needed (Fig. 16–12).

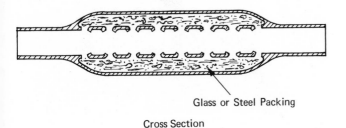

Glass or Steel Packing

Cross Section

Fig. 16–11 Cutaway view of a straight-through packed muffler

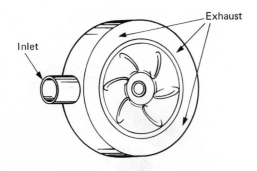

Exhaust

Inlet

Fig. 16–12 A typical swirl-type muffler

DIAGNOSIS AND SERVICE

Four-Stroke Diagnosis

Other than outside rust or obvious damage, there are seldom any problems with an average stock four-stroke exhaust system. Major dents can cause severe gas-flow restriction and require the replacement of the banged-up part. In rare instances, internal deterioration or factory defects

may cause some unbelievable frustrations to the mechanic. A bike can have good compression, perfect ignition, fresh gas, good carburetion, proper valve lift and timing, but really run poorly on one cylinder because that exhaust pipe is blocked. Consider the possibility of a restricted exhaust passage when you think you've checked everything else. This rare problem occurs on systems with double-thick pipes that are used to keep the chrome from overheating and bluing (Fig. 16–13).

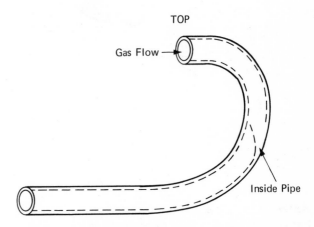

TOP

Gas Flow

Inside Pipe

Fig. 16–13 Internal exhaust blockage showing inside pipe blocking gas flow

The same problem also occurs on old mufflers where the internal baffles have rusted off and block the escape of exhaust gases.

The best way to test for a blocked exhaust is to remove the old exhaust pipe and inspect it visually. If it seems suspect, borrow and install an identical pipe and see if the problem goes away. Remember, this is an extremely rare occurence, so don't borrow your neighbor's right-side headpipe and muffler everytime you forget to turn on the gas. *Check everything else first.*

Two-Stroke Diagnosis

The exhaust system of a two-stroke motorcycle should be a regularly scheduled maintenance item. On bikes equipped with oil injection systems, it should be serviced every 3000 to 4000 miles and more frequently on pre-mix machines. If you notice a gradual, slight loss of power at high rpm, your exhaust system could be clogging up. This condition is illustrated in Fig. 16–14).

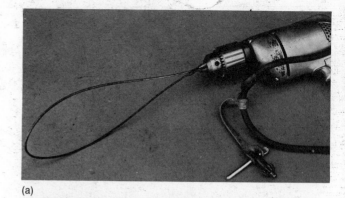

(a)

(b)

Fig. 16–15 Drill and cable trick, showing cable (a) inserted in drill chuck and (b) being used to clean pipe

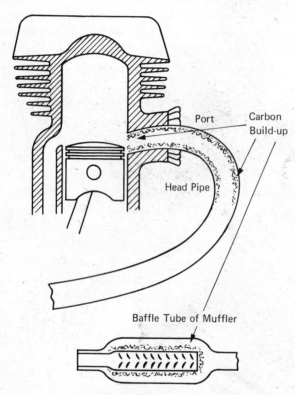

Fig. 16–14 Carbon buildup in two-stroke engine showing carbon in port, head pipe, and baffle tube

Servicing

Servicing the exhaust system is a simple task and can be handled in several ways. All these techniques require removing both the muffler baffle and the exhaust system from the bike.

Hand-Scraping Method. This technique involves the use of screwdrivers, wire brushes, and carbon scrapers to physically scrape the carbon from the exhaust port, head pipe, and muffler baffle. Carefully wipe the loose carbon away and reassemble the exhaust system onto the bike.

Drill and Cable Trick. Loop an old inner speedometer or clutch cable into a 1-foot loop and clamp the ends into a 3/8-inch drill (Fig. 16–15). Insert the loop into the head pipe and spin the loop with the drill. The technique reaches places you can't get to with hand scraping and it works especially well on small trail bikes with tight bends in the head pipe.

Soda and Water Trick. Stuff a potato up the muffler end of the pipe to block it off. Then fill the pipe with a solution of one-half box of baking soda and a gallon of warm water. Let this stand overnight, then wash out the carbon and soda water in the morning (Fig. 16–16).

Propane Torch Trick. Baffles can be cleaned pretty well by heating them cherry red with a torch, then quickly drenching them in cold water. The sudden cold causes the carbon to flake off, leaving only the baffle. Be careful not to melt the baffle; it is very fragile, thin metal.

New Parts Trick. If your bike is in excellent condition except for a hopelessly clogged, rusted exhaust system, avoid the "tricks" outlined

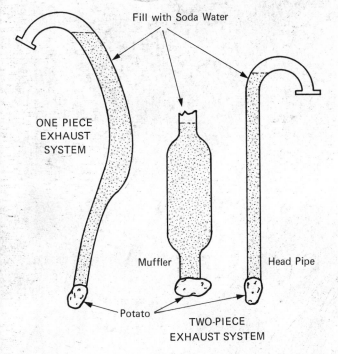

Fig. 16–16 The soda water trick, showing one-piece and two-piece exhaust systems stopped with raw

new, shiny exhaust system. Remember: motorcycles consume three things—gas, oil, and parts.

Appearance. Keep your chrome exhaust system shiny with some of the good chrome cleaners your dealer sells. The less abrasive types take more time but they don't scrape away as much of the chrome each time you clean the pipes.

If you have a trail bike with a flat black muffler and head pipe, you can pretty them up when they are off for decarbonizing. Remove the chrome heat shield and sand muffler and pipe with about a 280 grit sandpaper until it's smooth to the touch. Hang the pipe and muffler from a wire and wipe it down with paint thinner. After it dries, apply five or six light coats of flat black high-temperature header paint from a spray can. Wait an hour or two, reinstall the heat shield and bolt the unit back onto the bike. You'll be surprised how much a new looking exhaust system adds to a bike's appearance.

above for rescuing exhaust systems. Do yourself a favor by going to a dealer and buying a nice,

Primary Drive and Clutch

Many of the earlier units in this book were devoted to the study of both two- and four-stroke engines. By now you probably have a pretty good understanding of how a motorcycle engine generates power and how to maintain engines. The question now is: "What is the best way to get power from the end of a spinning crankshaft to the rear wheel where it can do some good?"

Most manufacturers currently, favor using a chain drive to the rear wheel with a clutch to allow the power flow to be interrupted. A gearbox with about five ratios helps to give the vehicle more power flow variation.

The basic parts of the power train in a typical motorcycle are the primary drive (from the engine to the clutch), the clutch, the transmission, and the final drive (from the transmission to the rear wheel). This setup is shown in Fig. 17–1.

PRIMARY DRIVE DESIGN

Because of the high rpm necessary for a lightweight engine to produce plenty of power, motorcycle engines operate much faster than car or truck engines. A speed reduction must take place, therefore, even before the power flow reaches the transmission. So when coupling the engine to the clutch, which is mounted adjacent to the transmission, the engineers provide about a 3-to-1 speed reduction. This allows the engine to turn three times faster than the clutch.

Types of Primary Drives

The engine can be connected to the clutch either by a pair of gears, as shown in Fig. 17–1, or by a chain and two sprockets, as shown in Fig. 17–2.

Chain Drive. In a chain-type primary drive, the clutch turns in the same direction as the engine. This requires a transmission with a layshaft so that the power goes in and out of the transmission on the same axis. The components of a chain-type primary drive include a drive sprocket, the chain, a driven sprocket on the clutch hub, and a chain tensioner.

The drive sprocket is a splined or tapered sprocket that fits securely to the crankshaft. The sprocket may accommodate a single, dual, or even a triple roller chain. Sometimes link belt-type chains are used because of their quiet operation and excellent strength. A typical triple roller chain primary drive set is shown in Fig. 17–3.

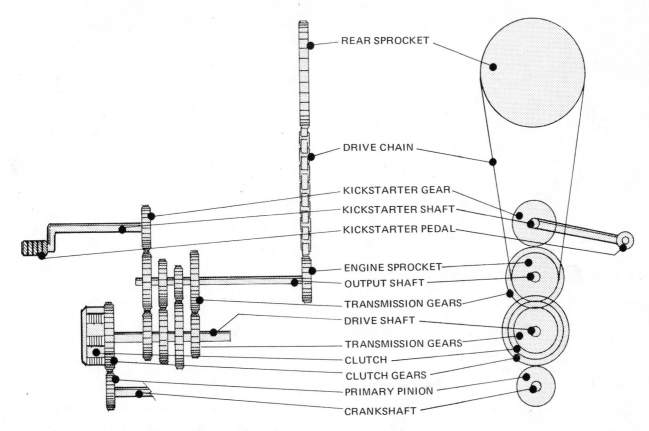

Fig. 17-1   Motorcycle drive train (Kawasaki Motors Corporation)

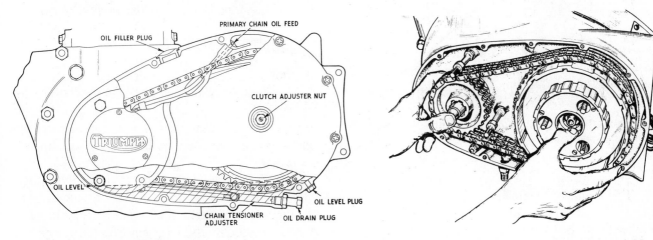

Fig. 17-2   Typical chain drive primary (Triumph Norton Incorporated)

Fig. 17-3   Triple roller chain primary drive (Triumph Norton Incorporated)

The driven sprocket is actually the clutch outer hub with chain teeth fashioned right into its circumference. Tabs on the fiber driving plates fit into slots of the clutch outer hub and transmit power to the driven plates splined to the clutch's inner hub (Fig. 17-4).

Because all chains stretch with use, some device is needed to adjust the tension of the chain for proper operation. Generally, some type of "shoe" or "slipper blade" is used at the bottom of the chain between the two sprockets to eliminate chain slack. A typical approach to this adjustment requirement is shown in Fig. 17-5.

The specified chain adjustment is usually about 3/8 inch for unit construction engines, but check your service manual for the exact setting.

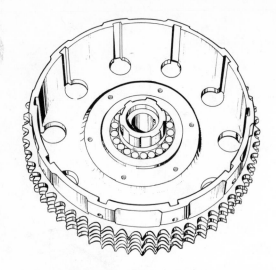

Fig. 17–4 Outer clutch hub (Triumph Norton Incorporated)

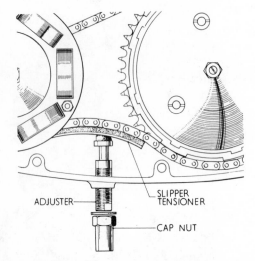

ADJUSTER

SLIPPER
TENSIONER

CAP NUT

Fig. 17–5 Primary chain adjuster (Triumph Norton Incorporated)

The primary chain, like any other chain, requires lubrication, adjustment, and cleanliness. Since it's hidden behind a primary cover, it takes a few minutes to check it. If you take the time to service it when major clutch adjustment is made it will probably last as long as the rest of the machine. Keep this in mind when reviewing the service section later in this unit.

Gears. On most small motorcycles and some road machines the primary drive is usually a set of two gears—a small gear on the end of the crankshaft and a large gear on the clutch. Their difference in size allows the engine to turn about three times faster than the clutch. This gear reduction, you remember, is part of the primary

drive's duty in addition to transferring engine power to the clutch and transmission.

There are two types of gears used on motorcycles as primary gears: straight-cut gears and helical gears (Fig. 17–6).

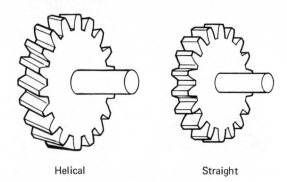

Helical   Straight

Fig. 17–6 Helical and straight primary drive gears

A straight-cut gear has teeth running straight across the edge of the gear. This approach is strong, efficient, and cheap to manufacture, but it has the drawback of being a bit noisy. Of course, this isn't too great a concern in some smaller bikes where strength and cost considerations are more important.

The helical gear has teeth running at an angle across the edge of the gear. It is very quiet but less efficient than the straight-cut gear. This loss of efficiency is caused by friction that is generated by the sliding motion of the teeth as the gears mesh. In addition, helical gears are more expensive to manufacture and generate side thrusts that must be controlled by heavy washers and extra lubrication.

Honda combines the benefits of both straight-cut and helical gears in their offset straight-cut primary drive gears. These are essentially two straight-cut gears side by side that are one-half tooth out of phase. This construction enables the gears to be firmly meshed, yet run quietly. In addition, it doesn't rob efficiency by producing excess friction as helical gears do (Fig. 17–7).

The gear-type primary drive turns the clutch opposite to the direction of the engine rotation. For this reason most machines with this type of primary use a constant-mesh transmission that has power going in one shaft and out another to counteract the rotation reversal that takes place in the primary.

The parts of the gear drive primary are even simpler than those of chain-type primaries. A drive gear mounted on the crankshaft and a driven gear on the outer clutch hub are the major parts. No adjustment provision is needed, although spacers and washers are used to keep the gears aligned properly.

Fig. 17–7 Straight-cut offset primary drive gears

CLUTCH DESIGN

The clutch is located between the primary drive and the transmission. It allows the engine to keep running while the bike is stopped and serves to "disconnect" the engine from the transmission during shifts.

The clutch has several friction plates and steel plates called drive plates and driven plates. These plates are stacked alternately, with the drive plates connected to the primary-driven outer clutch hub, and the driven plates splined to the transmission-mounted inner clutch hub (Fig. 17–8).

When the drive and driven plates are squeezed together by the clutch springs, the engine is linked directly to the transmission. There is also a mechanism that compresses the springs even further, which allows the plates to release each other and rotate independently. In this situation the clutch is disengaged so that the engine

and transmission are disconnected. This permits re-shifting or getting underway.

Remember, friction plates have radial tabs on their outside edges that fit into slots on the edge of the clutch outer housing. The driven plates have teeth on their inner edges that fit into splines on the clutch inner hub (Fig. 17–9).

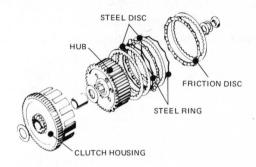

Fig. 17–9 Clutch hub splines (Kawasaki Motors Corporation)

The clutch hub rides in the center of the clutch housing and is splined to the transmission input shaft. The clutch outer hub is also centered on the input shaft, but a special bearing enables the housing to turn freely on the shaft.

Turn back to Fig. 17–1 and carefully review the power flow to the transmission. The engine turns the primary drive gear, the primary drive gear turns the clutch housing, the clutch housing carries the friction plates, the friction plates rub against the steel plates, causing them to turn. The steel plates on the clutch inner hub turn it, passing the power to the transmission. When the release mechanism is operated, the plates are free to sep-

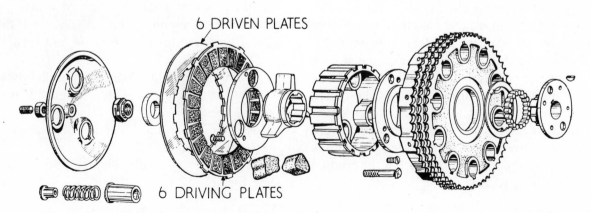

6 DRIVEN PLATES

6 DRIVING PLATES

Fig. 17–8 Clutch assembly (Triumph Norton Incorporated)

arate from each other and slip. The engine, primary drive, clutch housing, and friction drive plates continue to turn, but the steel driven plates, clutch hub, transmission, and motorcycle can remain still.

Many machines use a screw-type clutch release mechanism. The inner half of the release mechanism runs like a screw in the threads of the outer section. This action transmits the pull of the clutch cable into the direct pushing motion needed to disengage the clutch (Fig. 17–10) giving the rider a considerable mechanical advantage.

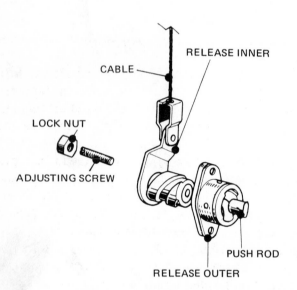

Fig. 17–10   Screw-type clutch release mechanism (Kawasaki Motors Corporation)

Some manufacturers use a cam-type clutch release. In this type the clutch cable attaches to a lever on the outside of the clutch cover. Figure 17–11 shows how a cam and lever system operates. Pulling the clutch handlebar lever causes the clutch lever to rotate in the clutch cover. Note that as cam lever (A) turns, it pushes the clutch pressure piece (B), clutch disc (C), clutch cover (D), clutch cage (E), and cage cover (F) toward the engine. This action compresses the clutch springs (G) and relieves tension from the friction discs (H), allowing the clutch hub to rotate freely.

Regardless of which type of clutch-release mechanism is used, they require careful adjustment and proper lubrication.

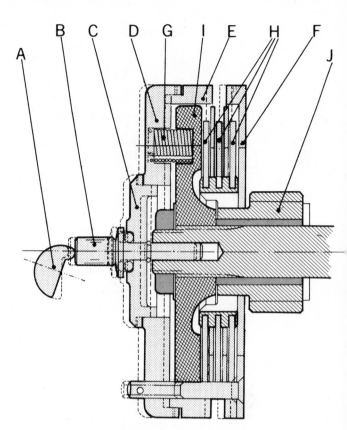

Fig. 17–11   Cross section of cam-type clutch release mechanism, showing disengaged clutch. Dashed lines show engaged position. (Pabatco)

Clutch Diagnosis

The approach for diagnosing clutch problems follows the method outlined for other systems on the motorcycle. Isolate and identify the real problem as quickly and easily as possible. Make sure that the problem is in fact inside the primary drive or clutch before pulling the side cover off the engine. Check the final drive chain and sprocket.

Is the chain tight? Are the sprockets worn?

How about clutch rod adjustment? Is it set to factory specs?

Are the cable and lever in good shape? Are they well lubricated?

Is the primary chain adjusted and lubricated? (See Fig. 17–12.)

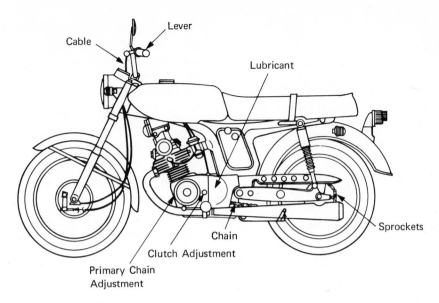

Fig. 17–12 Clutch diagnosis pre-check points

If the outside factors check out okay, try to identify or get a clue to the source of the problem from the noises and operational symptoms of the bike.

Gear Primary Drive Diagnosis. In a bike having straight-cut primary gears, some gear whine and racheting noises are normal. If the machine seems to be much noisier than other bikes of the same model, check the gear wear and the nuts, spacers, and washers that retain the gears. Don't discount the possibility of worn crankshaft and transmission bearings or bushings, which allow the mesh of the gears to vary during operation. Of course, any primary that has been contaminated with water and/or dirt should be disassembled and cleaned before any worn parts are replaced.

Keep in mind that gear drive primaries are generally reliable and maintenance-free. Therefore, most abnormal operation in a geared primary system can be traced to the clutch and its linkage. Chain drive primaries are another story, however.

Chain Primary Drive Diagnosis. Chain drive primaries can often be diagnosed by the noises they produce. Sometimes noises from the primary sound like engine lower-end noises, so

check the primary first when you suspect lower-end noises.

A rattling noise indicates the possibility of a loose chain or broken rollers. Often a damaged chain will destroy the sprockets in a short time, so correct these problems as soon as they become evident.

A rumble or "groaning" noise could be a primary chain that is too tight. Tightness causes the chain to strain and wear itself and the sprockets very fast. This extra tension also causes severe wear on the crankshaft bearing and the transmission shaft bushings.

Clunking noises that occur when the clutch is operated can often be traced to a loose chain or worn rubber pieces in the cushion-drive section of the clutch. When in doubt about the condition of the rubber cushions in cush-drive clutches, replace them.

A grinding noise could be caused by the chain sprockets or clutch rotating against the engine case or outer cover of the adjuster. Look for worn or rubbed spots on a stationary part that is adjacent to a moving part. Often a forgotten or misplaced spacer or washer causes this problem just after reassembly.

Clutch Action or Lack of Action Diagnosis. Several operational characteristics must be remembered when diagnosing a clutch. When the

191

clutch plates are separated, the drive plates are free to turn independently. When the clutch plates are forced to mesh by the springs, the engine is coupled to the transmission shaft. During the transition period, the drive plates rub on the driven plates, causing them gradually to transmit power to the transmission. Because of this rubbing and the frequent action of the springs, the discs and clutch springs must be replaced from time to time.

There are two general categories of clutch problems: clutch slippage and clutch drag. Other clutch problems can generally be traced to the lever, cable, and release mechanism.

Slippage. Clutch slippage can result from tight adjustment, worn friction plates, glazed friction plates, burned steel plates, weak springs, or improper assembly of the clutch mechanism. The replaceable parts in the clutch can be measured to determine if they are beyond their wear limits found in the models shop manual. If they are found to be worn, replacement is the only answer to the slipping clutch problem. The improper assembly problem can be remedied by following the assembly sequence called for in your shop manual. A parts book usually has a clear breakdown of the clutch assembly that will show the proper assembly sequence.

Clutch Drag (Won't Properly Disengage). Clutch drag causes the bike to creep forward in gear, stalls the engine, and makes neutral very hard to find. Nearly all clutches drag when they are extremely cold or extremely hot. Try to be gentle with a cold clutch until it frees itself and reaches operating temperature. A slipping clutch often heats up excessively and starts to drag. Try to correct slippage problems by proper adjustment before they get to this point. You might be replacing fewer parts that way.

Other causes of clutch drag can be loose adjustment, a broken cable, stuck plates, improper assembly, or a broken release mechanism.

Clutch Service

Keep in mind when servicing clutches and primary drives that a properly adjusted and lubricated primary drive almost never causes a problem. The clutch plates and springs, on the other hand, are replacement items and are designed to wear slightly with each engagement and disengagement.

The most frequently required services on clutches are lubrication and adjustment of the release mechanism, and clutch disc and spring replacement.

Lubrication requirements vary from bike to bike, but most call for a 20- to 40-weight oil to lubricate the clutch, whether lubrication comes from a separate primary case or is integrated directly from the engine lubrication system. Make sure there is enough of the right kind of oil and that it is not homogenized with water. Condensation or rain will often combine with oil under pressure to form a white frothy substance that make a poor lubricant for the clutch and primary. If this happens, drain the affected oil and refill with the proper lubricant. Run the bike for an hour or so then change the lube again to make sure you've gotten rid of all the homogenized oil.

After checking and remedying any lubrication problems, adjust the clutch release mechanism. Conventionally, this is done in several steps.

1. Screw in the clutch hand-lever adjustment to gain the greatest possible amount of slack in the clutch cable.

2. Loosen the clutch adjuster lock nut at the release mechanism (Fig. 17–13).

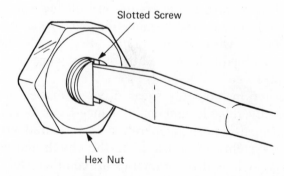

Fig. 17–13 Adjustment of clutch release mechanism

3. Lightly screw in the adjusting screw until it contacts the clutch push rod (you will feel a light resistance at that point).

4. Unscrew the adjusting screw 1/4 to 1/2 turns and tighten the lock nut.

5. Replace any access covers you had to remove, and

6. Readjust the clutch cable to give the proper free play at the handlebar lever.

Some machines, including many popular Honda models, use another method to adjust the clutch, so always check your factory service manual before attempting this procedure.

Take another look at the clutch release mechanism in Fig. 17–10. This mechanism must be cleaned and well lubricated if the clutch is to operate properly. The release system often becomes bound up from contamination, especially on dirt bikes. Service this section of the clutch before disassembling the clutch itself since many clutch problems can be traced to the release mechanism. Be sure that the clutch cable, ferrules (the cable end protectors) slack adjustors, and levers have been inspected, adjusted, and lubricated prior to disassembling the clutch for service.

Before actually pulling the primary cover to begin a clutch service job, make sure the bike is very clean to prevent contamination from ruining your clutch job. Remove any foot pegs, exhaust components, or accessories that might get in your way during the overhaul. After draining the oil and removing the primary cover (Fig. 17–14), the next step is to remove the clutch cover that is held in place by the clutch spring nuts. Removing this cover will give you access to the springs and the clutch disc pack (Fig. 17–15).

Clutch springs can lose their strength with time and use and should always be measured for proper free length if the clutch is slipping (Fig. 17–16). This measurement is given in the shop manuals for each model. Sometimes the tabs on the friction plates pound notches in the edges of the clutch housing fingers. The tabs can catch in the notches and prevent the clutch from fully engaging. The common problem, however, is worn friction plates. The fiber friction plates should be checked against the thickness specifications listed in the shop manual for that machine. The thickness to be measured, of course, is that distance from the surface of one fiber pad to the pad on the opposite side of the disc (Fig. 17–17).

Another important item to check is clutch plate warpage. All of the clutch plates should be

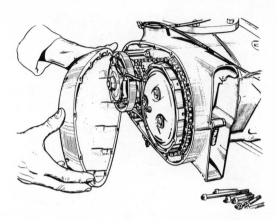

Fig. 17–14   Primary cover removal (Triumph Norton Incorporated)

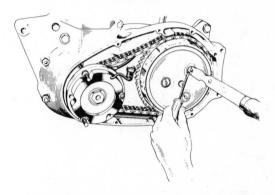

Fig. 17–15   Removing the clutch cover (Triumph Norton Incorporated)

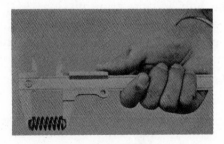

Fig. 17–16   Measuring the clutch springs (Yamaha International Corporation)

perfectly flat. The steel driven plates should be free from discoloring due to scorches or hot spots, and the fiber drive plates should be unglazed. If either condition is apparent, replace the damaged part (Fig. 17–18).

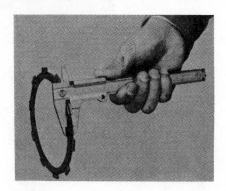

Fig. 17–17 Measuring friction disc thickness (Yamaha International Corporation)

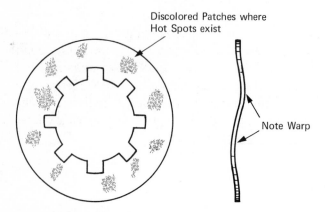

Fig. 17–18 Clutch warpage and hot spots

Some clutches use a cushioning device between the hub and the transmission shaft. This consists of rubber pads and holders mounted between the hub and shaft. These rubber pads are shown in the exploded view of a Triumph clutch in Fig. 17–19.

To remove the rubber pads for inspection or replacement, remove the three retaining screws holding the shock absorber cover plate and pry off the plate. The shock absorber rubbers can be pried out with a small screwdriver by levering out the smaller rubbers first. If the rubbers show *absolutely* no signs of punctures or cracking, you can use them again. Remember, however, that a slight puncture or crack in the rubber can ultimately result in the rubber disintegrating (Fig. 17–20).

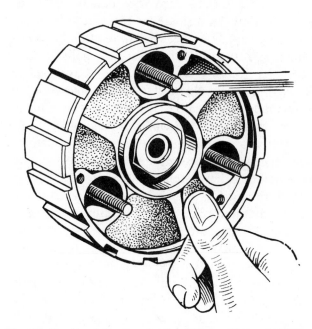

Fig. 17–20 Servicing the clutch cushions (Triumph Norton Incorporated)

In addition to the springs and plates, you should thoroughly inspect the pressure plate inner and outer hubs, thrust washers, and spring cups, and replace or recondition any part that is in doubtful condition.

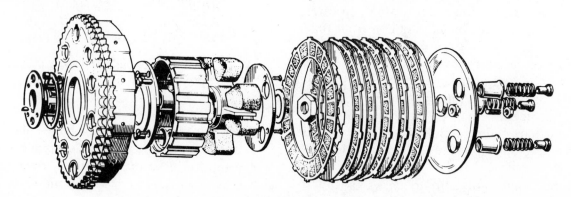

Fig. 17–19 Clutch and cushioning device (Triumph Norton Incorporated)

Clutch Reassembly. There are three critical points to remember when reassembling a clutch:

1. If the clutch is a wet clutch, oil it thoroughly during reassembly.
2. If it is a dry clutch, keep it dry!
3. Replace all parts in *exactly* the same order in which they were removed.

The shop manual or parts manual is the best guide to follow for the order of parts reassembly. If you mix up the order of the plates or forget or misplace a washer, your new clutch job can be ruined. Don't get careless at "button up time."

Many European bikes require clutch cover adjustment to prevent clutch drag. This step involves adjusting the spring retaining screws or nuts so that the clutch cover will rotate "wobble free." It is important that these spring nuts are tightened evenly to keep the plates parallel. Often the normal setting is for the outer face of the nut to be flush with the end of the stud. Check the accuracy of the spring setting by pulling the clutch lever and rotating the pressure plate by using the kickstarter. Any unevenness should be taken out by readjustment of the appropriate springs (Fig. 17–21).

The final step in a clutch job is to refill with the specified lubricant, adjust the release mechanism and cable, and then road test the machine. Give the clutch a chance to break in and allow the oil to circulate through the splines and plates. A few miles of gentle riding with frequent engagement and disengagement of the clutch should satisfy this requirement. Readjust the clutch after the initial road test and be sure to change the lubricant after 500 miles or so.

Remember, there's nothing mysterious about the clutch and primary drive system of a motorcycle. It just needs occasional lubrication and adjustment. Should you encounter one that's been abused, servicing it isn't any mystery either—just get the replacements parts required and repair the unit by following the guidelines in this chapter and the procedures in the proper service manual.

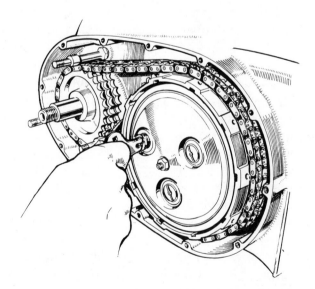

Fig. 17–21 Adjusting clutch springs (Triumph Norton Incorporated)

unit 18

Transmissions

The motorcycle engine is a wonderful piece of engineering. It is light, compact, efficient, and develops tremendous power for its size. Its one drawback, like most internal combustion engines, is that it is only really efficient over a relatively narrow range of rpm. At low rpm it doesn't develop much power, while at high rpm it wears out quickly. These characteristics of the engine require that a multiple-speed transmission be used to allow the engine to operate in its efficiency range. The transmission allows the engine to run in this narrow rpm range while the rear wheel's rotating speed varies greatly.

The typical motorcycle engine runs fast: at 2000 rpm and up on most bikes. At 60 mph the rear tires are only turning about 800 rpm while the engine is revving about 4000 rpm. Since the engine must turn five times faster than the rear wheel, an overall reduction of about 5 to 1 is required. Part of this reduction is provided by the primary drive which was covered in Unit 17. Other gear reductions are handled by the transmission, which allows the rider to select from four to six different ratios on most machines. The lower ratio gears allow the engine to get the mass of the machine and rider underway without straining the clutch or engine itself. The high ratio gears allow the engine to operate in its efficiency range at faster cruising speeds.

Figure 18–1 shows a layout of the basic parts of the power train in a typical motorcycle. It shows the primary drive (from the engine to clutch), the clutch, the transmission, and the final drive (from transmission to rear wheel).

The transmission is located behind the engine and receives its power through the clutch. The clutch connects and disconnects the engine from the transmission to allow the rider to select various transmission ratios and to start and stop efficiently.

GEAR RATIOS

When a small gear drives a larger one there is an increase in torque or twisting force and, simultaneously, a decrease in rpm at the driven gear. Figure 18–2 shows this principle. The gear reduction pictured is a 3-to-1 ratio. The smaller gear must turn three times in order for the larger gear to turn once. Doesn't it make sense that the torque force of three revolutions of the smaller gear is transferred to the larger gear that is making one revolution? Of course, it does.

Now, if we could combine several gear sets like this in such a manner that we could activate and deactivate them at will, we would have a transmission.

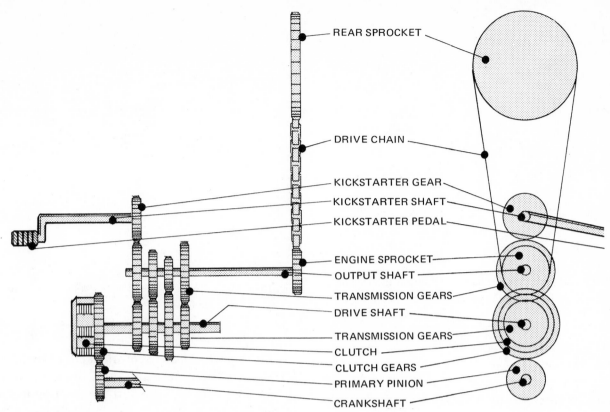

Fig. 18–1 Motorcycle power train (Kawasaki Motors Corporation)

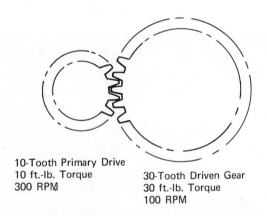

10-Tooth Primary Drive
10 ft.-lb. Torque
300 RPM

30-Tooth Driven Gear
30 ft.-lb. Torque
100 RPM

Fig. 18–2 1-to-3 gear ratio, showing 10-tooth primary and 30-tooth drive gear

TRANSMISSION DESIGNS

Conventional transmissions use steel gears to accomplish the ratio reductions. The transmission consists of two parallel shafts upon which the gears are mounted. These are commonly called the drive shaft and the output shaft, but they may be referred to in some manuals as the mainshaft and the countershaft or layshaft.

Each shaft carries four to six different sized gears, as many as there are "speeds" in the trans-mission. Each gear meshes with a corresponding gear on the other shaft. To obtain each of the different reduction ratios or speeds, the varying sized pairs of gear sets are used individually.

There are two types of motorcycle transmissions basically. Their difference lies in how the various gear ratios are selected. The more common type uses sliding gears on the shafts to select the gear set to be used. The less common constant-mesh transmission uses a cluster gear on one shaft and a countershaft to which a matching gear can be fixed to transmit power. More on the constant-mesh transmission later—after we discuss the more popular sliding-gear transmission.

Sliding Gear Transmissions

Gear shifting in a sliding-gear transmission is accomplished by forks that fit into circumferential grooves in the hubs of the gears (Fig. 18–3). Usually a four-speed transmission will have only two forks, but a five- or six-speed box needs three forks. Each gear is splined to its shaft so it can slide, but not rotate independently. These slider gears have "dogs" or tabs on their side faces that protrude to engage holes or slots on adjacent

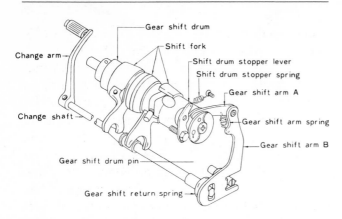

Fig. 18–3 Shifting fork mechanism (Yamaha International Corporation)

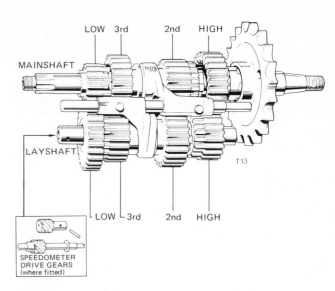

Fig. 18–5 Transmission components (Triumph Norton Incorporated)

gears. Each adjacent gear is constantly in mesh with a companion gear on the other shaft, but it spins freely until it is engaged by a sliding gear which locks the gear to the shaft. Even though all of the gears can be meshed simultaneously, only one gear set will be transmitting power. The other pairs of gears all have one gear spinning freely. When the transmission is in neutral, none of the sliding gears are engaged with adjacent gears, so the output shaft doesn't turn with any force! It does try to spin a little though, because of the friction of the gears spinning on it. Follow the sequence of events in this paragraph while studying Fig. 18–4. Another good orientation picture is presented in Fig. 18–5 which shows the gears, shafts, and shifting forks.

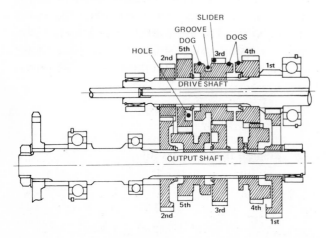

Fig. 18–4 Transmission cross section (Kawasaki Motors Corporation)

The shift forks are controlled either by a shifter drum or a cam plate. The function of the drums and plate is to convert the rotating motion of the shifter to move the sliding gears into and out of engagement (Fig. 18–6).

Fig. 18–6 Shifter drum and fork operation (Kawasaki Motors Corporation)

The shifter drum is a kind of cam with slots in its surface in which pins on the forks ride. The forks themselves may be supported by the drum or by separate shafts. Either way, their lateral movement and positions are controlled by slots in the shift drum (Fig. 18–7).

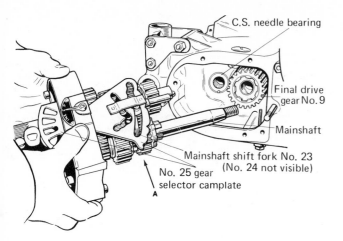

C.S. needle bearing

Final drive gear No. 9

Mainshaft

Mainshaft shift fork No. 23 (No. 24 not visible)

No. 25 gear

selector camplate

A

Fig. 18–7 Gear selector cam plate (Triumph Norton Incorporated)

As the drum rotates, the forks are moved sideways to shift the gears. Each gear change requires only a few degrees of drum rotation. Most five-speed transmissions need only 1/6 of a turn of the drum, or 60°, for each gear change. The end of the drum has a set of pins that work in conjunction with hooks and levers to rotate the drum the proper amount each time the gear-shift lever is moved. A spring-loaded gear-set lever holds the pins to lock the drum in each gear position. Sometimes other detent (or holding devices) are used, but the objective is the same — to hold the shifter drum in position (Fig. 18–8).

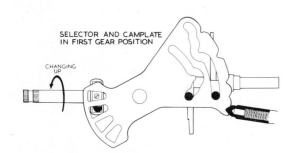

SELECTOR AND CAMPLATE
IN FIRST GEAR POSITION

CHANGING UP

Fig. 18–8 Spring loaded detent (Triumph Norton Incorporated)

Constant-Mesh Transmissions

Instead of sliding gears and dogs, some smaller bikes use the constant-mesh ball-lock type transmission. These transmissions use a one-piece cluster gear with four, five or six different gears formed on it. This cluster gear is called the mainshaft. The gear teeth on this unit engage directly with the countershaft gears that are free to rotate on the countershaft. Any one of these

countershaft gears may be locked to the shaft by the shafts four locking balls (Fig. 18–9).

Hodaka is one of the popular machines that uses this approach to transmissions. Referring to their transmission and shifter drawings (Fig. 18–9), you can follow the transmission operation. Gear selections are made by raising or depressing the foot gear change lever. The lever is connected by a shaft to a rachet device on either side of the shafts axis. (See Fig. 18–10.) After the lever has been operated, the rachet spring automatically returns the lever to its central position. Also, during lever operation the foot change shaft key engages the rachet which, in turn, moves the shifter arm assembly a selected distance into or out of the transmission countershaft. A sliding pin is fitted to the tip of the shifter arm to engage the spool end of the control shaft.

As the shift mechanism moves the control shaft to and fro within the countershaft, the ball receiver pushes a set of steel balls out of their pockets in the countershaft (Fig. 18–11). These steel balls then lock the selected gear to the countershaft since they now protrude out of the countershaft into depressions in the gear selected. All other gears on the countershaft are free since they are only riding on the countershaft, not locked to it.

Figure 18–12 shows a cross-sectional view of the transmission with the gear engaged. Note that the ball receiver has forced the balls out, to lock high to the countershaft. The engagement of the steel balls permits engine power from the mainshaft to be transmitted through the selected gear to the output sprocket attached to the end of the countershaft. The chain then transmits the power to the rear wheel (Fig. 18–12).

Transmission Service

Lubrication. Some four-stroke motorcycles use the engine oil to lubricate the clutch, transmission, and primary drive systems. The components are designed to function with a specific type and grade of oil. Follow the manufacturer's recommendation and change the oil often for good transmission protection. These oil changes

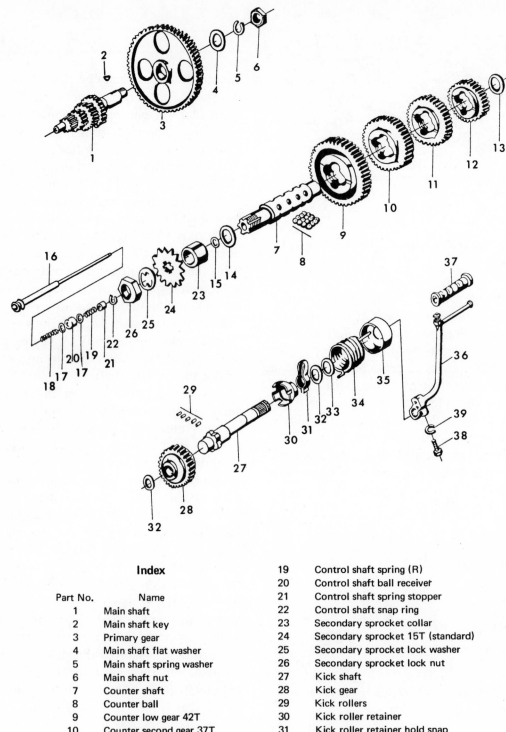

Fig. 18–9 Constant mesh transmission showing the various parts (Pabatco)

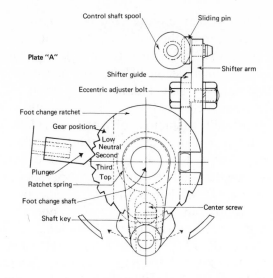

Plate "A"

Control shaft spool
Sliding pin
Shifter guide
Shifter arm
Eccentric adjuster bolt
Foot change ratchet
Gear positions
Low
Neutral
Second
Third
Top
Plunger
Ratchet spring
Foot change shaft
Shaft key
Center screw

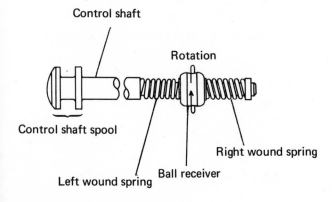

Plate "B"
Neutral position

Plate "C"
Low gear engaged

Plate "D"
Second gear engaged

Fig. 18–10 Shift mechanism (Pabatco)

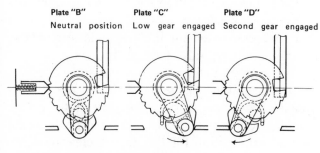

Control shaft

Rotation

Control shaft spool

Right wound spring

Left wound spring

Ball receiver

Fig. 18–11 Ball receiver (Pabatco)

should be frequent (every 300 to 400 miles) for the first 1500 miles to insure proper mating of new contact surfaces during the break-in period.

In many four-stroke bikes, and in most two-strokes, the transmission oil is used to lubricate the clutch, kick-starter, transmission and primary drive. Because the clutch friction discs operate in the transmission lubricant, use only the types of oil recommended for the bike model. "Miracle" oils, exotic detergents, and thick additives are of-

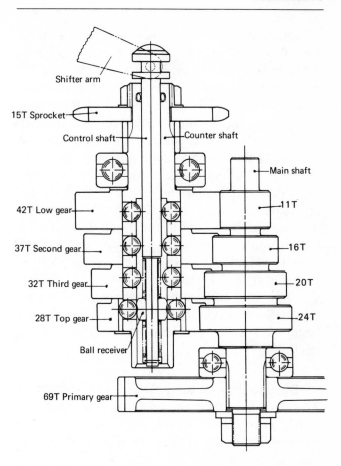

Shifter arm
15T Sprocket
Control shaft
Counter shaft
Main shaft
42T Low gear
11T
37T Second gear
16T
32T Third gear
20T
28T Top gear
24T
Ball receiver
69T Primary gear

Fig. 18–12 Cross section of engaged fourth gear (Pabatco)

ten so slick that the clutch discs slip and burn up when these products are used. It's far wiser to stick with the recommended oil and change it of-tener than indicated in the manual.

When changing transmission oil, tilt the bike to the side several times to insure that the oil has drained from the clutch area completely. Never overfill a transmission because the oil will pour out of the breather spout onto the rear tire or possibly even damage the transmission seals, causing permanent leakage. The service manual also gives the exact amount of oil to use.

DIAGNOSING TRANSMISSION PROBLEMS

Complaints about transmission problems are like complaints about carburetor problems. These two systems are so poorly understood that they get blamed for everything.

Don't tear into a transmission before eliminating a few other possible problems. Is the shifting lever and linkage clean, lubricated, and adjusted properly? Has the lever been bent or damaged recently in a fall? Is there enough of the proper lubricant in the transmission? Are the sprockets and chain in good condition, lubricated and adjusted? Is the primary chain adjusted and lubricated? Are the clutch cable and control levers lubricated and adjusted properly? Is the clutch rod adjustment at factory specs? Is the clutch slipping or dragging? (See Unit 17 for clutch diagnosis.) Is the shifting too slow or too fast? Are the kick and electric start systems in proper working order? (See Fig. 18–13.)

Only after these other possible problems are eliminated by checking and road testing may you begin to suspect problems in the transmission itself.

Diagnosing Sliding-Gear Transmissions. The two most frequent and major problems on sliding-gear transmissions are bent, broken, or worn shift forks and worn or damaged engagement dogs.

If poor gear engagement or jumping out of gear seems to be the problem, check the shift linkage first to be sure that it is rotating the drum inside the transmission. There are many different setups used for shift linkage to the drum. Follow your manual closely for specifications and design. Be especially suspicious of worn or broken lever return springs and pawl or detent springs. If the linkage seems to be in good working order, disassemble the transmission and inspect its internal parts. REMEMBER: many of the spacers, washers, circlips, and even the gears appear nearly identical in motorcycle transmissions. DON'T CONFUSE THE ORDER OF THE PARTS AS YOU DISASSEMBLE, CLEAN, AND INSPECT THE COMPONENTS. Take whatever steps are necessary to organize your work area so that you can overhaul the transmission neatly, cleanly, and correctly the first time.

Worn forks will appear scored and galled on the surfaces that engage the sliding gears. If this area is excessively worn on the gear that is giving trouble, replace the fork. Manufacturers often give a specification for the proper clearance between the fork and the groove in the gear. If this specification is exceeded, the fork and/or gear should be replaced (Fig. 18–14).

Some sliding transmissions use a slotted drum to move the shift forks. Others use a slotted cam

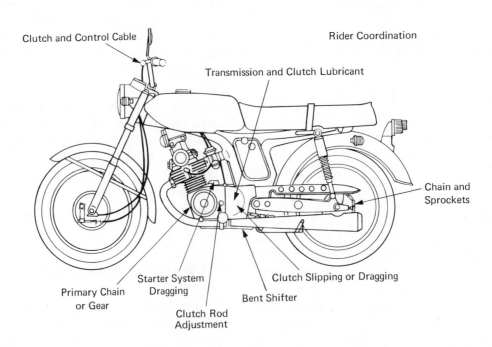

Clutch and Control Cable

Rider Coordination

Transmission and Clutch Lubricant

Chain and Sprockets

Primary Chain or Gear

Starter System Dragging

Clutch Rod Adjustment

Bent Shifter

Clutch Slipping or Dragging

Fig. 18–13   Transmission problem pre-checks

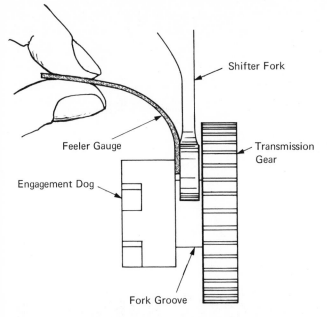

Fig. 18–14 Checking the fork groove clearance, showing shifter fork in groove and feeler gauge measurement

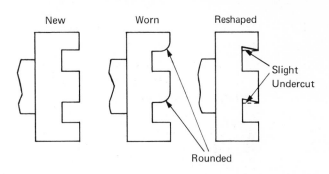

Fig. 18–15 Engagement dogs, showing a new dog, worn dog, and refiled dog with proper undercut

plate. With either method there are stresses and wear in the cam grooves. Check these grooves for wear or galling. Sometimes galled grooves can be refinished by careful filing and sanding, but generally these parts should be replaced if they are really damaged.

Engagement dogs bear the brunt of shifting. They are slammed into engagement at extremely high speeds under great pressure. Eventually, the corners of the engagement dog teeth get worn and rounded, causing poor shifting and jumping out of gear (Fig. 18–15). If new gears are not available, the dogs can sometimes be trued up or refaced by careful grinding or filing. Try to duplicate the original under-cut angle as much as possible, and don't grind away so much material that you weaken the gear. Remember, this is only a temporary emergency measure and is *not* a permanent repair!

Notice that transmission work is mostly a "disassemble, inspect, and replace the bad parts" routine. Therefore, reassembly is the most critical step. The service manual for the machine has an exploded view drawing of how the unit is reassembled. Use some light grease to lubricate the shafts and gears during reassembly. Be especially sure to replace the seals and gaskets carefully so the transmission doesn't leak. After it is refastened in the motorcycle frame refill the transmission with the correct amount of recommended lubricant, then check the other systems on the motorcycle before you road test it. After a few gentle passes up and down through the gears, the transmission should shift firmly, but not too stiffly. It should not jump out of gear under acceleration or deceleration, and neutral should be as easy to find as ever.

If your transmission overhaul meets the standards of the road test, you've done a good job. All that remains is to change the oil *frequently* for the first 1500 miles. Then the transmission should give good service for the life of the machine.

Final Drives

The motorcycle drive chain, losing only about 1 per cent of its efficiency to friction, is a lightweight, straightforward way to get power to the rear wheel. Nearly all motorcycles use a chain for their final drive, so it is important for the cycle repairman to understand what the chain drive system consists of, and how to repair and adjust it.

CHAIN DRIVE COMPONENTS

The driving member (Fig. 19–1) of a chain drive system is the countershaft sprocket that is attached to the transmission. This sprocket has from 12 to 23 teeth and is made of hardened steel. The chain connects the front and rear sprockets, transmitting the engine's power from the transmission to the rear wheel. Chains comes in several different sizes to match different service requirements.

The rear or driven sprocket is usually made from steel, though some aftermarket sprockets are fashioned from aluminum. The number of teeth on a rear sprocket ranges from about 30 to as many as 72 for special applications.

The rear sprocket sometimes bolts directly to the rear wheel, but often it bolts to a cushioning hub that helps to soften the load on the chain and sprockets. Generally, this device is simply two separate hubs with rubber bushings or cushions between them.

Chains have been improved quite a bit from the leather link belts used on early Triumphs and machines of the early 1900's. The use of chain drives in industrial applications has contributed important discoveries that are directly applicable to motorcycle drive chains. Seamless rollers, permanently lubricated chains, and self-lubricated sprockets are among the advances that have helped the motorcycle's drive system.

There are three main categories of chain used for final drive systems on motorcycles. These are the split roller, seamless roller, and permanently lubricated solid roller chains. Since split roller and seamless roller chains are similar in construction, they can be discussed together as "conventional roller chains."

Conventional roller chains are made up of inner side plates, outer side plates, pins, bushings, and rollers (Fig. 19–2). The only difference between the split roller chain and the seamless one is the construction of the roller. On cheaper chains, the roller is cut from seamed tubing, while higher-quality chains use rollers cut from more

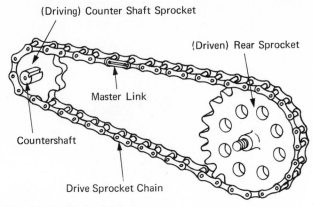

Fig. 19–1 Chain drive system

(Driving) Counter Shaft Sprocket

(Driven) Rear Sprocket

Master Link

Countershaft

Drive Sprocket Chain

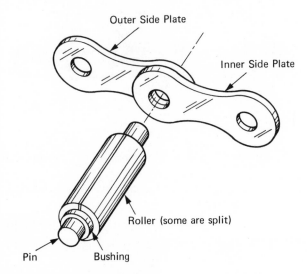

Outer Side Plate

Inner Side Plate

Roller (some are split)

Pin

Bushing

Fig. 19–2 Chain construction

Fig. 19–3 Master link swedging tool

Because chains are so vastly overtaxed on modern "superbikes" some accessory companies have tried to improve the design by doubling the chain. A set of twin front and twin rear sprockets are included with the double chain. This design appears much stronger than the original setup, but only time will tell if it will take the place of conventionally designed chains on the bigger bikes (Fig. 19–4).

Fig. 19–4 Dual chain showing sprocket engagement

expensive seamless tubing. The seam in the roller of a split roller chain is just another place for dirt to enter the bushing area.

Usually a clip-type master link is used to join the ends of a conventional chain, although a rivet-type master link is sometimes used for extra reliability. The rivet-type master link requires a special swaging tool for proper installation (Fig. 19–3).

Some chains are permanently lubricated; that is, their rollers are made of a self-lubricating oilite-type material. The rollers do not rotate on this type of chain, but rely on the lubricity of the roller itself to ease the friction as the chain passes over the sprocket. These chains require no oiling and certainly help to keep oil spots off the back of your jacket.

Overall gear ratios, which greatly affect top speed and acceleration, can be altered simply by changing sprockets. A larger rear sprocket or smaller front drive sprocket lowers the gear ratio to give more power at lower speeds and better acceleration. Conversely, a smaller rear sprocket or a larger front sprocket gives a higher gear ratio that yields less acceleration and pulling power, but more top speed if the engine can deliver the power. For the mechanic working on street machines, a change of more than two teeth on the front sprocket or six teeth on the rear sprocket is generally too drastic to be beneficial.

Second only to lubrication as a critical factor in chain life, chain adjustment is often overlooked by the average rider. Chains that become loose and sloppy on their sprockets may hop off. This can strand a rider on a lonely roadside with a damaged chain, or even break the engine cases. A tight chain, on the other hand, rapidly accelerates chain and sprocket wear due to unusual friction and tension. Chain and sprocket life can be prolonged by maintaining chain slack in the proper range. Usually 1 inch total movement is about right, with the bike loaded (Fig. 19–5).

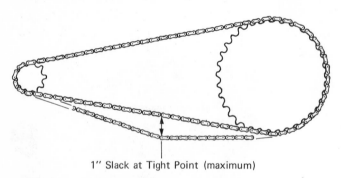

1" Slack at Tight Point (maximum)

Fig. 19–5 Drive chain showing maximum allowable slack

Shaft Drive

A few of the larger road machines (BMW, Moto Guzzi and Honda 1000) eliminate chain problems by using a driveshaft from the engine through a universal joint to a spiral bevel gear on the rear wheel hub. The enclosed rear-end gears operate in an oil bath and require virtually no service. Though expensive to manufacture, the shaft drive mechanism is smooth, quiet, and trouble-free. Figure 19–6 shows the major components of a typical unit. Service should not be attempted

with out the special tools and accurate specifications necessary for permanent repair.

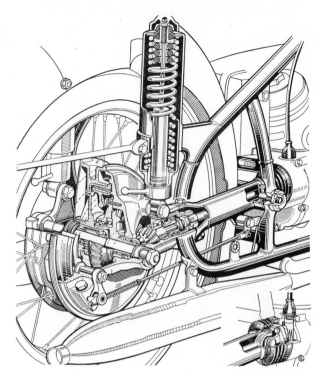

Fig. 19–6 A typical shaft drive unit (Intertech Publishing Corporation)

Diagnosis and Service

Lubrication. A motorcycle chain should be lubricated with a quality brand chain lubricant everytime the gas tank is filled. Simply prop the machine up on its center stand, rotate the rear wheel, and apply lubricant to the seams between the sideplates and rollers as the chain approaches the sprocket (Fig. 19–7).

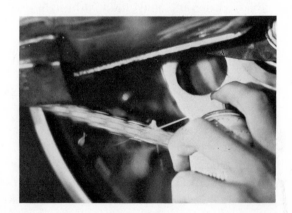

Fig. 19–7 Lubricating the chain with aerosol spray

Full-Service Cleaning and Lubrication.

Several times during the riding season, the chain should be completely cleaned and lubricated.

Using needlenose pliers, separate the chain at its master link and attach a couple of feet of extra chain to one end with the master link. Pull the spare chain over the drive sprocket so that both ends are still accessible, then disconnect the drive chain (Fig. 19–8). Leave the spare chain on the drive sprocket so you can attach the newly serviced chain and pull it over the sprocket without removing the housing.

Using a parts brush, clean the chain with Varsol, kerosene, or a "Safeticlean"-type solution. Don't use gasoline or any thin solvent because they will only embed the dirt in the center of the chain.

Shake the solvent off the chain and wipe it dry before immersing it into a heated pan of 90- or 140-weight gear oil. Gear oil isn't the only lubricant that works well. Every cycle shop mechanic or racer has his own formula that may include STP, graphite, molybdenum disulphide, or any number of other lubricants. The principle is the same — get some good, thick lubricant, heat it until it's thin, then cook your chain in it for about half an hour so the grease penetrates the rollers. Hang up the chain on a nail and let the excess drip back into the pan for next time. This treatment should be done with an old cookie canister and a hot plate rather than on the kitchen stove, because hot gear oil has a distinct residual odor.

Reattach the cleaned and lubricated chain to the piece of spare chain on the bike. Carefully draw the serviced chain over the drive sprocket, remove the spare chain, and reclip the master link, making sure the closed end is facing forward (Fig. 19–9).

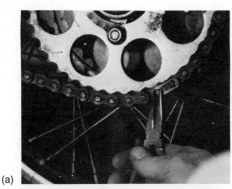

(a)

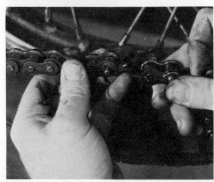

(b)

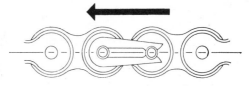

Fig. 19–9 Master link direction (Yamaha International Corporation)

(c)

Fig. 19–8 Installation of spare chain: (a) needlenosed pliers are used to separate the chain; (b) attach extra chain to one end with master link; (c) pull spare chain over drive sprocket so both ends are accessible.

Now is a good time to safety-wire the master link to the side plate. This old Enduro riders' trick just about eliminates master link problems. Use the fine wire that's available in small spools at the hardware store to wire the link clip in place. Make sure that the wire fits between the side plates of the chain so it doesn't interfere with contact between the roller and the sprocket. Three or four wraps of the wire and a nice tight twist will insure a secure master link (Fig. 19–10).

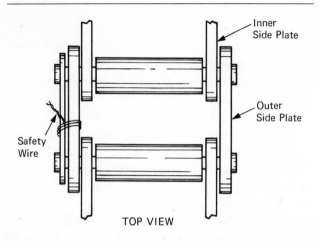

Fig. 19–10 Safety wiring the master link, showing an overhead view of link with safety wire in place

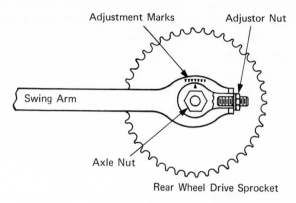

Fig. 19–11 Chain adjustment system

Chain Adjustment. A new chain should be adjusted after about 100 miles and again at 500 miles. Thereafter, the chain should be checked every 1000 miles and adjusted when necessary. If the chain is kept well lubricated, it won't need adjustments very often. Most manufacturers call for 1/2 to 1 inch of total up-and-down travel on the chain. To check properly, the bike should be taken off the center stand and weighted with the rider. The chain should be at its tightest spot when determining the amount of total free-play. If the chain has loose spots with 2 1/2 to 3 inches of free play when the tight spot is adjusted, better buy a new chain.

If the chain appears to need adjustment, remove the cotter pin and loosen the axle nut (Fig. 19–11). Sometimes you must also loosen a pair of chain adjuster side nuts. After the axle is free to be positioned in the swing arm slots, loosen the swing arm adjuster lock nuts. Turn the swing arm adjuster positioning nuts an equal amount on both sides of the wheel to keep the rear axle in alignment.

Some bikes have chain adjustment or wheel alignment marks to help you align the rear wheel properly when adjusting the chain. Many bikes, however, don't have any such marks, so you'll have to align the rear wheels in a more conventional manner. There are several basic ways to check.

Chain Sprocket Alignment. If the chain tends to cling or favor one side of the sprocket, this is an indication that the rear axle may be out of alignment. Compensate for this misalignment by loosening the appropriate chain adjuster until the chain is centered on the rear sprocket as it spins (Fig. 19–12).

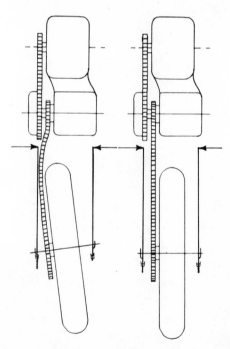

Fig. 19–12 Chain sprocket alignment (Intertech Publishing Corporation)

Tape Measure Trick. Check the distance from the center of the swing arm pivot to the center of the rear axle on both sides of the bike. Equalize these two measurements by readjusting the chain tensioners. This step usually corrects rear wheel misalignment if there are no chain adjustment marks on the swing arm (Fig. 19–13).

Two-by-Four Technique. The rear wheel may be aligned by using two straight-edged two-by-fours. With the bike off the stand, the boards should be placed alongside the wheel. They should be about 4 inches off the ground. When both are touching the rear tire on both sides, the front wheel should be midway between them. In

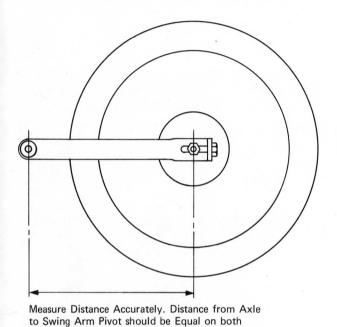

Measure Distance Accurately. Distance from Axle to Swing Arm Pivot should be Equal on both Sides of Bike.

Fig. 19–13 Measuring axle to swing-arm pivot distance

addition the front wheel should be parallel to both boards. If the wheels don't appear just as the ones in the center section of Fig. 19–14, correct the misalignment and then reset the chain tension.

Chain Length Changes. If you have kept your chain well lubricated and properly adjusted, you probably won't ever have to repair it or replace any sections. However, changes in sprocket sizes often require that several pitches be added or removed. If you should have occasion to repair, lengthen, or shorten a chain, a rivet extractor or chain breaker and a few spare parts is all that is necessary. A chain repair kit is available at your cycle shop and costs only a few dollars. The chain breaker can also be obtained at the cycle shop. Avoid small, cheap, flimsy chain breakers. Buy only those rivet extractors that are heavy enough to give a lifetime of reliable service. There's nothing quite as frustrating as a broken chain rivet extractor. To use the chain breaker, retract the drive pin by turning the screw counterclockwise until the jaws can be placed around the chain roller. Allow the spring to clamp the jaws around the roller and drive the pin from the chain by turning the screw clockwise (Fig. 19–15). You should remove two adjacent pins from the chain

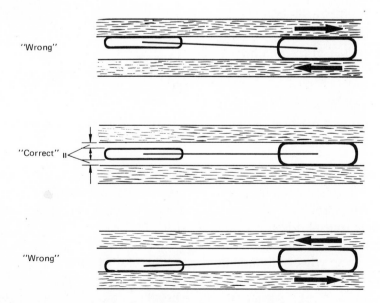

Fig. 19–14 Aligning the front and rear wheels (Triumph Norton Incorporated)

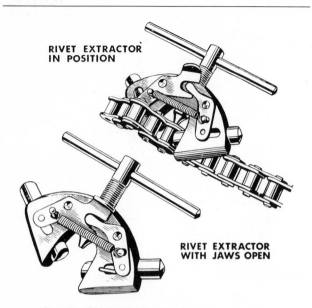

Fig. 19–15 Chain breaker (Triumph Norton Incorporated)

because it makes separating the chain much easier.

Several repairs can be made to your chain, once you've removed it. See Fig. 19–16 for the procedures necessary to cure your chain problems.

Chain Wear Tests. To test for a worn chain with the chain still installed on the bike, grasp the chain and try to pull it away from the rear sprocket. If you can see more than half of the sprocket tooth under the chain, start thinking about a new chain (Fig. 19–17). If the chain is already off the bike, lay it out full length on a clean flat surface and compress it end to end. Stretch the links, observing the amount of movement. If more than 1/4 inch of movement per foot of chain is noted, the chain should be replaced.

Sprocket Wear. It's a good idea to examine sprocket teeth for wear each time the chain is removed for cleaning. Worn sprockets will ruin even a new chain in a short time. Look for knife-edged sprocket teeth, hooked teeth, broken teeth, or side wear caused by poor wheel alignment. *Never* fit a new chain over worn sprockets or a worn chain over new sprockets. Sometimes sprockets can be "flopped over" if they are flat.

To SHORTEN a chain containing an EVEN NUMBER OF PITCHES remove the dark parts shown in (1) and replace by cranked double link and single connecting link (2).

To SHORTEN a chain containing an ODD NUMBER OF PITCHES remove the dark parts shown in (3) and replace by a single connecting link and inner link as (4).

To REPAIR a chain with a broken roller or inside link, remove the dark parts in (5) and replace by two single connecting links and one inner link as (6).

Fig. 19–16 Chain alterations (Triumph Norton Incorporated)

This trick will permit you to get some extra mileage out of a sprocket that is wearing out. Generally, replace sprockets with every other chain (Fig. 19–18).

Servicing Cushion Drive Mechanisms. Often there is a cushioning device between the rear sprocket and the wheel hub. This arrangement eliminates sudden shocks to the chain, hub,

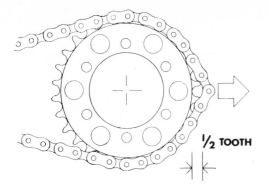

Fig. 19-17 Checking for excessive chain wear (Yamaha International Corporation)

clutch, and transmission. The cushion drive consists of some rubber or neoprene discs or spacers between the sprocket mounting hub and the rear

wheel hub. If there is excessive play or movement between the wheel and sprocket, replace the cushioning spacers.

Shaft Drive. The shaft drive system used on some sophisticated touring bikes requires almost no maintenance. Check the oil level when lubricating the machine every 2000 miles or so. The only other problems that occur seem to be an occasional leaking seal that allows oil to pass into the rear brake drum. A simple seal replacement usually cures the problem. Major repair work requires special tools and instruction best provided by the manufacturer.

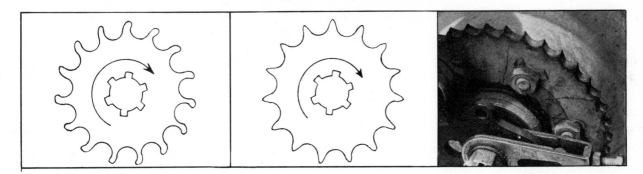

Fig. 19-18 An example of sprocket wear showing sharp sprocket teeth at left and center. Worn, rounded teeth are highlighted at right.

Charging Systems

ELECTRICAL THEORY

Electrical energy ignites the air-fuel charge in the combustion chamber, powers head and tail lights, and operates other components on the motorcycle. An understanding of the basic principles and theory of electricity is necessary to become a top mechanic. This unit is designed to get you started in that direction.

Electron theory states that all materials are composed of tiny parts called atoms that in turn are made from electrically charged particles, including electrons that have a minus (−) charge and protons that have a positive (+) charge. These particles are constantly moving or vibrating and the outer electrons are able, under the right conditions, to drift or flow some distance from the original atom (Figs. 20–1, 20–2).

Some substances, metals in particular, with loosely held outer electrons are good electric conductors because the electrons are able to drift through the material freely. Substances with tightly held outer electrons are insulators. Those materials with outer electrons that can be moved, but not as readily, are referred to as resistors.

When a source of extra electrons, (−) or negative charge exists in one part of a conductor and a source lacking enough electrons to be neutral, (+)

or positive charge is connected to another part of the same conductor, the electrons will mostly tend to drift in the same direction. The electrons will drift toward the positive source, creating what is called a current flow (Fig. 20–3).

Units of Electricity

We need to be able to describe how much current is flowing, how much electrical difference exists between two points, and how much difficulty the electrons will have traveling or drifting from one point to another. The words that describe these values are voltage, amperage, and resistance.

Voltage. The difference between the excess electrons available at one source and those lacking at another source is called voltage, and sometimes it is also referred to as electromotive force (emf). We also refer to voltage as potential difference. The measured unit is the volt with the symbol V (and sometimes E).

Amperage. The amount of electron drift or flow is called amperage. The measured unit is the ampere (sometimes amp) with the symbol A (and sometimes I). We also call amperage "current."

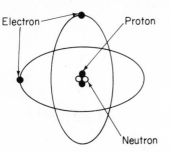

Fig. 20-1 Structure of an atom (Herbert E. Ellinger, *Automechanics*. By permission of Prentice-Hall, Inc.)

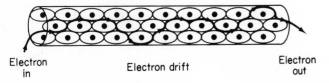

Electron in

Electron drift

Electron out

Fig. 20-2 Electron drift (Herbert E. Ellinger, *Automechanics*. By permission of Prentice-Hall, Inc.)

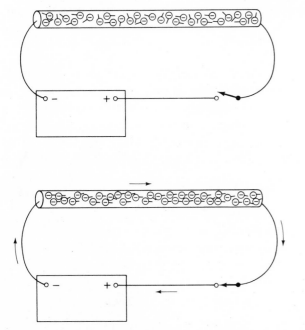

Fig. 20-3 Current flow, showing battery at lower left connected to conductor. The electron move toward the positive pole. (Herbert E. Ellinger, *Automechanics*. By permission of Prentice-Hall, Inc.)

Resistance. Electrons move or drift through some materials more readily than others, and some not at all. When a material is capable of allowing current flow, the ease or difficulty of flow or drift can be measured, and this difficulty is called electrical resistance. The resistance unit is the ohm with the symbol Ω (and sometimes R).

These units are more easily understood when they are compared to water running through a pipe. Voltage would be the *pressure* available to make the water flow. You can have voltage or electrical pressure and not have current or flow, just as you can have water pressure in a pipe and not have flow. Amperage or current flow is similar to the *amount* of water coming out of the end of the pipe or flowing past any given point in the pipe for a given period of time (Figs. 20-4, 20-5).

Electrical resistance can be compared to water flow *resistance* created by making a pipe smaller in diameter or longer (Fig. 20-6). It takes a greater pressure to force water to flow at a given rate (gallons per hour) through a pipe 1000 feet long compared to a pipe 10 feet long. Electric wire has the same effect; a long wire of a given size requires a greater voltage to obtain the same

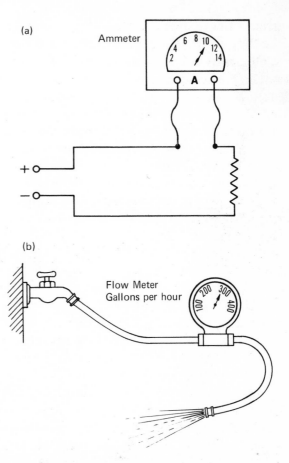

Fig. 20-4 Ammeter (a) on circuit and flowmeter (b) on pipe, showing ampere and gallons per hour readings

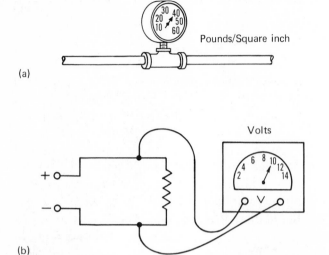

(a)

(b)

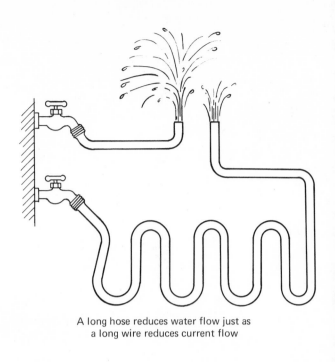

A long hose reduces water flow just as
a long wire reduces current flow

Fig. 20–5 Voltmeter (a) and pressure meter (b), showing readings

Fig. 20–6 An example comparing electrical wire resistance to the resistance in a water pipe

current flow, amperage, than if the same wire were shorter. Increasing the diameter of a wire allows the current to flow more easily. Decreasing the diameter of the wire increases its resistance (Table 20–1).

Ohm's Law. A definite relationship, known as Ohm's law, exists among the three electrical units. Using the symbols discussed earlier—I for amperage, R for resistance, and E for voltage—Ohm's law can be expressed by the formula:

$$I = \frac{E}{R}$$

It means current (I) equals voltage (E) divided by resistance (R). If you know the values of any two, you can find the value of the missing one. An example would be where an ignition coil had a resistance measured at 1.2 Ω (R) and was supplied a voltage of 6 V (E), the current flow would be:

$$\frac{E}{R} = \frac{6}{1.2} = 5 \text{ A (I)}$$

The relationship could also be written as:

$$E = I \times R \quad \text{or} \quad R = \frac{E}{I}$$

Table 20–1   *Resistances of Wire Sizes for Copper Wire*

Wire Gauge	Diam. (Thousandths)	Ohms Resistance Per Foot Length
10	.102	.0010
12	.081	.0016
14	.064	.0025
16	.051	.0040
18	.040	.0064
20	.032	.0100
22	.025	.0160

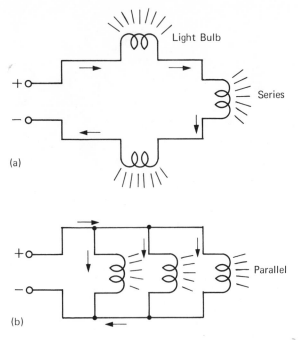

Fig. 20-7 Three light bulbs connected in series (a) and in parallel (b).

Fig. 20-8 Selecting voltage scale on meter

Parallel and Series Circuits

A discussion of electricity must include what is meant by a series or parallel circuit, the circuit being the path that electricity follows as current flows. Using three light bulbs as components to be connected together, you could connect them as shown in Fig. 20-7. The bulbs in parallel will have the same voltage on either side while the bulbs in series will not. Try making the connections after you learn to use electrical meters and see for yourself. The light bulbs are one kind of resistance. Other kinds of resistances found on motorcycles include the wiring, horn, ignition system components, and other electrical accessories. The wiring used to connect these accessories to the power supply can be combinations of parallel and series circuits.

Meter Use

Don't let the talk about flow and current and electromotive force stop your reading and force you into just changing tires. What really counts is your ability to measure electrical values and determine if a part or a circuit is operating properly. Knowing what kind of meter to use, how to connect it correctly and take an accurate reading are the first skills you need to be a fine motorcycle electrical troubleshooter.

Voltmeters. The typical voltages to be measured on a bike are in the 0-10 or 0-20 volt ranges. If the meter has more than one scale, turn the meter selector switch to a scale where the highest voltage reading exceeds the voltage you expect to measure (Fig. 20-8). The test leads are then connected in parallel to the circuit voltage to be tested. Parallel connection means that current flow of the circuit will *not* have to run through the meter for the circuit to operate.

You must also be careful to observe correct polarity (+ and −) when connecting the meter. A red test lead is connected to the positive (+) side of the circuit, and a black lead to the negative (−) side. Connecting leads backwards or in series with the circuit could damage the meter. The symbol for a voltmeter is —Ⓥ— (Fig. 20-9).

Ammeter. Ammeters are connected in series with the circuit to measure the actual current

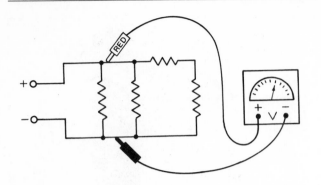

Fig. 20–9   Parallel connection of voltmeter

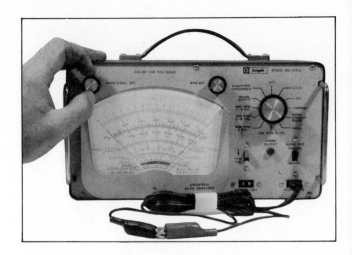

Fig. 20–11   Adjusting an ohmmeter to zero

flow. Be careful not to connect an ammeter in parallel with the circuit (Fig. 20–10). A meter capable of reading 10 A will satisfy most service work. Again, polarity must be carefully observed when connecting the meter.

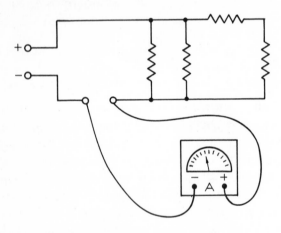

Fig. 20–10   Series connection of ammeter

Ohmmeter. Resistance of a component or circuit can be measured only with a meter when there is no current flowing through the circuit. An ohmmeter has its own low current supply that, when the meter leads are attached to the circuit, allows a small current to flow. The voltage drop through the circuit indicates the resistance of the circuit.

To read a circuit's resistance, first turn the meter to the desired resistance scale. Then connect the test leads together and adjust the meter to a zero reading (Fig. 20–11). The leads are then connected to the circuit. There is no polarity to observe. A low or zero reading indicates current will flow very easily. An infinite reading indicates no current will flow—an open circuit.

In other words, when an ohm meter reading of less than infinity exists, the current has found a continuous path along which it can travel—continuity exists! The ohmmeter is used to determine if there is continuity in a circuit. Infinite resistance indicates no path exists for electricity to flow, and this is referred to as an open circuit.

A very low or zero resistance reading indicates electricity has a very direct or short path to follow—possibly finding a route not intended by the manufacturer, a "short" or short circuit.

Multimeters. Several different meter functions can be packaged in one case; the resulting unit is a multimeter. A volt-ohmmeter-milliampmeter (VOM) and the diagnostic service testors sold by the different bike makers are examples of multimeters you might use (Fig. 20–12).

Use special care when selecting the meter function. A wrong selection could damage the meter. Make your selection before connecting leads and be sure you don't leave the instrument in an ON position when you are through using it. Battery-powered ohmmeters left in an ohm reading scale selection will soon have dead batteries. All types of meters that you will use are fragile. Banging around, grease and dirt, along with improper connections will run your equipment expenses out of sight. A handy trick is to cut a window in a styrofoam container so you can read and

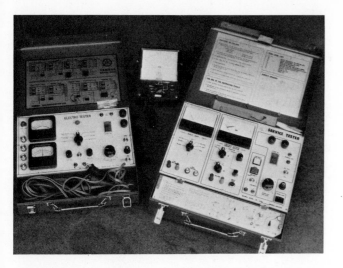

Fig. 20–12 Multimeters and diagnostic service testers

Fig. 20–13 Cutaway of a motorcycle battery

operate the meter. Then tape the remaining styrofoam around the meter and add a wire handle. These steps protect the meter in case of a fall and the wire handle makes it handy to hang on handlebars while using it.

BASIC CHARGING SYSTEMS

Battery

The battery is the basic unit in most motorcycle electrical systems. Current is made available to the circuit by a chemical reaction that takes place in the battery. The construction consists of the case, which is plastic or rubber, and three or six cells connected in series, each producing approximately 2 volts. The size and number of positive and negative plates in each cell determines the capacity (amperage) of the battery (and hour rating). Batteries are rated in amperehours: current discharged times the hours of available discharge (Fig. 20–13).

The positive plates in a cell are made of lead peroxide, and the negative plates of sponge lead. The cell is filled with an electrolyte made of dilute sulpheric acid. Insulators between the plates are called separators. A single vent and plastic vent tube serves all cells.

When current flows through a circuit from the negative plate to the positive plate, a chemical reaction takes place, supplying more free electrons. Supplying electrons from a generator to the battery reverses the chemical reaction, or recharges

the battery. A higher voltage, up to 14.5 in a 12-V system, than the battery provides is necessary to reverse the reaction, so generators or alternators typically are designed with output voltages higher than the battery voltage.

Alternators, Generators, and Magnetos

All of the mechanical generators produce current by the movement of a magnetic field through a conductor. This causes an electric current to flow through the conductor. Permanent magnets fixed in the rotor are spun rapidly, moving a magnetic field through the field coils, inducing current. This current is used to charge the battery or power circuits on the motorcycle. Revolving the coils past the magnetic field has the same desired results: an electrical current will flow (Fig. 20–14). Current flow can be increased by increasing

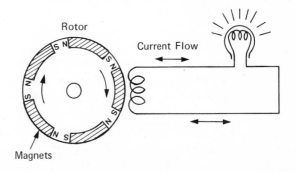

Fig. 20–14 Alternator, showing movement and current flow

the magnetic field strength, increasing the number of turns of the coil, or increasing the speed of rotation of the coil or the magnet.

Alternators. The two basic types of alternators are those with permanent rotating magnets and stationary stator windings (Fig. 20–15), and those with coil type electromagnets that rotate and produce the magnetic field that cuts the stator windings to produce the current flow (Fig. 20–16). This second type has the advantages of being able to vary the magnetic field strength by varying current flow through the field windings, and thereby varying alternator stator output.

Fig. 20–15 Alternator, permanent magnet type: (1) F mark, (2) alignment mark

Fig. 20–16 Two typical electromagnetic field coils (Kawasaki Motors Corporation)

The alternator has several advantages over a direct-current (d-c) generator. Voltage output is higher at all speeds in the alternator, so battery charging can take place even at idle speeds. Less mechanical force is needed to turn the alternator, and a lower current is needed through the brushes for a given output than is required for the d-c generator's commutator brushes. An alternator does produce alternating current (ac) that requires the addition of rectifiers to the charging circuit. Rectifiers change ac to pulsating dc (Fig. 20–17, 20–18).

Magneto. Flywheel magneto systems are similar in action to alternators. The engine flywheel has a magnet or magnets cast into it. Mounted on the stator is an ignition primary coil. There may also be a generating coil or coils for lighting or charging if the system has a battery. The addition of generation coils increases current output. A switch system can direct magneto coil output into the lighting system of the motorcycle when desired (Fig. 20–19).

Rectifiers. Rectifiers are devices that are used to change alternating current to direct current. They do this by allowing current to travel through them in only one direction. Selenium rectifiers, common on motorcycles, do have some resistance to current flow in the proper direction and do permit a very slight current flow in the reverse direction. These disadvantages are not enough to outweigh their relatively low cost and current-carrying ability (Fig. 20–20).

Four silicone diodes, used together as a type of rectifier, are in many alternator circuits for rectification. The bridge circuit shown in Fig. 20–21 is typical in larger motorcycles with alternators. Each diode allows current to flow only in one direction. Their placement in the "bridge" changes ac to dc.

Generator. The parts of a generator are field windings that are stationary and produce a variable magnetic field, an armature with many separate windings that rotate through the magnetic field, and a commutator. The commutator is a segmented rotating conductor to which the armature windings are attached. Brushes ride on the commutator and pick up current from the armature windings as it is generated by the passing of these windings through the magnetic field. All the current generated must pass through these brushes, and then is used for charging the battery or operating the ignition or other circuits (Fig. 20–22).

At low operating speeds this system does not produce sufficient voltage to charge the battery. The brushes must be heavy to carry the high current loads. The d-c charging system does not require rectifiers.

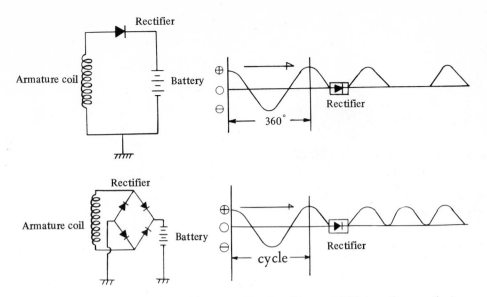

Fig. 20–17 AC current flow line wave with and without rectification (Kawasaki Motors Corporation)

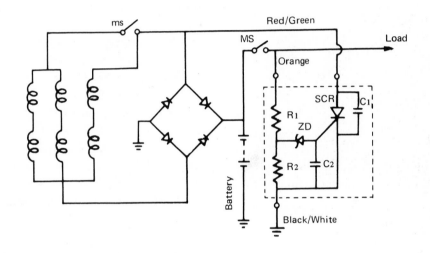

Fig. 20–18 AC generator schematic showing generator, rectifier, regulator (U.S. Suzuki Motor Corporation)

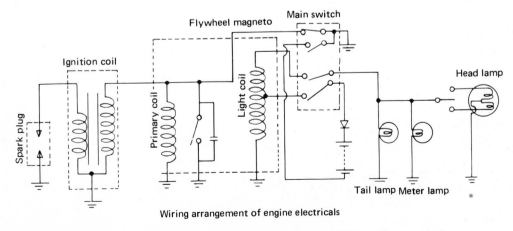

Wiring arrangement of engine electricals

Fig. 20–19 Flywheel magneto-type charging system schematic (U.S. Suzuki Motor Corporation)

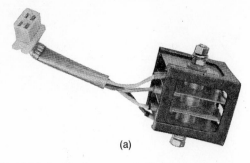

(a)   (b)

Fig. 20–20 At left, (a) shows a selenium rectifier (American Honda Motor Company) and at right, (b) shows a silicone diode (Kawasaki Motors Corporation)

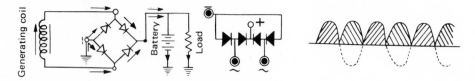

Fig. 20–21 Full-wave rectification (U.S. Suzuki Motor Corporation)

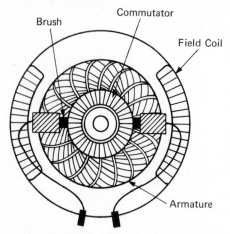

Fig. 20–22 DC generator schematic showing relation of field and armature

Regulating Charging Circuits

A fairly common practice on smaller bikes is to have no regulating system in the charging circuit; instead, output voltage of the generating system is limited by switching output coils OPEN when not needed, or by designing the alternator or magneto voltage output low enough so as not to excessively boil away battery water. It is a good idea to check battery fluid level more often on bikes of this type. Pointless and point-type regulators are the types you will need to understand.

Point-Type Regulators. Output regulation of a generator or alternator can be controlled by several methods. If the current developing system is constructed with permanent field magnets, the current is dependent only on the speed of rotation of either the field magnets (alternator and magneto) or armature (d-c generator). Some systems have field windings where the magnetic field is produced by sending electricity through coils wound over iron cores. This current produces the magnetic field necessary for generator or alternator output. The amount of current allowed through the field coils determines the magnetic field strength and, therefore, generator or alternator output.

The point-type regulator (Figs. 20–23a and b) has a small electromagnet and spring that control the opening and closing of contact points in the field circuit. When the points are open, there is no strong field (the iron core retains some magnetism) and generator or alternator output is low. When the points are closed by spring tension, field strength is high and output is high. If the voltage of the generator or alternator becomes excessive, the regulator magnet draws open the regulator points, reducing field current and lowering output. In operation the points open and close very often (rapidly) and are said to "vibrate." This vibration of the regulator points maintains a controlled output regardless of the

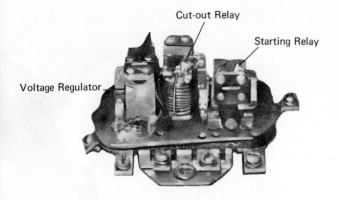

Cut-out Relay

Starting Relay

Voltage Regulator

(a)   Point Type

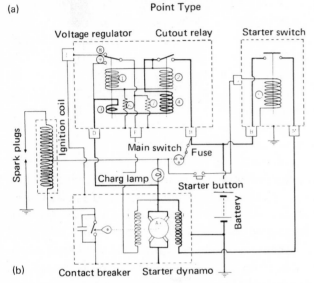

(b)

Fig. 20-23 At top, (a) shows a point-type regulator (American Honda Motor Company). Below, (b) shows the schematic for this kind of regulator (Kawasaki Motors Corporation)

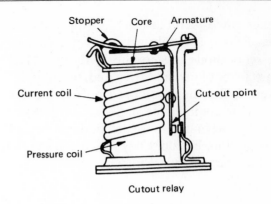

Stopper   Core   Armature

Current coil

Pressure coil

Cut-out point

Cutout relay

Fig. 20-24 Cutout relay (American Honda Motor Company)

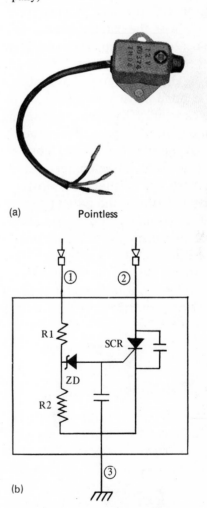

(a)   Pointless

R1

ZD

SCR

R2

③

(b)

Fig. 20-25 At top, (a) shows a pointless type regulator (Kawasaki Motors Corporation). At bottom, (b) shows the schematic for this type regulator (Kawasaki Motors Corporation)

overall demand placed on the generator or alternator.

An additional device found in d-c generator regulators is a cutout relay—another electromagnetically controlled set of points. Their purpose is to disconnect the regulator from the charging circuit when output voltage becomes lower than battery voltage. This keeps the battery from discharging through the generator and becoming dead when output is too low (Fig. 20–24). Alternator circuit diodes prevent the battery from discharging back through the alternator.

Pointless Regulators. Silicon-controlled rectifiers (SCR), or pointless rectifiers as they are called, have no moving parts (Fig. 20–25 a and b). They are triggered by an electronic device called a zener diode—a diode that does allow current to reverse flow, but only above a specific voltage. The zener diode triggers the SCR which will not allow current flow until triggered, but then allows current to flow until voltage is no longer being applied. This combination maintains output voltage from the alternator to a specific level regardless of generation, but does not regulate when output is below the needed voltage.

Service Procedures

Battery. Battery service is most easily and safely done with the battery out of the bike. Disconnect it (ground strap first) and go to a work bench. Remove the caps and fill to the proper level, using distilled water if available. Charging should be done at very low rates, 1 to 2 amps, with the caps off. Charging at a rate higher than the manufacturer's specs will generate excess heat, warp the cell plates, and cost someone a new battery. Turn off the charger before you disconnect it from the battery. Explosions have resulted from sparks at the battery terminals igniting the excess oxygen and hydrogen vapors that are produced during the charging process.

The state of the battery charge can be checked by measuring the specific gravity of the battery fluid with a hydrometer (Fig. 20–26). A specific gravity of 1.280 at 60°F indicates a full

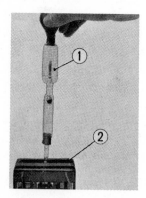

Fig. 20–26 Measuring specific gravity of a battery (a) hydrometer, (2) battery (American Honda Motor Company)

charge. Higher or lower temperatures will result in less accurate hydrometer readings.

Battery cables, cases, and terminals should be cleaned before the battery is replaced. A coat of vaseline or grease on the connections after they are tightened will help to prevent corrosion. Battery vent tubes should be routed carefully because an overflow will corrode parts of the bike. The vent tube slit should be near the battery.

Alternator. Cleaning, testing, and replacing defective units are the normal alternator service procedures. The electrical tests include checking resistances, grounds, and open circuits and, when the unit is operating, voltage and current.

Output. The first test to make on most alternators is the charging voltage test with the engine running at the specified rpm. Observe polarity on the connecting leads and check the voltmeter reading against the service manual. On 12-volt systems it should be in the 14–15 volt range. Checking the output of a bike with the battery or other components removed is risky with the new electronic components. Heavy loads or reversed grounding can destroy them. Look at all components for cracks and breaks. Charging current is also checked as a sulfated battery may not accept a charge at the normal output voltage.

Field. If the field is a permanent magnet type there is no regular way to test its magnetic strength. Some mechanics place the magnet on the side of a metal cabinet; if it slides off or falls, it is too weak. When alternator output is low and all other components are checked out as OK, then replacement is necessary—after determining why the magnet lost its magnetism. Banging around, hammering on, overheating, and strong electric currents can all damage a magnet. Coil types should be checked for correct resistance and shorts with an ohmmeter. Infinite resistance (full scale) should be the reading between the winding and its base (Fig. 20–27). Slip rings should be clean and the brush lengths should fall within manual specifications.

Stator Windings. Look for poor insulation, broken wires, and signs of heat deterioration. Check the windings for the right resistance. Shorts (too low a resistance) and opens (a very high resistance) show replacement is necessary. Unless the cure with electrical parts is obvious

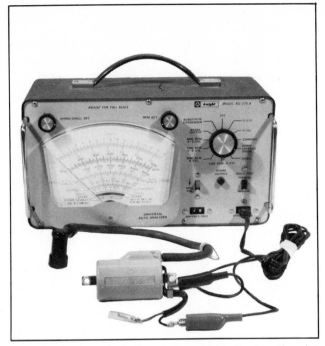

Fig. 20-27 A typical ohmmeter used to check coil resistance between windings and base

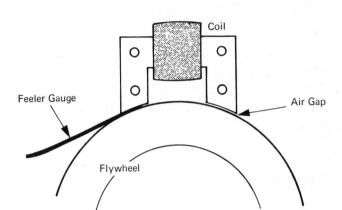

Flywheel to Coil Airgap

Coil

Feeler Gauge

Air Gap

Flywheel

Fig. 20-28 Adjustment of flywheel to coil air gap as measured with feeler gauge

and easy, replacement is the best way to go—after the cause of the problem has been corrected.

Magneto. These systems are similar to alternators except the ignition circuit is in close relationship, the coils for lighting and ignition are both stationary, and the rotating magnets are always permanent. The lighting coil is tested with an ohmmeter and its output with a voltmeter at a specified (in the manual) rpm. Defective or suspected parts are replaced. Substitution of new parts to see if output improves is one way to test the system. Be sure the part won't be damaged in the substitution or you won't be making much of a profit.

When coils are movable within the flywheel, be sure the air gaps between the flywheel and the coil core ends are properly adjusted. Feeler gages are the tools to use (Fig. 20-28).

Regulator. The solid state or pointless regulators can be tested and must be replaced if defective. As there are almost as many types as there are bike manufacturers, close use of workshop manuals for testing connections and specifications is the way to go. An ammeter is sometimes

used to determine if there is current flow at a given voltage (Fig. 20-29).

Point-Type Regulator. Pitted points can be restored by filing to a smooth flat surface (Fig. 20-20). Fine sandpaper or fingernail emery boards are recommended by some manufacturers for this job, but be sure to clean out any grit that may remain on the points. Point-type regulators are usually adjustable by a screw-type adjustor or by bending the tang that holds one end of the points spring (Fig. 20-31). Changing the spring tension of the points changes the output voltage that the regulator is set at.

Check the cutout relay, if the regulator has one, by starting the bike with a voltmeter attached to the charging system and observe what voltage the cutout functions at—anything less than above battery voltage (12.5–13 V is normal for a 12-V system) is telling you to try to adjust it. If adjustment fails, replace the regulator. The points and spring in the cutout relay are cleaned and adjusted the same as the voltage relay. Coil resistance on relays may be specified and should be checked.

D-C Generators. These generators have an armature made of many coils, each connected to two segments of the commutator. The output cur-

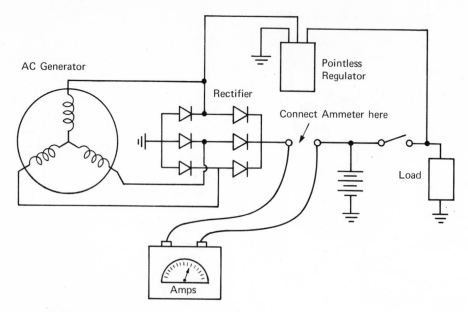

Fig. 20-29 Schematic of charging circuit with ammeter to test output

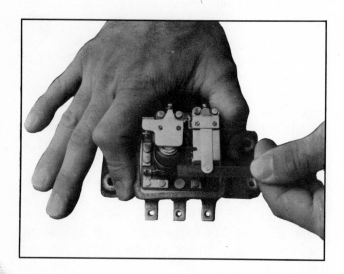

Fig. 20-30 Filing points on a regulator with an emery board

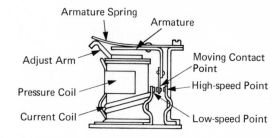

Fig. 20-31 Regulator output adjustment: to change spring tension adjustment, bend adjusting arm

SYMBOLS AND DIAGRAMS

Wiring diagrams in the different shop manuals follow no standard and often are a combination of electrical schematics and pictorials. The following is a list of symbols and pictorials you may encounter and some notes on their meanings:

Battery

Resistance

Light Bulb   or

Capacitor   or

Coil

rent is transferred from the armature by the commutator segments through the brushes. Burned, unevenly worn, and short brushes are replaced in pairs. The commutator may be polished with flint or garnet sandpaper. If it is very rough or pitted, place the armature in a lathe and cut or turn down the commutator the minimum necessary to regain a clean surface. Undercutting of the mica segment insulators with a ground hacksaw blade is then needed (Fig. 20-32). The segments and insulation can be checked for shorts with an ohmmeter. Replace it if it is shorted.

Ammeter ─(A)─

Voltmeter ─(V)─

Rectifier ─▷├─

(Current will flow through only in one direction—right to left on this diagram)

Switch ──o⌒o── or ──□□──

Fuse ──o⌒o──

Ground ─┤|├ or ⏚

(The frame on most bikes is used as ground. Current flows through the frame to electrical components on a negative ground system.)

Wiring Connection ──●──

Wire Cross ─┴┬─ or ─┼─

(not connected)

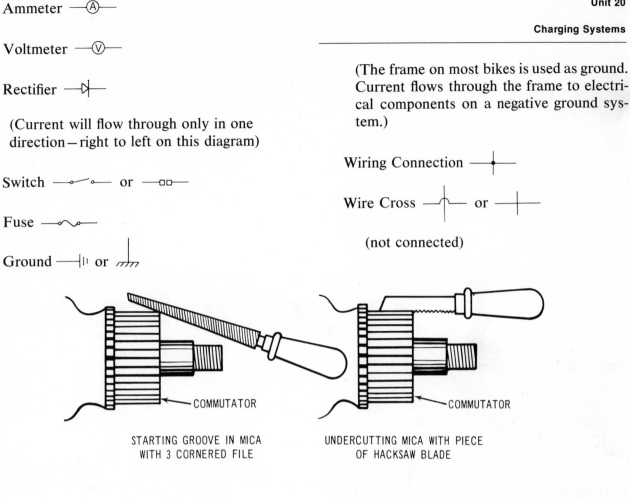

STARTING GROOVE IN MICA
WITH 3 CORNERED FILE

UNDERCUTTING MICA WITH PIECE
OF HACKSAW BLADE

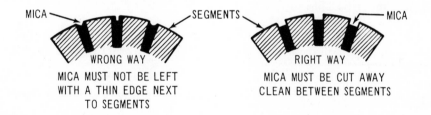

WRONG WAY
MICA MUST NOT BE LEFT
WITH A THIN EDGE NEXT
TO SEGMENTS

RIGHT WAY
MICA MUST BE CUT AWAY
CLEAN BETWEEN SEGMENTS

Fig. 20–32 Undercutting mica segments on a dc generator (AMF Harley-Davidson Motor Co., Inc.)

Ignition Systems

All motorcycles currently use a spark plug and high voltage spark to ignite the air-fuel charge in the combustion chamber. The voltage necessary is over 10,000 volts. Several systems are used on different kinds of bikes, including magneto ignition, battery coil ignition, and capacitator discharge ignition.

The ignition system must be able to:

1. Rapidly develop high voltage necessary to fire a plug.
2. Have the spark occur at exactly the right time in the power cycle.
3. Be able to repeat the cycle millions of times without service.
4. Function properly over a wide variety of temperatures, moisture levels, and rpm.

The timing of the spark is particularly important in relation to the power output of the engine. On a two-cycle engine running at 8000 rpm, an ignition spark must occur 133 times a second. For maximum power, the timing of these sparks should be accurate to 1° of a revolution of the crankshaft. At 8000 rpm, the spark must be accurately timed to 2/100,000 of a second. To maintain this kind of accuracy is your job. So, first, let's discuss how the various systems work.

KINDS OF SYSTEMS

Battery Coil

The parts of the battery coil system include an ignition coil with two windings, a current supply, a set of points, points cam, a capacitor, and the spark plug set up similar to that in Fig. 21–1.

Battery. This is the source of direct current used to power the system.

Ignition Coil. The coil is composed of a primary winding of relatively heavy copper wire (0.5 to 1.0 mm) wound around a laminated soft iron core, and a secondary winding with many more turns of fine copper wire (0.05 to 0.1 mm) wound over the primary winding (Fig. 21–2).

Points. The points act as a heavy duty switch to allow current to flow through circuit.

Capacitor. This is also called a condenser — a storage unit for electricity.

Points Cam. The points cam is a mechanically rotated ramp for opening and closing the points.

Spark Plug. The plug provides an accurate electrically insulated air gap in the combustion chamber.

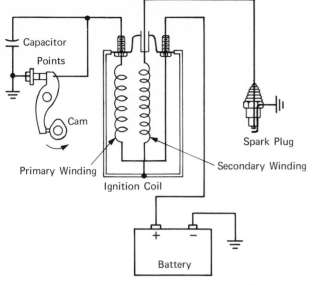

Fig. 21–1 Wiring diagram of a battery-coil ignition system

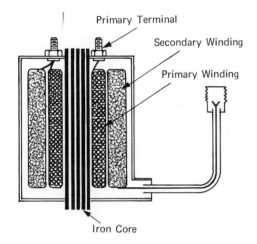

Fig. 21–2 Cross section of MC coil showing core, primary, and secondary windings

All of these parts work together in this sequence to produce the timed ignition spark. Current is supplied from the battery through ground, in Fig. 21–1, through the points when they are in the closed position, through the primary winding of the coil to the positive terminal of the battery. The current flowing through the coil develops a strong magnetic field in the coil. When the cam turns and opens the points, current in the primary coil winding stops flowing. The magnetic field collapses very rapidly. This collapse generates (by self-induction) a strong counter voltage in the primary coil many times greater than the initial battery voltage. The capacitor at this point helps stop current from continuing to flow across the points, as they begin to open, by providing a place

for the current to flow—by charging the capacitor. This charging also boosts the countervoltage by developing a highly positive area on the coil side of the capacitor.

The high countervoltage in the primary winding (up to 300 V) induces a very high voltage (mutual induction) in the secondary winding which jumps the spark plug gap and ignites the air-fuel mixture. Each time the points open the spark plug "fires." Without the capacitor the points would become pitted from arcing across the gap as the points open. Higher primary countervoltage is also possible because of the capacitor.

The cam opens and closes the points at a rate determined by crankshaft speed. The position of the cam follower on the points in relationship to the cam determines spark timing (Fig. 21–3). Rotating the points plate in the direction of cam rotation retards or delays spark timing and turning the plate the other way advances the spark timing. Often bikes with two cylinders have two point sets operated by the same cam, two capacitors and two coils to fire the two spark plugs. Other combinations of points sets and coils are also used for multicylinder engines.

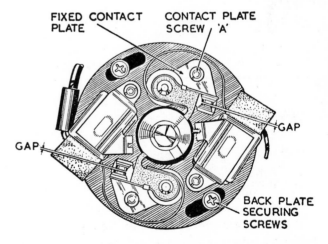

Fig. 21–3 Cam and points plate with arrow to show plate rotation movement (Triumph Norton Incorporated)

Magneto Ignition

An ignition system that uses a magnetic induction generator for the primary current source is called a magneto. In Fig. 21–4 you can see that

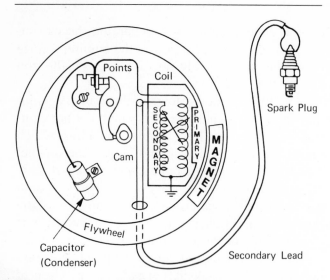

Fig. 21-4 Wiring diagram of magneto ignition system

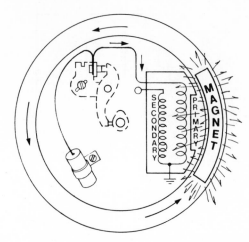

Fig. 21-5 Magnet moving past coil showing the current induction direction

the components are much like the battery coil system. You still need a points set, cam, capacitor, primary, and secondary coils. One major difference is that the primary current is supplied by the action of the magnet rotating past the primary coil, causing a high induced voltage in the primary coil. Most motorcycle magnetos fire on the field coil build-up, not its collapse.

A Magneto has several advantages that can be useful:

1. A battery and separate generating system are not necessary.
2. It has a simple construction of high reliability.
3. It provides a small engine with additional inertia at low speeds for smooth running.

An additional primary coil can be built in the "mag" for providing additional current to power lights and other accessories.

Some bikes have an external self-contained magneto added to replace the original ignition system. These optional equipment mags are designed to produce a very hot spark for severe operating conditions.

The "mag" system, except energy transfer types, works like this:

1. The magnet rotates past the coil, inducing a high primary current as shown in Fig. 21-5. (In some "mags" the coil rotates past the magnet).

2. The primary current develops a strong magnetic field around the primary coil (Fig. 21-6).
3. The ignition points are opened by the cam, causing a rapid collapse of the magnetic field (Fig. 21-7).
4. The condenser prevents current from arcing across the points by providing an alternate place for it to go. This charges the condenser (Fig. 21-8).
5. Even higher current is induced in primary winding by the rapid collapse of the magnetic field (self-induction) and condenser discharge (Fig. 21-9).
6. A very high voltage (10,000 to 30,000 V) is induced in the secondary winding by mutual induction when self-induction occurs in the primary winding (Fig. 21-10).
7. The high secondary voltage jumps the spark plug gap to complete its circuit and "fire" the plug (Fig. 21-11).

All this takes place in a time period measured in millionths of a second, and is repeated up to 200 times a second.

Electronic Ignition

The major type of electronic ignition system found on bikes is the capacitor discharge system. Basically, a large capacitor is charged with direct current of from 100 to 400 volts. A rotating signal magnet induces current that triggers (gates) a part called a thyristor which then allows the capacitor to discharge through the ignition coil primary.

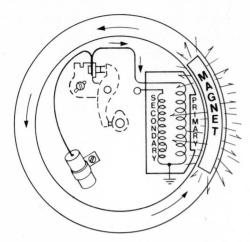

Fig. 21-6 Coil with a magnetic field opposite the magnetic field of magnet

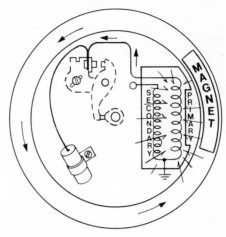

Fig. 21-7 Diagrammatic mag system: points open and primary field collapsing

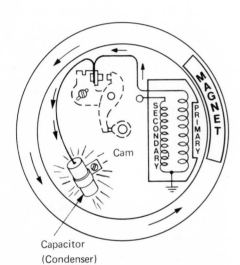

Fig. 21-8 Diagrammatic mag system: condenser receiving charge

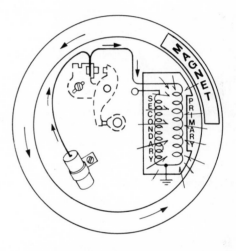

Fig. 21-9 Diagrammatic mag system: primary field collapse and condenser discharge

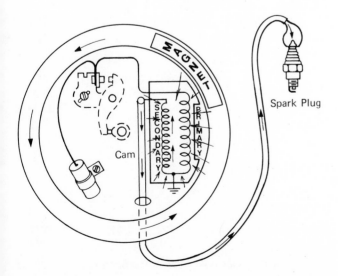

Fig. 21-10 Diagrammatic mag system: high voltage in the secondary

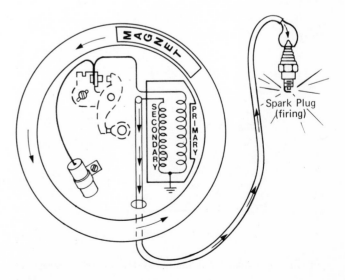

Fig. 21-11 Diagrammatic mag system: spark plug firing

The rest is similar to a conventional battery coil ignition system.

The capacitor can be charged by either bat- tery current or magnetic induction current. Let's look at both ways (Figs. 21–12, 21–13). In the in- duction system a coil, called an exciter, generates current much like a generator. The alternating current is run through a diode that converts it to dc and then to the capacitor for running up a high charge.

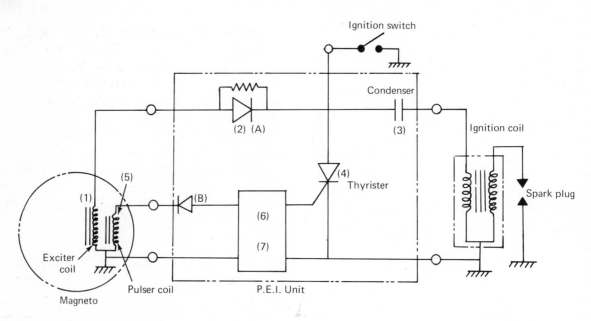

Fig. 21–12   Capacitor discharge system diagram: magneto induction (U.S. Suzuki Motor Corporation)

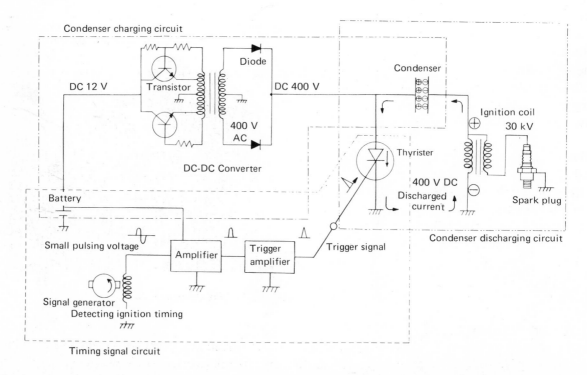

Fig. 21–13   Capacitor discharge system diagram: battery charging of capacitor (Kawasaki Motors Corporation)

At the same time the pulser or trigger coil induces current that is run to a zener diode. Both coils are located in a position similar to a regular magneto condenser points set. The zener diode will not allow current to flow in the reverse direction until a specific designed voltage is reached. Then the current flows readily on to the thryister. Most diodes allow current flow only opposite the direction the arrow points (──▷⊢). The zener diode will reverse above design voltage.

The thyristor, similar to a diode, keeps current in the capacitor from flowing until a gate voltage is applied. The current can flow through a thyristor only in one direction — and only if a gate voltage is applied. It could be called a signal voltage switch.

When the capacitor is allowed to discharge through the primary side of the ignition coil, very high voltage is induced in the secondary, causing a spark at the plug gap. Timing of this ignition system is determined by the location of the pulser coil in relation to the rotating magnet on the shaft, similar to the location of the points cam follower and cam in a battery coil system.

The battery-supplied current type "CD" system is very similar to the one just described (Fig. 21–13). The difference is that there is no exciter coil and the capacitor is charged by current from the battery. A special unit changes 12-volt dc to ac by using transistors, a transformer to step up the voltage to 300 to 400 ac, and diodes to convert the ac back to dc. All this is to get 300 to 400-volt dc to charge the capacitor so it can be discharged through the ignition coil.

Advantages of the CD system are:

1. No points to become burned or misadjusted.
2. Ignition timing, once set, does not change.
3. Higher secondary voltages are possible.
4. Electronic switching provides faster voltage rise times for better ignition.
5. Sealed units provide a more moisture-proof ignition system.

SERVICE PROCEDURES

Ignition service is the most critical factor in keeping a bike running at peak performance. If you understood all of the theory discussed, then application through performing careful service adjustment, testing, and replacement will make good sense.

Points Adjustment and Replacement. With the proper cover removed, inspect the ignition points, looking for blackened or burned contact surfaces, pitting, or metal transfer (Fig. 21–14). Minor unhealthy conditions can be cleaned up with a points file (Fig. 21–15). Rough points should be replaced. Slight metal transfer from one point to the other is normal on most motorcycles. Excessive transfer indicates condenser problems. Be sure no oil is on the point contact surfaces. They can be cleaned with spray contact cleaning solvent.

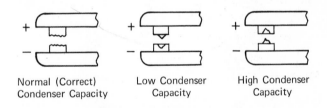

Normal (Correct) Condenser Capacity   Low Condenser Capacity   High Condenser Capacity

Fig. 21–14 Points-condenser relationship: points normal, deposit positive, deposit negative

Fig. 21–15 Points being filed

To install new points, first run a strip of clean, dry paper between them to remove any oil or wax left from their manufacture. Look to see if they are making proper contact (Fig. 21–16). Tighten in the primary wire and capacitor if connected there firmly with the correct size screwdriver. Lubricate the cam with a *small* amount of grease, and the points pivot with one drop of oil. If the cam has a felt pad, use oil instead of grease.

Be sure the wires that connect the point set do not contact the breaker plate or points cover. This commonly made mistake grounds the primary current before it can reach the contact points themselves.

When the points are correctly fastened, turn the engine over until the points cam follower is on the cam lobe—widest point opening. Adjust the points to the correct gap, using a feeler gage; 3 to 4 mm (0.012 to 0.016 inch) is normal for most bikes. Tighten points adjustment screw, turn engine through several times, and recheck gap to insure accuracy.

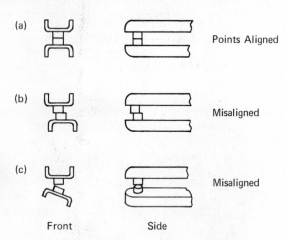

Fig. 21–16 Points correctly aligned (a), and points misaligned side to side (b), and angle contact (c)

Ignition Timing. With most bikes, ignition is timed to occur before the piston reaches top dead center (TDC) on the compression stroke. You will need the correct "specs" for the one you are working on to properly check and adjust the timing. Be sure the point gap is right before you start.

Timing can be done with the engine stopped (static) or running (dynamic). The second is more accurate, but requires the use of a strobe timing light. To time an engine statically, first rotate the

crankshaft until the piston to be timed approaches TDC. On four-strokes, make sure you are on the compression and *not* the exhaust stroke.

Engines differ, but here are some of the approaches used:

1. Alignment of timing marks on flywheel and case (Fig. 21–17).
2. Alignment of timing marks on alternator rotor and stator (Fig. 21–18).

Fig. 21–17 Alignment of engine timing marks, showing flywheel and case (Pabatco)

Fig. 21–18 Timing marks, showing (1) stator index, (2) RF mark, and (3) generator rotor (American Honda Motor Company)

3. Measuring piston travel with dial gauge before TDC (Fig. 21–19).
4. Pin fitting through case into flywheel slot (Fig. 21–20).

Others can be found by using the shop manual. Once the crankshaft is correctly positioned, the points plate is loosened and rotated. The place at which the points just open is the correct static timing. This can be found by:

Fig. 21-19 Timing with a dial gauge

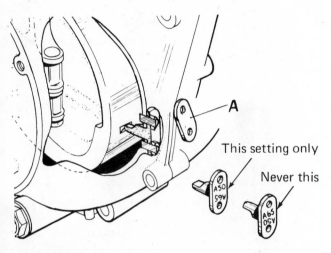

Fig. 21-20 Timing: pin through case (Triumph Norton Incorporated)

Fig. 21-21 Points-meter connection

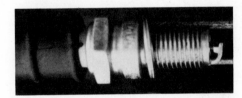

Fig. 21-22 Spark plug out and connected: rotate engine
until plug fires

1. Connecting a points tester in the circuit
and stopping where the meter jumps from low to
high resistance (Fig. 21 a and b).

2. On battery ignition systems with the ignition on, a spark plug out, and connected to the
high tension lead, rotate until the plug fires (Fig.
21-22).

3. With battery current on and test light
across the points, rotate the plate until the light
just lights. The current will go through the points
until they open and then the light will come on
(Fig. 21-23).

Dynamic timing is checked by properly connecting the timing light into the circuit and observing where the strobe shows the timing mark
to be. Manufacturers specify a particular rpm for
strobe timing, so be sure the engine is at the right
speed. Also check the timing advance at the
higher rpm when the specification is listed. Capacitor discharge (Cd) ignition systems that are

Fig. 21-23 Test light across points, switch on

Fig. 21–24 Checking ignition timing by use of a timing light

battery powered can be timed only dynamically because the impulse rotor must be moving to generate the trigger voltage (Fig. 21–24).

Remember, timing is one of the most important places to be really accurate. Too much advance puts holes in pistons, and too much retard causes severe overheating.

Condenser Testing. Test ignition condensers for shorting, leakage, and capacitance. The test for shorting is made by setting your ohmmeter to zero with the probes connected, and then touching the probes to the pig tail and case of the condenser (Fig. 21–25). The resistance should be

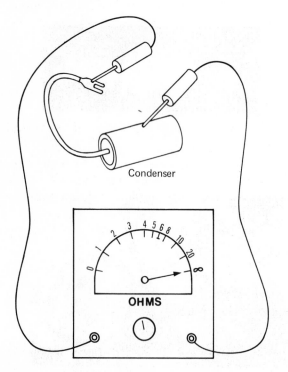

Fig. 21–25 Condenser-ohmmeter leakage test

infinity. Be sure to discharge the condenser before and after this test by touching a wire from the positive to the negative side of the condenser (Fig. 21–26). This will prevent meter damage and shocks.

Current leakage is checked by charging the condenser 5 seconds directly across a battery, allowing it to stand for 5 minutes, and taking a voltage reading. The voltmeter should deflect to at least 9 volts when charged with a 12-volt battery. Check the initial charged reading against the 5-minute delay reading. The difference is leakage.

Capacitance is tested with a meter reading in microfarads (Mf. or μF). The normal-size capacitor for most bikes is 0.25 Mf.

Fig. 21–26 Shorting condenser pigtail to case (Yamaha International Corporation)

Points Plate and Advance Mechanisms. Points plates need to be flat, clean, and have good threads for attaching the points. If someone has been in there prying and has bent something, the camshaft or crankshaft seal may leak all over the points. You should replace a bent points plate or one that has damaged threads or a leaky seal.

Advance mechanisms on some bikes have the points cam attached to the driving shaft by means of spring-loaded counter-weights (Fig. 21–27). As the speed of the shaft increases, centrifugal force moves the weights out against the spring action. As the weights move out, the points cam turns forward in relation to the driving shaft. This advances the spark timing. Weight size and spring tensions determine how soon and how far the ignition timing is advanced. A bike that is timed at 5° before TDC at idle speed may be advanced at 40° BTDC by the time it reaches 3000 rpm.

Dirt and rust can "freeze" up the advance mechanism and heat can change spring tension.

Fig. 21-27 Spark advancer weight assembly (American Honda Motor Company)

Check the advance curve of the engine's timing against the factory specs at the rpm listed. Cleaning and light lubrication can free the parts. If the springs are weak and allow too early or too much of an advance, they will have to be replaced.

Coil Testing. A quick test of the coil is to remove a spark plug, reconnect the plug wire to the plug, hold the plug about 1/8 inch from the engine, and touch the point wire to ground. As the wire is touched the spark should jump the distance from the plug to the engine and have a blue-white color. No spark, faint or yellow color, or very thin spark indicates a weak or defective coil. Replacement is the solution. Be sure the points, plug, condenser, and wiring are good before you spend your pennies (Fig. 21-28).

Fig. 21-28 Spark coil distance test: plug wire is held within the 6-7 mm spark jumping distance

Most bike manuals give resistance specs for both primary and secondary winding in a coil.

Check the windings with an ohmmeter against the specs.

If you have a coil tester, make the connections according to the tester manual. The spark between the electrodes in the tester should be regular. On the testers, the coil puts out with regularity. On the stationary gap models, you want to find the minimum voltage required to get a regular spark. Watch out for accidential grounding. The coil output voltage is high! Applying too much voltage can damage the coil. Heat, oil soaking, and getting battered around are three ways coils become damaged. One other way to test a coil is to compare its output with another coil that's new or you know is good. Get rid of your junk parts as soon as they are proven defective so they don't keep getting in your way.

Magneto Service. Servicing the mag is similar to the procedures just described for coils, points, condensers, and mounting plates. The parts are disassembled, cleaned, and inspected. The condenser is tested, the points are filed or "stoned," and the primary and secondary windings of the coil are tested for resistance, shorts, and grounding.

Additional service includes:

1. Point spring tension is checked on some models with a proper gauge.

2. The point rubbing block can be inspected for excessive wear.

3. Flywheel magnet can be checked for rubbing against coil ends. Many bike makers list a specified end clearance that is set with a feeler gauge (Fig. 21-31).

4. Test lighting coils for continunity, shorts, or grounding.

When everything is cleaned and put back in place, the ignition timing needs to be set.

Capacitor Discharge Ignition Testing. Two major points must be remembered when you test a CDI system:

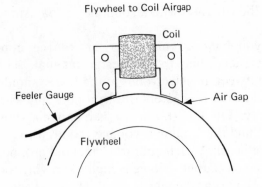

Flywheel to Coil Airgap

Coil

Feeler Gauge

Air Gap

Flywheel

Fig. 21-29 Using a feeler gauge to check flywheel to coil distance

Fig. 21-30 Head with too short reach plug installed

1. Any one test or reading that does not fall within specification tolerances generally requires the replacement of the whole unit.

2. Connecting any lead incorrectly can damage electronic components in the unit and lead to replacement.

As each manufacturer has a different design, you will need the proper shop manual to get the right test sequence and proper connections to make for the bike you are working on. Some of the specialized analyzers also have their own hook-up for a given CDI system. Follow the directions carefully.

Pulser coils and, where they are used, exciter coils are tested for proper resistance. Leads into the sealed unit may be tested for continuity, correct resistance, amperage, and voltage. Don't try it if the manual doesn't list the expected readings and show the meter connections to make.

Spark Plugs and High Tension Wiring. The right plug in good condition has a lot to do with how a bike is running and stays running. First, make sure the bike you're working on has the right size plug. Too short a reach fouls the plug hole threads and reduces combustion efficiency (Fig. 21-30). Too long a plug will run hot or may be struck by the piston, possibly breaking it.

The heat range of a plug is one thing a mechanic should know how to select. When a bike is generally ridden hard, a colder plug is required.

The slow, cautious rider will need a hotter than standard plug installed to keep the bike running well (Fig. 21-31). Only change one step at a time in plug heat range or you may cause excessive fouling or burned piston crowns.

The spark plug's condition is a good indicator of changes to make in selecting a new plug as well as other problems that will require attention:

1. Normal plug condition (Fig. 21-32).

2. Burned plug (Fig. 21-33). Need cooler plug, richer air-fuel mixture, or have improper plug reach. Ignition timing might be way off its proper setting.

3. Dry, sooty plug (Fig. 21-34). Need hotter plug, leaner mixture, or plugs are old and need cleaning or replacement.

4. Oil-fouled plug (Fig. 21-35). Need hotter plug or leaner mixture. May have too much oil in two-strokes or possibly the bike is being "lugged" rather than being ridden properly. Could be poor rings or valve guides, excessive choking or restricted air filter, retarded timing. Correct the cause of the oil fouling as well as the plug.

Changing a spark plug sounds simple, but requires care in this sequence:

1. Loosen old plug and blow dirt away from the plug and head.

2. Remove old plug and check its condition.

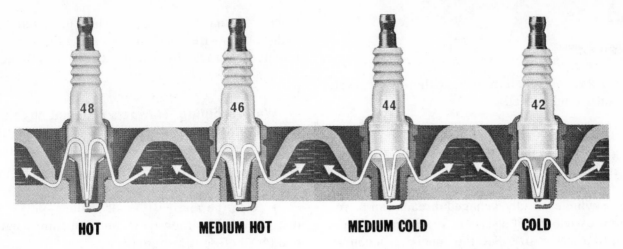

HOT   **MEDIUM HOT**   **MEDIUM COLD**   **COLD**

Fig. 21–31   Spark plug heat range difference (AC Spark Plug Division of General Motors Corporation)

Fig. 21–32   Spark plug, normal condition (AC Spark Plug Division of General Motors Corporation)

Fig. 21–34   Carbon-fouled plug (AC Spark Plug Division of General Motors Corporation)

Fig. 21–33   Burned plug (AC Spark Plug Division of General Motors Corporation)

Fig. 21–35   Oil-fouled plug (AC Spark Plug Division of General Motors Corporation)

3. If the plug is still good, clean it by gently scraping the built-up deposits away from the electrodes. Abrasive blasters shorten plug life and may leave grit to get in the plug threads and cylinder.

4. Set the gap on the new or used plug.

5. Insure the plug gasket is in the proper position. A new gasket on a reused plug will help heat dissipation.

6. Apply a small amount of graphite or grease on the plug threads, but don't get it on the ceramic insulator.

7. Install plug with fingers to prevent cross-threading.

8. Use a torque wrench to get the correct gasket compression for heat removal and not strip the plug threads in the head. If you don't have a torque wrench, tighten the plug finger-tight and

turn 1/2 to 3/4 of a turn more with a new gasket, 1/4 on an old gasket.

If a plug thread in the head is tight, a special plug tap will clear the dirt or carbon from the threads or repair minor cross-threading. Removing the head for this work keeps metal chips out of the cylinder. Badly damaged threads can be repaired by using coil inserts or redrilling and tapping to a larger size. See the special procedures section in Unit 23 for directions.

Plugs sometimes misfire with no visible problems due to internal shorting, gas leakage, or insulator current conduction. If you're sure what the problem is, substituting a new plug is a quick test.

High-tension wiring insulation deteriorates over a period of time due to heat, oil, and aging of the material. Look for cracking and pin holes caused by arcing. Running the engine in a dark place will make any current leakage from the high-tension wires evident. Replacing the wires, if possible, periodically is good, cheap insurance.

Waterproofing. Having a bike quit any time it gets a little wet or when you go through a little stream takes a lot of the enjoyment out of riding.

Four things can do a lot to eliminate the problem:

1. Use the marine type of sealing sprays on disassembled ignition wires and put things back together before the spray dries.

2. Use the silicone type of sealer on case and timing covers and where secondary wires come through the case.

3. Vent magnetos in such a way that condensation will be driven out when the bike gets warm, but so water can't run in. Some models are vented to a vacuum line on the carb.

4. Use a real tight spark plug boot with a liberal dose of spray sealer when it's installed on the plug wire.

unit 22

Electrical Accessories

WIRING DIAGRAMS

The first time a mechanic or motorcycle owner looks at the wiring diagram for the motorcycle that he needs to diagnose or repair, it looks like the Los Angeles freeway system to a farmer from Kansas. Like most complex systems, you don't try to understand it as a whole, but just read one section of the diagram or one part of the system at a time.

Let's start with a particular diagram and see how they are drawn to represent the actual wiring harness of a bike. For discussion we use the Honda CL 90 (Fig. 22–1). Before trying to trace a particular circuit, notice that electrical wires in most bikes are color coded. The insulation on the wire is colored and there may also be a second color as a spiral or dotted line.

When you look at the diagram, remember that the real wires won't be the same length as those in the diagram and aren't necessarily next to the wires indicated. A wiring harness is wrapped up and not flat out. It is very important to know what is connected to what—not how it gets there.

BASIC COMPONENTS

Get to know what the basic parts of an electrical system are before trying to figure out a particular problem. Remember the symbols used in wiring diagrams, back in Unit 20? Check back if you don't remember the symbols for a battery, switch, fuse, and different kinds of loads. Electrical systems have current suppliers—battery and generator—fuses to protect the system from too high demand, switches to control current use, and the different users—loads—such as lights, horn and ignition system. You would expect to find the parts in the right order: battery, fuse, switch and load.

Have you found the battery in the wiring diagram? It's not labeled and doesn't have the usual symbol; just a rectangle with a + and − sign. The one and only fuse in this particular system is right next to it in the red (R) lead. Trace that red lead further and you come to the main switch. When wires cross on a diagram there is usually no connection unless indicated by a (—+—) on the diagram. Don't forget that the frame of the bike is a major path for electrical current to follow in many circuits. The ground symbol (—‖ı) or (—⧚) indicates current is coming through the frame.

Lighting Systems

Figure 22–2 shows the same wiring diagram as 22–1 with the headlight and taillight circuits

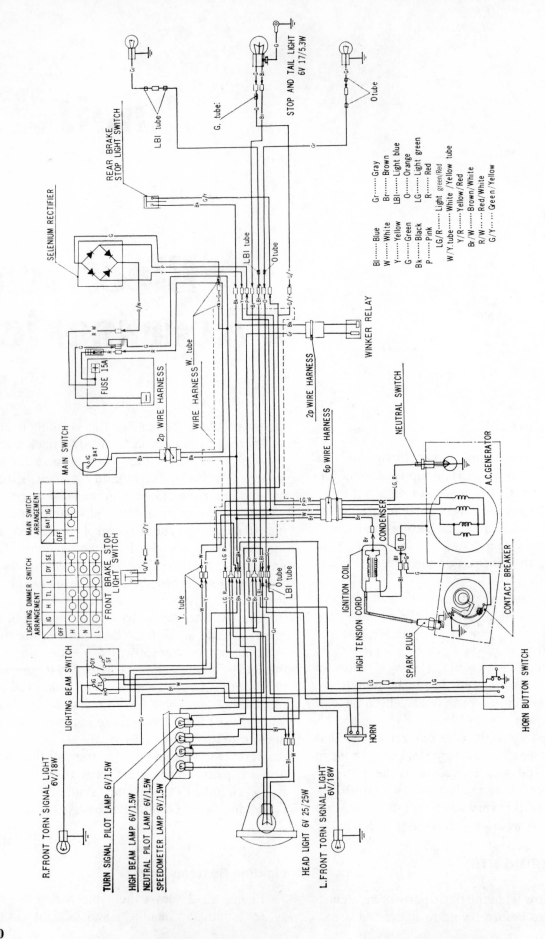

CL 90, CL 90 L U.S.A. EXPORT TYPE

MAIN SWITCH ARRANGEMENT

	BAT	IG
OFF		
I	○—○	

LIGHTING DIMMER SWITCH ARRANGEMENT

	IG	H	TL	L	DY	SE
OFF						
H						
N						
L						

Bl······Blue
W······White
Y······Yellow
G······Green
Bk······Black
P······Pink
LG/R······Light green/Red
W/Y.tube······White /Yellow tube
Y/R······Yellow/Red
Br/W······Brown/White
R/W······Red/White
G/Y······Green/Yellow

Gr······Gray
Br······Brown
LBl······Light blue
O······Orange
LG······Light green
R······Red

R.FRONT TURN SIGNAL LIGHT 6V/18W

TURN SIGNAL PILOT LAMP 6V/1.5W

HIGH BEAM LAMP 6V/1.5W

NEUTRAL PILOT LAMP 6V/1.5W

SPEEDOMETER LAMP 6V/1.5W

HEAD LIGHT 6V 25/25W

L.FRONT TURN SIGNAL LIGHT 6V/18W

LIGHTING BEAM SWITCH

FRONT BRAKE STOP LIGHT SWITCH

MAIN SWITCH

FUSE 15A

SELENIUM RECTIFIER

REAR BRAKE STOP LIGHT SWITCH

STOP AND TAIL LIGHT 6V 17/5.3W

WIRE HARNESS

2p WIRE HARNESS

2p WIRE HARNESS

6p WIRE HARNESS

WINKER RELAY

NEUTRAL SWITCH

A.C.GENERATOR

CONDENSER

CONTACT BREAKER

IGNITION COIL

HIGH TENSION CORD

SPARK PLUG

HORN

HORN BUTTON SWITCH

Fig. 22-1 A typical wiring diagram for a Wiring diagram for a Honda 90 model (American Honda Motor Company)

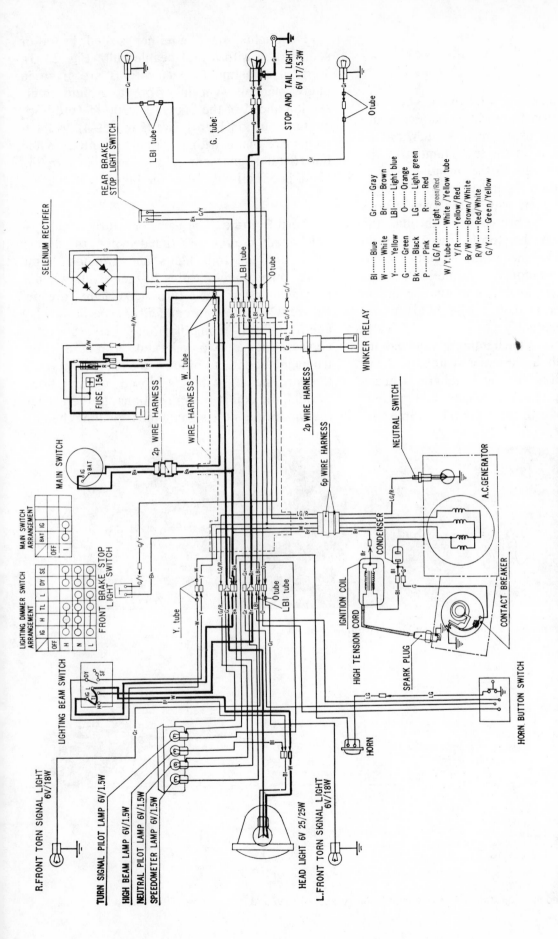

Fig. 22-2 Wiring diagram with headlight and taillight circuits darkened (American Honda Motor Company)

darkened so you can easily trace them. The headlight circuit starts from the positive battery terminal through the fuse to the main switch, on the lighting beam switch, to the low filament of the main beam, and returns to the negative battery terminal by the green ground wire. The taillight circuit follows the same path to the switch, goes to the taillight by the brown wire, through the taillight filament (not the stop filament) to an indicated ground. This means the circuit is completed through the motorcycle frame back to the negative battery terminal. The grounding of the negative battery terminal does exist, but is not indicated on this diagram.

The components of the lighting system can include a lighting switch, a dimmer switch, the head light, shock mounting for the headlight, a headlight adjustment system, the taillight, and grounding either by wire or through the bike frame.

Headlights may be either sealed beam or semi-sealed with a replaceable bulb (Fig. 22–3). Vertical adjustment specifications are given in many manuals, varying from a ground intersection ahead of the bike (150–200 feet) to horizontal when on high beam (Fig. 22–4). Adjustments are made with the rider mounted. When horizontal adjustment is provided, be sure the beam is directly ahead of the bike.

Turn Signals. The parts of a turn signal system usually are the turn signal switch, the flasher relay, and the four lights and grounds. Some newer bikes have warning buzzers and switches to remind riders their turn signal lights are on. Figure 22–5 shows a condenser-type flash relay and turn signal wiring diagram. The flasher relay consists of a two-coil and iron-core electromagnet, contact points, and a capacitor. When the turn signal switch is closed, current flows through the coil in both directions, to the capacitor and through the signal bulbs. As long the cur-

Fig. 22–3   Headlight replaceable bulb (American Honda Motor Company)

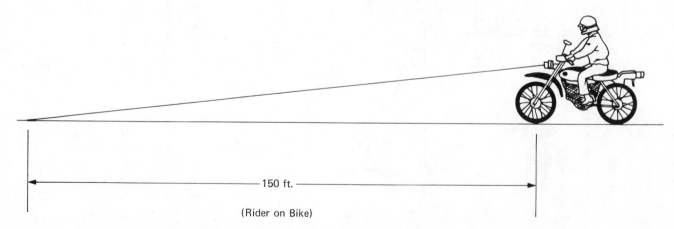

150 ft.

(Rider on Bike)

Fig. 22–4   Correct headlight adjustment, showing light beam parallel to road and intersecting 150-ft. ahead

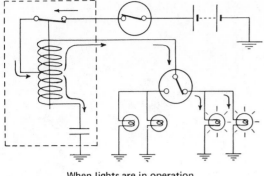

When lights are in operation

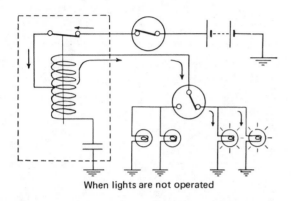

When lights are not operated

Fig. 22–5 Wiring diagram for turn-signal flasher relay (U.S. Suzuki Motor Company)

rent flows both ways through the coil, the electromagnetic fields are self-cancelling and the points are not opened; the signal lights remain lighted.

When the capacitor becomes fully charged, current flows only one way through the coil, opening the points, which remain open until the capacitor discharges fully. This discharge current holds the points open, but it is not sufficient to light the bulbs. When the capacitor is discharged, the cycle repeats.

Referring to Figs. 22–5 and 22–1, notice that the system has four directional signal bulbs: one for the front and rear for each side, and a pilot bulb usually near the speedometer group. Major problems encountered with turn signal systems are burned out bulbs, loss of grounding, defective relays, and switch malfunctions. The use of a test light to trace current availability will help to locate the trouble. Relays are designed for a specific wattage load and will not cycle at the correct frequency if the load is greater or less than designed for.

Heat type of relays are also very common. They use a bimetalic strip that bends when heated. The heat is developed by current flow through the flasher, which causes the bending strip alternately to make and break the circuit. The turn signal lights flash in relation to the alternate operation of the relay.

Indicator Systems. Most motorcycles are designed with several indicator lights to inform the rider of special conditions. These lights can include:

1. Neutral indicator light
2. Low oil pressure warning
3. Charging system warning
4. High beam indicator
5. Ignition on indicator light

As bikes become more and more sophisticated, more will be added to the list. On the CB-350 wiring diagram (Fig. 22–6) the indicator lights and wiring are shown for neutral, high beam, and turn signals.

Most of these systems operate through the action of a switch that completes the circuit to ground. These switches aren't often repairable if they become defective and must be replaced. The location of the neutral switch and sometimes the oil pressure switch may make them difficult to check, because they may be inside the engine or transmission. It's a good idea to inspect and test the action of these switches any time the cases are apart for engine or transmission repair. Replacing a rough, gritty switch at that time is cheaper than taking the bike apart just to replace the switch later.

Brake Light Systems. Most motorcycle brake light systems have three major components; the stop-light switch(es), the light bulb, and the ground system. A separate fuse just for the taillight is also found in some systems. (See Fig. 22–11.) Many new bikes have switches for both front and rear brakes to light the taillight; older bikes often have only a switch controlled by the rear brake operation.

The rear brake switch is usually mechanical in both action and connection to the rear brake link-

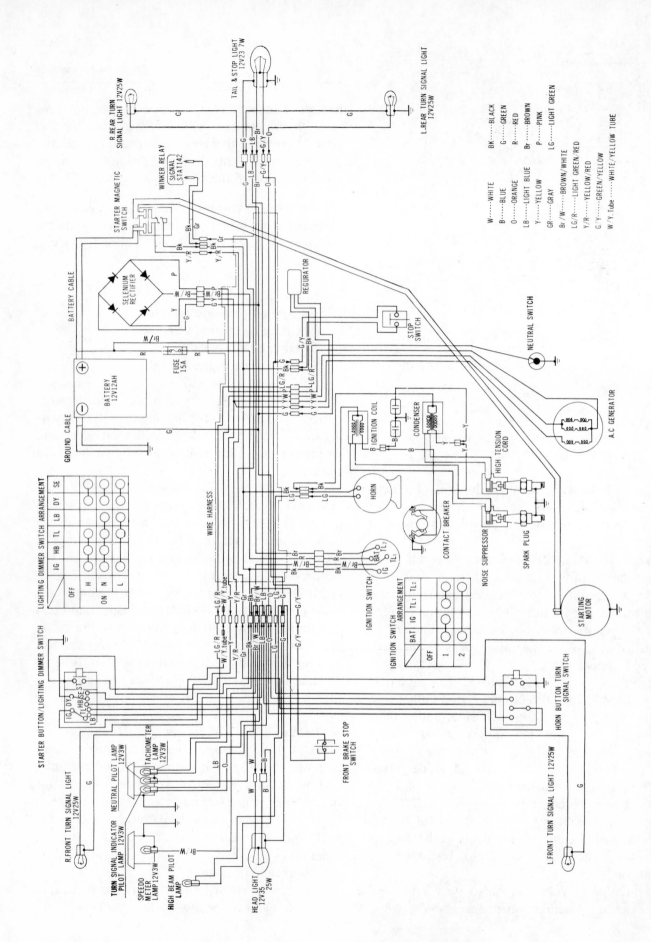

Fig. 22-6 Wiring diagram for a Honda 250/350 (American Honda Motor Company)

age. Adjustment should be set so the bulb lights with only a small amount of brake linkage travel. With the front brakes going to discs and hydraulic operation, hydraulic brake switches, which do not require adjustment, are bound to become more common. These switches are simply tested to see that the circuit is complete when hydraulic pressure is applied. Defective switches are replaced.

The maintenance required for brake light systems is:

1. Check the taillight light bulbs to see if "good" or burned out—both parking and brake filament.

2. Check the ground circuit with an ohmmeter—resistance should be very low between bulb socket interior and the frame ground.

3. Check the taillight fuse if there is one.

4. Check the stop light switch(es) with an ohmmeter (disconnected from motorcycle power supply) for proper operation. The resistance should be almost zero when the switch is operated.

5. Adjust brake light switch(es) so it (they) operate with very little pedal or lever travel. Hydraulic switches should operate when light pressure is applied to the lever.

Starter Systems

Starter systems generally consist of two separate circuits—the power circuit, consisting of the battery, cables, main current side of the solenoid or magnetic switch, starter motor, and the drive mechanism—the control circuit that has a starter switch or button, the energizing side of the solenoid, the neutral or safety switch, and sometimes a clutch override (Fig. 22–7). Let's look at the control circuit first.

The starter switch shown in Fig. 22–7 allows current to flow from the battery through the main or ignition switch, through the starter relay or solenoid, then through the starter switch to ground. This circuit design requires only one wire to be routed to the switch on the handlebar. Other circuits that require two wires to the starter switch place the switch before the relay, with the current going from the relay directly to ground (Fig. 22–8). The control circuit allows a low current switch (starter switch) to activate a high current (up to 150 amps) relay or solenoid switch.

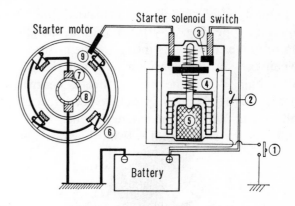

① Starter button switch ② Ignition switch
③ Contact unit ④ Excitation coil ⑤ Plunger ⑥ Pole
⑦ Brush ⑧ Armature ⑨ Field coil

Fig. 22–7 Starting system wiring diagram for the Honda 250/350 (American Honda Motor Company)

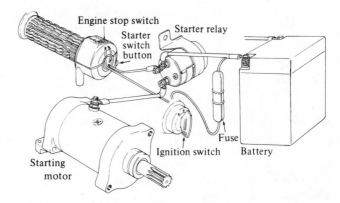

Fig. 22–8 Starting system wiring diagram for a Suzuki 750 (U.S. Suzuki Motor Corporation)

The power circuit has heavy cables from the battery to the relay or solenoid, and from the relay to the starter motor. The current travels from the battery through the heavy relay switch to the motor to ground.

Starter motors have two basic designs: the combination starter-generator, used on some small displacement motorcycles, and the conventional starter motor. The starter-generator is usually mounted directly on the crankshaft and is of low-torque design. The larger bikes' starter motors drive the crankshaft through a chain or gear arrangement and require some type of engagement device such as a clutch.

One type of starter clutch used is the roller and ramp type (Fig. 22–9). Rotation of the starter motor moves the rollers into a wedge position between the starting sprocket hub and the clutch outer hub. When the engine starts, centrifugal force, due to the higher sprocket speed, forces the rollers out against the roller springs and disconnects the starter motor from the sprocket.

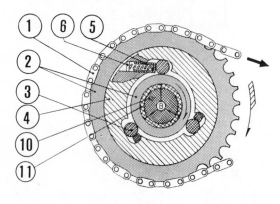

① Starting chain ② Starting sprocket ③ Roller
④ Clutch outer ⑤ Roller spring cap ⑥ Roller spring
⑩ Left crankshaft ⑪ 21 mm bushing

Fig. 22–9 Roller and ramp starter clutch (American Honda Motor Company)

The relay or solenoid construction shown in Fig. 22–10 is typical. The magnetic coil is activated by the starter button. The magnetic field pulls the plunger toward the center of the coil against the force of the return spring. The contact plate attached to the plunger makes a heavy electrical connection between the terminals, allowing current to flow through the starter motor. Release of the starter button allows the return spring in the solenoid to disconnect the power circuit.

Two other switches may also be a part of the starter control circuit, either separately or in series. They are the neutral switch and the clutch switch. Their operation together may require the use of a starting motor safety unit (relay) (Fig. 22–11). In the CB-750 diagram the bike must be in neutral, the clutch must be disengaged, and the starter button pushed on before the solenoid (starter magnetic switch) will complete the power

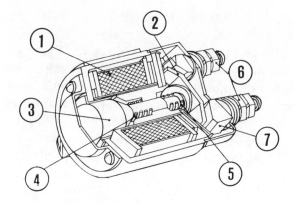

① Magnetic coil (primary coil)
② Contact (operating side) ③ Plunger ④ Return spring
⑤ Contact return spring ⑥ Terminals
⑦ Contact (fixed side)

Fig. 22–10 Starter solenoid relay (American Honda Motor Company)

circuit. When these conditions are met, the relay allows the current to flow to ground, completing the circuit.

Horn System

Whether it goes beep, buzz, or toot, there isn't a lot of difference in the horn systems of the different bikes. Power supplied by the battery through the horn button reaches the electromagnet(s) of the horn. The magnetism pulls the horn diaphragm and at the same time opens the horn contact points. This stops the magnetic field, the diaphragm returns to its original position, and the points close, starting the cycle over again. The very rapid vibration of the diaphragm caused by this cycle produces the horn sound or tone (Fig. 22–12). A resistance is often connected across the points to eliminate arcing. Single-wire horn buttons simply ground or complete the circuit. Two-wire horn buttons work by allowing current to flow to the horn that has the ground at that point.

Maintenance of this circuit could include:

1. Checking the power supply with a voltmeter to see that voltage is available at the switch and horn. Defective switches are replaced. Fuses are a part of this or the overall bike electrical system, so check the fuse if no voltage is available.

2. Some horns have an adjusting nut or screw

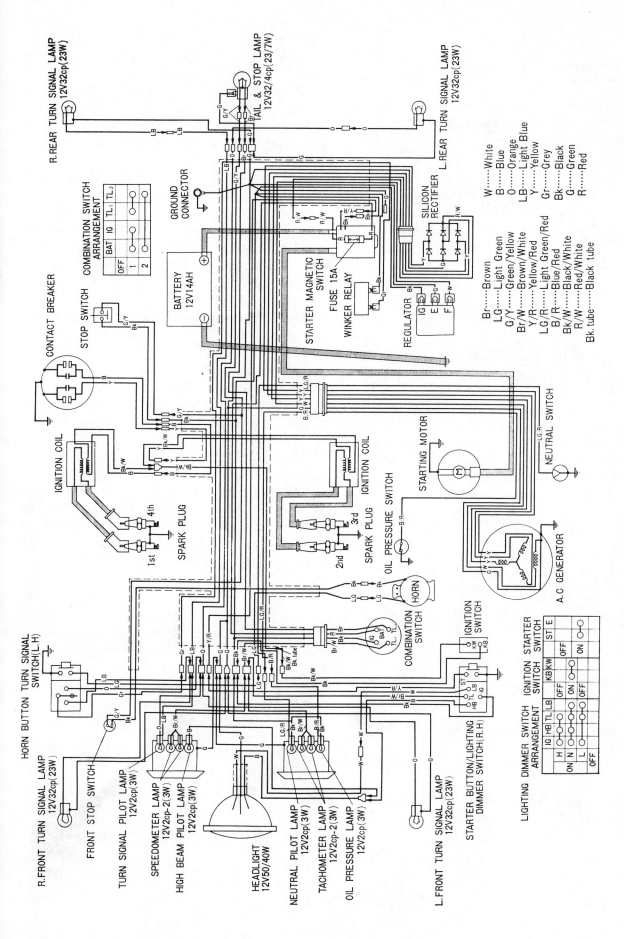

Fig. 22-11 Wiring diagram for starter motor safety unit relay

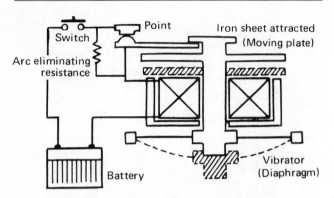

Fig. 22-12 Cross section of electrically operated horn (U.S. Suzuki Motor Corporation)

for the diaphragm tension. Tone and volume can often be adjusted by these fasteners.

3. Horn vibrating points can be cleaned with a point file and the tension adjusted for vibration frequency.

4. On sealed horns, make sure they are carefully resealed against water so they can't corrode. Some types are not repairable or adjustable and must be replaced.

Accessory Loads

Sooner or later it seems everyone wants to put some kind of electrical accessory on his bike. Commonly installed extras include: bigger horns, turn signals, additional lights, gages, and theft-warning devices. There are right and wrong ways to do it and some kinds of jobs that just shouldn't be attempted. What should you think about when the electrical accessory bug hits? Ask yourself such questions as:

1. Can the electrical system handle the additional load?
2. Is there a good way to make the needed connections?
3. Is the accessory you plan to install compatible with your bike? From the standpoint of voltage and grounding?

Question 1 will take some figuring. The manual can give you the charging system's maximum output. If the current required by those systems already on the bike and the new load you want to add don't exceed the generator output, you can start figuring how to hook it up. If the load is too great, you could find yourself in the dark on a night ride.

Three good rules to remember and use when connecting electrical accessories are:

1. Have it operate through the main switch. It will be automatically turned off when the bike is shut down, and you won't come back to a dead battery.
2. Fuse each new accessory separately with the appropriate size fuse. Too often, main wiring harnesses get fried because an addition to the system wasn't fused.
3. Use good mechanical electrical connections, such as soldering or commercial connectors (Fig. 22-13). Twisting two wires together and taping will give you trouble sooner or later.

When you start to wire something in, don't tap into the nearest wire. Run a new wire back to the beginning of the power source, near the battery, but after the main switch. If you do decide to hook in before the switch, you run the risk of leaving the accessory on and running the battery down. Use your wiring diagram to help make the decision.

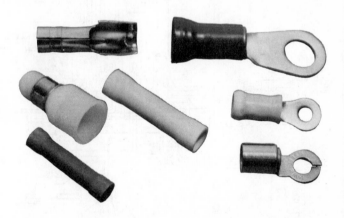

Fig. 22-13 Seven typical electrical connectors

unit 23

Special Repair and Service Tips

SOLDERING

Soldering is the process of joining two pieces of metal together with a third metal having a lower melting temperature. The solder we commonly use is a 50–50 mixture of tin and lead. It is possible to buy solder with mixtures of 60–40 and 70–30 that have a lower tin volume and also a higher melting temperature. These are less desirable because of the need for using more heat. Fifty-fifty solder melts around 400°F.

Attention to three points will produce a strong, solid connection every time:

1. The two pieces to be soldered must be *clean*.
2. Use the proper *flux*.
3. Use enough *heat* to allow the solder to *flow* easily through the joint.

Wires should be freshly cut, with insulation stripped clear of the joint. Acid fluxes should *not* be used for electrical connections. Don't use acid core solder, either.

Try this procedure when joining two or more wires for any electrical connection:

1. Cut fresh ends on the wires.

2. Strip the insulation back 1/2 inch.
3. Twist the wires together.
4. Apply a paste-type nonacid flux. A small dab will do.
5. Hold the wires near the insulation, using needle-nose pliers. This will keep excess heat from melting the insulation (Fig. 23–1).
6. Using a soldering iron or gun, heat the wires until the flux flows.
7. Apply solder to the wire (not to the soldering iron) until it melts and flows through the joint.
8. Remove the heat and hold the joint still until the solder is hard. Early movement causes a weak joint.
9. Don't allow your soldering iron or gun to overheat because this will ruin the tip.

Soldering a new end on a clutch or brake cable is done the same way. You do have to fray the cable end so it won't pull out of the soldered tip you are building. Make the end oversize and shape it with a file or sand paper.

TAPS AND DIES

A tap is used to cut internal threads. Here's how:

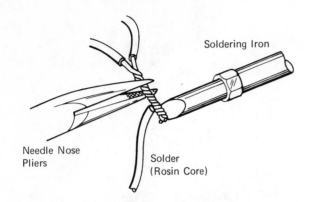

Fig. 23-1 Soldering a wiring connection

1. Locate the center for the new threaded hole by careful measurement, then center-punch the location.

2. Drill a small (1/8″) hole, being careful to remain centered on the punched location.

3. Using the chart in the tap and die set, select the proper tap drill and drill the small hole out to the full tap drill size. Using cutting oil on iron or steel will increase cutting speed and save drills.

4. With the proper tap fastened in the tap handle, start the tap in the hole by applying pressure while turning slowly in a clockwise direction. Check for squareness.

5. After cutting about 3/4 of a turn, back the tap up until the chip that has developed breaks off. Use plenty of cutting oil in steel, but tap cast iron dry. Aluminum requires mineral oil or soluble oil.

6. Remember to back the tap and break the chip after each 3/4 turn of cutting.

The process for touching up damaged threads is also easy. With the *correct* tap and proper lubricant, simply run the tap slowly through the threaded hole. If any serious resistance is felt, back the tap out and clear the hole with low-pressure compressed air. Wear safety glasses!

Cutting external threads with a die is a similar process. Select the proper die and secure it in the die stock (handle). Be sure you have the side of the die you start the threads with toward the stock to be threaded. Prepare the stock by grinding or filing a taper on the end. This will

help the die start the threads more easily. Using the proper lubricant and moderate pressure, turn the die stock clockwise about a full turn. Then back it up the same as you would a tap (Fig. 23-2).

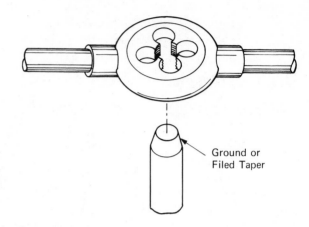

Ground or
Filed Taper

Fig. 23-2 Starting external threads, showing tapered stock, die and diestock

When deciding what size threads to use, consider the following:

1. Soft metals like aluminum have good holding power with coarse threads.

2. Two small fasteners are sometimes more effective than one large fastener.

3. Fine threads are used where small adjustments or precise torque is important.

4. Thin sections may require finer thread.

Thread Repair

External threads may be cleaned up or repaired by using a proper size die to remove metal where the threads have been banged or distorted. Often shafts that have threaded ends have been flattened or mushroomed by careless hammering or use of the wrong puller. A three-corner file is then used to remove the excess metal, being careful to maintain the original shape of the thread.

A third repair method is to purchase a special thread file. These are available in both American and metric thread sizes, and a size to match the threads under repair must be selected. (See Fig. 12-25.) A file may have up to eight different thread sizes on the one file.

Internal threads that are damaged are repaired in three ways. The first effort is to run a special chasing tap through the threaded hole.

These taps differ from standard taps in that they have six or eight flutes for cutting rather than four. The spark plug repair set shown in Fig. 23–3 is an example of chasing taps.

Fig. 23–3   Spark plug chasing tap set

If the threads are too far gone for simple clean-up with a chasing tap, a more drastic solution could be necessary. Redrilling and tapping to a larger size is one option. Another option is the use of one of the special thread inserts available. The inserts generally come with the proper drill and tap or combination drill-tap necessary for their use.

First, the old threads are either drilled out or used as the drawing power for the special drill-tap. The new, larger threads are used to support the coiled wire type of insert that is put in and cut off to the proper length. Figure 23–4 shows the process. Some of the inserts on the market are solid types requiring an allen head type of installation tool.

REMOVING BROKEN STUDS

It's sure not uncommon to have someone bring in a bike with a stud broken off even with the case. You may break one yourself on occasion. Phillips head screws that have been badly misused can present the same kind of problem. Here's how you remove them:

1. Center punch the end of the broken stud. You must be very accurate! Any off-centerness will make removal of the stud more difficult.
2. Drill down the center of the stud with a small-sized drill bit (1/16 to 3/32). Care is necessary to have the drilled hole perfectly centered and not break the drill bit.
3. Select a drill bit just smaller than the root diameter of the threads, and drill the stud hole out

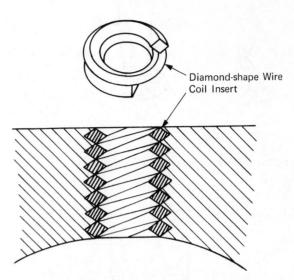

Diamond-shape Wire Coil Insert

Fig. 23–4   Cross section showing coil-type thread insert

to that size. If your first hole is slightly off-center, use a smaller drill bit so as not to cut into the threads.
4. Insert a hardened stud remover in the hole. (See Fig. 3–14.) Tap it lightly with a soft hammer. Turn the stud, remove counter-clockwise. The stud is supposed to come out (Figs. 23–5, 23–6, 23–7, 23–8).

REMOVING VALVE GUIDES

A very good way to remove stubborn insert-type valve guides is:

1. From the rocker arm side, using an appropriate tap, cut threads about 3/4 inch into the guide.
2. Screw a spare bolt into the valve guide until it lightly bottoms out on the newly cut threads.
3. Turn the head over and, from the combustion chamber side, use a hammer and drift directly against the bolt to drive out the guide (Fig. 23–9).

KICKSTARTERS

You've probably seen motorcycle racers "run and bump start" their engines by pushing the bike and then releasing the clutch lever. This tech-

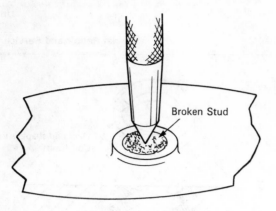

Fig. 23-5   Center punching a broken stud

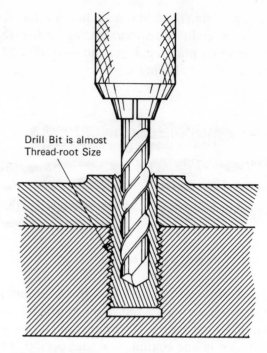

Fig. 23-7   Root drilling a broken stud

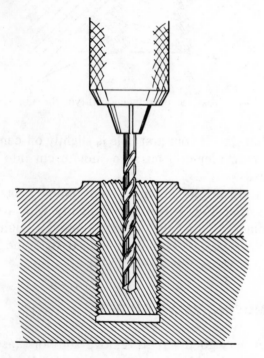

Fig. 23-6   Center drilling a broken stud (cross section)

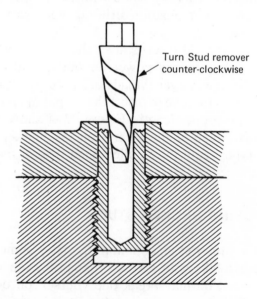

Fig. 23-8   Inserting the stud remover

nique of "bump starting" permits the rider to use the momentum of a rolling bike to spin the engine over sufficiently to start it.

Of course, this method would be very inconvenient to use with your daily transportation bike or your woods scooter. Therefore, it's important that you understand the design, operation, and repair of kickstarters.

Basic types

Most kickstarters found on modern motorcycles are simply a spring-loaded one-way racheting device, indirectly geared to the crankshaft.

The "one way" features may be a roller type, lock pawl type, or a regular rachet type. All three of the popular approaches are illustrated in Figs. 23-10, 23-11, and 23-12. Just remember that these devices have but one function—to rotate a shaft in one direction, but still allow it to turn freely in the other.

The roller-type kickstarter in Fig. 23-10 has a set of rollers riding between the foot-activated

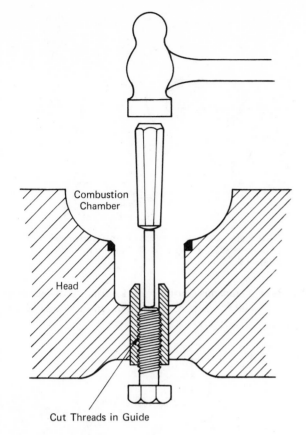

Fig. 23-9 Removing valve guide insert

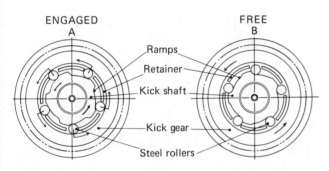

Fig. 23-10 Roller-type kickstarter mechanism (Pabatco)

"kickshaft" and a "kick gear" connected to second gear in the transmission. When you depress your foot, the steel rollers become lodged tightly between the shaft and the gear turning second gear in the transmission which is connected to the primary drive which, in turn, rotates the engine. In effect, using the kickstarter is just like "bump starting" the bike in second gear. When the engine starts, the rotation of the kick gear by the engine disengages the rollers, allowing the assembly to run freely.

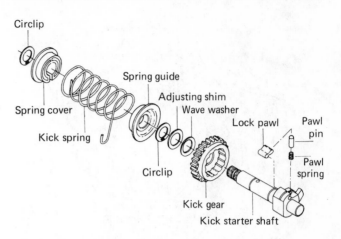

Fig. 23-11 Lock pawl-type kickstarter assembly (Yamaha International Corporation)

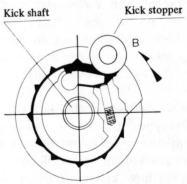

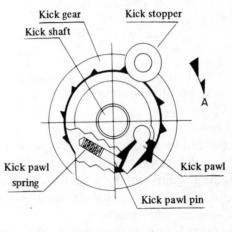

Fig. 23-12 Lock pawl kickstarter action

The lock pawl or pawl rachet kick-start mechanism (Fig. 23-13) also has the rachet mechanism located in the kick gear, but its design is a bit different. Figure 23-13 shows that when the kick

Special Repair and Service Tips

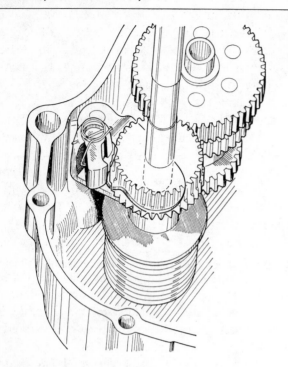

Fig. 23-13 Rachet-type kickstarter mechanism (American Honda Motor Company)

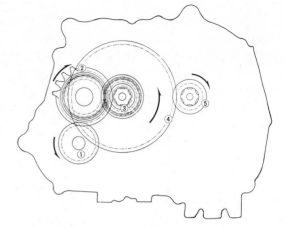

1 Kick starter pinion   4 Primary driven gear
2 Counter shaft low gear   5 Primary drive gear
3 Main shaft

Fig. 23-14 Transmission-type kickstarter showing gear interlock power flow (American Honda Motor Company)

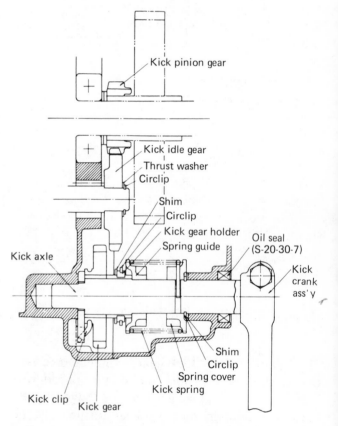

Fig. 23-15 Primary drive-type kickstarter power flow (Yamaha International Corporation)

shaft is rotated by the kick lever, the kick pawl is pushed into the inner teeth of the kick gear. The pawl rotating against the kick gear then transmits that motion to the crankshaft of the engine through several other gears.

The rachet-type kickstarter mechanism is very simple. By rotating a shaft-mounted rachet flange and forcing it to engage the small kickstarter pinion gear, foot power can be transmitted to the engine through the countershaft low gear (Fig. 23-14).

If you're confused by the short descriptions of the various types of kick-start mechanisms, refer to your specific model manual for an elaboration and clarification of what you will be working with.

Realizing how kick-start mechanisms work, you are probably curious as to how the power is transmitted to the crankshaft. There are two popular approaches to this problem. Conventionally, the kickstarter operates directly on either the clutch or the transmission as shown in Fig. 23-15, a typical approach to gear interlock for kickstarters. Any type of kickstarter drive that is geared to or through the clutch should be used only with the clutch engaged and the transmission in neutral. To make a stalled engine easier to start, designers developed the primary kick-start gear. This system activates the primary drive system rather than the clutch and transmission. With primary kickstarting an engine may be started in any gear simply by disengaging the clutch. This is a nice feature for trail riders or new riders who may have difficulty finding neutral. A kick idle gear is often used to connect the kick gear to the kick pinion gear on the primary drive gear.

Diagnosis of Kickstarter Trouble

There's not much that goes wrong with kickstarters. There are, however, quite a few complaints at the dealership such as: "my kicker won't work" or "the kickstarter is hard to turn." Of course these problems are usually really from locked or siezed up engines. If a kickstarter isn't functioning properly, the nature of the malfunction can give you a clue to the problem. The most common problems are broken return spring, worn or broken rachet mechanism, or worn shaft bushing in the case. Often damage may result from abusive kicking of the engine when it won't start. On some models, the starter rest or step bumper may become broken or worn. This allows the starter mechanism to interfere with other devices in the case such as the shifting linkage.

If there is no damage to the shaft mounts, stops, or spring mounts, kickstarter repair is as simple as replacing the worn or broken parts. Follow your service manual closely when doing the repair because there are quite a few washers and spacers that can become misplaced during reassembly.

WATER COOLED ENGINES

History, Principle and Theory, Components and Workings, Radiator, Thermostat, Water Pump

Motorcycle engineers and racers have known for years that an engine will run best in a rather narrow temperature range. If it is too cool, the fuel will not vaporize properly as it enters the cylinder; if it is too hot, the engine may seize up.

Air cooling an engine by finning its external surfaces has been the traditional approach to cooling a motorcycle engine. This system is dependent on an airstream moving across the fins to remove the heat. The temperature and speed of the moving air are also important. If the air is already hot, say 100°, and the bike isn't moving through it very fast, say, in a traffic jam, there could be a problem. For instance, a piston seizure or at least scoring of the cylinder walls. Conversely, on very cold days a bike will often require a great deal of time to warm up. If it's an old two-stroke, chronic plug fouling, possibly even terminal plug fouling, may result.

Water cooling has the benefits of narrow-range operating temperature, quick cool-weather warmup, and adequate protection against hot weather seizures. The only draw-backs are the extra components, coolant, and weight that are inevitable in a water-cooled engine.

Recently, with the development of lighter, more compact components and better coolant additives, water cooling has become feasible for larger touring machines and has also advanced in popularity among road racers.

Currently, Suzuki produces a 750-cc water-cooled, two-stroke triple that has been well received by riders. It has the snappy power of a highly tuned two-stroke, yet is nearly seizure-proof and much quieter than comparable water-cooled models. The Suzuki triple appears to be a forerunner of more water-cooled production models to come, so in this section we'll examine the GT-750 cooling system (Fig. 23–16).

Basically, the Suzuki system works exactly like the cooling system in your automobile. A water pump or impeller circulates water through the engine and a radiator. A temperature-sensitive valve called a thermostat restricts the flow of water through the system until the engine reaches the proper operating temperature. When the engine begins to reach the upper limits of its operating range, the thermostat opens fully, allowing greater amounts of water to circulate, cooling the engine back to the proper temperature. This event could take place under severe load on a hot day. Figure 23–17 shows how a thermostat operates, allowing water to pass as needed.

Something must be done to prevent the water in the system from boiling at 212°F or 100°C as it normally does in an open container. In order to raise the boiling point to over 250°F, the system is pressurized to about 15 psi by using a pressure-

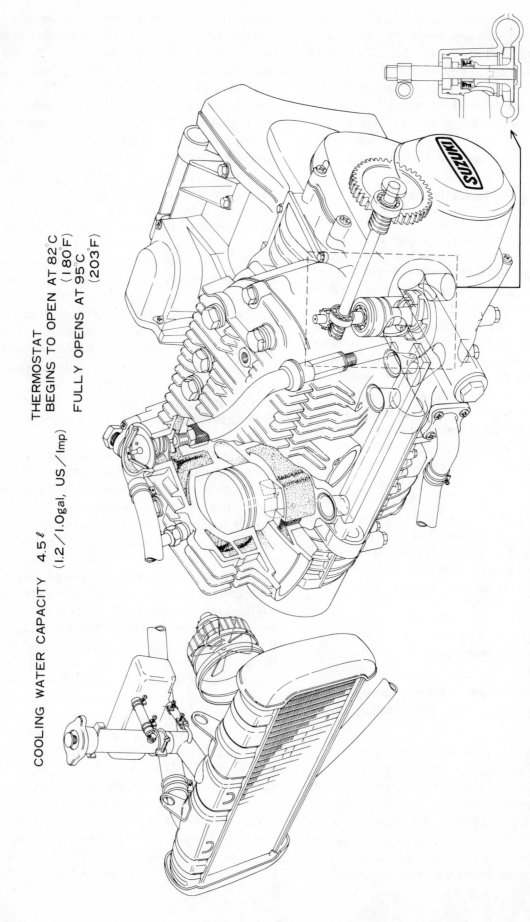

COOLING WATER CAPACITY 4.5 ℓ
(1.2／1.0gal, US／Imp)

THERMOSTAT
BEGINS TO OPEN AT 82°C
(180°F)
FULLY OPENS AT 95°C
(203°F)

Fig. 23–16 Suzuki GT 750 Cooling System (U.S. Suzuki Motor Corporation)

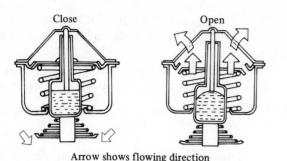

Close   Open

Arrow shows flowing direction

Fig. 23–17 Thermostat operation (U.S. Suzuki Motor Corporation)

sensitive radiator cap and by including additives in the coolant. The charts in Fig. 23–18 indicate the temperature at which various mixtures of permanent antifreeze and water will boil or freeze.

The water pump is needed to circulate the coolant through the system. Suzuki uses a six-bladed impeller, centrifugal-type pump mounted in the transmission chamber at the bottom of the crankcase. The pump is driven by a shaft that is geared to the crankshaft on one end and the impeller shaft on the other. Figure 23–19 is a detailed drawing of the Suzuki pump, showing not only the pump components, but also the oil and water seals and the shaft bearing.

The radiator itself is a set of funnel tubes and chambers very much like the radiator found in most cars. Since radiators are made of soft copper or aluminum they must be carefully mounted. Rubber and steel mounting hardware is used to protect the radiator from vibration damage. Should any damage or problems plague a Suzuki radiator, a regular automotive radiator shop should have no trouble cleaning or repairing it.

Another component that may cause difficulties is the cooling fan. Suzuki has mounted a small electrically powered fan behind the radiator to help cool it in traffic. If the fan fails to operate,

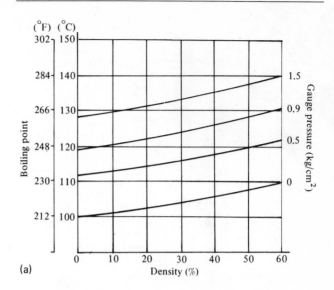

(a)

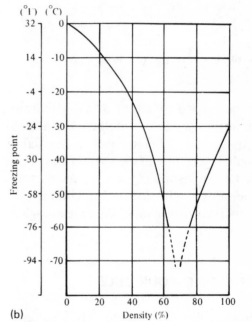

(b)

Fig. 23–18 Boiling point graph (a) and (b) pressure temperature graph

Table 23–1 REQUIRED AMOUNT OF ANTI-FREEZE COOLANT AT EACH TEMPERATURE

Temperature under which	°C	−10	−15	−20	−25	−31	−39
your motorcycle is used	°F	14	5	−4	−13	−24	−38
Mixing ratio of anti-freeze	%	30	35	40	45	50	55
Amount of anti-freeze	ltr	1.35/3.15	1.60/2.90	1.80/2.70	2.00/2.50	2.25/2.25	2.50/2.00
/distilled water	US.pt	1.40/3.30	1.70/3.10	1.90/2.90	2.10/2.60	2.40/2.40	2.60/2.10
for 4.5 ltr (4.75/3.95 qt, US/Imp) of cooling solution	Imp.pt	1.20/2.75	1.40/2.55	1.55/2.40	1.75/2.20	2.00/2.00	2.20/1.75

Note: This table applies to the use of GOLDEN CRUISER 1200 Coolant only. (U.S. Suzuki Motor Corporation)

Special Repair and Service Tips

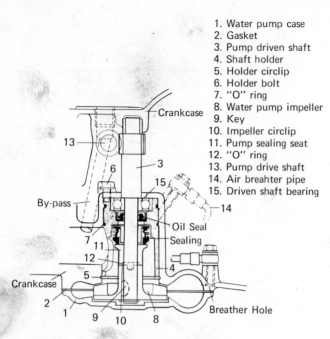

1. Water pump case
2. Gasket
3. Pump driven shaft
4. Shaft holder
5. Holder circlip
6. Holder bolt
7. "O" ring
8. Water pump impeller
9. Key
10. Impeller circlip
11. Pump sealing seat
12. "O" ring
13. Pump drive shaft
14. Air breahter pipe
15. Driven shaft bearing

Fig. 23–19   Cross section of a water pump

it may be caused by either a faulty thermostatic switch in the engine or a defective fan motor.

The Suzuki GT-750 service manual has a thorough description of the system and contains a detailed troubleshooting guide. As motorcycles become more sophisticated and complex, having the proper service manual becomes more important.

HIBERNATING YOUR BIKE

Motorcycles are delicate. They suffer "shelf damage" if they are simply parked for several months. Before storing your bike for any lengthy period, take the time to perform some preventive maintenance.

Follow this list and when you can get back to the real world your bike will be all rested and ready to go:

1. Remove the battery. Charge it slowly and fully. Store the battery in a dry above-freezing place above the floor. Recharge every six months.

2. Get the bike off the ground—on the center stand with an extra prop so the tires don't touch.

3. Be sure the bike is fully lubricated, including fresh oil and grease, and that the cylinders have a couple of teaspoons of oil each. Turn the engine through several times after the oil has been added to the cylinders.

4. Carefully clean all surfaces of the bike—both chrome and paint. Give everything a good wax job.

5. Apply a coating of rubber lubricant or brake fluid to the tires and all other exposed rubber parts.

6. Fill the gas tank to the top and include a cup of dry gas. Drain the sediment bowl and carburetor float bowls. A full tank won't rust from condensation. If the bike is going to sit for a real long time, take the tank off, drain it, fill it with a quart of oil, and slosh the oil well over the inside. Drain out the excess.

7. Cover the bike with something that "breathes." Don't use a plastic cover that holds the moisture under it. A canvas cover that fits a little loose is good.

8. Visit the bike occasionally. You will both feel better!

Glossary

ac or *a-c:* abbreviation for alternating current

Allen head: a kind of screwdriver that fits six-sided (hexagonal) screw heads that have no slots.

A.T.V.: abbreviation for all-terrain vehicle

bell mouthing: flaring at the mouth

brake fade: failure of brake lining to grip brake drum surface and reduce speed, often caused by overheating and glazing of brake linings

braze: to join metal parts by flowing melted brass between them

break-in: a period of gentle operation during which new or different parts fit together better from surface wearing

BTDC: abbreviation for before top dead center

buddy seats: seats large enough for two riders

buttoning up: final reassembly and testing after repair or overhaul work

caster effect: the tendency of a pivoting wheel to follow the driving force

cc: abbreviation for cubic centimeter

CDI: abbreviation for capacitor discharge ignition

centimeter (cm): a small unit of metric measurement (one one-hundredth of a meter), equal to 0.39 inch

clearance: the distance between parts that move inside or beside one another

clutch: a device that couples or disengages the engine from the rest of the drive train

clutch drag: when the clutch parts will not disengage, usually when very cold or very hot

clutch slip: when the clutch parts do not engage properly, causing heat-up by friction

cm: abbreviation for centimeter, equal to 0.39 inch

compression ratio: the numerical relationship between the volume of fuel mixture in the cylinder at the start of the compression stroke and the volume the mixture is squeezed down to when the piston reaches top dead center — say, from 100 cc squeezed to 10 cc, a 10-to-1 ratio

dampening: using shock absorbers to get smoother riding

db: abbreviation for decibel

dc or *d-c:* abbreviation for direct current

decibel: a unit of sound measurement

degree: a unit of temperature or arc measurement meant by the sign °

displacement: the volume of the cylinder when the piston is at bottom dead center, usually specified in cubic centimeters

drag: resistance that holds down speed

drive train: the mechanical parts that transfer power from the engine to the rear wheel

emf: abbreviation for electromotive force

Enduro: a timed motorcycle competition event where specially designed machines are ridden through rough terrain

fairings: streamlined shields that reduce drag by smoothing air flow when a vehicle is moving

flapper valves: valves that are opened by vacuum and closed by pressure

flogging: abusive, aggressive treatment of a motorcycle

flux: a material, such as rosin or borax, that is used to speed the fusing of metals during soldering or brazing

foot: unit of English linear measurement meant by the sign ' and the abbreviation ft.

foot pegs: foot rests; some fold in close to the frame when not in use

four stroker: an engine that completes the combustion cycle with four strokes of a piston in each cylinder

frame flex: movement of frame parts, especially when a vehicle is not designed well

gear box: the transmission

gear ratio: the numerical relationship between the number of times a gear must turn to rotate a larger gear once

hard-tails: bikes without rear suspension systems

hex: abbreviation for hexagonal (six sided)

hot dog: a rider who shows off, regardless of safety

hp: abbreviation for horsepower

inch: unit of English linear measurement meant by the sign " and the abbreviation in.

knobbies: tires with treads that bite into dirt and mud

leading shoe: a brake show that is self-assisting because the rotating drum has a tendency to rotate the shoe on its pivot and force it into the drum with greater force

lean: an air-fuel mixture that has too much air for good combustion

linkage: parts that transmit motion or control from the rider to a part or system on the machine. Linkages are made from cables, rods, cams, springs, and pivots in various configurations

lock-up: stopping a wheel from turning, often by using brakes too hard. The term may refer to engine seizure also

lower end: the crankshaft, connecting rods, and engine case sections

lugging: making an engine work harder than necessary by not using proper gear combinations at lower speeds

micrometer: a finely adjustable instrument used to measure small sizes or angles

millimeter: very small unit of metric measurement (one thousandth of a meter) meant by the abbreviation mm, equal to 0.04 inch

min: abbreviation for minute

mini-bike: any small youth's motorcycle whose wheel diameters are 12 inches or smaller

minute: unit of time or arc measurement meant by the sign ' and the abbreviation min

mm: abbreviation for millimeter, equal to 0.04 inch

motorcross: a motorcycle race conducted on a rugged closed course

mph: abbreviation for miles per hour

multicarb: having more than one carburetor

peen: a hammer with one ball or wedge head used to bend or indent metal

Phillips head: a screw that has two crossed slots in its head; also the screwdriver that fits such screws.

port: passageway through which intake or exhaust mixtures pass on their way into and out of the combustion chamber

psi: abbreviation for pounds (of pressure) per square inch

re-ring: to install new piston rings

resonance: a vibration of large amplitude in a mechanical or electrical system

rev: abbreviation for revolution; to speed up then slow down an engine repeatedly *rich:* an air-fuel mixture that has too much fuel for good combustion

rpm: abbreviation for revolutions per minute

SCR: abbreviation for silicon-controlled rectifier

second: unit of time or arc measurement meant by the sign " and the abbreviation sec

seizure: heat expansion of one part so it does not slide as it should over or in another surface

siamesed: term (from Siamese twins) that describes the merging of two exhaust pipes into one

skid plate: a plate that protects engines from skid damage

slipping clutch (See clutch slip)

specs: abbreviation for specifications (makers' instructions or dimensions)

sprocket: a tooth or projection shaped to fit a gear or chain

sprocket wheel: a toothed wheel used to drive a chain or gear

stroke: the distance a piston travels inside its cylinder

swing arm: the pivoting member that attaches the frame of a motorcycle to the rear wheel

tach: ("tack"): abbreviation for tachometer

tailgate: to ride very closely behind the vehicle in front

TDC: abbreviation for top dead center

teeth (See also sprockets): projections along the rim of a wheel that are spaced to fit the same kind of projections on gears or into chains

telescopic forks: front suspension assemblies that expand or contract to absorb road shock by means of springs in tubes that slide over one another

timing advance: the precise moment at which ignition takes place in a cylinder before the crankshaft reaches top dead center position. It is measured in crankshaft degrees or piston distance from the top of its stroke

top end: the head assembly, piston rings, top end of the rod, and cylinder assembly

torque: rotational force delivered by a turning part, such as a crankshaft

trail bike: a motorcycle specially designed for travel off of paved roads

trailing shoe: a brake shoe that tends to pivot away from the brake drum when the brakes are applied

transmission: a group of gears that transfer engine power to different turning speeds and torque of the rear wheel, fast or slow, enabling the rider to tailor necessary road speed to engine rpm

truing: making sure that wheels, with and without tires, are round and straight

twins: engines that have two cylinders

two-strokers: engines that complete the combustion cycle with two strokes of a piston in each cylinder

undampened: springs that are used without shock absorbers

upper end: same as top end

V: abbreviation for volt

VOM: abbreviation for volt-ohmmeter-milliampmeter

wind screen: plastic or other material used to shield a rider from wind and dirt

WOT: abbreviation for wide open throttle

zener diode: an electrical device that regulates the charging current to the battery by converting excess current to heat, usually housed in a finned heat sink

Index